Interpersonal	Factorial	Relational-Systemic	Relational-Feminist	Integrative-Evolutionary	Integrative-Systemic
Sullivan, Leary, & Benjamin	Frances & Widiger; Eysenck, Costa, & McCrae	Bowen, Ackerman, & Guerin	Rogers, Gilligan, Baker, Miller, & Jordan	Allport, Murray, & Millon	Wachtel & Magnavita
Deductive Inductive	Deductive	Deductive	Inductive	Deductive Inductive	Deductive
Abstract Realistic/Idealistic Objective/Subjective Intro/Extro-spective	Observation near Realistic Objective Extrospective Formal	Abstract Idealistic Subjective Introspective Formal	Abstract Idealistic Subjective Introspective Informal	Observation near Realistic Objective Extrospective Formal	Abstract Idealistic Subjective Extrospective Informal
Clinical utility Self-understanding Predictive ability	Practical utility Predictive ability Ability to generate research	Clinical utility Insight into human nature Ability to understand behavior	Clinical utility Insight into human behavior Ability to understand behavior	Clinical utility Practical utility Insight into human nature Ability to understand complex behavior	Clinical utility Ability to understand complex behavior Insight into human nature
▪ Interpersonal ▪ Attachment ▪ Defensive ▪ Cognitive	▪ Behavioral ▪ Neurobiological	▪ Relational ▪ Systems	▪ Relational ▪ Cultural	▪ Affective ▪ Cognitive ▪ Neurobiological ▪ Defensive	▪ Affective ▪ Cognitive ▪ Interpersonal ▪ Defensive ▪ Systemic
Somewhat complex terminology	Limited application to complex issues	Difficult to empirically validate	Limited to women and lacks empirical evidence	Many component systems	Many components are not clearly defined and easily measurable
Good balance of empirical with depth of understanding	Good empirical approach and sound results	Offers a novel and valuable perspective	Offers a fresh culturally sensitive perspective	Breadth and depth of coverage	Flexibility for understanding multiple levels

Theories of
Personality

Theories of
Personality

Contemporary Approaches to the Science of Personality

Jeffrey J. Magnavita

University of Hartford

JOHN WILEY & SONS, INC.

Library of Congress Cataloging-in-Publication Data:
Magnavita, Jeffrey J.
    Theories of personality : contemporary approaches to the science of
personality / Jeffrey J. Magnavita.
        p. cm.
    Includes bibliographical references and index.
    ISBN 0-471-37890-9 (alk. paper)
        1. Personality.   I. Title.
    BF698 .M24 2002
    155.2—dc21

                                                        2001026638

Printed in the United States of America.

10 9 8 7 6 5 4 3 2 1

To Annie and our daughters—
Elizabeth, Emily, and Caroline

Personality is a field of study that has captured our attention for centuries, but the modern era of "scientific" approaches did not arrive on the landscape until the late nineteenth and early twentieth centuries. The twentieth century heralded a remarkable interest in the topic until about the midpoint of the century. There is much written about this body of work, much of which is now considered classic, and numerous textbooks have described these developments, many going through successive editions to try to keep up with these rapid developments. The interest in personality theory and personality as a construct lost much momentum in the 1960s during the "Dark Age" of the field. After almost 20 years of quiescence, the field was revitalized in the 1980s and has continued to grow and expand at a rapid rate. This period, from the 1980s to the beginning of the twenty-first century, is considered to be the phase of contemporary personality theory. The impetus for writing this text has been the rapid growth of the field in my professional life. Over a century of developments, many of which have taken place in the last quarter of the twentieth century in the fields of psychology, psychiatry, genetics, evolutionary psychology, psychopathology, computer technology, statistical methods, and neuroscience, has fueled the emergence of the field of contemporary personality. Many other newer and related disciplines, such as affective science, relational science, and developmental science, and other scientific models, such as general systems theory, chaos theory, and evolutionary theory, have offered new insights in the quest to understand ourselves and answer the age old questions philosophers have wrestled with: Who are we? and What is consciousness?

The student and professor of personality may wonder what makes this book different from the array of fine textbooks on this topic. I would respond that this text was conceived to fill a void in the field. Rapid developments in the past 20 years in a number of related disciplines as well as in personality theory have changed the theoretical landscape substantially. Personality is a field in a phase of exponential growth, with new developments reported almost daily. It is a topic that holds interest for most of us and has applications to many disciplines of study beyond psychology. It is truly a multidisciplinary topic!

I have enjoyed tremendously the experience of finding and reading many of the classic works on personality, which have always been on my reading list. Whenever possible, I have provided material from the original works so that the reader will have an appreciation for the excitement of many of the conceptual developments and paradigmatic shifts that are reported by various pioneers. I hope that this inspires readers to seek out original works. Although I endeavored to at least mention many of the major developments during the past century, to limit this text to one volume, many important psychological discoveries have been omitted. The most challenging aspect of this project was to identify the components of personality theory that are most relevant to contemporary theory. Older texts have chapters devoted to individuals who are not even cited in this one or are given only minimal coverage. This is not to place a value judgment on the work of so many important contributors. I believe that the major theoretical models presented in this volume give the reader a sound foundation from which to grow and, I hope, find passion in a subject that never seems to lose interest for many and can provide a life-long learning experience. There are many other fine texts available for those interested in the history of the field and for those who seek greater detail of the lives and work of major historical figures.

This text emphasizes the major theories of contemporary personality theory and provides the reader with the necessary background perspective from which to appreciate and understand the evolution of these developments. The main goals of this text are to:

- Present a historical and theoretical background so that the themes and challenges inherent in the study of contemporary personality theory will be evident.

- Present a brief introduction to Freud's psychoanalytic model, along with variants offered by his early disciples, both for its historical value as well as for its continuing influence on many contemporary theories of personality.

- Present an overview of the component systems and newer scientific disciplines that have emerged in the last half of the twentieth century that are required to understand contemporary personality theories. These new developments in cognitive, affective, developmental, and relational theories and neurosciences have a direct influence on theoretical models and will continue to offer fresh perspectives as well as empirical evidence.

- Present the major contemporary theoretical models of personality currently seen in the literature. Many theoretical models and trends have gained prominence and then fallen out of favor. In part, this evolution represents the scientific process in operation.

- Present theoretical models from all levels of the biopsychosocial matrix, each of which offers an insight into personality through its own unique lens.

- Offer a standard format for each of the main theoretical chapters that allows for an examination of the pertinent issues that need to be considered, as well as examples of how the model is applied in real-world situations.

Organization of Material

This text is organized into five sections. Section One provides an introduction to the topic of personality and begins to pose some of the questions a reader is probably beginning to ponder. In this section, basic constructs are introduced that will be seen throughout the text so that the reader begins to develop a conceptual vocabulary. A brief history of the field of personality is presented, beginning with early Greek theoretical formulations, followed by later nineteenth-century attempts at establishing scientific psychology.

Section Two provides the reader with a basic overview of modern scientific personality theory, starting with Freud, and progresses through the work of Freud's disciples and the controversy they sparked.

Section Three summarizes and defines various disciplines that comprise the components needed to understand essential aspects of human nature, personality, and the relationship between the mind and brain.

Section Four, the major body of the text, presents the major contemporary theoretical models using a standard format for each of the seven chapters. Each chapter begins with a review of the main historical figures, followed by a presentation of the current theory. At the end of each chapter, a sample of relevant research is presented in a separate section with a citation for each so that interested readers may select the ones that they are interested in pursuing further. The philosophical underpinnnings and assumptions, notions of normal versus abnormal, assessment strategies and tools, applications of the model, how cultural differences are understood, as well as strengths and limitations are offered. Each chapter is summarized and the major concepts highlighted.

Section Five contains one chapter devoted to a number of important topics and issues that are relevant to the field.

For instructors, an *Instructor's Manual* is available from the publisher that provides a template for using this text for a college course.

JEFFREY J. MAGNAVITA

I would like to express my deep appreciation and thanks to my wife, Anne Gardner Magnavita, for her unflagging support during the time it took me to research and write this volume. Her organizational ability kept our life and family running when I was preoccupied with aspects of this project along with teaching and clinical responsibilities. My daughters, Elizabeth, Emily, and Caroline, have graced me with the opportunity to witness the unfolding of their unique personalities. I want to thank them for delivering cups of coffee and snacks, along with smiles and hugs while I was working.

I would like to extend a special thanks to Dr. Theodore Millon, who was one of the main impetuses for accepting the challenge of this project. He has been exceedingly kind and supportive, giving feedback, filling me in with his encyclopedic knowledge when there were numerous holes in my own, and reading drafts of portions of the manuscript. His work, presented in this text, establishes him as one of the main figures in the field of contemporary personality theory. I have truly appreciated and benefited from our collaboration. Dr. Millon is not only a seminal thinker in the field but an artist as well and has graciously allowed us to use his drawings of some of the prominent figures in psychology. These are seen throughout the text.

I would also like to thank Jennifer Simon, associate publisher, who extended the original offer to develop a proposal, believing a theory of personality text was a worthwhile project. She has done an amazing job shepherding this project along from shortly after its inception to the finished product. She strongly believed that there existed a need for a personality theory text that was "out of the box" and gave me the freedom to allow my unorthodox approach to take shape, carefully crafting it to fit the needs of the reader. A special thanks also goes to Isabel Pratt for her thoughtful input, calm consistent presence, and organizational ability. I would also like to thank the staff at Publications Development Company of Texas for their diligent copy editing and production work on this text. Their work has made it much more coherent.

I would also like to express my thanks to a colleague, Dr. Dorella L. Bond, who teaches personality theory and at the inception of this project loaned me texts. More important, she offered her ideas and insights about what she thought would make a useful text.

A number of academicians, some who teach personality theory and others from related areas, kindly took time from their hectic schedules to read an early draft of a portion of the manuscript. They provided incisive and critical commentary that truly helped in the evolution of my thinking and in the final product. My thanks go to an anonymous reviewer who provided a useful critique. I would especially like to thank Dr. Jack Powell, University of Hartford; Dr. Dean Murier, Mills College; and Dr. Peter Bieling, McMaster University, Canada.

J. J. M.

Chapter 2

History of Personality from the Ancients to the Mid-Twentieth Century

Section Four
Contemporary Models of Personality

Chapter 5
Psychobiological Models of Personality

Chapter 6
Contemporary Psychodynamic Models of Personality   **191**

Chapter 7 _____

Behavioral Models of Personality   237

Chapter 8

Cognitive and Cognitive-Behavioral Models of Personality **275**

Chapter 9
Interpersonal and Factorial Models of Personality   303

Chapter 10
Relational Models of Personality   **329**

Chapter 11 _____

Section Five
Special Topics

Chapter 12
Applications, Research, and Future Directions

INTRODUCTION AND HISTORICAL FOUNDATION TO THE STUDY OF PERSONALITY

What Is Personality? Basic Constructs and Challenges of Contemporary Personality Theory

1

Chapter

Introduction—Our Interest in Personality and Knowing Ourselves

Contemporary society is intrigued with the notion of human behavior as it expresses itself in our **personality.**

How do we explain why people do what they do when their actions seem self-defeating to outside observers?

Our current interest in this topic is evident in our near-obsessive preoccupation with the lives, behavior, and tragic deaths of celebrities such as Princess Diana and John F. Kennedy Jr. and the self-sabotaging behavior of politicians such as William Jefferson Clinton, the recent president of the United States. During the last decade of the twentieth century, millions of people were glued to their television set to watch the unfolding of the Clinton sexual scandal and postelection saga. How could such a brilliant, charismatic leader risk the office of the most powerful man in the world to have a sexual relationship with an intern nearly the same age as his daughter? More surprising, how could he do so while a major investigation was taking place regarding his alleged "mistreatment" and "inappropriate" relationships with women? Numerous books were written on the subject of Clinton's character, as have been written about other controversial presidents such as John F. Kennedy, who, although widely admired, was noted for his promiscuous sexual behavior and association with organized crime figures while in office.

Is jealousy learned or an evolutionary endowed mechanism to ensure survival of the species?

The Clinton Syndrome: The President and the Self-Destructive Nature of Sexual Addiction (Levin, 1998)

In a book about Clinton, Levin traces the roots of Clinton's personality back to his experiences being raised in an alcoholic family system (see dysfunctional personologic systems, Chapter 10). Many of the defenses that are observed in his behavior today may have been incorporated as a way to adapt to an alcoholic system where compartmentalization and denial were key survival tactics. Not only was alcoholism a central theme, but also violence and abandonment, which are also said to have been major contributing factors to what Levin describes as a false self or one that is erected to glean acceptance, love, and approval from others. Being raised in an alcoholic family may have set the stage for much of the behavior that led to Clinton's public humiliation resulting from his reckless behavior. Levin speculates that Clinton suffers from a sexual addiction that serves the same function as alcoholism or any other addiction: to fill up the empty self. We discuss theories of narcissism in Chapter 6.

The Nature of Jealousy and Violence toward Women

We were also intrigued and shocked by the murder of Nicole Simpson and her companion, which many individuals believe was carried out by her enraged and jealous husband. Some mental health professionals described O. J. Simpson as manifesting the profile of a **batterer,** which is generally a male who intimates, threatens, and physically and emotionally abuses women to keep them from abandoning him. The evolutionary psychologist David Buss writes (2000b): "But the irony of jealousy, which can shatter the most harmonious relationships, is that it flows from deep and abiding love. The paradox was reflected in O. J. Simpson's statement: 'Let's say I committed this crime [the slaying of ex-wife Nicole Brown Simpson]. Even if I did, it would have to have been because I loved her very much, right?'" (pp. 55–56). The personalities of those involved in this nationally broadcast trial, the prosecuting attorney and the defense attorneys and their entourage, were often more compelling than those involved in the event itself. Questions about the nature of jealousy have been of interest to a new breed of **evolutionary psychologists** who believe that many aspects of personality are shaped by evolutionary challenges to adapt. In his book about the evolutionary basis of sexuality, Buss (2000a,b) theorizes that sexual jealousy has evolved as an early detection system for infidelity. In some Middle Eastern countries, women are severely punished if they show more than their eyes in public. Is this an adaptation to reduce the opportunity for activating pathological jealousy? Or does it create a hothouse where sexual jealousy is intensified? Buss also found that individuals with narcissistic personality characteristics are more likely to be unfaithful. He describes narcissism, which is discussed in Chapter 6, thus:

> *Perhaps most central for infidelity, narcissists typically lack empathy for the pain and suffering they cause others. They are so preoccupied with their own needs and desires, they neglect to consider how their actions might hurt others, even those closest to them. Finally, narcissists are frequently envious of others, resentful of those who might have more success, power or prestige. Their envy may be linked to their fragile sense of self-esteem, since narcissists oscillate between feelings of grandiosity and feelings that they are worthless. Good behavioral markers of narcissism include showing off one's body (exhibitionistic), nominating oneself for a position of power (grandiosity), taking*

the best piece of food for oneself (self-centered), asking for a large favor without offering repayment (sense of entitlement), laughing at a friend's problems (lack of empathy), and using friends for their wealth (interpersonally exploitative). All of these qualities seem conducive to gaining gratification outside of marriage. (D. Buss, 2000a, p. 149)

In his research, Buss (2000a) identified some of the signals that are indicative of emotional infidelity. These include (1) declaring that love has left the marriage; (2) emotional disengagement: not saying "I love you" when a partner expresses love; (3) forgetting important events such as anniversaries and special dates; and (4) displays of guilt, such as difficulty maintaining eye contact or acting guilty after sexual relations.

Are we creatures of our evolutionary adaptations not far from the Neanderthal, or are we influenced by cultural and family factors?

The Dangerous Passion: Why Jealousy Is as Necessary as Love and Sex (D. Buss, 2000a)

Here are a few real-life examples of violence triggered by sexual jealousy.

The first case is told by a woman, age 19, whose husband started beating her shortly after they got married: "Tim [her husband] is really jealous. I remember once when we were at my girlfriend's house. I had to use the bathroom. The bathroom is upstairs. Well, my girlfriend's brother's room is next to the bathroom. I stood in front of his door and talked to him for a minute on my way back downstairs. When I got to the stairs Tim was waiting for me. He called me a whore and a tease and slugged me on the side of my head. I fell down the stairs. I can't blame Tim, though. I guess I shouldn't have talked to my girlfriend's brother. I mean, I know Tim's real jealous."

In a second case, "The wife, confronted with yet another round of accusations and cross-questioning about a boyfriend she had before marriage and with whom she had a child, responded that at least her previous lover had been man enough to get her pregnant. This touched on the husband's fears about his potency and fertility, and triggered a furious assault" (pp. 101–102).

Will we see future defense of Simpson-like cases calling forth the evidence from evolutionary psychology that this type of response is hardwired and not under control?

Are humans violent by nature or is violence shaped by sociocultural influences?

The Wave of Violence in Schools: What Are the Root Causes?

The tragic mass murder at Columbine High School in Littleton, Colorado, and many others that have followed stunned the nation, shaking our sense of security and basic trust in the safety of our children while at school. Mental health and educational professionals, sociologists, and politicians searched for every possible explanation for the behavior of these "privileged" adolescents who engaged in an orgy of senseless mayhem and random mass murder. The cold-blooded nature of these killings left many of us in the mental health profession wondering about the two killers' degree of **psychopathy,** which is seen in individuals with **Antisocial Personality Disorder** and indicates a lack of empathy for others and an inability to experience guilt. Our schools were no longer the relatively safe harbors where children go to learn and be socialized, but were places where seemingly inexplicable violence was being perpetrated by other children. Children in many schools had to submit to searches, lost their lockers, and had to carry see-through backpacks. To many, a culture of **paranoia,** a pathological level of suspiciousness and mistrust, was being engendered.

Why are aggression and violence so much more common in men than in women?

Mass Murders Perpetrated by Extremists

The bombing of the Edward Morrow Jr. building by a white supremacist was another incident of senseless mass murder that propelled the nation into a sense of despair and grief. Little satisfaction was gained in our trying to understand the motivation and inner workings of the mind of the bomber, Timothy McVeigh, who remained defiant and remorseless, even after being sentenced to death. Many believe that McVeigh was suffering from a psychopathic (antisocial) personality disorder and feels no normal sense of guilt as others would. This type of personality seems to be attracted to certain political philosophies that show a lack of empathy for those who are different. This also seemed to be the case of many in Adolf Hitler's inner circle who were responsible for the genocide of the Holocaust. Many of those who were caught and tried at Nuremberg used various **defense mechanisms** such as denial, rationalization, or minimization to explain their involvement in the mass murder that took place during World War II. Many books have been written that tried to understand the inner workings of Hitler, one of the most infamous figures of the twentieth century. Various authors have utilized psychoanalytic concepts to explain such behavior. His early childhood experiences have been microscopically examined for clues about his developmental and familial experiences that may have shaped his personality into the demigod that he became.

Why do some individuals become violent and others from the same family system, with "similar" upbringing and genetic endowment, eschew violence?

Insane or a Social Reformer? The Unabomber

Another complex personality that has captured the nation's attention, Theodore Kaczynski, known as the Unabomber, carried out a reign of terror for over two decades, sending bombs in the mail to scientists, maiming and killing many. He felt his actions were justified because the ends justified the means. He wanted to undermine the technological/industrial complex, which he and other, less "deranged" individuals thought would be responsible for the ultimate destruction of the planet. Kaczynski was a Harvard graduate and PhD scientist, whose manifesto was "greeted in 1995 by many thoughtful people as a work of genius, or at least profundity, and as quite sane" (Chase, 2000, p. 44). The manifesto was a 35,000-word essay titled *Industrial Society and Its Future* was published in the *Washington Post* and the *New York Times*. Kaczynski's brother recognized the writing, which led to his capture. Kaczynski was believed to be a paranoid schizophrenic by some mental health professionals; however, many others who have read his manifesto believe that his writings are coherent and indicate otherwise. The clarity and depth of his writing have led others to be cautious about this diagnostic pronouncement. Kaczynski himself was concerned with how his psychological status would be judged if he were captured alive. The media were quick to dismiss him as crazy (Chase, 2000), and Kaczynski wrote of this inevitability: "I intend to start killing people. If I am successful at this, it is possible that, when I am caught (not alive, I fervently hope!) there will be some speculation in the news media as to my motives for killing. . . . If some speculation occurs, they are bound to make me out to be a sickie, and to ascribe to me motives of a sordid or 'sick' type. Of course, the term 'sick' in such a context represents a value judgment . . . the news media may have something to say about me when I am killed or caught. And they are bound to try to analyse my psychology and depict me as 'sick.' This powerful bias should be borne [in mind] in reading any attempts to analyse my psychology" (p. 47).

Is it ethical to conduct psychological experiments on students that may cause harm or about which they are not reasonably informed?

To add another interesting twist to this story, Chase (2000), in an article in the *Atlantic Monthly*, investigated the link between Kaczynski's actions and his experience in a psychology experiment conducted by the famous personality theorist Henry Murray, who was at Harvard when Kaczynski was an undergraduate. In a long-term study that was supposed to be investigating techniques of personality assessment, Kaczynski, as were other student volunteers, was subjected to what under today's ethical guidelines would be considered deceitful if not unnecessarily abusive treatment. Chase describes this procedure:

Is aggression a basic human drive, or is it stimulated and shaped by violent images and abusive treatment by parents and others responsible for children?

> When the subject arrived for the debate, he was escorted to a "brilliantly lighted room" and seated in front of a one-way mirror. A motion-picture camera recorded his every move and facial expression through a hole in the wall. Electrodes leading to machines that recorded his heart and respiratory rates were attached to his body. Then the debate began. But the students were tricked. Contrary to what Murray claimed in his article, they had been led to believe that they would debate their philosophy of life with another student like themselves. Instead they confronted what Forrest Robinson describes as a "well-prepared 'stooge' "—a talented young lawyer indeed, but one who had been instructed to launch into an aggressive attack on the

subject, for the purpose of upsetting him as much as possible. . . . Not surprisingly, most participants found this highly unpleasant, even traumatic, as the data set records. (Chase, 2000, p. 55)

Can life events shape our personality?

Chase (2000) questions the purpose of these experiments and wonders whether they were intended to assist the CIA in determining "how to test, or break down, an individual's ability to withstand interrogation" (p. 56). Regardless of the ultimate goal of these psychological experiments, the question is whether this experience was a turning point that in some way led to or shaped Kaczynski's attitudes about the scientific/technological advances in society: "Thus did Kaczynski's Harvard experiences shape his anger and legitimize his wrath" (p. 63).

Why is violence perpetrated on those who are culturally different or who have a different sexual orientation?

Manifestations of Homophobia in Society

Other critical events were also widely publicized, such as the senseless hate crimes and gay bashing reprehensible to most people. In one nationally broadcast event, a Black man was chained to a truck and horrifically dragged to death by two White racists. In another equally heinous act, two men tied a gay man to a post, beat him, and left him to die. These and other senseless events left many of us disoriented and wondering what was next. Psychoanalytic theorists believe that underlying homosexual impulses in the homophobic individual generates this type of reaction. When encountering someone who is perceived as homosexual, these individuals project their anxiety and fear in a massive destructive rage.

Is personality real, and what exactly does it mean?

Personality Theory and Theorists

An important element of understanding what occurred in the above described events and many others mentioned throughout this volume is explained by **social scientists** and **personality theorists** by the concept we know as **personality** and, in pathological versions,

personality disorder. Personality theorists are psychologists who devote their scientific careers to the development of **paradigms** or models that attempt to explain the complexity of human behavior.

The Construct of Personality

The term personality has become part of common parlance. We speak of people as having an "annoying" or "off-putting" personality; we describe others as "being laid back" or "irritable" or "hyper." Individuals may be described with adjectives such as cruel or empathic. We all seem to have inner **adjective checklists** whereby we rate those in our life. We use various **scales** of polar traits, such as weak versus strong. We might further break down these characteristics into **traits,** or stable characteristics, such as shy, outgoing, hostile, or provocative. Personality, however, is a **construct**—something we cannot see but for which we make **subjective** or **objective ratings.** We also make **theoretical inferences** about individual motivation and behavior. We ask, *Why did he or she act in this way or that? Was it in character?* We are often shaken and uncomfortable when someone we know acts in a way that we do not expect or would not have predicted.

Is the study of personality really scientific or just speculative pondering by those with advanced degrees repackaging commonsense notions?

Various theoretical constructs are presented in this text. Some of them have been validated in part by the scientific method using various forms of empirical research. However, for the most part, the science of personality theory is in its infancy, and many of the theoretical models remain speculative at best. Personality theorists approach the study of personality from differing perspectives using various **empirical methods.**

Factor Analytic Models

Personality can be empirically studied using methods of advanced statistics known as factor analysis. In this approach to understanding personality, various attributes are listed and then subjected to rigorous statistical calculations that reduce these attributes to common factors. This is primarily a **lexical study of personality.** This means that the language used to describe personality characteristics is usually the starting point to begin to explore the way ideas about personality are encoded in language. For example, all the words in the dictionary used to describe personality are recorded and then subjected to factor analysis to distill these to the essential or core factors. Most researchers have identified three to five factors that can be used to account for the individual variations in personality.

Clinical Psychopathological Models

Much of what we have come to understand about personality comes from **clinical observation** and **psychometric testing** of individuals with disordered personalities and from abnormal psychology. Clinical observations in the form of case summaries that have been gathered over the past century and published by psychologists and psychiatrists are the foundation for many theories of personality and have led to the current system of classification of mental disorders, both personality disorders and **clinical syndromes,** which are the manifestations of symptoms of depression, anxiety, and other mental states. Most of the theories of personality presented in this text that form the basic fabric of current personology evolved from years of painstaking observations of patients in various mental health settings who availed themselves of psychotherapy and other medical forms of treatment.

Intensive Study of Individuals

Another way personality is empirically studied is by in-depth examination of an individual. This is the type of approach that Henry Murray did with Ted Kaczynski and other, less infamous Harvard students. Often, groups of individuals may be subjected to extensive testing and interviews so as to study various features of personality. This method can also be done in a longitudinal fashion, wherein the subjects are retested over time to examine changes in the individual (Brody & Siegel, 1992). This provides information about the stability and malleability of personality, along with other important data.

What is the difference between the study of personality and psychotherapy? Aren't they really the same subject?

Psychotherapy and Personality

Rychlak (1973) makes the observation that the understanding and advancement of personality theory is inextricably linked to developments in the field of psychotherapy. Psychotherapy became a clinical and scientific branch of psychology during the twentieth century. As we shall see in Chapter 3, the birth of modern psychotherapy can be traced to Freud's developing a comprehensive theory of psychic functioning, which until that time had never been attempted. In fact, Rychlak believed that the questions What is personality? and What is psychotherapy? are relevant when asked together. In one of his classic texts, *Introduction to Personality and Psychotherapy* (1973), he stated:

> *The two questions are not unrelated, however, since it is historical fact that many of our major personality theorists have come from the medical profession, or they have taken considerable interest in man's level of psychological health even as they were explicating his temperament, character, or "personality." . . . We want to write theories about what makes some people differ from others. . . . Personality theorists are drawn to discriminal theorizing—at least, the classic personality theorists were. And one of the most dramatic forms of difference among people is the level of normalcy they reflect. There are "good" ways to be normal, of course, such as by excelling in a sport, having a popular personality, or achieving success in one's job. But such individuals are not causes for concern. A profession dedicated to studying them and helping them to achieve or be all the more popular does not seem to make sense. It is more important to help the negatively deviant—the criminals, mentally retarded, or insane—return to the fold of socially defined normalcy, or to help the average person excel in some fashion. (pp. 17–18)*

Rychlak brings a number of interesting points to our attention. He mentions a style of theorizing called **discriminal,** by which he means trying to tie together behavioral sequences. He contrasts this to **vehicular** theorizing, which is an analysis of the laws that tie behavioral sequences together. This text emphasizes contemporary theorists who are primarily discriminal in their theorizing, although an attempt is made to include those who have provided many of the building blocks that contemporary theorists use.

We can also see another noteworthy trend since Rychlak's text was published in 1973. Psychologists, psychiatrists, and other mental health professionals are concerned not only with the "deviant" members of our society but with the functioning of the "worried well." We see evidence of this in a number of areas, from the growth of marriage and family therapy, to sports psychology, to behavioral medicine. Each of these areas has developed to fulfill needs of a more affluent and psychologically minded population.

Psychotherapy continues to be an important lens through which to view personality. Much of psychotherapy is concerned with behavior or personality change. Psychotherapy continues, since Freud's time, to be a major experimental forum in which to measure, diagnose, and treat personality and related disturbances. Historically, many of the seminal personality theorists were psychiatrists (Freud, Jung, Sullivan, Ferenczi) or clinical psychologists (Carl Rogers, George Kelly). "Though these men were healers, they did not confine their comments on man to the abnormal. How could they? A well-rounded theory of man was required if there was to be a place for the sick or abnormal man within the picture" (Rychlak, 1973, p. 18). This has resulted in a marriage between psychotherapy, one branch of clinical science, and personology, the study of what makes us unique. In a more recent article, Rychlak (2000) discusses science and psychotherapy:

> *When one works closely with people—seeing their lives through their conceptual eyes, struggling with them to help set things straight, looking for something better, including the spiritual—it is just plain silly to view them as being moved by meaningless impulsions of the billiard-ball (efficiently caused) variety. Life is fraught with hopeful aspirations, self-delusions, plans not carried out, achievements to be proud of, misunderstandings, and empathic insights. This is what I think the modern student is seeking to capture in her or his theorizing, and unfortunately these students are blaming the scientific method for this disenchantment as if it were the messenger of mechanism rather than the disinterested testing vehicle of the paradigmatic theoretical assumptions advanced by the dominant language community in psychology. (p. 1131)*

Aren't the terms temperament, character, and personality interchangeable?

Temperament, Character, and Personality

Central to the notion of personality are the related constructs temperament and character. Throughout this text, we use various terms based on the theoretical model being presented to describe personality and its components.

Temperament

When personologists speak of temperament, we are referring to an individual's basic biological dispositions that many believe are innate at birth; for example, we might describe Cindy as a high-strung person or Karen as irritable. Developmental psychologists have observed and rated the temperamental variations in infants, and theorists who ascribe to the **psychobiological model** use this as a basis of understanding the underlying biological substrates of temperament.

Character

Character is a commonly used term that generally refers to the basic enduring aspects of a person, such as integrity, honesty, morality, and stability. Character assessment views or judges how a person acts in various contexts. For example, in the case of McVeigh, what type of character would explain this apparently remorseless individual? Characterological explanations are most often seen in the psychodynamic literature to describe and understand the inner workings of such people.

Traits

Traits are specific features of one's personality, such as persistence, integrity, and honesty. Trait psychologists have done extensive studies to reduce these to factors that can account for the variance in personality. Generally, most traits can be reduced by a process called factor analysis to three to five superordinate ones. For example, we might ask what types of traits are evident in individuals with homophobia.

Personality

Personality is an individual's habitual way of thinking, feeling, perceiving, and reacting to the world. Although some believe that personality is stable and immutable, others view personality as a more fluid concept that is influenced by a number of external factors such as culture and family systems. Integrative and relational models of personality attempt to understand the multidimensional factors in constant interrelationships. Others look at biological, cognitive, or behavioral systems to explain personality.

Prototypes/Typology

Certain constellations of temperament and traits may be characterized in a stereotypic way or in more sophisticated, scientifically validated ways. Prototypes combine a **type of personality** with a **dimensional scale.** For example, the construct of the **authoritarian personality** developed by Adorno, Frenkel-Brunswik, Levinson, and Sanford (1950) is one such example. A cluster of **traits** that include excessive conformity, overcontrol of feelings and impulses, rigid thinking style, and ethnocentrism characterizes the authoritarian personality (Krech, Crutchfield, & Ballachey, 1962). Such individuals also are preoccupied with status and power and tend to identify with others who are authoritative. They tend to be hostile to groups of people they consider "outsiders," usually members of minority groups. The interest in this personality type emerged from interest in understanding the anti-Semitism that fueled the Holocaust. The authoritarian personality was measured by something called the F-scale (for fascism). Another finding is that individuals high on the F-scale tend to see things in black and white. Individuals who are raised with parents who are high on the F-scale tend to be more authoritarian than those whose parents score lower. Evidence suggests that those raised under very strict parental control, which was standard child rearing in pre-World War II Germany, are more likely to be obedient to authority and repress their anger only to displace it on those they see as lesser and weaker. The description of the authoritarian personality was very similar to what was considered the "ideal" personality of a Nazi.

How do you know the difference between "normal" and "abnormal" personalities? Is personality best conceptualized as a category, or does it exist on a dimensional level?

Distinguishing among Normal Personality, Trait Disturbance, and Personality Disorder

The theories of personality presented in this text have to contend with a critical question: *how to differentiate between what is considered normal and what is pathological personality functioning.* This is a source of many polemics in the field of abnormal psychology, clinical psychology, and psychiatry and has major implications. For example, severe personality disturbance is classified as a mental disorder, and thus treatment is covered under many medical insurance plans. Conferring the status of a mental illness, such as Antisocial Personality Disorder, on a pattern of conduct such as criminal behavior has major implications for how society will react. Calling one type of personality pattern disordered and declaring another within normal range thus has important societal and financial implications.

Where does "normal" personality end and abnormal or disordered personality begin? The way this question is posed suggests that personality and personality disorders exist on a continuum and that as we proceed along the points, normal personality becomes abnormal. However, the major classification and diagnostic system of mental disorders of the American Psychiatric Association uses a categorical approach. This approach assumes that there are discrete categories of personality disorder—you either have it or you don't, so to speak. Our assumptions about what we are measuring and what is normal can be viewed through various lenses, each offering a view of the reality of a complex phenomenon.

Don't other disciplines, such as literature, theology, and philosophy, deal with personality?

How Related Disciplines View Personality

Personality is not only the province of behavioral sciences. Other disciplines are also concerned with personality and character and understanding the basic forces that operate within all human beings. Later in the text, we examine the contributions of anthropology, philosophy, and biology; each has offered useful perspectives and metaphors for understanding the cultural aspects of personality.

Philosophy and the Study of Human Nature

Psychology emerged from its sister discipline, philosophy, which is concerned with understanding the nature of man. Strong philosophical underpinnings are apparent in various systems of psychological thought. Early philosophers speculated on the nature of humankind.

The Greek philosopher Aristotle was one of the earliest systematic thinkers who strove to know. In fact, the definition of **psyche** is *substance that is capable of receiving knowledge:* "To Aristotle, psyche basically meant living" (R. I. Watson, 1971, p. 54). Psychology and personality theory have their roots in two disciplines: philosophy and natural science (see Figure 1.1).

Literature and the Understanding of Human Nature

Much can be learned about the inner workings of men and women from reading literature. Writers offer a view of human beings that often shows profound insight into the basic struggles of existence and how these are navigated by people from various times and cultures. Our fascination with literature is in large part our attempt at understanding the struggles of human existence and the impact that environmental, family, and genetic factors exert on fictional or real characters. Elements of classical literature can be seen in many theories of personality. In the development of psychoanalytic theory, Freud drew directly from Greek mythology and Shakespeare; for example, the Oedipal complex borrowed directly from the play *Hamlet,* and the roots of our current conception of narcissism come from the Greek myth of Narcissus.

Religion and the Understanding of Human Nature

Religion offers another valuable perspective on the nature of humankind. Theology attempts to understand humankind and our relationship to a greater power. Various religious groups make assumptions about the nature of good and evil and which features we

Figure 1.1

The Relationships among Philosophy, Natural Science, and the Emergence of Twentieth-Century Personality Theory.

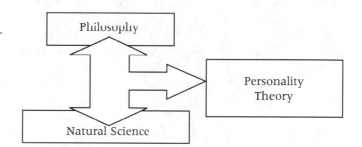

should strive to emulate that will bring us closer to God. Theological systems of thought offer alternative understandings concerning the nature of humankind and the possibility of transformation.

Murray's Scientific Personology

Henry Murray (1938) advanced the field of personality with his systematic study of personality. He coined the term **personology:** "The branch of psychology which principally concerns itself with the study of human lives and the factors that influence their course, which investigates individual differences and types of personality, may be termed 'personology' instead of 'the psychology of personality,' a clumsy tautological expression" (p. 4).

Murray (1938) was very concerned about establishing the study of personality as a valid scientific endeavor. He challenged the scientific community to rise to the task of organizing the data into coherent theoretical constructs, to which he devoted much of his scientific career. He wrote: "Personology, if it is ever developed, will rest upon an organized collection of facts pertaining relevantly to the long

course of complex events from human conception to human death. They will be contained for the most part in case histories based on observations of behavior in natural and experimental situations, together with the subject's memories and introspections. The questions: what are facts? how are they discovered? and how proved to others? will always be fundamental to the science. But the discipline will not advance until it is possible to transform the raw data of experience into adequate abstractions" (p. 23). Murray commented on the process of scientific advancement: "To study human nature patiently, to arrive at understanding, to gain some mastery; there would be little hope in the enterprise if it were not for the history of science, the steady, unassertive, conquering pace of disinterested observation, experiment and reflection. Three centuries ago did the fancy of the most imaginative men foresee the miracles of thought and technics that would mark the way of science? Absorbing this tradition, man may now explore his soul and observe the conduct of his fellows, dispassionate to the limit, yet ever animated by the faith that gaining mastery through knowledge he may eventually surmount himself" (p. 35).

I hope readers and students of personology after reading this text will come to the conclusion that we have accomplished much of what was spelled out in Murray's (1938) volume, *Explorations in Personality*. The field has amassed a tremendous amount of data through observation in clinical settings, empirical research, and theory building. Much needs to be done, but we can rest assured that the twentieth century was an exciting one indeed for pioneers in personology.

Isn't personality something that, once developed, stays with you for life without much change?

Is Personality Stable or Mutable?

Our intuitive understanding of personality suggests that our personality is stable. You will probably agree that most people you know have stable or consistent characteristics at various times and in various situations. This notion—that we are identifiable to those who know us—suggests a certain degree of predictability in our personality. Further, we know that when certain individuals are the unfortunate victim of brain damage, spectacular changes in personality often result. In some cases, individuals who were severely aggressive have become more docile and individuals who were nonviolent have been observed to become violent when certain parts of the cerebral cortex were damaged by accident or war injuries. We will see how the field of neuroscience has shed much light on the underlying substrate on which personality is built.

When I am in a "blue" mood and withdraw and avoid others, hasn't my personality changed?

Trait versus State Differences

In our journey to understand personality, it is vital to introduce the concepts of trait and state. **Trait** refers to the stability of a personality factor that is consistent in various conditions; **state** refers to a condition that fluctuates, such as a mood. At times, these differences are a matter of polemics but are nevertheless vital to our understanding of personality. For example, an individual who is depressed may withdraw from his or her surroundings and appear preoccupied and difficult to engage interpersonally. If we assessed personality at this time, we may arrive at the inaccurate conclusion that the individual is introverted. Later, when the depression lifts, the person might become more outgoing and socially responsive. Thus, we say that the personality was influenced by the **affective—mood state**—of the individual.

Are there tools that can be used to assess and compare various theories?

Rychlak's Fundamental Dimensions of Theory

The root word for theory is the Greek work *theoria*, meaning to view or contemplate. The *Random House College Dictionary* (Stein, 1975) defines theory as a "coherent group of general propositions used as principles of explanation for a class of phenomenon." Wilson (1998) describes the importance of theory: "Nothing in science—nothing in life, for that matter—makes sense without theory. It is our nature to put all knowledge into the context in order to tell a story, and to re-create the world by this means" (p. 52).

In a classic text, *A Philosophy of Science for Personality Theory*, Rychlak (1968) devotes a great deal of consideration to the topic of theory. Understanding these fundamental dimensions are crucial in the critical assessment of the various theoretical systems of personality presented in this text. The dimensions Rychlak discusses are presented in Table 1.1.

Abstraction

Theoretical **constructs** are abstractions "made from a given point of view, a refined perspective, a biased position, or the like. The elements to be included in the construct will depend upon the general nature of the theory, its purpose, the purpose of the theorists who subscribe to it, and so on" (Rychlak, 1968, p. 13). The dimensions of abstraction range from lesser to greater levels. Behavior

Table 1.1   **Rychlak's Theoretical Features**

Abstract	Observation Near
Concepts tend to be esoteric and can be interpreted differentially.	Data are emphasized and constructs follow in the form of laws.

Realistic	Idealistic
The perspective that there is an observable external world that is immutable.	The perspective that reality is subjectively observed and constructed.

Objective	Subjective
Assumes that experience can be reliably observed when the proper criteria are used.	Assumes that there is a level of knowledge that is personal and not observable.

Introspective	Extrospective
The belief that the observer can realistically observe the self.	The belief that the observer cannot accurately observe the self and must be detached from the point of observation.

Formal	Informal
Laws and postulates are clearly articulated and logically connected.	Laws and postulates are loosely formulated and connected.

theory and psychoanalytic theory, as you shall read in the following chapters, were at odds with one another early on in the evolution of personality theory and are thus useful to compare and contrast (see Table 1.2). Classic behavior theory attempted to keep as close to the **observable** data as possible and used as little, if any, abstraction as possible. Psychoanalytic theory lies at the opposite end of the continuum and is highly abstract, often accused of using esoteric terminology that has various levels of meaning. In each position, something is lost and something gained. Behavior theory stays close to empirical truths but may lose much when it attempts to describe the complexity of the personality system. In psychoanalysis, the theory and language are rich and the explanatory potential great; yet, psychoanalytic language can also be murky, with

Table 1.2   **Comparison of Behavioral and Psychoanalytic Models**

Behavior theory	Little abstraction, terms precisely defined	Close to empirical observation	Avoids theory and derives laws from data
Psychoanalytic theory	Highly abstract, terms loosely defined and esoteric	Removed from empirical observation	Complicated theory, fits data into theory

multiple meanings for the same term, and often strays a great deal from the data points.

In the observation of human behavior and personality, we need terms to describe what we see as well as "a way of organizing the mass of potential variables fluctuating before our eyes" (Rychlak, 1968, p. 13). Various theorists have developed and refined terms to classify what they see and these are often not interchangeable.

Realism versus Idealism

Theories are also developed along a continuum of realism and idealism. **Realism** refers to the position that the world (sometimes phrased "external world") of perception and cognition has an immutable existence all its own, entirely independent of the perceiver. Scientists use abstractions to map a reality to gain scientific knowledge. **Idealism** refers to the stance that there is no external reality apart from the perceiver. Humans view the world through their unique and limited perceptions and senses. Reality is created and coconstructed between observer and subject. "Abstractions are ordered percepts, given a name; but to assume that they map anything having a clear-cut, literal, or unchanging existence really adds nothing to our theoretical activity, and it may even hamper us" (Rychlak, 1968, p. 17). As Rychlak very astutely describes, " 'meaning' is a relational concept; it suggests that some item to which one refers bears a certain relationship to other concepts already 'grasped'—i.e., placed in an interpenetrating relationship. The meaning of 'love,' though vague and at times difficult to point to, is carried by this

term's relation with many aspects of experience, including senti-
mental songs, party experiences, jealousies, lust, a quiet solitude, a
sharing, and so on. Now, to tie this directly into our present dimension, a realist would hold that the relational aspect of his constructs
is provided in *nature*, entirely independent of his intellect or his behavior" (p. 18).

Objective versus Subjective

Objective refers "to the view that abstractions, and hence the relationship between abstractions, transcend the individual abstractor,
and may be grasped or understood by all individuals in a specified
class" (p. 22). **Subjective,** "on the other hand, implies that our abstractions and relations between them are somehow private, and
difficult or impossible to circumscribe, much less to generalize beyond the behavior of the abstractor in question" (p. 23). When discussing objectivity and subjectivity, we also should understand two
other terms, **nomothetic** and **idiographic:** "Nomothetic study essentially presumes that a theoretical abstraction can be made which
has general applicability for several members of a given class (i.e.,
distribution). Idiographic study, on the other hand, emphasizes the
uniqueness of personality manifestation" (p. 24).

Introspection versus Extrospection

The position of the observer is also important in the development of
a theory of personality: "If the theorist takes an introspective attitude and perspective, his constructs will be formulated from the
point of view of the *object of study*" (p. 27). "If the theorist takes an
extrospective perspective or frame of reference, he defines his vantage point as observer, regardless of the point of view of the study"
(p. 27). In academic psychology, there was an attempt to reject the
use of introspection; with the rejection of introspectionism, the importance of consciousness was also sidestepped.

Formal versus Informal

Formal theory is stated in as uniform and specific a way as possible
and is "written to bring together all the loosely joined tenets,
hypotheses, and validated facts into a consistent, interdependent

unity" (p. 35). **Informal theory** "is theory which has not been stated explicitly, lacks a clear unifying abstraction, and, since it often goes unrecognized, does not have as its implicit goal the formulation of a logically consistent and mutually interdependent body of knowledge" (p. 35).

Rychlak's schema helps us conceptualize the differences in various theoretical approaches so that they can be compared and contrasted on their essential features. There is no correct or incorrect way that personality theory ought to be constructed; one theory may have more utility in one aspect of prediction or understanding than another. For example, behavior theories are often better suited at predicting behavior in many cases, but psychodynamic theory may be better suited for clinicians who are attempting to understand certain pathological states.

What makes a theory "scientific" as opposed to something someone dreamed up that doesn't have any validity?

Psychological Science of Personality

All branches of science require a way of **classifying the data,** a **set of propositions,** and a **theory** for organizing the data into a comprehensible framework that can guide further developments and pose testable hypotheses. The theory must then stand the test of **empirical** examination that will either confirm or refute the theory, allowing for outright rejection or modification.

Classification

The first stage in the emergence of a new scientific discipline is the effort to classify the domain of its interest. For example, in the early stages of the development of biological science, great strides were made in advancing knowledge by organizing the various classes of plants and animals by similarities in characteristics and functions. Thus, biological scientists were able to organize the millions of species into more manageable classes with distinguishing features and commonalties. In the development of the science of personality theory, early scientific interest was directed toward classifying human personality into various groups based on repeated observations of human behavior. Although many of these early systems, such as the four humors from the early Greeks and phrenology from the nineteenth century, were based on faulty assumptions, their attempt at classification of different personality types was the beginning of the scientific study in its elementary form. As the reader shall see, these models have areas of convergence with modern-day theoretical formulations, which we hope are based on sounder foundations.

A Set of Propositions

Once sufficient data have been accumulated and organized into coherent categories, scientists then begin to develop propositions about how these elements interact and influence each other. These propositions are considered to have greater **validity** when they are accurately describing the data and are **reliable** if they are testable and reproducible by other investigators. In fact, one of the main elements of the scientific method is the validation of results through repeated experiments. The scientific method requires that findings be subjected to peer review and that the specific steps in arriving at the conclusions be made public so that other investigators can prove or refute the findings. The sine qua non of scientific investigation is considered by many to be the **experimental method,** a process in which the factors being investigated are manipulated by comparing an experimental group and a control group and the experimenters and their assistants are blind to the various groups.

Building a Theory

Usually, the next, more advanced stage of scientific development of a discipline requires the building of a theoretical model that explains how the components of the model interrelate. For example, in the biological sciences, major advances were made when investigators began to develop theoretical models of how pathogens cause disease. Even though the viruses and bacteria responsible for the spread of disease and decimation of large numbers of people had been identified, little progress was made until a theory was put forth as to how these agents invisible to the unaided human eye cause so much devastation.

One of the major advancements in knowledge was achieved by Charles Darwin when, after years of observation and classification of the natural world, he advanced the theory of evolution that explained the diversity on earth with the concept of natural selection. His model of evolution has informed and influenced many disciplines; later, we spend some time seeing how this model has been applied to the study of personality.

Testing the Theoretical Components

Before a theory is accepted, it needs to be subjected to scientific inquiry. If the propositions of the theory are not validated, the theory will eventually fall out of favor. This happened with the field of phrenology, which we discuss later. Although the study of the contour of an individual's head made some sense at the time, the propositions failed to be supported and thus phrenology became an extinct theory of personality.

There seem to be so many elements that make us unique, how can I organize all the various components?

Observing Different Levels of Abstraction of Component Systems

There are various levels of abstraction that can be used to view the observations we are organizing. A concept developed by Engel (1980), which he termed the **biopsychosocial model,** is useful in understanding the various levels of abstraction that we may use to understand human behavior (see Figure 1.2).

We may abstract various phenomena **microscopically** or hypothesize what is going on at an unobservable level because we have no instrument to see. For example, on an intrapsychic level, Freud postulated the inner workings of the psychic agencies of the id, ego, and superego; he did so not by direct observation, as these are explanatory constructs that do not exist, but by listening to the free associations of the patients he was treating. On another microscopic level of abstraction, we may be concerned with how the neurotransmitters in the brain function and their effect on personality. On a **macroscopic** level, we can observe the phenomena directly, with the unaided eye, as in the interpersonal interaction between a married couple; we can note their emotions, the content of their communication, body posture, vocal intonations, and so forth.

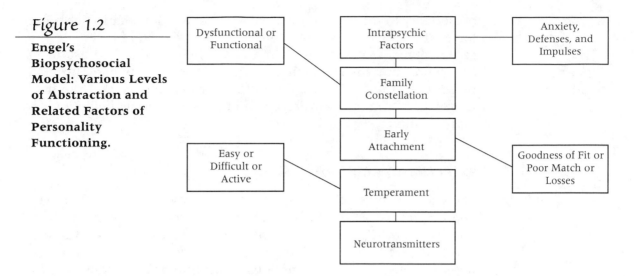

Figure 1.2

Engel's Biopsychosocial Model: Various Levels of Abstraction and Related Factors of Personality Functioning.

Metapsychology

Meta refers to a higher order or transcending construct; therefore, metapsychology refers to constructs that transcend basic psychological principles.

Why are there so many theories of personality that seem at times to contradict one another?

Convergence of Personality Theories

Over a quarter of a century ago, Rychlak (1973) wrote: "The area of personality theory is immense and confusing, and even the great thinkers in the field do not have a clear picture of one another." What he said then still applies to the current state of the field of personality, although much less so. Major advances and interdisciplinary cross-fertilization have spawned a period of exponential growth. There are now many well-established theoretical models that in many ways begin to show signs of convergence as they evolve. As we can imagine, the variables are infinite, but good theory makes the confusing morass more manageable and comprehensible. We are not at the point in the development of the science of personality to make accurate predictions of an individual's behavior; for example, we cannot accurately predict who will be violent at a given moment. We do, however, have theories that are useful in deepening our understanding of the way people work. This text presents a sample of these, but the reader is reminded that the field is broad and complete coverage of all the aspects of the field requires many volumes.

Eclecticism and Integration

The theories presented in this text are to varying degrees eclectic and integrative. At the early stage of theoretical development, theorists were much more iconoclastic in their views. For example, psychoanalytic and behavioral models seemed to be vehemently opposed in most of their assumptions about humankind, philosophical underpinnings concerning the philosophy of science, and **epistemology**—how we come to know what we know. With advances, a dialectic process occurs: Aspects of a rejected system are slowly absorbed as the system evolves. As the field evolved and many theories that had gained ascendancy fell out of favor, only to be rediscovered in a new form, there has been a continual movement toward more eclectic or integrative models. Gordon Allport (1968) began his book *The Person in Psychology* with reference to this topic:

> *Eclecticism is often a word of ill-repute. An artist or composer, even a psychologist who is "eclectic" seems to lack a mind and a style of his own.*
>
> *Yet in a wide sense there is surely some portion of truth in every thoughtful theory or observation. How shall the broadminded theorist take this fact into account unless he holds an eclectic perspective. (p. 3)*

Allport (1968) defines eclecticism in psychology as "a system that seeks the solution of fundamental problems by selecting and uniting what it regards as true in the several specialized approaches to psychological science" (p. 6). Although, as he believed, it is probably not plausible to unite all theoretical systems, synthesis is a warranted goal. He urged the field to embrace a "systematic eclecticism."

Is personality something that can be measured?

Assessing Personality

Over the past two decades, there has been exponential growth in the development of instruments to measure personality. The main categories of instruments used to measure personality include structured interviews, objective tests, projective tests, and rating scales. Numerous instruments have been developed to assess both normal and abnormal personality. These are briefly reviewed and examples of one or two of the most notable provided.

Structured Interviews

These interviews have structured questions that are asked of the subject by a research interviewer. Structured interviews are generally preferable to the self-administered instruments, as they are thought to reduce potential problems with self-report. Some of these are designed to assess the range of personality traits and others are specifically designed for a type of personality disorder. Structured interviews are often pathology-based assessment instruments used in research. One commonly used and revised instrument by Spitzer, Williams, and Gibbon (1987) is the Structured Interview for *DSM-II* (SCD-II), which consists of 120 items. This has been used for research studies in personality disorders.

Objective Tests

These are standardized instruments that are self-administered and have numerous scales that are empirically derived. These instruments are often computer scored because of the complexity of hand scoring. The best known of these is the Minnesota Multiphasic Personality Inventory (MMPI), which has been extensively validated. It consists of 550 statements to which a true or false response is given by the subject. Probably the next most utilized instrument of this type, developed by Millon (1977), is the Millon Clinical Multiaxial Inventory (MCMI), which has been through a number of revisions since its inception. These instruments were developed to measure personality disorder and psychopathology. Other instruments of this type were developed for measuring normal as well as abnormal variants using a dimensional model. The most cited of these, developed by Costa and McCrae (1985), is the NEO Personality Inventory (NEO-PI-R), which is based on the Five-Factor Model of Personality covered in Chapter 9.

Projective Tests

These instruments are based on the assumption that people constantly perceive the world through their own idiosyncratic perceptual field. For example, it was discovered that if you show individuals an ambiguous stimulus, they will project the content of their unconscious process, which then can be analyzed for content and thematic elements. By far the most popular of these instruments is the Rorschach Inkblot Test, which continues to spark controversy about its usefulness and validity not only among psychologists but in the popular press (Goode, 2001). The other famous projective instrument still widely used in research and clinical practice is the Thematic Apperception Test (TAT), developed by Murray and Morgan (1943). The TAT is covered in greater detail in Chapter 9, as it was derived from interpersonal theory.

Rating Scales/Checklists

These instruments have various categories and are administered by an examiner or self-administered. They contain a variety of items that the subject or examiner is asked to check if present. The results are then scored and compared to criteria. An example of a widely used rating scale is the Psychopathy Checklist–Revised (PCL-R), which was developed by Hare (1991) to measure two factors (lack of empathy and erratic behavior) present in antisocial or psychopathic personalities.

The use of psychological instruments to determine personality type and disorder has been a major challenge and stimulus to the growth of both academic and professional psychology. Sophisticated computer programs, powerful personal computers, and advanced statistical methods provide access for researchers and clinicians to efficiently and cost-effectively measure personality. The turn-around time is often immediate, unlike in the past, when hand scoring using complex logarithms required considerable time. These often highly sophisticated instruments have been incorporated into many sectors of society, including assessment of police, clergy, military, child custody, executive placement, and pupil and personnel placement and employee assistance programs.

Cultural Bias in Psychometrics

It should be noted that although the development of assessment instruments to measure intelligence and personality has been a major accomplishment of twentieth-century psychology, there are problems with the field that need to be underscored. Sue and Sue (1999) raise objections to the use of testing and the classification that often results. There is a clear danger that psychometric instruments to measure both personality and intelligence are severely skewed in favor of White, Euro-American, middle-class persons and biased toward minorities. They describe one example of this phenomenon: "The personality test that reveals Blacks as being suspicious, mistrustful, and paranoid needs to be understood from a larger social-political perspective. Minority groups who have consistently been victims of discrimination and oppression in a culture that is full of racism have good reason to be suspicious and mistrustful of White society" (p. 15). They remind us that definitions of health are culturally derived by the attitudes of dominant cultural values: "Definitions of mental health such as competence, autonomy, and resistance to stress are related to White middle-class notions of maturity" (p. 14). The political use of pathological labeling and hospitalization can become a form of political control. Sue and Sue label this phenomenon **ethnocentric monoculturism,** which they view as dysfunctional in a pluralistic society (p. 32). They describe five components of this process: (1) belief in superiority of the dominant culture; (2) belief in inferiority of others who are different; (3) the power to impose standards; (4) manifestation in institutional settings of the beliefs of the dominant cultural values; and (5) the "invisible veil" that racism, sexism, and homophobia have on attitudes and behavior of society (pp. 32–34). Sue and Sue eschew this ethnocentric monoculturism and urge that a **culturally diverse** perspective be adopted. The reader of this text should keep in mind that the main theoretical models of the twentieth century, using Sue and Sue's framework, are derived from this ethnocentric monoculturism.

Personality Theory in the New Millennium

The study of personality should not be limited to those with an interest in psychology. An understanding of personality theory has major benefits for students from various disciplines. In Edward Wilson's (1998) book *Consilience*, he attempts to provide a unified theory of knowledge that has as an essential element the discipline of psychology, whose subdiscipline is the study of human personality.

Personality theory is essential to a comprehensive understanding of various related social sciences, including economics, anthropology, art, sociology, literature, history, and archaeology.

The future of the field of personality theory has its greatest utility in enabling social scientists to offer insight into the nature of humans and why we do what we do. This will be a step in helping us resolve some of the age-old problems of aggression, mental illness, poverty, economic imbalances, racism, environmental destruction, and so on, by assisting in the development of a unified theory of human personology. One important challenge will be to develop models of personality that are culturally diverse. These theoretical advancements can then be applied to the various challenges that humankind faces in the new millennium. It will also require that those who are interested in resolving the challenges ahead be well versed and grounded in personality theory so that a superficial understanding of human beings will not guide national and world policy and political action.

Using Personality Theory as a Lens for Understanding

How do we address the complex issues raised at the beginning of this chapter? Personality theory provides a lens through which we may attempt to make sense out of information about individuals, dyads, and larger systems that may not make sense initially. Readers will find themselves attracted to one or more theories in this book, often depending on the intuitive sense they make. The remaining chapters primarily focus on the contemporary advances in the last quarter of the twentieth century and provide the reader (as much as possible in a text of this size) with discussions of the classic theorists and foundation concepts. In the following chapter, we explore some of the historical roots of contemporary personality theory and offer an additional approach to Rychlak's for assessing the various theoretical models presented in this text.

Summary

This chapter serves as an introduction to the topic of personality theory, a highly diverse field that attempts to understand human nature, much like its mother discipline, **philosophy,** in which it originated. Various individuals have been the subject of fascination in contemporary society, as have past infamous figures such as Hitler and brilliant and creative ones such as Michelangelo, Mozart, and Leonardo. As a result of our curiosity to understand their often incongruent, self-defeating, or abhorrent actions or their brilliant contributions, we are compelled to try to understand their personalities. All of us use personality theory in our everyday life. On a conscious and nonconscious level, we continually assess, rate, and categorize the people we interact with. It is a normal and natural process, one probably shaped by evolution to provide a mechanism to guarantee our survival. Personality theorists attempt to systematically organize this material so that it will be useful in creating a better understanding of the complexity of humans. Theory represents a formal attempt to arrange the various observations we make in a coherent fashion that tells a story.

One important way the study of personality diverges from philosophy is its emphasis on the empirical or scientifically based attempt to build a cogent theory. Murray, who coined the term personology, attempted to establish personality as a credible discipline interested in the study of human lives and individual differences. It is crucial to differentiate between the key concepts trait (a stable personality factor) and state (a fluctuating element of the personality system). The main elements of a psychological science of personality include a system of classification for the data, a set of propositions, a theory model, and a means by which to test the theory's integrity.

There are various levels of abstraction by which we can view the multiple factors that make up personality. A biopsychosocial model is essential for comprehensive understanding of personality. These factors range from the biological substrates to the cultural. Personality variables can be looked at microscopically or macroscopically, as can any complex biological and social system. Thus, we can focus on the action of neurons and their various neurotransmitters as well as look at the cultural impact of a phenomenon such as immigration.

There has been a strong trend toward convergence in personality theory as more interdisciplinary cross-fertilization has taken place. There has been an integrative-eclectic process that has been described as an integrative movement or systematic eclecticism. There is a very close relationship among the fields of personality theory, psychotherapy, and abnormal psychology. Various instruments have been developed to measure and assess intelligence and personality, which has been a major advancement in scientific psychology. Unfortunately, many current measures may be biased toward minorities and are representative of ethnocentric monoculturism. A number of new disciplines have made major progress in clarifying the component systems of personality. The field has advanced at a remarkable rate during the twentieth century, especially in the last quarter of the century. There is a remarkable void in theoretical models of personality that are culturally diverse, the development of which represents an important challenge to twenty-first-century personality theorists and researchers.

Selected Reading

Murray, H. A. (1938). *Explorations in personality.* New York: Oxford University Press.
Sue, D. W., & Sue, D. (1999). *Counseling the culturally different: Theory and practice* (3rd ed.). New York: Wiley.

History of Personality from the Ancients to the Mid-Twentieth Century

2

Chapter

Introduction

This chapter presents the reader with some of the origins of the field of personality, dating from the time of early civilization. Presentations of the main influences leading to the developments in contemporary theory are briefly reviewed.

Although many of these ancient "systems" and later ones may seem humorous to us from the perspective of the twenty-first century, it will become clear that these early conceptualizations represent the germination of the seeds of later comprehensive scientific theories about the nature of humans and personality. Also covered in this chapter are some of the major historical paradigmatic shifts that occurred in a variety of areas in scientific psychology in the late nineteenth and early twentieth centuries. A number of major developments and minor influences have integrally shaped contemporary psychology and the field of personality. Some of the major influences that converged in the late nineteenth and early twentieth centuries include:

- The emergence of psychology as a discipline separate from philosophy.
- The challenge of the scientific revolution.
- Emergence of and methods of experimental psychology.
- The development of the field of statistics.

- The publication of the landmark work *Principles of Psychology* (James, 1890).
- The birth of psychoanalysis.

The first five developments are reviewed in this chapter; psycho-analysis is discussed in Chapter 3.

Ancient Conceptualizations of Personality

The study of psychology and personality has a long, documented lineage in the history of humankind. In this section, some of the early conceptions of the ancient era formulated by physicians, theologians, and philosophers are briefly presented to illustrate the compelling fascination that humankind has with itself as consciousness and civilization developed in tandem. Many thinkers tried to understand the differences and similarities manifest in human personality, as well as the causes and amelioration of human illness and emotional suffering. The professions of medicine and philosophy and later psychology emerged from this rich intellectual soil.

The Early Middle East

Psychosomatic Medicine: As early as about the fourth millennium B.C.E. in Babylon, concepts about medicine, the mind-body interaction, and psychology were beginning to develop. A primitive system of psychotherapy was developed by the early Egyptians, who endorsed soul-searching on the part of ill patients similar to modern conceptions of psychosomatic illness (Alexander & Selesnick, 1966). Spiritualism, mysticism, and astrology dominated the medical and psychological system.

Hysteria and the Uterus: Egyptian physicians hypothesized a link between the uterus and the emotional disorder later termed hysteria by the Greeks. Erroneously, "they believed that the symptoms were caused by the malposition of the uterus and therefore fumigated the vagina, hoping to lure the vagrant uterus back to its natural position" (p. 21). Later in Greece, Plato and Hypocrites endorsed a similar treatment. This primitive conceptualization of female sexuality was elaborated in the later nineteenth century in conceptions about hysteria and the repression of female sexuality and sexual abuse.

Blaming/Projection: In the history of Israel, one can see the identification of the psychological mechanism known as projection. In some early Talmud writings, a case is reported of an anti-vice crusader who "accused the people of Jerusalem of committing precisely those crimes of which in fact he himself was guilty" (p. 22). This psychological mechanism was later elaborated on in the theory of psychoanalysis and has become a major feature of object-relational models.

Early India

Meditation: In approximately 500 B.C.E., Gautama Buddha, a Hindu prince known for his tremendous empathy, developed the psychological technique of meditation (Alexander & Selesnick, 1966). Through meditation, one attempts to experience pure being and renounce worldly desires. Through successive mastery of various stages of meditation, one may be able to reach the state of nirvana— a state of extreme tranquillity devoid of all earthly longings. In the twentieth century, the West adopted this method and it is being increasingly incorporated into healing practices.

Emotional Centers: Ancient Hindu medicine of about 800 B.C.E.– 1000 C.E. in the works of Charaka "suggested that powerful emotions may be related to peculiar behavior" (p. 25). Also, certain personality characteristics were said to be located in the body: "For example, ignorance was located in the abdomen, passion in the chest, and goodness in the brain" (p. 25). A rudimentary psychological system for classifying human emotional functioning was being developed and used to understand adaptation and personality. Harmony and balance in the proper proportions among the various substances, such as phlegm, bile, and air, were thought necessary for health. These conceptual elements were also seen in Greek conceptions of personality.

The Classical Period: Greek Philosophers

The classical period in intellectual thought began in approximately 1000 B.C.E., when Homer described people suffering from mental illness because they had offended the gods. Their punishment was to act strangely. This moral insanity notion would continue to dominate many societies up until the nineteenth century and even later in some cultures. By the sixth and seventh centuries B.C.E., an intellectual movement toward rational thought emerged (Alexander & Selesnick, 1966).

The Four Humors

Over 25 centuries ago, the Greek physician Hypocrites put forth the first recorded systematic classification of personality. This structural system was based on the four humors or body fluids and their relationship to temperament. Depending on the predominance or imbalance of these fluids, an individual would likely manifest one of four temperamental predispositions: **choleric,** related to an excess of yellow bile; **melancholic,** related to an excess of black bile; **sanguine,** related to an excess of blood; and **phlegmatic,** related to an excess of phlegm.

As Millon (Millon & Davis, 1996a) points out, centuries later, this early categorization of the humors was modified by Galen, a surgeon to the gladiators, who associated these four temperaments with emotional states. Galen described the **choleric** temperament as having a tendency toward irascibility; the **sanguine** as a tendency to be optimistic; the **melancholic** as a tendency toward sadness; and the **phlegmatic** as a tendency toward apathy. It is interesting to note that modern neurobiological models of personality, reviewed later in this book, share common beliefs with this early model. Modern-day biological psychiatrists do not attribute personality disturbance to the humors being "out of balance." Instead, these modern psychopharmocologists highlight deficiencies and imbalances in neurotransmitters to explain emotional predispostion toward depression, anxiety, mania, and aggressiveness, which they believe are the major components of personality. Too much or too little of a neurotransmitter might produce affective dysregulation, the hallmark of borderline personality.

Early Greek Interest in Describing Character

Over the millennia, humans have expressed a keen interest in character and the complexity of human relations. This was expressed in the early Greeks' interest in drama; in fact, the word *personality* is derived from the masks that the Greek actors wore in their productions. Later, the meaning of *persona* shifted from the mask to the self. Millon (Millon & Davis, 1996a) writes of the Greeks' early interest in character: "Allport has referred to 'character writing' as a minor literary style originating in Athens, probably invented by Aristotle and brought to its finest and most brilliant form through the pen of Theophrastus. Presented as 'verbal' portraits, these depictions of character are brief sketches that capture certain common types so aptly as to be identified and appreciated by readers in all walks of life. In these crisp delineations, a dominant trait is brought to the forefront and accentuated and embellished to highlight the major flaws or foibles of the individual. In essence, they are stylized simplifications that often border on the precious or burlesque" (p. 35).

Writing about character types experienced resurgence with the development of psychoanalytic theory in the early twentieth century. Some of the most eloquent descriptions of personality and manifestation of various traits abound in the classic writings of many analytic pioneers. Millon, one of the major contemporary theorists, has also fine-tuned his capacity to describe the various character styles and personality disorders.

Alexander and Selesnick (1966) write: "We may disregard most ancient theories and observations, but we cannot emphasize too strongly the historical importance of the rationalistic approach, the mentality of ancient Greece, which was inaugurated and established as a tradition during this unique phase of human history—the Classical era" (p. 48).

Emergence of the Science of Psychology from Philosophy

In the history of science, psychology is a relatively new discipline that emerged from the much older branch of knowledge called philosophy. Philosophy is concerned with the investigation of being, knowledge, and conduct; its major tool is logical thought. Thus, the essential meaning of life and existence was a major focus of philosophers for thousands of years. The questions posed include Who are we? and What is the meaning of our existence? Much of the writing of early philosophers such as Aristotle, Plato, and Socrates is an attempt to understand human psychology. Rychlak (1973) summarizes:

Man's earliest formulations concerning the world were quaintly anthropo-morphized accounts. Nature was made up of human-like gods and demigods having intentions, moods of vengeance or lust, hopeful aspirations, and so forth. Philosophy and thereby science is often said to have begun when Thales of Miletus (640?–546 B.C.) and his student, Anaximander (611–547 B.C.), began giving accounts of nature in terms of the basic "stuff" which presumably made it up—"water" or the "boundless" as their respective views expressed it. Heraclitus (540–480 B.C.) and Parmenides (515–456 B.C.) raised the issue of change, of whether anything really happened in this world of days and nights, and thus introduced a concern for the "fabric of movement" or impetus in events across time. Heraclitus was also instrumental in bringing another notion to the fore, the logos *by which events flowed. The movement of time was patterned into a rational order which was not random. Based on this preliminary belief Democritus (460–370 B.C.) was later to say that there was no such thing as "chance" in the universe for everything is subject to patterned laws. (p. 3)*

Psychology developed from philosophy, but to do so required the birth of modern empiricism. The scientific revolution provided the impetus for psychology to leave the introspective realm of philosophy and evolve into modern scientific psychology: "The seventeenth century must be given credit for laying the first foundations of the modern world" (Alexander & Selesnick, 1966, p. 89). Underlying the advances of this century were two approaches: "The first emphasized deductive, analytical, and mathematical reasoning; the second empirical and inductive reasoning" (p. 90).

Dialectical Nature of the Universe

The Greeks were intrigued with the dialectical nature of the universe: Truth and error were part of the process of knowing. Socrates and Plato developed the art of dialectic discourse as a way of advancing knowledge. Socrates would pose a question and then have his student defend the opposing position. The Socratic method was used to explore the dialectical meaning of the universe and to generate new ways of understanding. The history of science in some way may be a dialectical process that can be seen in the evolution of the contemporary theories of personality presented in this text.

The Scientific Revolution

The British philosophers Sir Isaac Newton (1643–1727) and Sir Francis Bacon (1561–1626) were the fathers of the empirical approach.

They assumed that there were no intentions in nature and that phenomena must be explained only in material and causal terms. Thus, terms could be reduced to lower levels of abstraction, even to those not observable by the human eye. This **reductionism** in scientific investigation assumed that knowledge was made of lower-level abstractions or substrates of reality. Knowledge advances by operationally defining constructs.

John Locke theorized that humankind's ideas are merely maps of one's experience with reality and that each mental construct has a circumscribed meaning: "The Lockean model provided the initial impetus in natural science and still holds sway in psychological theories of the so-called tough-minded variety" (Rychlak, 1973, p. 9). Immanuel Kant believed that the categories used to organize information influence our assumptions, which should be empirically tested to demonstrate their validity.

In the late nineteenth century, psychology began to distinguish itself from philosophy: "When psychology gained its independence from philosophy and became a science in the second half of the nineteenth century, its goal was to use a laboratory-based introspection to discover the basic elements of mental life" (Hjelle & Ziegler, 1976, p. 21). After the phenomenal growth of psychology during the twentieth century, the discipline continues to grow at an exponential rate, with more and more subdisciplines developing all the time. Many of the component systems that constitute modern scientific personality are covered in Chapter 4.

False Starts in the Development of Theories of Personality

Phrenology: A Precursor to Modern Neuroscience

Phrenology was an early attempt by Franz Joseph Gall (1758–1828) at developing scientific personality theory based on suspected specialized brain functions associated with various areas of the cerebral cortex. Gall emphasized the "correlation" among contour variations in the skull, erroneously believing that these reflected underlying brain structures. Gall, a physician, known as a top-notch neurophysiologist, discovered through dissections that the larger the amount of cortex a species possesses, the higher the intellectual functioning (Hunt, 1993). He also discovered the connection between the two halves of the brain known as the commissures. In spite of his advances in knowledge of brain structure and function, he is most remembered for his interest in **phrenology.** He believed that physical character- istics noted in the skull represented various cortical areas responsi- ble for different traits. He and a colleague examined hundreds of subjects and identified various regions of the skull and their associ- ated personality traits. By feeling the bumps on an individual's head, a profile of the individual was developed. Each area of the original 27 areas (later expanded to 36) was supposed to relate to an under- lying area of the cortex. In vogue for almost a century, phrenology finally fell out of favor for lack of empirical support. Although based on faulty assumptions, phrenology was the precursor of modern neuropsychology that was dramatically advanced based on observa- tions of the effects of brain injuries and their resulting behavior changes. This is an important example of how science evolves from theory to practice and empirical verification.

Another surgeon, Pierre Flourens (1794–1867), did actual psy- chosurgical procedures removing small portions of the brain from animals and then observing their behavior; thus, phrenology was definitively refuted (Hunt, 1993). Even though the areas of the brain associated with specific traits was not supported, the theory that the brain has areas of specialized function was accurate! Through his methodical work, Flourens discovered that although there are localized brain functions, "perception, judgment, will, and memory were distributed throughout the cerebral cortex" (p. 105). Hunt comments on the advances made by Gall and phrenology: "Gall's pseudo-scientific theory thus led to the first experimental studies of the localization of brain functions. Moreover, his theory, though wrong in all its details, survived Flouren's assault, since later neurophysiologists, following Flouren's lead, were able to identify particular areas of the brain as being responsible for visual percep- tion, auditory perception, and motor control. Flourens was right that memory and thinking are distributed throughout the cortex, but a limited number of lower and even some higher mental pro- cesses are indeed localized" (pp. 105–106).

Body Morphology: A Precursor to the Psychology of Typology

Ernst Kretschmer (1925) attempted to empirically validate the rela- tionship between physical appearance and personality. Kretschmer believed that body type was related to personality. He "observed" that short, fat individuals were predisposed to being cheerful and jolly and that tall, thin individuals were more likely to be shy and withdrawn.

Sheldon (Sheldon & Stevens, 1942; Sheldon, Stevens, & Tucker, 1940) advanced these ideas, developing a system of classifying personality that was somewhat more empirically based. Using photographs, he identified several thousand college students on the basis of three body *somatotypes* or builds, which he termed endomorphy, mesomorphy, and ectomorphy. In this system, the **endomorph** tended to be short and fat, the **mesomorph** muscular, and the **ectomorph** tall and slender. To make the system more precise, everyone was rated from 1 to 7 on the three body types; he then correlated the three physical types and their variations with dimensions of temperament using clinical rating scales. Relaxation and an extroverted disposition typified the endomorph; mesomorphs were thought to more likely be energetic and aggressive; ectomorphs were withdrawn and restrained.

Sheldon assumed that this **correlation** between somatotypes and personality was innate thus best explained by genetics. However, as you have learned in introductory psychology courses, correlation does not imply a causal (cause-and-effect) relationship but only that two variables regularly are observed together. Sheldon did not take into account a competing hypothesis: that one's somatotype dynamically interacts with the social systems such as family and peers, whose response dynamically influences and shapes personality.

Wundt and the Birth of Experimental Psychology

Setting the Stage for the Development of Scientific Personality Theory

Although humans have been experimenting in various forms since appearing on the earth, it wasn't until later in history that science began to become more widely accepted (Lathrop, 1969). Another movement that set the stage for the development of the field of contemporary scientific personality was experimental psychology. Lundin (1969) describes the emergence of this major scientific discipline and its impact on the field: "In the year 1913 there began to take place what may be called a major revolution in psychology. All the excitement was started by the publication of an article by John Watson, in which he threw the mind and other unobservables out of psychology. Of course, any drastic change which takes place in the history of a subject does not come without preparation. Psychological laboratories had already been in operation for some time, and those who worked in them believed they were taking a very systematic and careful approach toward the analysis of the mind. Wilhelm Wundt was credited with starting the first psychological laboratory in Leipaig, Germany, in 1879; so, in this sense, Wundt is the founder of modern experimental psychology" (p. 30).

Wilhelm Wundt (1832–1920) was one of academic psychology's early pioneers and considered by many to be "the first modern psychologist" (R. I. Watson, 1971, p. 283). Wundt was the founder of structuralism and created a small research laboratory called the Psychologische Institute. Wundt (1904) taught the first course in physiological psychology, later publishing the landmark two-volume *Principles of Physiological Psychology,* in which he outlined a new domain of science. He sought to understand the mind and consciousness through perceptions, sensations, cognitions, and feelings but emphasized doing so with empirical methods. Wundt's institute "became the mecca of experimental psychology and attracted countless students, many of them Americans, and is recognized as the model for subsequent psychological laboratories" (Hillner, 1984, p. 35). Many luminaries in psychology studied there, including Cattell and Spearman (presented in this chapter). "To Wundt, the use of the experimental method, whenever possible, was mandatory" (R. I. Watson, 1971, p. 267). Although somewhat narrow in his focus, he solidified psychology. Probably his greatest contribution was his emphasis on research methodology to investigate various domains of psychology. Although his emphasis was on quantitative methods, modern psychology also uses qualitative ones where appropriate.

Experimental Methods: Qualitative and Quantitative Approaches

There are various categories of experimental design that are used in psychological science. Generally, we can distinguish between two broad categories of psychological research: qualitative and quantitative. **Qualitative research** uses logic and various types of evidence, such as historical material, self-report, participant observation, and interviews to support the hypotheses that are offered. **Quantitative research** relies on the experimental method and uses statistical analysis and procedures to determine whether the hypotheses are accepted or rejected. Isaac and Michael (1979) identify nine functional categories or research methods. Each has advantages and disadvantages. Some emphasize certainty at the cost of more penetrating analysis; others, the ease of carrying out the method in a natural environment. These factors are evident in the descriptions below. The qualitative approaches are described in 1 through 4 and 9; 5 through 8 are quantitative:

1. *Historical:* In this type of research, an investigator attempts to reconstruct the past in an accurate and objective manner. This type of research has often been used in psychobiographical research and can have a great deal of bias, as well as be illuminating.

2. *Descriptive:* In this type of research, an effort is made to describe certain phenomena in an accurate and factual manner. This approach has been used extensively in describing various types of personality and traits.

3. *Developmental:* In this type of research, the investigator observes changes over time in function and growth. Erickson's (1959) developmental stages are an example of the use of this approach.

4. *Case or field:* In this type of research, a social unit—individual, dyad, triad, or larger system—is intensively observed and conclusions are drawn. This has been the major approach employed by clinicians, developmental psychologists, and psychotherapists from various approaches ascribing to different models of personality.

5. *Correlational:* In this type of research, the investigator observes and measures how variations in one factor will affect others using correlation coefficients. This method of research is primarily employed by the factor theorists but is common in many approaches.

6. *Causal-comparative:* In this type of research, the investigator looks through existing data to see if a determination of a causal relationship among variables can be inferred. This method is common to many clinical theorists. For example, an

investigator may look at the medical/psychiatric charts of all hospitalized patients diagnosed with Borderline Personality Disorder to see if a report of early abuse in their history is suspected of being a causal factor.

7. *True experimental:* In this, the most difficult type of method to employ, the investigator is looking for a cause-and-effect relationship and does so by randomly assigning subjects to either a control or an experimental group. Different treatment conditions are then compared and the results analyzed to determine whether significant differences exist.

8. *Quasi-experimental:* In this type of research, the investigator attempts to replicate the conditions of a true experimental design but is unable to manipulate all the relevant variables. For example, two groups of hospitalized patients who receive different forms of group therapy are compared on a measure of self-esteem after treatment is completed. Random assignment has not been made, but the investigator does his or her best to assess any differences in composition of the groups that might affect the outcome.

9. *Action:* In this type of research, the investigator develops a new approach in an applied setting. For example, a new type of skills training group is offered to a group of socially phobic outpatients (Isaac & Michael, 1979, p. 14).

Modern scientific psychology could not have advanced as it has without the contributions of the experimental psychologists, who sought to create a new empirical science and developed methodologies to do so. But more would be required to firmly establish this new science and legitimize the study of the self, consciousness, and personality. William James, who emerged during the same period, would pave the way.

James and the Birth of Modern Scientific Personality Theory

William James (1842–1910) was born in New York City to affluent and socially prominent parents (Hunt, 1993). James was one of the most influential psychologists who bridged the gap from the nineteenth-century philosophers to twentieth-century psychologists.

He studied at Harvard Medical School but discontinued when he lost interest and traveled to the Amazon to explore the subject of natural history. He hated this subject and decided to resume medical school. He was plagued by various physical and emotional aliments and left medical school again, returning to Europe to study with Helmholtz and other leaders of the new psychology. He also sought relief in the baths from his physical and emotional suffering. When he returned to finish medical school, he was 27 but did not elect to practice medicine, as this was not intellectually challenging enough for his broad-ranging interests and keen intellect. Instead, he studied psychology and became a professor at Harvard.

In 1890, he published his landmark *Principles of Psychology.* It took him 12 years instead of the two projected to finish *Principles,* but the success of this endeavor was remarkable beyond what the publishers had imagined. Even today, one sees James's *Principles of Psychology* on the bookshelves of many bookstores, as over a century later it remains a popular text. Hillner (1984) comments: "The book club to which my wife belongs recently read *Principles;* but it was read from the perspective of being an introduction to *contemporary* psychology, a fact that illustrates both the common-sense and layman's orientation of functionalism and cultural saliency which James' work still enjoys" (p. 66).

In *Principles,* James (1890) declared that "psychology is a natural science" (p. 183) and proceeded to outline the field of psychology and its various topics, spawning a century of investigation (Magnavita, in press-a). James wrote: "Psychology is the Science of Mental Life, both of its phenomena and their conditions. The phenomena are such things as we call feelings, desires, cognitions, reasonings, decisions, and the like; and, superficially considered, their variety and complexity is such as to leave a chaotic impression on the observer" (p. 1).

Many consider James to be one of the most brilliant psychological theorists and observers, who had a "profound influence" on the field of psychology (Hillner, 1984, p. 65). James wrote about the component systems of personality, such as emotion, self, will, cognition, memory, and consciousness, that are primary components of the contemporary science of personality. The twentieth-century innovations and theoretical formulations summarized in this book and many other contemporary ones (Millon, 2000) reflect the inspiration they continue to offer and the influence they continue to have

(Magnavita, in press-a). However, he was a man of many contradictions. Hunt (1993) comments on this often controversial luminary: "What is one to make of a distinguished professor of the new science of psychology who denies that it is a science? Who praises the findings of experimental psychologists but loathes performing experiments and does as few as possible? Who is said to be the greatest American psychologist of his time (the late nineteenth century) but never took a course in psychology and sometimes even disavows the label of psychologist?" (p. 144).

James was responsible for introducing the new discipline of experimental psychology to the United States. Prior to this, the main psychological subject taught in universities was phrenology. Although he hated conducting experiments, James designed some elegant ones, such as disputing a theory accepted for centuries that memory is strengthened by practice (Hunt, 1993). James was a voracious reader and developed interests in education, philosophy, and religious experience, among others. "In 1894 he was the first American to call attention to the work of the then obscure Viennese physician Sigmund Freud, and in 1909, though ailing, he went to Clark University to meet Freud on his only visit to the United States and hear him speak" (p. 153). Freud's visit and lectures at Clark University would have a profound effect on American psychology and personality theory. Freud presented the first comprehensive theory of personality ever developed and, although controversial and novel, it intrigued the academic and professional community of psychologists in the United States. Most individuals who heard or read his theories reacted strongly one way or the other.

Rejection of Dualism

James was uncomfortable with the notion that the mind and the body are independent entities. He "was an implicit mind-body interactionist dualist and avowed pragmatist, both of which positions found expression later in functionalism's focus on the utility value of consciousness in relation to the organism's adaptation to the environment" (Hillner, 1984, p. 66). However, he did not believe that psychology was ready to solve the riddle of how mind and body interrelate. This puzzle is still a crucial one to our topic of personality theory and will be explored in Chapter 4 in the section on the nature of consciousness. Humans are thought to be the only species capable of considering the self and who possess consciousness to ponder our mortality and existential issues about the meaning of our existence and purpose. This consciousness has allowed for the development of civilization not evident in any other species. James believed that consciousness was not a mosaic of separate elements but a continuous, unbroken stream.

The Conception of Self

James was very interested in conceptions of the self, which he divided into three categories: the **material self,** the **social self,** and the **spiritual self.** These correspond loosely to domains of biological-temperamental, social-interpersonal, and intrapsychic systems presented later in this text. He believed that there are often conflicts among the various sectors of the self and describes the rivalry in his colorful way:

> *I am often confronted by the necessity of standing by one of my empirical selves and relinquishing the rest. Not that I would not, if I could, be both handsome and fat and well dressed, and a great athlete, and make a million a year, be a wit, a* bon-vivant, *a lady-killer, as well as a philosopher; a philanthropist, statesman, warrior, and an African explorer, as well as a "tone-poet" and saint. But the thing is simply impossible. The millionaire's work would run counter to the saint's; the* bon-vivant *and the philanthropist would trip each other up; the philosopher and the lady-killer could not well keep house in the same tenement of clay. Such different characters may conceivably at the onset of life be alike* possible *to a man. But to make any one of them actual, the rest must more or less be suppressed. (James, 1890, pp. 309–310)*

James did not believe the field of psychology during his time was prepared to tackle the problem of the mind-body connection and thought it should be put aside until the future. He thought that psychology should concern itself instead with describing and explaining various processes, such as memory, imagination, feelings, will, and perception. "From James's time on, this would be the dominant view within many branches of American psychology—the study of personality and individual differences, educational psychology, abnormal psychology, child development studies, social psychology; everything, indeed, except experimental psychology, much of which would be behaviorist and anti 'mentalist' for many decades" (Hunt, 1993, p. 155).

Another development was also crucial in providing the social sciences with a powerful tool for analyzing the data made available by experimental methodologies. What was needed was a statistical system.

The Development of Statistics

The Study of Intelligence

The study of intelligence and of personality share some common foundations and are the two great domains of interest of early psychologists. The development of the field of statistics has been seminal in the evolution of social science, marking the transition from philosophy to modern scientific psychology. Sir Francis Galton, a cousin of Charles Darwin, was interested in the transmission process of intelligence and began to study the intellectual capacities of great families of Britain. His evidence suggested that intellectual ability ran in families (Galton, 1892). Although Galton tried to devise an intelligence test, his efforts were unsuccessful (Herrnstein & Murray, 1994); they were too simplistically conceived.

Mental tests were an area of interest to investigators at the end of the nineteenth century, but it was not until Galton devised what is termed the correlation coefficient that a breakthrough in understanding and measuring intelligence could occur. Karl Pearson, a disciple of Galton's, refined the concept with the development of the correlation coefficient, called **Pearson's r.** This statistical breakthrough allowed one to determine how much of a relationship exists between two variables, on a scale ranging from −1 to +1. A − 1 represents a perfectly negative relationship between two variables and a + 1 a direct correlation.

Factor Theory: Intelligence and Personality

Another approach to the study of personality is factor theory, which assumes that all complex behavior can be accounted for by a limited number of underlying variables or factors that can by measured by psychometric tests and rating scales. The English psychologist

Spearman (1904) pioneered this approach in his study of intelligence. A variety of tests, which can be quantitatively scored, are given to subjects and the results of these are reduced to factors. Spearman noticed that when many people were given a variety of mental tests, their scores were positively correlated. He believed that this indicated evidence of two kinds of factors in intelligence: a **general** factor, measured by all the tests, and a specific factor that is unique to each test.

Later, this factor theory, applied to personality, was advanced in the United States by Thurstone (1938). He believed that by examining subjects' responses to a series of self-ratings and likes and dislikes, personality could be evaluated. The responses (raw data) are collected and subjected to a statistical technique, factor analysis, which determines how the variables correlate with one another. On the basis of these correlations, common factors can be found and given a label. These factors then become the dimensions or **personality traits.**

A Lexically Derived Trait Theory

Gordon Allport's trait theory exemplifies another important development in the study of personality based on lexical analysis. Allport and Odbert (1936) conducted an exhaustive review of the words in the English language used to describe personality, recording a total of 17,953. When these were reduced through factor analysis, composite traits emerged. Allport believed that traits were the most fundamental aspect of personality structure. Traits are the characteristic manner in which we respond to stimuli in our environment. The way our traits are patterned reflects our unique personality. There are traits that are prominent and others that are minor; these prominent traits can override the personality.

Cattell's Factor Theory and Statistical Analysis

Raymond Cattell (1860–1944) is a seminal figure in the development of personality psychology. Cattell, who was English, attained his undergraduate degree in chemistry before his doctorate in psychology. One of his major contributions to personality was his incorporation and elaboration of research methodology and the use of statistical procedures. Cattell served as "Wundt's self-appointed first assistant" (R. I. Watson, 1971, p. 391), so he had a strong empiricist perspective. He annexed powerful statistical tools such as correlation, factor analysis, and multivariate techniques in the study of personality (Winter & Barenbaum, 1999). The development of these powerful statistical tools was a major advancement for the social sciences. It allowed researchers to investigate relationships among variables as never before. Although we take statistics for granted in our modern life, their development and use in the social sciences represented a major leap in establishing an empirical basis for the social sciences. Various techniques of **inferential statistics** are used in social science research. Inferential statistics is a form of mathematics that is used to determine the likelihood that certain relationships are chance occurrences. The following statistical techniques are often used in personality, psychopathology, and psychotherapy research studies:

- *Correlation:* Two or more variables are measured and it is determined whether changes in one will affect the others with a certain degree of probability. Although a valuable tool, correlation does not imply a cause-and-effect relationship, as unknown variables may be responsible for the change. This is why it is usually preferable that experiments be done with experimental and control groups where subjects are randomly assigned and even the researcher does not know which group is which. This is known as a double-blind study and is most often used in studying the effects of drugs so that placebo effects can be factored out.

- *Factor analysis:* Another powerful statistical tool often used by personality researchers is factor analysis. In this technique, multiple variables are correlated so that they can be reduced to essential factors. Factor analysis of personality attempts to determine and measure the basic components of personality. This is a primary tool of factor theorists and was essential in developing the Five-Factor Model of Personality (presented in Chapter 9), as well as Eysenck's Three-Factor Model (presented in Chapter 7). As with most statistical methods, factor analysis has limitations in that it does not address the individual personality in its complexity. But it is a powerful tool for looking at aggregates of traits and average tendencies. It can encourage investigators to test their theoretical formulations empirically but is useful for measuring only factors that are easily operationalized. There are different types of rotations or solutions that factor analyses can be subjected to, such as oblique and principal factors. The results will be somewhat different depending on the solution chosen (Amick & Walberg, 1975).

- *Multivariate analysis:* Even more powerful statistical techniques for analyzing large amounts of data and multiple variables are known as multivariate analysis; these include multiple regression analysis and discriminant function analysis. **Multiple regression analysis** plots a line that best fits the data points depicted on a graph. This shows the algebraic relationship among the data points on the x and y axes. The resulting equation can then be used to predict future behavior. **Discriminant function analysis** is used to classify data into categories based on several variables or measurements (Amick & Walberg, 1975). For example, if one wanted to classify a person as either dependent or avoidant personality, one could take various objective psychological measurements and subject them to a discriminant function analysis and confirm which category fits the subject. This technique considers the various weights of the variables as well as the best combination for making the prediction.

- *Meta-analysis:* Meta-analysis, a more recently developed technique, is a powerful statistical technique for combining the results of multiple studies in an aggregate to increase the validity of findings (Dillard, 1991; Eagly, Makhijani, & Klonsky, 1992). Meta-analytic techniques are often incorporated in studies of psychotherapy so that results of multiple studies can be used to form valid conclusions. One classic study aggregated 2,400 patients over 30 years and showed that after 8 sessions of psychotherapy, 50% were measurably improved and by 26 sessions, 75% were improved (Howard, Kopta, Krause, & Orlinsky, 1986).

Trait Reduction through Factor Analysis

Cattell (1945) sought to reduce the enormous data set by using correlation and multivariate statistical procedures. He was interested in isolating the underlying factors in the list of 4,504 traits that was originally derived by Allport and Odbert (1936). Cattell reduced this list to 171 different traits and then further reduced the list to 35 trait clusters. Others then studied various cardinal traits and it was suggested that personality could revolve around some of these, such as authoritarian.

Cattell defended the use of the **lexical approach** (using words from common language that describe personality traits) and believed that language covered all aspects of personality. This approach continues to have relevance for the contemporary factorial models presented in this text, although, as we shall see, the use of factors based on Western language may not have cross-cultural application. The success that was seen in the early twentieth century in the measurement of intelligence "convinced many personality psychologists that personality could (and should) be measured in a similar way, by scales of 'items' " (Winter & Barenbaum, 1999, p. 3).

According to Hillner (1984), Cattell "(1) institutionalized American psychology's concern for individual differences, (2) fostered psychology as an applied discipline by organizing the Psychological Corporation, (3) solidified academic psychology by serving as professor and head of the Psychology Department at Columbia University for 26 years, and (4) experienced the prestige of being the first psychologist elected to the National Academy of Sciences" (p. 68).

The Combination of Research Methodology and Statistics

By combining these and other statistical methods and powerful research methodologies using both experimental and quasi-experimental designs (Campbell & Stanley, 1963; Cook & Campbell, 1979), Cattell created an unparalleled opportunity to study the complex components of human personality. Instead of relying purely on introspection, observations and theories could be subject to empirical examination, allowing for the rapid acceleration in the twentieth century of scientific knowledge in all fields. The rise of rationalism as a philosophical movement in the seventeenth and eighteenth centuries insisted that knowledge be gained through observation and reason (Lathrop, 1969).

Experimental methods, powerful statistical models, and trait theory—potent as these developments are in enabling us to understand personality, something was missing in this fertile mixture. That missing element was the study of **cultural forces** and the impact they have on personality. The rising prominence of anthropology, a sister science, offered the missing perspective by emphasizing cultural influences. The advancement of the field of personality theory in the twenty-first century will probably rest in part on the ability of theorists and researchers to address this virtually neglected but vital area.

Cultural Diversity, Anthropology, and the Western Perspective

In the middle of the twentieth century, Margaret Mead (1964) wrote: "We are entering an era in history when an understanding of cultural change is essential" (p. 81). Unfortunately, by and large, personality theorists did not heed her words. The personality theories presented in this text, with the exception of the Stone relational model of women's psychology presented in Chapter 10, are primarily constructions of the Western perspective, that of White, educated, male professionals. Other, feminist perspectives were offered by some of the pioneering women in psychoanalysis presented in Chapter 3. As reviewed in this chapter, based on centuries of Western philosophy concerning the nature of humankind and epistemology (the study of systems of how knowledge is attained), a primarily individualistic system of personality unfolded.

An alternative perspective that will assist us in the journey through the various theoretical models in this book and toward culturally sensitive ones in the future is offered by the discipline of anthropology. Leeper and Madison (1959) incorporated the new findings that were emerging from the growing field of anthropology to better understand personality theory. In trying to answer the questions of personality theory about the development, potential, and nature of humans, they remind readers of the limitations of Western science:

> We need to realize that almost all the observations of personality by psychotherapists and by experimental psychologists have been made under rather limited sets of conditions. The persons who have been scrutinized in each of these conditions have been even more restricted; they are the conditions that have molded the personalities of relatively well-educated, economically well-off, and socially favored individuals of this modern Western culture.

As a general scientific procedure, this is seriously open to questions. Any limitation of the conditions under which observations are made imposes restrictions on the generality of whatever conclusions are drawn from the data. Since characteristics of human beings and of all natural phenomena can vary enormously, observations made under special and restricted conditions may give a very faulty picture of what might be discovered under a wider range of conditions. (p. 100)

Cultural Bias

The presence of cultural bias in the development of personality theory is substantial, and the reader should bear this in mind throughout the text. It is also true that the major interest in and development of personality theory has been primarily a Western endeavor, so it is understandable that this view predominates the theoretical models. Whether these theories can be applied to other cultures is not clear at this time and will be explored in greater depth in Chapter 12. Cultural bias seems to be a ubiquitous problem: "Human beings have always had difficulty in understanding and respecting those who are different from themselves. Other people, outside a given culture, have always been regarded as barbarians—their customs and mode of life have been merely something to disparage" (Leeper & Madison, 1959, p. 103).

Anthropologists' Early Interest in Psychological Concepts

Anthropologists were keenly interested in the use of psychology to broaden their level of analysis. Early pioneers such as the renowned anthropologist Margaret Mead, who married and collaborated with the natural scientist and innovator Gregory Bateson (1944), a major figure in the application of general systems theory to family process (covered in Chapter 10), were also interested in the process of character development. Mead (1964) saw that a marriage of anthropology and psychology provided a powerful dual lens for understanding character development and culture: "Any systematic attempt to include the psychological structure of individuals must rely, of course, not only upon an adequate psychological theory, but also upon adequate cultural theories regarding the process of cultural standardization of behavior, the nature of character formation, and the way in which idiosyncratic behavior is to be referred systematically to a cultural and societal base" (pp. 65–66).

In spite of Mead's interest and work, the influence of cultural processes has been minimally considered in the development of personality theory during the twentieth century. Anthropologists considered questions that seem highly relevant to personality, although not pursued by the psychological community. For example, Mead (1964) mentions the impact of immigration on personality and how individual character may be shaped:

> In primary culture contact the impact on character formation will differ systematically as between the effects of the new environment on the personalities of the immigrants and the effects of such immigration on members of other cultures on the personalities of the native members of the community. Among immigrants we find a variety of adjustments, all derived from the fact that the immigrant brings to the new environment a personality shaped in a previous and different environment. He may, while living and working in the new culture, continue to refer all of his behavior to the values of his original culture, adjusting only to the concrete realities of this new situation—learning proper names, bus routes, how to give change—but continue to interpret these activities in old terms. He may enter the new culture so determined to become part of it that he actually succeeds in putting large sections of his former life and values out of his consciousness, and even his use of his mother tongue may become stumbling or disappear altogether. (p. 70)

Behavior may change dramatically from one generation to the other as assimilation occurs: "Thus the personality type which develops where most of the rearing adults have experienced secondary cultural contact reflects on the one hand the native's sense of a shattered outer world, which comes from the rapid impingement of immigration, technological change and urbanization, and, on the other, the sense of internal disorientation of the immigrant" (p. 79).

Mead's Warning to the Orthopsychiatric Association

In a 1947 symposium address with Franz Alexander, a prolific writer whose varied work is presented throughout this text, at the annual meeting of the American Orthopsychiatric Association, an interdisciplinary society interested in children, Mead presented a

paper titled "The Role of the Scientist in Society." In this paper, she wrote of the potential and realized dangers of the developing social sciences:

The final and perhaps the central problem of the position of human relations scientist in society concerns manipulation. Once the possibility of discovering and applying principles of human behavior is granted, what possible safeguard can society develop against the misuse of this power? The examples of recent decades in which a very little knowledge of human behavior has been used in commerce, in government, and in war to bemuse, befuddle, subjugate, corrupt, and disintegrate the minds of men, breed a very justified fear that a society with a real grasp of human behavior would be a monstrous society in which no one would willingly live. It breeds the belief that it may be better to accept every human ill to which flesh is heir—disease, famine, war, insanity—than to risk the inevitable destruction of human dignity in the controlled world, in which those in absolute power have been absolutely corrupted by that power. (1964, p. 89)

An example of the realization of Mead's fear can be seen in various societal manifestations, but one classic that most people have heard of is the book *Clockwork Orange*, which depicts social scientists running amuck.

Leeper and Madison (1959) summarized the liabilities of the Western cultural perspective that they believed should be kept in mind when studying personality:

- An excessive respect for science and the products of technology to the neglect of human values.
- The tendency to reductionism in our thinking.
- The terror-and-danger theme in our culture (pp. 121–122).

They then summarize their perspective: "Biological factors do not compel human personality to develop in one narrow way. They create a wide range of potentialities, and it is the culture of a people, broadly speaking, that determines which of these potentialities will be developed and which will be muted" (p. 126).

Throughout the remainder of this text, an emergent theme is the degree to which various personality theories emphasize *nature versus nurture*. Although most theories recognize the multifactorial nature of personality, different theorists emphasize one aspect over another. Leeper and Madison (1959) write:

> It might be protested that when we ask psychologists to recognize the dependence of personality on field factors, we are not talking about concepts that are subject to experimentation, and that such an approach would keep psychology from being "scientific." But this seems like a travesty on the task and responsibility of psychology. People do not turn to psychology merely for a summary tabulation of the findings of experiments that have been obtained to date; they turn to psychology, and quite legitimately, to obtain as truthful and basic a picture of human nature as can be furnished. If, to get this picture, we need to enlarge the kinds of data that we consider, well and good. The aim of the scientist must be the clearest possible thinking and the most instructive factual observations he can find. (p. 130)

The Technological-Human Interface

Another cultural phenomenon important to personality theorists is the impact of rapid technological developments that have the capacity to transform humans into organisms that have primary interaction with computers and other technological advances.

This text endeavors to live up to the challenge posed by Leeper and Madison (1959) by offering multiple perspectives that can be used to advance the rapidly evolving science of personality.

Black Identity Development, the Legacy of Slavery, and Personality

The influence of racism on identity development of Blacks of African American descent who have experienced the multigenerational legacy of slavery is an important topic that has not been sufficiently addressed by personality theorists (see Grier & Cobbs, 1968; White & Parham, 1990). Sue and Sue (1999) report that when African Americans are given personality tests, they are often found to be more suspicious and mistrustful than White subjects: "Some educators have used such findings to label African Americans as paranoid" (p. 13). For example, African American men are often seen as "angry" or "enraged" (Grier & Cobbs, 1968). Grier and Cobbs view this "rage" as a phenomenon of **culturally induced** paranoia; they suggest it may be more disturbing or pathological when Blacks don't exhibit this normal level of suspiciousness. These findings need to be understood in the broader sociocultural context, which spawns what is probably a healthy adaptation to a society. Overt and subtle forms of racism persist; one recent example is **racial profiling,** using the race of an individual to predict the likelihood of criminal behavior. Those who are unaware of the cultural biases that exist in mental health and academia can pathologize normal and adaptive behavioral and defensive responding (Jones, 1985). Sue and Sue report how some Blacks have responded: "In response to their slave heritage and a history of White discrimination against them, African Americans have adopted various behaviors (in particular, behaviors toward Whites) that have proven important for survival in a racist society. 'Playing it cool' has been identified as one means by which Blacks, as well as members of other minority groups, may conceal their true thoughts and feelings. A Black person who is experiencing conflict, anger, or even rage may be skillful at appearing serene and composed. This tactic is a survival mechanism aimed at reducing one's vulnerability to harm and exploitation in a hostile environment" (Sue & Sue, 1999, p. 13; White & Parham, 1990).

Another aspect of the African American experience for males is the detrimental health effects of discrimination and racism (Franklin, 1998): "For many African American men there is an inner struggle with feeling that genuine talents are invisible to others in society. Personal respect and dignity as a man within the African American community are often challenged by intolerance and disrespect from the racism experienced outside of the community" (p. 239). African American men have a plethora of health problems and one of the lowest life expectancies of all minorities due to murder. African American males are significantly overrepresented in prisons. "To fulfill societal gender role expectations of provider and protector, African American men must contend with impeding racial barriers, such as disproportionate underemployment, as well as racial/gender notions that are disparaging, such as the stereotype of African American men as unreliable" (p. 243).

African American Families and Women's Role: Women tend to head African American families that have often been described as "matriarchal" in a pejorative way (Sue & Sue, 1999). Often ignored are the strengths in these extended family systems that provide economic and emotional support through closely established kinship bonds not often present in White families to the same degree. Spiritual beliefs are often highly valued and church is an important aspect of the cultural system. African American women also seem to be underserved by the health care system (see Chapter 12).

Evaluating Personality Theories

Making a determination of the usefulness of the various theories of personality presented in this text and elsewhere is not always straightforward. Various theoretical models may have useful application in one arena but not in another. Some theoretical models may make perfect sense in deepening our understanding of abnormal behavior or understanding the nature and evolution of humankind; others may have more microscopic usefulness, such as predicting the type of individual prone to cardiac disease. No current theoretical model is capable of being all things to all people. There are distinctive differences as well as many basic similarities in many of the theoretical models presented in this text. Readers may be assisted by a breakdown of the various ways in which theory can be assessed as to its usefulness by asking certain questions of each model.

- *Clinical utility of the theory: Is the theory useful to clinical practitioners in their conceptualization and treatment of emotional and personality disturbances?* A theory, even if not empirically validated, may have usefulness to mental health clinicians in conceptualizing and guiding treatment. Psychoanalytic models of personality were very useful to clinicians conducting assessment and practicing psychotherapy.
- *Practical utility of the theory: Does the theory have practical utility?* Some theoretical models have substantial practical application to the problems of humankind. Behavior models have demonstrated practical utility in a variety of areas, including education, health, behavior modification, and child rearing.

- *Predictive ability of the theory: How effective is the theoretical model for predicting behavior?* The prediction of behavior is a major focus of psychology. Some theoretical models are more effective than others in their prediction of human behavior. Psychoanalytic models for the most part have low predictive strength, whereas factor models have more.

- *Insight into human nature: Is the theoretical model useful for providing insight into human behavior and nature?* Some theoretical models have a much greater depth of understanding complex behavior and the nature of humankind. Psychodynamic and modern evolutionary-based theoretical models seem to make intuitive sense to many concerning the often confusing behavior of humans demonstrated in war, violence, and destructiveness.

- *The ability to provide self-understanding: Is the theoretical model useful in creating personal awareness and deepening self-understanding?* Some theoretical models are capable of producing personal insight or understanding about the way we act and live. Psychodynamic and cognitive models are very helpful for many people in understanding why we act the way we do. Others, such as factor models, do not concern themselves so much with individual motivation but are more concerned with group prediction.

- *The ability to generate new research: Is the theoretical model useful in generating new lines of research?* Some theoretical models are very generative in sparking new areas of research. Other models may be self-limiting, and if they don't continue to generate research will fall out of favor.

- *The ability to understand complex human behavior: Is the theoretical model capable of understanding complex human behaviors?* Some theoretical models are more capable of understanding complex human behaviors, such as domestic violence or child abuse. Some are better at understanding less complex behavioral sequences, such as simple learning sequences.

- *The ability to generate cross-disciplinary fertilization of ideas: Is the theoretical model capable of generating cross-disciplinary lines of thinking and research?* Some theoretical models are extremely useful for generating interest in other disciplines. For example, systems theory has generated much interdisciplinary theorizing and investigation.

One Final Advance: Computer Technology

The final advance presented in this chapter is the development of computer technology. Computers were seen as a potential tool for psychology early in their development in the mid-twentieth century. Computers have advanced significantly since that time, and the tremendous power that was once available only to large institutions is now available in most desktop computers. Computers have allowed for complex computational functions that have been seminal to the development of modern psychometrics (see Chapter 11 and the review of the Millon inventories). Another fascinating use of computers is to model personality (Tomkins & Messick, 1963). For a variety of reasons, this movement, unlike artificial intelligence that uses computers to create models of intelligence, the personality-computer simulation movement did not take hold. This will be discussed in Chapter 12 in a section on future directions. In the following chapter, we continue our journey exploring the birth and evolution of the contemporary science of personality with an examination of the groundbreaking development of the first comprehensive model of the mind and personality, Freud's psychoanalysis.

Summary

The focus of this chapter is on selected developments that have set the stage for the evolution of psychological science and contemporary personality theory. Early societies began to formalize systems to explain human nature and the human experience. These systems, representing rudimentary theory, can be viewed as the foundation of later attempts to develop an empirical science of personality and human behavior. Many of the early conceptions had a grain of truth, but it was not until more systematic thinking developed during the classical Greek era with rational systems of thought proposed by philosophers that great gains were made in understanding the nature of humankind. The next major development representing the birth of the scientific revolution occurred in the seventeenth and eighteenth centuries, sparked by the new rationalism of Locke, Bacon, and Hume among many others. This period set the stage for the development of modern scientific psychology in the late nineteenth century and saw the emergence of psychology as a discipline distinct from philosophy. This movement was sparked by Wundt's developments in the new discipline of physiological psychology, emphasizing psychology becoming an empirical science. Wundt's advancements and landmark publication *Principles of Physiological Psychology* had substantial impact on many in the new discipline of psychology. William James, in his landmark volume *The Principles of Psychology,* described many of the component systems, such as affect, cognition, self, will, perception, and memory, necessary for the study of personality and consciousness. There were false starts as well, such as Gall's phrenology and Sheldon's body somatotypes, on which theories of personality were postulated and refuted through empirical verification. Although refuted by later workers, these efforts propelled the field of personality science, demonstrating the power of the scientific model for behavioral science.

Both experimental methods using randomization and quasi-experimental methods attempting to control factors in natural settings were applied to the study of behavior and personality. Statistical procedures such as Pearson's correlation coefficient coming out of studies in genetics and intelligence offered new methods of inferential statistics to quantify the results of experiments. The study of intelligence, a major domain of scientific psychology, and its search for factors led others, such as Allport and Cattell, to apply this approach to the search for the traits and essential factors that constitute the basic structure of personality. Assisted in these developments with new multivariate statistics such as factor analysis, researchers were able to reduce thousands of words taken from the dictionary, in a lexical approach, to describe personality and reduced them to their basic factors.

The development of the field of anthropology offered another vital perspective overlooked by personality theorists concerning the cultural impact on personality. The influential anthropologist Margaret Mead urged social scientists to adopt a cultural perspective and warned about the need for ethical behavioral science. Also discussed is the bias that exists in applying dominant cultural models of normality and psychopathology to minority groups. A blatant example of this type of racial bias exists in the way African American males have been affected by the legacy of racism and social marginalization. Often, responses that have been labeled pathological represent healthy adaptation to prejudice. This is an area of great importance to the future viability of the field to respond to increasing cultural diversity. Last, the development of computers has enabled researchers to process data at a level never before possible, making the complex calculations necessary in a discipline with so many influences.

Suggested Reading and Tapes

Alexander, F. G., & Selesnick, S. T. (1966). *The history of psychiatry: An exaluation of psychiatric thought and practice from prehistoric times to the present.* New York: Harper & Row.

James, W. (1890). *The principles of psychology.* New York: Henry Holt and Company.

Kors, A. C. (1998). *The birth of the modern mind: An intellectual history of the 17th and 18th century: Parts I & II* (audiocassette series). Springfield, VA: The Great Courses on Tape, The Teaching Company Limited Partnership. (1-800-832-2412).

White, J. L., & Parham, T. A. (1990). *The psychology of Blacks.* Englewood Cliffs, NJ: Prentice Hall.

MODERN PERSONALITY THEORY

Freud and His Followers: The Birth, Evolution, and Controversy of Twentieth-Century Psychoanalytic Psychology

3
Chapter

Freud and the Birth of Psychoanalysis
   A Note on the Importance of the Personality and Sociocultural
      Setting of the Founding and Influential Theorists
   Brief Biographical Sketch and Historical Background

Theory of Psychoanalysis

The Structural Components of Personality
   Id: The Instinctual Force
   Ego: The Reality Agency
   Superego: The Seat of Conscience
   Instinctual Organization: Sex and Aggression

Map of the Mind
   Repression and Resistance
   Anxiety
   Mechanisms of Defense
   Neurosis and Symptom Formation

Stages of Psychosexual Development
   Oral Stage
   Anal Stage
   Phallic Stage
   Latency Stage
   Genital Stage
   Character Traits and Disorders and Psychosexual Development

Methods and Techniques of Psychoanalysis
   Dream Analysis

The Evolution of Psychoanalysis
   Jung and the Collective Unconscious
   Ferenczi and the Impact of Trauma
   Fenichel, Reich, and Character Analysis
   The Women of Psychoanalysis

Freud and the Birth of Psychoanalysis

The "discovery of the unconscious" and the development of the psychoanalytic method as a form of "scientific" inquiry heralded the birth of modern psychology and stands as one of the intellectual milestones of the twentieth century (J. Schwartz, 1999). Freud's once esoteric terminology permeates contemporary language and shapes culture to a remarkable degree. Hardly a day goes by that one does not hear these terms used by economists, homemakers, and newscasters as well as friends and family members. There is a surprisingly common knowledge, outside of the professional psychological community, of many of these seminal constructs, such as defense mechanisms, unconscious process, and intrapsychic structure: **id, ego,** and **superego.** We often hear people talk of **repressing** their feelings and memories, projecting, sublimating, and so forth. The word ego has become a mainstay of popular culture. Few biographers fail to incorporate various aspects of psychoanalysis for those they write about. In fact, Freud and many others undertook the psychoanalytic study of numerous historical figures, using the tools of inquiry to come to deeper understanding.

What Freud set into motion with his unifying system of constructs or **metapsychology,** for better or worse, was our focus on our inner workings, hidden motivations and dark forces that influence behavior and shape our interpersonal relationships. His theoretical constructs provided a new and exciting, if not murky, way to see the world in its multilayered splendor. His theoretical formulations, in spite of attack and attempts to discredit them, remain the cornerstones for many, if not

Freud and Einstein—Cassandra's Daughter: A History of Psychoanalysis (J. Schwartz, 1999)

The dominant image of Freud is the Severe. His penetrating gaze sees deep into our souls. In his presence, any word, any gesture betrays our secrets. If Einstein is the god of the incomprehensible, then perhaps Freud had become a god of judgement, an all-seeing father figure from whom nothing can be hidden. But Freud's fame, unlike Einstein's, is multi-faceted. Whereas everyone shares the same image of a long-haired, incomprehensible, genius Einstein, there are multiple Freuds—hero and villain, healer and charlatan, sexual liberator and sexual betrayer, revolutionary and reactionary. In the language of psychoanalysis, Freud is the target of the manifold projections of the feelings of disappointment, fear, love, and longing that we can visit on the famous. (p. 17)

most, contemporary theories of personality. The psychoanalytic model remains the most ambitious system for attempting to understand human personality and psychopathological adaptations.

Sigmund Freud's contributions to the development of psychology, although controversial during our time, are considered by many equivalent to the discovery of Einstein's theory of relativity. Bischof (1970) writes: "There is a unique parallel between the careers of Freud and of other intellectual giants. Freud, Darwin, Einstein, Dewey all pioneered certain aspects of their professional fields, [and] lived rather long and certainly productive lives" (p. 31).

At the time Freud undertook his study and attempted to develop a theoretical system of human mental functioning, there was little else to offer deep insights into human nature outside of the study of philosophy, which did not directly address the concept of personality in a scientific way.

A Note on the Importance of the Personality and Sociocultural Setting of the Founding and Influential Theorists

In keeping with the subject of this book, it is important to understand both the personality and cultural influences of the theorists presented. It is significant, therefore, to place Freud's work in the context of the time in which he developed his groundbreaking theory. Freud was raised in the rather repressive puritanical society that was the norm in post-Victorian society. He grew up in a culture where sexual expression, especially among the bourgeoisie, was very restricted. Eastern European society was quite restrictive about what was acceptable. Therefore, Freud's life experience was not one that enjoyed open discussion or even recognition of human sexual expression (Gay, 1988). The members of society that he tended to treat, first with hypnosis and then psychoanalysis, unduly suffered from this level of societal repression. What Freud observed and taught about repression was not unknown to previous intellectuals and philosophers. When society or an individual is under the force of severe repression, outbreaks of the impulses are not uncommon. Freud was therefore faced in the consultation room with many reports of incest, which he first took at face value and later modified in his theory to be fantasy. As we discuss later in this chapter, this is one of the great and most volatile controversies and considered by some to be the most painful Freudian legacy.

Cassandra's Daughter: A History of Psychoanalysis (J. Schwartz, 1999)

Cassandra, a princess of Troy, was given the power of prophecy by Apollo. But when Cassandra spurned Apollo, he decreed she should never be believed. Apollo, to whom the great temple at Branchidai was erected, was the patron god of the Pythagoreans, a grouping of rich industrialists and merchants. So too was science the patron god of the rich industrialists and merchants of the late nineteenth century. And so, too, did science give psychoanalysis the power of prophecy. And, as it is told, psychoanalysis has spurned the discipline that gave it birth and has not been believed.

But unlike the newly prosperous bourgeoisie of the nineteenth century who sought to invent roots for itself by approaching the myths of antiquity, we are now too mature to rely on the Greeks for our narratives. The story of psychoanalysis is not the story of Cassandra, but the story of Cassandra's daughter, a strange, not entirely welcome newcomer on the world stage. We do not know the story of Cassandra's daughter. We have to write it ourselves. (Preface)

Brief Biographical Sketch and Historical Background

Sigmund Freud was born in Freiburg, Moravia, on May 6, 1856, the oldest of seven children. He entered medical school at the University of Vienna in 1873 and was awarded his medical degree in 1881. He died on September 23, 1939. His first position was at the Institute of Cerebral Anatomy, where he conducted research comparing fetal and adult brains. He entered private practice as a neurologist because of the limited financial rewards of research and an anti-Semitic attitude that was prevalent in academia at the time. He was strongly influenced by his studies with Jean Charcot, a well-known specialist in the treatment of hysteria with hypnosis. He was inspired, as were many others, by Charcot's dramatic clinical demonstrations. Freud's interest in neurology gave way to his new passion for psychopathology and the study of hysteria.

Freud met Josef Breuer at the Institute of Physiology in the 1870s and they became intimate friends and scientific collaborators: "Inspired by Charcot and impressed by Breuer's results, on his return to Vienna from Paris in 1886 Freud actively collaborated with Joseph Breuer on the problem of hysteria" (J. Schwartz, 1999, p. 44).

Hysteria: A Debilitating Disorder

The symptoms of hysteria were spectacular. They included convulsions, disturbances of vision, deafness, loss of the sense of taste and smell, numbness of half the body, paralysis of the limbs, dumbness and contractures—permanent spasms holding an arm or a leg in a contorted position. In convulsions the so-called *grande mouvements* were, unlike movements in epilepsy, powerful, highly coordinated motions and contortions which frequently led to loss of consciousness. Disturbances of sight included a loss of colour vision, selective colour blindness (particularly violet), double vision and seeing things at twice or half their normal sizes. The contractures, anaesthesias, paralyses, and tremors were highly labile and could be transferred symmetrically to the other side of the body leaving the original area completely normal. Psychologically, patients could present as highly irritable or as melancholic and depressed. Heredity, in the form of an inherited hysterical disposition, was seen to be the ultimate cause of hysteria. (J. Schwartz, 1999, p. 36)

In 1886, Freud married Martha Bernays. They had six children; the most prominent, Anna, became a psychoanalyst and advanced the work of her father, particularly the application of his theory to the treatment of children. In 1909, Sigmund Freud was invited to the United States to give a series of lectures sponsored by Stanley Hall, a prominent American psychologist at Clark University. These lectures introduced his theories to the world. Psychoanalysis took off in the United States with the formation of many psychoanalytic institutes. Freud was forced to leave Austria prior to World War II and settled in England. He suffered tremendously from cancer of the jaw, probably caused by his prodigious—30 a day—cigar habit. He endured 32 operations but succumbed to the disease.

Theory of Psychoanalysis

Psychoanalysis is a theory of the mind and personality: "The theory of dynamic psychology developed by Sigmund Freud, is based primarily on the influence of unconscious forces such as repressed impulses, internal conflicts, and early traumas on the mental life and adjustment of the individual" (Goldenson, 1970, p. 1038). In his book *Open Minded: Working Out the Logic of the Soul,* Jonathan Lear (1998) compares the goal of psychoanalysis to the aim of early Greek philosophers: to examine and understand who we are. He writes: "The idea that The Unconscious is itself a mindlike structure, itself a locus of its own rationality and intentionality, seems, then, not so much an empirical discovery as a conceptual requirement" (p. 83).

Psychoanalysis was born when Freud abandoned hypnosis in favor of the technique of **free association,** the uncensored expression of feelings, thoughts, and fantasies. "The patient talks, tells of his past experiences and present impressions, complains, confesses to his wishes and his emotional impulses" (Freud, 1966). The development of the technique of free association was a radical departure from hypnosis, the major technique used by the French neurologist Charcot in his treatment of hysteria. Freud's theoretical formulations were primed by the work of Charcot (1982), who believed that certain mental contents exit out of consciousness and exert a powerful influence on the pathological development of thoughts, feelings, and behavior (Eagle & Wolitzky, 1992; Ellenberger, 1970). "Analogous to Galileo's use of the telescope to explore previously unknown structures in the night sky, the development of the analytic hour created an instrument that opened up an entirely new way to explore previously unknown structures in the human inner world" (J. Schwartz, 1999, p. 40). Breuer was also very influential in Freud's interest in hypnosis, which later became a source of frustration: "Originally Breuer and I myself carried out psychotherapy by means of hypnosis; Breurer's first patient was treated throughout under hypnotic influence, and to begin with I followed him in this. I admit that at that period the work proceeded more easily and pleasantly, and also in a much shorter period of time. Results were capricious and not lasting; and for that reason I finally dropped hypnosis. And I then understood that an insight into the dynamics of these illnesses had not been possible so long as hypnosis was employed" (Freud, 1966, p. 292).

From 1894 to 1896, Freud presented seven papers concerning the origins of hysteria as the result of sexual seduction. "Freud described severe cases, some coming to him after long unsuccessful institutional treatment, all of whom suffered trauma which had to be 'classed as grave sexual injuries; some of them positively revolting'" (J. Schwartz, 1999, p. 66). This discovery was profound and would create controversy for the next century, not only because Freud retracted it and developed his Oedipal explanation; as we shall see, the controversy continues in its current form in the "false memory syndrome."

"Fundamental to Freud's thinking about the mind was a simple assumption: If there is a discontinuity in consciousness—something the person is doing but cannot report or explain—then the relevant mental processes necessary to 'fill in the gaps' must be unconscious" (Westen & Gabbard, 1999, p. 59). Freud had a desire to go deeper into the complexity of the human experience and did not avoid the dark side of human nature that he is known for bringing to our attention. According to Westen and Gabbard, "Freud (1923, 1961) defined psychoanalysis as (1) a theory of the mind or personality, (2) a method of investigation of unconscious processes, and (3) a method of treatment" (p. 58). Freud believed that the conscious mind was only one small element of personality and spent much of his professional life mapping the unconscious landscape. He likened the conscious mind to the tip of an iceberg and the unconscious to the larger portion of the iceberg that is underwater and out of sight.

The Legacy of Freud Bashing

According to Diamond (2001), the two irreplaceable scientists of the past two centuries are Freud and Darwin. Why, then, is "Freud bashing" so common? Diamond, a professor of physiology at UCLA School of Medicine, suggests that Freud is castigated much more for his omissions and errors than is Darwin. He believes that Freud's failures have a much more direct impact because they affect how we understand the lives of those suffering from mental disorders. This is especially notable in his rejection of his findings about the prevalence of child abuse in late nineteenth- and early twentieth-century European society, discussed at the end of this chapter. Another reason for criticizing one of the greatest scientific pioneers is that he was "outstandingly ungenerous: He denied credit to others, was intolerant of rivals, hated many people, and surrounded himself with unquestioningly loyal admirers" (p. B11). Diamond continues: "Freud's detractors remain numerous, even though they take for granted many of his concepts and contributions" (p. B11). Two other factors may also drive this "unfair" treatment: It is often pointed out that many newer therapies are more effective, and Freud is inappropriately blamed for delaying new discoveries in biological psychiatry, most notably, the need to treat bipolar illness with medication, discovered after Freud's time.

The Structural Components of Personality

Psychoanalysis is a *structural theory* in that it offers us a schema for the structure of the psyche and the interplay among the various agencies. The three major structural components of this matrix are the *id, ego,* and *superego* (see Figure 3.1). Development proceeds from the id, which includes the drives we are born with, to the ego and superego: Infants are entirely driven by gratification of instinctual needs, without any concern for their effect; as development proceeds, the values of society are assimilated through parental figures or caretakers and are then *internalized,* forming the superego or conscience. The function of culture is to socialize humankind so that

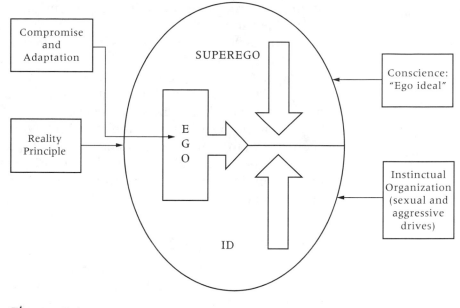

Figure 3.1

Structural Organization of the Mind: The Dynamic Interplay of the Id-Ego-Superego.

instinctual needs do not destroy society. War is the grandest way these instinctual forces, driven by primitive aggression, demonstrate the marginally effective control that culture places on human behavior.

Id: The Instinctual Force

The id is the part of the mind that harbors our instinctual organization (sexual and aggressive impulses), drives, and wishes, what Freud termed primary process. The id finds expression in the part of us that is influenced by our unadulterated drive for hedonistic gratification. It is the original matrix from which the ego and superego become differentiated. The id is the psychic agency closest to our physical being and from which energy is derived. The id constantly seeks to discharge any buildup of tension and to return to a state of comfort or homeostasis. The id operates by what Freud termed the **pleasure principle:** the attempt to avoid pain and maximize pleasure. There are two primary methods that the id utilizes in this attempt. **Primary process** discharges tension by using the imagery of an object to remove the tension. The memory image or hallucinatory experience represents a **wish fulfillment.** Primary process can be expressed in fantasy or in dreams; for example, almost everyone engages in some form of sexual or narcissistic fantasy to reduce tension. Individuals who are overly dominated by primary process are usually psychotic or engaged in autistic fantasy as a way of gaining primary gratification; in other words, real life has not been sufficiently gratifying to engage in. Simpler forms of organismic excitation are dealt with by built-in **reflex actions,** which are inborn physiological mechanisms such as sneezing or sighing when tension builds up.

Ego: The Reality Agency

The ego is the psychic agency that attempts to mediate the instinctual, gratification-seeking aims of the id with the demands of the external world. The ego works by the **reality principle.** The reality principle attempts to supersede the primary process, gratification-seeking pleasure principle of the id. The ego incorporates reality testing into its function so that realistic aims and plans can be carried out in the service of adaptation of the individual. The ego is considered to be the domain of executive function of the personality; therefore, cognitive functions are under the control of the ego. In other words, a secondary process of the ego is to problem-solve to seek appropriate satisfaction and preserve the individual's destiny. The ego works in conjunction with the id, attempting to balance impulses but also using the energy to provide drive, creativity, and motivation. When there is a breakdown of the ego, the individual loses most of his or her ability to adequately perceive reality and control the force of primary process, so that the constraints on behavior are often temporarily in abeyance.

Superego: The Seat of Conscience

The superego represents the internalized value system of society as portrayed by parental figures and social institutions. The superego represents the ideal state of how the individual should behave according to internalized parental expectations. It is formed from the punishment and praise provided by parents transmuted into superego function. Compared to the pleasure-seeking aims of the id and the reality orientation of the ego, the superego is concerned with ideals of morality and perfection. It serves as a constant judge for the actions of the ego. The **ego ideal** represents the internalization of the moral standards of the parental figures and is the yardstick against which all action is measured. Guilt arises in the system when there is a discrepancy between the ego ideal and an action. Most important, the superego contains the sexual and aggressive instinctual pressure exerted on the individual by the id, which, if allowed full expression, would destroy civilization.

The superego also attempts to modulate the ego's reality principle by highlighting the moral highroad in the executive functions of the ego. When one behaves in a manner that lives up to the ego ideal, one feels good and proud. However, as is often the case, when the standards of the ego ideal are not met, guilt becomes predominant. Guilt then serves the function of guiding the intrapsychic system by getting the individual back on track. This guilt is thought to be one of the major causes of neurotic behavior, when the individual seeks self-punishment as a way of reducing this uncomfortable state of tension.

Instinctual Organization: Sex and Aggression

Instincts are central to Freudian metapsychology. Freud postulated two primary instinctual drives: the sexual or libidinal and the aggressive. He theorized that these were opposing drives. The **libido** represents the **life instinct,** and aggression the **death instinct.** Psychoanalysis, although dualistic, emphasized the sex drive as the main source of psychic energy (Westen & Gabbard, 1999). Freud was convinced that aggression was a basic human drive that needed an elaborate psychic system to control: too little and the individual would suffer from a passive personality; too much is dangerous. When an individual is functioning well, he or she is able to use aggression in an appropriately competitive, self-protective, and assertive fashion. In many of his cases, Freud demonstrated how the aggressive impulses are channeled into various types of psychopathology, such as perversions, and characterologic disorders, such as hysteria, obsessional neurosis, and passive aggression. He believed that humans' attempt to gratify urges (pleasure principle) to reduce excitation is an attempt to attain a state of nirvana or nothingness (nirvana principle). This portion of his theory was never widely accepted and was considered overly speculative by many. However, his belief that humans are driven by aggressive and sexual instinctual organization is hard to dispute when one examines the content of popular culture or reads the history of the twentieth century, with two World Wars and frequent ethnic cleansing of millions of people by various cultures.

Map of the Mind

Freud's model of psychic functioning includes a formulation of the **topography** or map of the terrain of the mind (see Figure 3.2). This is not a map of real terrain but a theoretical conception of the way the mind organizes experience and how these various components interrelate. The main components include the **unconscious, preconscious,** and **conscious** sectors. These divisions of the mental apparatus have a central focus in Freud's metapsychology.

Figure 3.2

Topographical Depiction of the Mind and the Action of the Repressive Force of the Defense System.

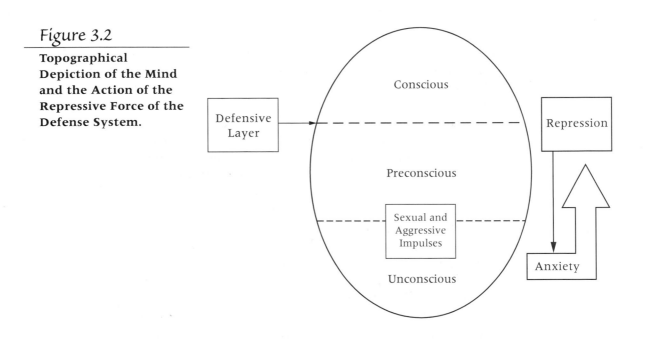

- *Unconscious:* Freud's notion of the unconscious refers to the portion of the mind where impulses, fantasy, and primary process reside out of awareness.

- *Preconscious:* The preconscious is the portion of the mind where unconscious material is transformed or "worked over" by defense mechanisms such as condensation and displacement.

- *Conscious:* The conscious portion of the mind contains aspects of ourselves of which we are aware.

Freud (1966) described this model of mental functioning:

> *The crudest idea of these systems is the most convenient for us—a spatial one. Let us therefore compare the system of the unconscious to a large entrance hall, in which the mental impulses jostle one another like separate individuals. Adjoining this entrance hall there is a second, narrower, room—a kind of drawing-room—in which consciousness, too, resides. But on the threshold between these two rooms a watchman performs his function: he examines the different mental impulses, acts as a censor, and will not admit them into the drawing-room if they displease him. You will see at once that it does not make much difference if the watchman turns away a particular impulse at the threshold itself or if he pushes it back across the threshold after it has entered the drawing-room. This is merely a question of the degree of watchfulness and how early he carries out his act of recognition. If we keep to this picture, we shall be able to extend our nomenclature further. The impulses in the entrance hall of the unconscious are out of sight of the conscious, which is in the other room; to begin with they must remain unconscious. If they have already pushed their way forward to the threshold and have been turned back by the watchman, then they are inadmissible to consciousness; we speak of them as* repressed. *But even the impulses which the watchman has allowed to cross the threshold are not on that account necessarily conscious as well; they can only become so if they succeed in catching the eye of consciousness. We are therefore justified in calling this second room the system of the* preconscious. *In that case becoming conscious retains its purely descriptive sense. For any particular impulse, however, the vicissitude of repression consists of its not being allowed by the watchman to pass from the system of the unconscious into that of the preconscious. It is the same watchman whom we get to know as resistance when we try to lift the repression by means of analytic treatment. (pp. 295–296)*

Repression and Resistance

Key concepts in understanding the dynamic interplay among the various components of the mind are repression and resistance. **Repression** is the mental process by which the energy associated with "unacceptable" impulses is retained but the memory is "lost." Symptoms are often the result of this repressive force. As the memory and affects of a particular event are isolated, the energy is then left to form symptomatic expression. This is the **dynamic** aspect of Freud's theory, which was based on a hydraulic fluid model. Thus, unconscious conflicts are often expressed in altered form by the preconscious through dreams, slips of the tongue, and daydreams.

Resistance refers to the manner in which the patient's characteristic defense patterns operate in the relationship with the therapist, the **transference relationship.** Freud (1966) describes this process of resistance: "Thus at times one has an impression that the patient has entirely replaced his better intention of making an end to his illness by the alternative one of putting the doctor in the wrong, of making him realize his impotence and of triumphing over him" (p. 290). In doing so, the patient is transferring his or her attitudes and expectations derived from early relationships and projecting them onto the blank screen that the therapist uses to facilitate this process. This process was termed the development of the transference neurosis. It was believed that the curative aspects of psychoanalysis lay in the transferring of these relationship qualities to the therapist and then in the analyzing of this transference relationship.

Anxiety

Freud's notion of anxiety included three basic categories: **moral, realistic,** and **neurotic.** All humans are familiar with the physiological state that is engendered when we are anxious. **Moral anxiety** refers to the anxiety generated when the id gains too much control over the ego. This is due to the fact that the superego demands that the individual live up to the ego ideal; when this does not occur, guilt is induced by the superego. **Realistic anxiety** is a rational response to danger in one's environment for which a flight-or-fight response is triggered. This is one way the human nervous system evolved to protect us from dangers in the world. Thus, anxiety signals an immediate response: Stay and fight or run and escape the danger. Anxiety prepares one for a rapid response.

Neurotic anxiety, on the other hand, has a kind of free-floating quality that is not related to any imminent threat. Terming it **expectant anxiety,** Freud believed that this type of generalized anxiety was one of the main features of neuroses. Anxiety of this type can often be converted into various symptoms, such as obsessional neurosis, wherein the individual engages in compulsions that serve the purpose of binding the anxiety so that it does not become overwhelming. Also, emotions that are not given full expression can be transformed into anxiety. Freud believed these affects or feelings exist both at the conscious and the unconscious levels. Anxiety, then, can be generated by repression by the superego or when a dangerous level of instinctual impulses threaten to break through to consciousness. Defenses are used to protect the system from becoming overwhelmed.

Mechanisms of Defense

One of the many of Freud's brilliant conceptualizations was that of defensive functioning (see Table 3.1). A mechanism of defense is a mental operation that protects an individual against anxiety that results when primary process material threatens to break through to the conscious or preconscious zone. For example, an alcoholic might defend against the anxiety that results from his drinking with **denial,** which may protect him from the associated anxiety from the hedonistic id that says "Drink" and the superego that condemns him for the pain he causes his family. Denial reduces the conflict but at a high cost to adaptive functioning.

Freud's identification and elaboration of many of the mechanisms of defense have added much to our understanding of personology and continues to influence our evolving understanding about the way defenses are used to adapt (Holi, Sammallahti, & Aalberg, 1999). Freud catalogued many of the basic defenses that he observed in his psychoanalytic explorations. His daughter, Anna Freud, went further in identifying defenses that are used to protect against anxiety.

Neurosis and Symptom Formation

Freud developed his theory to explain the development of the psychological symptoms common at that time, which he termed neurosis

Table 3.1   **Common Defense Mechanisms**

Defense	Definition	Example
Acting out	Conflicts are translated into action, with little or no intervening reflection.	A student disrupts class because she is angry over an unfair grade.
Denial	Refusal to acknowledge some painful external or subjective reality obvious to others.	A woman refuses to acknowledge a pregnancy, despite positive test results.
Devaluation	Attributing unrealistic negative qualities to self or others, as a means of punishing the self or reducing the impact of the devalued item.	The formerly admired professor who gives you a D on your term paper is suddenly criticized as a terrible teacher.
Displacement	Conflicts are displaced from a threatening object onto a less threatening one.	A student who hates his history professor sets the textbook on fire.
Dissociation	Conflict is dealt with by disrupting the integration of consciousness, memory, or perception of the internal and external world.	After breaking up with a lover, a suicidal student is suddenly unable to recall the periods of time during which they were together.
Fantasy	Avoidance of conflict by creating imaginary situations that satisfy drives or desires.	A student from a troubled home daydreams about going to college to become a famous psychologist.
Idealization	Attributing unrealistic positive qualities to self or others.	A student worried about intellectual ability begins to idolize a tutor.
Isolation of affect	Conflict is defused by separating ideas from affects, thus retaining an awareness of intellectual or factual aspects but losing touch with threatening emotions.	A biology student sacrifices a laboratory animal, without worrying about its right to existence, quality of life, or emotional state.
Omnipotence	An image of oneself as incredibly powerful, intelligent, or superior is created to overcome threatening eventualities or feelings.	A student facing a difficult final exam asserts that there is nothing about the material that he doesn't know.
Projection	Unacceptable emotions or personal qualities are disowned by attributing them to others.	A student attributes his own anger to the professor, and thereby comes to see himself as a persecuted victim.
Projective identification	Unpleasant feelings and reactions are not only projected onto others, but also retained in awareness and viewed as a reaction to the recipient's behavior.	A student attributes her own anger to the professor, but sees her response as a justifiable reaction to persecution.

Table 3.1 *(Continued)*

Defense	Definition	Example
Rationalization	An explanation for behavior is constructed after the fact to justify one's action in the eyes of self or others.	A professor who unknowingly creates an impossible exam asserts the necessity of shocking students back to serious study.
Reaction formation	Unacceptable thoughts or impulses are contained by adopting a position that expresses the direct opposite.	A student who hates some group of persons writes an article protesting their unfair treatment by the university.
Repression	Forbidden thoughts and wishes are withheld from conscious awareness.	A student's jealous desire to murder a rival is denied access to conscious awareness.
Splitting	Opposite qualities of a single object are held apart, left in deliberately unintegrated opposition, resulting in cycles of idealization and devaluation as either extreme is projected onto self and others.	A student vacillates between worship and contempt for a professor, sometimes seeing her as intelligent and powerful and himself as ignorant and weak, and then switching roles, depending on their interactions.
Sublimation	Unacceptable emotions are defused by being channelled into socially acceptable behavior.	A professor who feels a secret disgust for teaching instead works ever more diligently to earn the teaching award.
Undoing	Attempts to rid oneself of guilt through behavior that compensates the injured party actually or symbolically.	A professor who designs a test that is too difficult creates an excess of easy extra-credit assignments.

Source: Millon and Davis, 2000, p. 26.

(see Figure 3.3). **Symptoms** are a type of compromise formation that allows partial expression of the drive but also may include an aspect of self-punishment: One needs to suffer when one's instinctual organization is too close to the surface. When the memory and affects of a particular event are isolated, the energy is left to form into symptomatic expression. The energy is transformed, but the memory is "lost," often expressed in a disguised form in the symptom complex. For example, a choking sensation might represent a murderous impulse to choke someone with whom one is conflicted. This conflict zone is often expressed in altered form by the preconscious through dreams, slips of the tongue, and daydreams. The

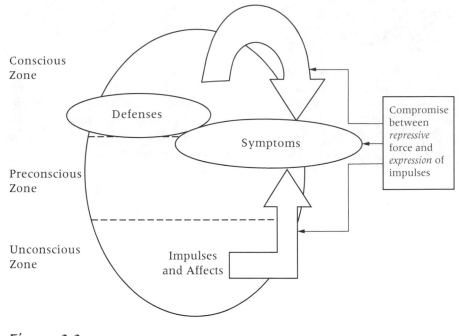

Conscious
Zone

Preconscious
Zone

Unconscious
Zone

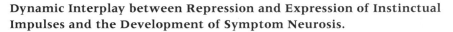

Figure 3.3

Dynamic Interplay between Repression and Expression of Instinctual Impulses and the Development of Symptom Neurosis.

conscious mind tries to repress or keep out of awareness painful or troubling memories or traumatic experience. Freud (1966) writes about this mechanism of repression and its function in the development of symptoms and neurosis:

> [Repression] is the precondition for the construction of symptoms, but it is also something to which we know nothing similar. Let us take as our model an impulse, a mental process and endeavours to turn itself into an action. We know that it can be repelled by what we term a rejection or a condemnation. When this happens, the energy at its disposal is withdrawn from it; it becomes powerless though it can persist in a memory. The whole process of coming to a decision about it runs its course within the knowledge of the ego. It is a very different mater if we suppose that the same impulse is subjected to repression. In that case it would retain its energy and no memory of it would remain behind; moreover the process of repression would be accomplished

unnoticed by the ego. This comparison, therefore, brings us no nearer to the essential nature of repression. (p. 294)

Symptoms are the way the unconscious mind transfers energy from the conflict into something that expresses the energy but hides the conflict from the suffering individual: "Symptoms, as we know, are a substitute for something that is held back by repression" (Freud, 1966, p. 298).

Stages of Psychosexual Development

Freud's theory of human development and personality formation was based on his notions about psychosexual development. The sexual instincts discussed previously, also referred to as libido, are one of the major forces in this developmental process; thus, Freud's is a theory of psychosexual development. The libidinal pressure, the **life instinct,** fuels development. The **death instinct,** a construct that was not widely accepted, derives from the aggressive drive. Psychoanalytic theory posits that individuals proceed through progressive stages of psychosexual development. Each of these stages emphasizes different developmental tasks. For a variety of reasons, an individual can become fixated in one of these stages, which will then set the stage for the development of different personality types.

Oral Stage

The first stage of life, up until about age 2, is termed the oral stage and is characterized by the need to suck, which is a biological survival reflex action. In this phase of development, gratification and satisfaction are primarily received through oral activities such as nursing, thumb sucking, and swallowing. The libido is distributed in the oral region. During the **oral sucking** period, the first eight months of this stage, weaning begins and then ends as other foods are offered. This can be traumatic if the weaning is abrupt or uncaring. The vestiges of this trauma can develop into character traits, as we shall discuss. During the second phase, oral biting, from 8 months to 2 years, the child uses biting as a weapon to express aggression; this is evident when the child begins to sense himself or herself as separate from the mother.

Anal Stage

The next stage, until about age 4, is the anal stage, when the primary source of pleasure is derived from voiding of feces. During this phase, the child is beginning to experience the intrusion of the outside world. This period of socialization generally sets the stage for the first conflict between parents and child. The ego starts to differentiate from the id and the reality principle starts to arise. Rewards are given for complying and disappointment for accidents. This is the beginning of crude superego function. With the onset of toilet training, the child can express autonomy by withholding, refusing to comply, or soiling himself or herself. This is termed the **anal expulsive stage,** which can occur anywhere from 2 to 3 years and is a period when the child learns how to manipulate parents by using elimination as a weapon. During the **anal retentive stage,** from 3 to 4 years of age, the child learns how to control and retain feces to control and punish and to present the feces as a symbolic gift when given in the right circumstances. This mastery can lead to a feeling of omnipotence.

Phallic Stage

The third stage of psychosexual development, the phallic stage, is from about 4 years to 7 or 8. During this phase of development, the primary source of gratification is derived from the genitals. This is the phase in which the child starts to experience pleasurable feelings from the opposite-sex parent and is the stage in which the Oedipal or Electra complex emerges. The child may touch, rub, or exhibit genitals as well as show interest in the anatomy of family members. Ideas concerning sex and birth are developing; this is characterized by the competition with the same-sex parent for the attention of the opposite-sex parent. There is a fear of castration of the male child because of his competitive feelings with the father over possessing the mother. The female child experiences a somewhat different process. In the **Electra complex,** the female child already believes that she has been castrated due to her lack of a penis. She searches for the person who did so and decides it was her mother. Blaming her mother, she increases her love for her father. After idealizing her father, she comes to terms with the loss and identifies with the mother. The resolution of the Oedipal and Electra complex results with identification with the parent of the same sex. The resolution of this phase results in the development of a more fully developed superego.

Latency Stage

The latency phase of development, from about age 6 to 12, is a time when preoccupation with sexuality lessens. The resolution of the Oedipus/Electra complex has been traumatizing and the child prefers to inhibit and repress sexuality. During this phase, much of the developmental energy is used to absorb the cultural and intellectual experiences that are available. Boys and girls tend to prefer playmates of the same sex. It is a relatively conflict-free and innocent time that will end with the entry into puberty, which marks the beginning of the genital phase.

Genital Stage

This stage of development, beginning about age 13, represents the fullest level of maturity, when the task is not the experience of pleasure in and of itself but the transformation of the libido into mature relationships with others. This is stimulated by the hormonal and biochemical changes that prime the individual for puberty. Romance is now a major interest. Initially, the interest tends to be homosexual because of fears of castration but then shifts to heterosexual relations, courting, and thoughts of marriage. During this phase of development, the narcissistic seeking of continual pleasure must be exchanged for mature love and caring for others. If successful, the earliest expression of the sexual instinct is essentially transformed to mature love. If individuals have had too much or too little gratification along the way, the outcome may result in disturbances in personality functioning.

Character Traits and Disorders and Psychosexual Development

Freud's conception of the way personality developes rested on the foundation of his model of psychosexual development (see Table 3.2). **Character** was derived from the Greek term for "engraving," which is the distinguishing feature of a person. As we shall see later in this

Table 3.2   **Stages of Psychosexual Development and Character Types**

Stage of Development	Approximate Age	Character Type
Oral stage	0 to 2 years	Dependency
Anal stage	2 to 4 years	Compulsive
Phallic stage	4 to 8 years	Narcissistic
Latency stage	6 to 12 years	Passive*
Genital stage	13 years	Hysterical

*Not included by neo-Freudian, but may be a logical type.

chapter, the development of a complex system of character types was elaborated by some of the pioneering psychoanalytic figures, such as Otto Fenichel and Karl Abraham.

Basically, the development of one's character is influenced by how the psychosexual stages of development are navigated. If there is a normal progression, the individual will develop a mature character. If, however, fixations occur at various stages, there will be a buildup of excessive libidinal energy related to the various errogenous zones. For example, an oral phase that does not have sufficient gratification can result in an oral hunger, later manifesting itself in excessive dependency.

Methods and Techniques of Psychoanalysis

As we have discussed, psychoanalysis is not only a theory of the mind but a method for treating emotional disorders. Freud used the investigative tools he developed to explore various aspects of mental processes, but was particularly concerned with the unconscious. Up until the discovery of psychoanalysis, there was little in the way of treatment for emotional disorders. Freud's method and technique of psychoanalysis relied on his observation that individuals tend to re-create their early relationship dynamics with the analyst in a process he termed transference. By transference, Freud (1966) meant "a transference of feelings on to the person of the doctor, since we do not believe that the situation in the treatment could justify the development of such feelings. We suspect, on the contrary, that the whole readiness for these feelings is derived from elsewhere, that they were already prepared in the patient and, upon the opportunity offered by the analytic treatment, are transferred on to the person of the doctor. Transference can appear as a passionate demand for love or in more moderate forms; in place of a wish to be loved, a wish can emerge between a girl and an old man to be received as a favourite daughter; the libidinal desire can be toned down into a proposal for an inseparable, but ideally nonsensual, friendship" (p. 442). Transference can have both positive and negative tones. What is important from a technical standpoint is that the development of the transference with the doctor is stimulated by the therapeutic stance the analyst assumes. Freud recommended that the analyst assume a position of technical neutrality so as not to influence the patient and to present himself or herself as a blank screen onto which the projection of the transference process would naturally occur. Freud's technique emphasizes the use of free association, the free expression of whatever comes to mind without censoring thoughts or feelings.

Freud advanced the work of his predecessors when he observed the power of the transferential relationship. As his method evolved, he considered the curative aspect of psychoanalysis to be the development of a **transference neurosis.** Because of the blank screen the analyst attempted to provide, the development of this transference relationship with the analyst resulted in this imaginary relationship. This became the hallmark of psychoanalytic process. If a transference relationship developed, it could be analyzed with the patient, who would then begin to develop a conscious awareness of his or her unconscious process. The patient could only imagine the doctor's reactions and feelings, which were never revealed to the patient.

Typically, Freud's patients lay on a couch with the doctor sitting behind. This was thought to keep the transference field clear by not allowing the analyst's reactions to be observed. The analyst refrained from giving advice or suggestions, and analyzed the material in a neutral manner. Lying on a couch seemed to provide an atmosphere in which it became easy for individuals to let their guard down and engage in free association.

Humankind's Fascination with the Meaning of Dreams

People have been fascinated with dreams, as seen in the earliest human records (Alexander & Selesnick, 1966). Dreams often were ascribed a spiritual significance that some cultures still hold. Dreams were often believed to be direct communication from the spirits. It is interesting that early shamans and healers were expected to report their dreams, not dissimilar to early psychoanalytic candidates being encouraged to analyze their dreams during free association; this training was necessary to undergo to qualify as a psychoanalyst. Such similar rites of passage of the psychological and spiritual healers are striking in this respect. Prior to Freud, there were many others who suggested that dreams offer important clues for understanding disturbances in mental functions. Dreams were one window into understanding symptoms as a disturbance of the whole personality.

The interpretation of dreams and the assumption that they reflect unconscious process have repeatedly come under fire during the past century, at various times being discredited as meaningless mental activity with no relationship to anything of concern in the individual's life. Others dismiss these attacks as being launched by those with a grudge who lack the introspective capacity in their own lives to see and experience the relevance of dreams. Which side of the debate is "right"? Interestingly, current findings from neuroscientists, covered in the following chapter, are beginning to shed some light on this controversial debate. The current thinking is in partial support of Freud's and the ancients' conceptions of dreams. Scientists studying dreams believe that when the brain is in a period of rapid eye movement (REM), during which dreaming occurs and incoming stimuli from the outside world are partially eliminated, the brain's activity continues as various neuronal networks and circuits fire. Current conceptions of how the mind works emphasize the organizing capacity and meaning-making processes of the brain while sleeping. It is believed that the brain continues to search for schema to organize the information that is being sent to the cerebral cortex in a way that often does not make rational sense. This is the brain's way of trying to make sense, the kind of unconscious activity that Freud observed in his analysis of dreams.

Dream Analysis

Another of Freud's pioneering developments was in the analysis of dreams. "The first edition of Sigmund Freud's *Interpretation of Dreams* published November 4, 1899, sold 600 copies in eight years, a disappointing accounting for any writer, much less one who likened his struggle with the manuscript to the biblical Jacob's wrestling match with an angel" (Goode, 1999, p. F4). From that inauspicious start, Freud's concepts have filtered through our culture in a deep way. Freud theorized that dreams are formed by the residual experiences of the day and conflicted unconscious material that, through the mechanism of condensation, was expressed symbolically in the dream. Freud considered his now classic text *The Interpretation of Dreams* to be the major work of his life. In this book, he presented his ideas about the symbolic meanings of various elements in dreams. Psychoanalysts use dreams as a way to access the patient's unconscious and make meaning out of life. Freud's ideas about dreams "still loom large on the landscape" (Goode, 1999, p. F4).

The Evolution of Psychoanalysis

As is the case with all great innovators, individuals soon seek them out and disciples are often created. Almost immediately, Freud developed a number of followers who recognized the groundbreaking discoveries he was making. Almost as swiftly, many of those in his inner circle, such as Carl Jung, Alfred Adler, and Sandor Ferenczi, began to develop theoretical systems and methods that veered too far afield for Freud's comfort. Typically, individuals who were close to him and considered potential heirs to Freud were ostracized, and hostile relationships ensued between the master and his students. Yet, even with all of the internecine rivalry, the new discipline of psychoanalysis could not be stopped and has shaped the nature of Western society with its tenets and perspective of the human struggle. Now that a century of evolving trends and figures is behind us, it is beyond the scope of this text to give more than the highlights of some of the significant contributions made by many of those who worked directly with and were in intimate relationships with Freud. For our purposes, we highlight those whose work has direct application to the topic of this text. This is in no way meant to diminish the work of countless other contributors. Psychoanalysis as a discipline has become so massive that there are those individuals who primarily study the historical developments in the field.

Jung and the Collective Unconscious

Carl Gustav Jung was one of the favored followers of Freud who was heir apparent to replace the father of psychoanalysis until he broke with Freud and developed his own theory and form of treatment. Jung's major disagreement with Freud centered on his refusal to accept the sexual instinct as the primary force in mental life. He is probably best known for his ideas about the **collective unconscious** and the concept of **archetypes.** The collective unconscious refers to the inherited possibilities or psychological structures that are built in to all people's brains, or ways we understand experience such as in parenting, maturing, and aging. His notion about the collective unconscious refers to the memories that are carried from one generation to another that are retained at the unconscious level and influence human behavior. Archetypes include common images, attitudes, and concepts, such as power symbolized as the sun or a lion. Other archetypes include God, the self, birth, death, the persona, and the wise old man.

Jung (1923) is also known for his development of the concept of psychological types, which are based on psychological activity in four spheres of functioning: **thinking** versus **feeling** and **sensing** versus **intuiting.** Thinking is used to describe individuals who approach life with a detached analytic tendency as opposed to those who use more emotional responding and subjective experiencing. Sensing refers to the use of one's sensory experience without interpretation and intuiting one's use of global impressions that are not given to rational process. Jung also observed that people orient themselves to their environment in two fundamental ways. Those who are introverts use **introversion** as a way of turning in to the self; these individuals tend to be loners and silent types. Extroverts use **extroversion,** turning outward; they tend to be individuals who like to be in the middle of everything, who like the natural world and being with other people.

The self develops through identification with the archetypes that exist in each person's unconscious. Our **persona** is the public self that we put forth that is constructed to respond to the expectations of others. In reality, all people have a shadow self that exits within us; there is a shadow self of a man in a woman and vice versa. Personality is influenced by the energy generated from the archetypes and how they are responded to by our preferred modes of responding to the external and internal worlds.

Ferenczi and the Impact of Trauma

Sandor Ferenczi, born in Budapest on July 7, 1873, is not often mentioned in the history of psychoanalysis, although his story is tragic and influence substantial to this day in clinical practice and theory. His work presaged current trauma theory and humanistic psychology, and he was the father of **active therapy,** now called short-term dynamic therapy, a major treatment modality for many types of personality disorders (Magnavita, 1997). "Ferenczi was Freud's favorite disciple and a man of exceptional clinical skills and great human warmth" (Masson, 1990, p. 152). Unfortunately, Ferenczi did not remain in such an esteemed position. According to Rachman (1997), "It is now a matter of record that Ferenczi's clinical work and theoretical ideas were suppressed, censored, and removed from mainstream psychoanalysis. Freud's once favorite son, most devoted pupil, and paladin and secret grand vizier suffered Freud's scorn and rejection, and was derided by his analytic colleagues, and was denounced by Freud, Ernest Jones, and Max Eitingon as an emotionally sick person" (pp. xv–xvi).

Why was Ferenczi so reviled? Ferenczi challenged the mainstream psychoanalytic movement in a number of ways. Most important was that he was the major proponent of the **seduction theory** and published a paper, "The confusion of tongues between adults and children: the language of tenderness and passion" (Ferenczi, 1933), whereby he attempted to reintroduce the theory that *real, not imagined* child sexual abuse leads to trauma. This paper was presented at the twelfth International Psychoanalytic Congress in 1932 at Wiesbaden. Freud objected to Ferenczi's presenting this paper and this led to much of the imbrogilo between them over the next 30 years (Rachman, 1997). Erich Fromm (1959) believed that the confusion of tongues paper was "one of the most significant contributions in the history of psychoanalysis" (Rachman, 1997, p. 414). Ferenczi's belief about the development of personality and psychopathological forms of adaptation was not in agreement with

A Hypothetical Letter to Freud from Ferenczi Concerning Their Disagreement on the Importance of Sexual Trauma

I know about the experience of sexual and emotional trauma first-hand. That is why I can acknowledge it in my analysands, that is why I can listen to them when they tell me they have been abused.

I want you to listen to the idea of sexual and emotional trauma in my COT [Confusion of Tongues] paper because you have always had difficulty with this idea. Originally you believed in trauma, but ever since you abandoned your clinical studies and focused on your oedipal theory you have been closed to this idea.

Early in my relationship with you, on your Sicily trip, I tried to get you to deal with the emotional components in our relationship, but you felt it was my problem.

Then in my analysis with you I tried to go deeper into our relationship and tell you of the trauma, but once again, you could not listen.

My COT presentation is my final attempt to convince you that I, like my analysands, have been traumatized by childhood experiences. What is more, I have also realized that I can repeat the analysand's trauma in the analysis when I behave in a detached, cool, clinical way, interpreting their needs as resistances. It was only when I liberated myself from the taboos of psychoanalytic technique and softened my analytic superego that I could respond to them in a human, healing way. This is the kind of response I want from you.

Why can't you give in to me? Why do you insist that I am trying to undermine your theories? Why do you condemn me for my clinical observations? Don't you see my pain? I am traumatized by your way of relating to me. You treat me like a bad child, who has disobeyed the parent.

You make me feel I am crazy because I have these ideas about trauma. . . . I know you can't deal with these issues in a direct, open way. You are too wedded to your theory and to being the father of psychoanalysis to hear me. But I know that my trauma, my analysands' trauma, and the trauma I am experiencing with you have similar elements. This is what I am trying to convey in my COT paper. (pp. 242–243)

SOURCE: *Sandor Ferenczi: The Psychotherapist of Tenderness and Passion (Rachman, 1997)*

Freud. As we have discussed, Freud believed that the internal process of the child as he or she navigated the stages of psychosexual development and resolved the Oedipal conflict was key. Ferenczi believed that in "addition, parental psychopathology—narcissism, rage, empathic failure, sadism, perversion—are considered the locus of trauma" (Rachman, 1997, p. 318).

Another of Ferenczi's controversial innovations was elaborated in the publication of the book *The Development of Psychoanalysis* (Ferenczi & Rank, 1925), which was "a landmark exposition of the shortcomings of psychoanalysis" (Rachman, 1997). Ferenczi and Rank feared that psychoanalysis had become overly intellectual at the cost of emotional experience and also suggested that the interpersonal aspects of analysis needed greater emphasis. This was another in a series of radical departures from mainstream psychoanalysis that fueled the Freud-Ferenczi conflict and led to its tragic outcome.

Ferenczi's Demise: May ??, 1933

Ferenczi was involved in a controversial disagreement with Freud concerning the etiology of psychopathology and the methods of psychoanalysis. In many ways, he was discredited and, according to Rachman (1997), was the target of a brutal character assassination by Ernest Jones, Freud's heir apparent, biographer, and translator of his works into English. In fact, Ferenczi analyzed Jones at the urging of Freud. The rivalry and political in-fighting among Freud and his followers has been well documented. Ferenczi seemed to be a most tragic example of these rivalries and hostilities. Rachman suggests that Jones "introduced the notion that Ferenczi was paranoid and conspiratorial" (p. 111) and proposes a variety of motivations for his doing so. There is no eyewitness confirmation to the commonly held assumption that Ferenczi died in a psychotic state. Rachman suggests that the existing evidence about Ferenczi's illness and death are consistent with pernicious anemia. However, Jones's "hateful version of Ferenczi's personal and clinical functioning" (p. 118) have generally been accepted by the psychoanalytic community. The results were that much of Ferenczi's pioneering work was suppressed, only later to be rediscovered by succeeding generations of clinical theorists and psychotherapeutic innovators.

Fenichel, Reich, and Character Analysis

Otto Fenichel was interested in exploring how certain mental complexes represent themselves in the character of the individual. He began to explore the terrain where the symptom formations overlap with personality, which we will later see has been reintroduced in a highly systematized way by the current-day theories of Theodore Millon. Fenichel (Fenichel & Rapaport, 1954) divided character traits into two groups: "those which are occasional and those which are habitual" (p. 203).

Wilhelm Reich, another pioneer in character analysis, was a highly controversial worker who came to a sad end, dying in a federal prison after a brilliant career that was derailed by mental illness in the final stage. Reich (1949) brought the concept of character into psychoanalysis. He was the first of Freud's followers to treat the character by interpreting the way defenses are used to protect the self by armoring the patient. Both Fenichel and Reich developed specific descriptive profiles of individual character typologies associated with phases of psychosexual development. Reich conceived of the phallic character as being preoccupied with success and exhibiting a tendency to be arrogant and brash.

Reich's Visit with Albert Einstein

We have compared some of the great scientific figures—Freud, Darwin, and Einstein—for the paradigmatic shifts that resulted from their conceptual breakthroughs. It is interesting that Wilhelm Reich, also a great thinker, attempted to enlist the help of Einstein. After writing to Einstein, he requested a meeting for what he felt was an urgent scientific matter. He believed he had found the solution to the mystery of life in a biological energy that he thought was different from other energy. After several requests that were ignored, Einstein met with Reich in Princeton and had a four-hour discussion. After Reich disclosed that many believed him to be mad, Einstein is said to have replied, "I can believe that" (Higgins, 2000).

The Women of Psychoanalysis

Anna Freud and Child Psychology: Anna Freud was the favored youngest of Sigmund and Martha's six children who carried on and extended her father's work. She acted as Freud's "secretary, nurse, and main exponent of his ideas" (Sayers, 1991, p. 145) and never married. She seemed to spend her life devoted to her father and unable or unwilling to find her own primary relationships. In her early life, her father dominated her. In fact, she was actually analyzed by her father, which has been the source of much controversy and questions concerning this unusual therapeutic arrangement. She began her analysis with her father in 1918 and continued until 1924, resuming again in 1926. Although this was considered scandalous by many, there has been little documentation of the nature of this relationship (Young-Bruehl, 1988).

When Freud turned 80, Anna presented him with the classic book she had written, *The Ego and the Mechanisms of Defense* (Young-Bruehl, 1988). This event "marked a reconfiguration of their lives; she was then the inheritor of her twin, the mother of

psychoanalysis; the one to whom primary responsibility for its spirit, its future, was passed" (p. 15). Anna Freud left a prodigious body of clinical and scientific papers in psychoanalysis. For many years, she worked and was director of the Hampstead Child Therapy Course and Clinic, an independent institute where she conducted her pioneering work applying psychoanalysis to the understanding, development, and treatment of children.

Karen Horney: Horney (1967) did not accept Freud's view of the psychosexual development of women. She challenged the notion of penis envy and believed that it was not women who grow up feeling inferior, but little boys. Horney (1945) formulated three types of interpersonal relations—**moving against, moving toward,** and

moving away from people—and three character types that display them: Moving against represents an **aggressive type,** moving
toward a **compliant type,** and moving away from a **detached
type.**

Individuals whose style is to move against have a need for controlling and exploiting others. Horney elaborated three subtypes: narcissistic, perfectionistic, and vindictive sadistic. The moving toward type has
a high need for approval and a willingness to deny self-assertion to
please others. Those individuals with a tendency to move away actively
attempt to avoid others because they fear closeness will result in conflict and frustration. In some cases, they are likely to become severely
alienated.

Horney (1937) also emphasized the role culture plays in the
development of the neurotic personality. Unlike Freud, she did not
assume a biologically related drive basis for the development of
psychopathology. She emphasized issues such as competitiveness
and how sociocultural influences such as economics shape who we
are and the conflicts we struggle with. She writes: "It seems that
the person who is likely to become neurotic is one who has experienced the culturally determined difficulties in an accentuated
form, mostly through the medium of childhood experiences, and
who has consequently been unable to solve them, or has solved
them only at great cost to his personality. We might call him a
stepchild of our culture" (p. 290). She also believed that children
can often withstand much trauma if they feel loved, but that in
neurotic personality development, "the basic evil is invariably a
lack of genuine warmth and affection" (p. 80). As we shall see later
when we talk about resiliency, she identified one of the major in-
gredients that can protect an individual from psychopathology: a
positive attachment. We can see in her work how the need for affection can result in the development of her various personality
types. Those who did not receive enough affection can turn against
people; others who are more conflicted might move toward the
perceived source and sacrifice their autonomous self or move away
because of the fear of rejection.

Melanie Klein: Melanie Klein was a noted child analyst who pioneered
theories and techniques of child psychoanalysis. She surprised people
when they found that she was not a big woman, as the force of her

personality was quite strong (Sayers, 1991). Her most controversial technique was providing deep interpretations to children without concern for timing or for the extraanalytic context. Klein (1975) believed that Freud's methods were overly circuitous. She challenged Freudian doctrine about the formation of the Oedipal complex, which created quite a stir and fueled the Anna Freud–Melanie Klein feud for many years. Basically, she believed that it was the aggressive cannibalistic needs that were aroused early in development, beginning with weaning, that gave rise to the primitive superego functions. Like Ferenczi, but working with children, she believed that the anxiety over these oral aggressive impulses needed to be brought to the surface by reactivating and relieving them in the therapy. Although she believed the medium of communication that the child used, play, was different from an adult's, free association, the same technical process should occur.

The Professional Feuding between Anna Freud and Melanie Klein

One of the noteworthy controversies in psychoanalysis emerged in the theoretical differences between Anna Freud and Melanie Klein. Klein believed that the superego does not emerge as a result of the Oedipal complex alone but is primed for this at the end of the first year of life. This is a result not of identification with the same-sex parent but as a result of the cannibalistic and sadistic impulses that derive from weaning. Klein looked to the anxiety experience of weaning as an accompaniment to oral aggression or sadism. From this, two very different techniques of child analysis were offered. Freud's stressed the importance of working in a psychoeducational manner with parents and gaining a detailed life history. She stressed the need to keep the child in close proximity to familial surroundings. Freud believed child analysis should be conducted differently from adult analysis. Klein believed that this was all unnecessary and that child analysis should be conducted as one would with adults, making deep interpretations of the child's play actions.

Klein was also interested in schizoid mechanisms, or how individuals manage contradictory experiences by splitting the good part from the bad part. She believed schizoid experiences were rooted in early childhood attachments. Klein also modified analytic techniques to treat psychotic patients. She helped to conceptualize the idea of projective identification as a defense mechanism. Projective identification occurs when affects of the patient are transmitted so powerfully by splitting them off that the therapist experiences these affects and then responds to the patient in a characteristic manner that the patient experienced from significant others in the past. This is a seminal concept used by various current-day psychotherapies, especially those that deal with severe personality disorders, where this defensive operation is not uncommon.

Helene Deutsch: Helene Deutsch, who trained and worked as a pediatrician before becoming a psychiatrist, was another of the pioneering women who subscribed to and advanced psychoanalysis. Her classic textbook *Psycho-Analysis of the Neuroses* presented her clinical world with vivid descriptions of her cases. "Deutsch's focus on mothering and her account of pregnancy and breast-feeding from the mother's rather than the child's standpoint is a major advance on Freud's father-centered account of female sexuality" (Sayers, 1991, p. 39). Deutsch (1965) published a number of case studies describing the clinical treatment and theoretical issues with various character types and issues related to identity formation and female sexuality.

The Controversy within and over Psychoanalysis

Over the past century, as one can expect with any major paradigm shift, Freud's work and life stimulated great controversy. Probably due to the nature of his theories, emphasizing sexuality and aggression, his view of humans as having powerful, dark, instinctual forces that exist in the unconscious of all of us stimulated many polar reactions. Some have credited him with being a genius, even a demigod. There is no question that psychoanalysis, as we shall see in later chapters, continues to provide foundation concepts for almost every theory of personality, even if the terminology has changed. For any serious student of personology, it is difficult to dismiss his contributions, although there are many aspects of his theory that have lost their utility or been dismissed as more refined ways of conceptualizing the clinical and empirical data have emerged. Psychoanalysis has been attacked on many fronts, ranging from Freud's own personality to the nonempirical, overly theoretical deductive thinking he employed based on what many would consider insufficient data. Yet others believe he has distilled some essential aspects of human mental functioning in an extraordinary and clear way. The main controversy, Freud's abandonment of the seduction theory and the reification of technical aspects of treatment, are probably the most valid.

The Seduction Theory

Probably one of the most controversial aspects of Freud's career and theoretical development concerned the seduction theory. Early in Freud's career, he came to believe that many of the middle-class patients he was treating for hysteria were being sexually molested by family members. Some believe that, when faced with this evidence, he abandoned the seduction theory so as not to expose this endemic problem and risk the attack and possible ruin of his career. "One hundred years ago, Freud had ample evidence to suggest that widespread cruelty to children—and, in the case of neuroses, sexual abuse—could well be the universal aetiological agent behind the disease" (J. Schwartz, 1999, p. 75).

In his book *The Assault on Truth: Freud's Suppression of the Seduction Theory,* Jeffrey Masson (1984) explores the issue of Freud's abandonment of the seduction theory. Ferenczi believed Freud was wrong in his discounting accounts of sexual abuse in childhood. Instead, according to Masson, the field of psychoanalysis suppressed the truth and did not take seriously patient reports of incest and abuse. Freud developed an elaborate theory to explain how these reports were fantasy productions of children who were engaged in wish fulfillment. This has the aura of blaming the victim. Many believe that this delayed the acceptance of trauma for many decades, causing undue suffering to those who have been the victims of incest and child abuse.

Freud's Ambivalence about the Seduction Theory

The Freud of 1896 was convinced that he was on the right track. A single aetiological agent (like Koch's tuberculosis bacillus)—childhood sexual abuse—could be seen to be the causative agent in all the major neuroses. The agent worked through the repressed, strangulated affect associated with the original experience. There was now no need for special pleading in the form of abnormal sensitivities or genetic predispositions or inherited mental degeneracy. Neurosis could be understood as a result of lived experience. The order of the day would be to develop not the neurology of neurosis but an exploration of its psychology, in particular the puzzle of why repressed memories have a pathogenic effect, whereas unrepressed memories do not. The mystery of hysteria seemed close to being resolved. (J. Schwartz, 1999, p. 73)

The Reification of Theory, Methods, and Techniques

Another criticism of psychoanalysis that should not be dismissed is the well-documented trend in the psychoanalytic movement to reject that which disagrees with the founder. This is evident throughout the evolution of psychoanalysis over the past century. Although it is not uncommon to have intense turf battles and feuds in any branch of scientific endeavor, psychoanalysis has been criticized by many for remaining hermetically sealed and thus being slow to evolve. Many observers and historians have felt that psychoanalysis, because of its failure to integrate the findings of other disciplines in cross-pollination, resulted in the discipline's becoming sterile and stodgy. In fact, there seems to be much truth to these criticisms. Psychoanalysis as a form of treatment has come near to extinction for a variety of reasons. In another work, *Final Analysis: The Making and Unmaking of a Psychoanalyst,* Masson (1990) makes a more general attack on the training, corruption, political infighting, and cultlike phenomenon that he experienced in his own training as a psychoanalyst and his appointment as the director of the Sigmund Freud Archives.

Summary

This chapter presents the major theoretical system of the twentieth century and the first effort at a comprehensive theory of personality created by Sigmund Freud and known as psychoanalysis. Psychoanalytic theory is a structural theory in which the mind is conceptualized as having the following structures: the id, primary drives of sex and aggression; the ego, reality agency; and the superego, the conscious. These represent the intrapsychic structure of the mind, which are in constant dynamic interplay. Freud's major tool for exploring the unconscious mental apparatus is free association, which is the uncensored free expression of all thoughts, impulses and mental imagery. The main innate drives within the human are sexual (life instinct) and aggressive (death instinct). The psychoanalytic model is also topographical in that the mind is divided into three regions: unconscious, preconscious, and conscious. Repression is the force that keeps primary process material unconscious so it does not overwhelm the individual with anxiety. In therapy, this repression is also expressed as resistance, so that the unconscious material related to conflictual experiences is not painfully remembered and brought into the open, the goal of psychoanalytic treatment. To contain anxiety over expression of primitive impulses, defenses such as intellectualization, rationalization, and projection are utilized. These are ego defenses. Neurotic symptoms serve as a compromise formation redirecting the energy and expressing the conflict in a hidden manner.

All individuals progress through oral, anal, phallic, latency, and genital stages of psychosexual development. Personality is formed based on the resolution or fixation an individual faces during his or her development. One's character then has certain traces of the conflict expressed in various character types; for example, oral is primarily concerned with gratifying oral needs, phallic is concerned with gaining admiration for potency.

A number of followers of Freud have elaborated and expanded his theory to include additional elements, many of which were controversial. The most controversial aspect of Freudian theory to the present day is his rejection of the seduction theory, the theory that child sexual abuse is responsible for many forms of emotional suffering witnessed by analysts of the time. Freud instead altered his thinking and, some believe, the course of psychoanalysis by postulating that sexual fantasy on the part of children toward their parents is natural and not necessarily the result of sexual abuse. This has been termed the trauma theory and was championed by Ferenczi, who was discredited by the analytic community until only recently.

Suggested Reading

Gay, P. (1988). *Freud: A life for our time.* New York: Norton.

Masson, J. M. (1990). *Final analysis: The making and unmaking of a psychoanalyst.* New York: Addison-Wesley.

PERSONALITY AS AN INTERDISCIPLINARY SCIENCE

Component Models of Personality

4

Chapter

Introduction

This chapter explores the major developments in various scientific disciplines, in the field of psychology as well as related areas, that have radically changed our understanding of the nature of humankind, the **mind,** the **self,** and **human personality** adaptations and functioning. These rapidly evolving fields are providing renewed interest and insight in the study of personality. Probably one of the major advancements in the twenty-first century in the field of personality will be the interdisciplinary nature of the field. D. M. Buss (1999) states, "No other branch of psychology except personality psychology aspires to the broad conceptualization of human nature" (p. 31). No longer can we be content understanding the complexity of personality theory from one perspective or discipline. Because of the exponential advances in science during the past century, we are forced to look at personality with an appreciation for new scientific thinking and often contradictory data that different perspectives offer. Modern theories of personality incorporate several of these scientific disciplines or component systems in either the assumptions they make or the well of empirical data from which they draw. Buss states, "Personality psychology aspires to be the grandest, most integrative branch of the psychological sciences" (p. 31). Hundert (1990) writes of the complexity of our topic: "Human thought and behavior are so complex that any given description or explanation of a human experience is best considered a perspective—a point of view rather than a point of fact. This is not to say that a description or explanation cannot be wrong. It is, rather, a reminder that no single description or explanation is truly complete, however accurate it may be" (p. 1).

To best understand the personality theories presented in the next section, it is critical to examine the **component systems** and some of the influential conceptual and empirical developments that have occurred in this rapidly growing field of personology and its related domains (see Figure 4.1).

Where Does Personality Reside?

The question Where is personality located? is important to the development of the science of personology. At first, we are tempted to answer that personality is located in the "person," or maybe in the "mind" or definitely in the "brain" or in the "soul." This question, however, is more complex and requires us to examine various subdisciplines of philosophy, psychological science, and neuroscience to have greater clarity about the answer or answers. Further complicating this puzzle is the observation by many animal behaviorists, as well as animal owners, that personality is not solely the domain of humans (Griffin, 1992) but is evident in nonprimates. However, because this text is concerned with human personality, we shall not delve into this interesting topic, more appropriately addressed in

Figure 4.1

Relationship among New Scientific Disciplines and Personality Theory.

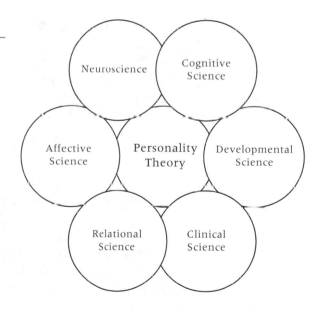

other areas of psychology, such as comparative, physiological, and animal behavior.

Philosophical and scientific advancements provide us with a clearer vision of the mosaic and many of the component pieces, but we are still not at the point of having an acceptable answer to the question What is human nature and how do we account for consciousness and explain personality? As we shall see, assumptions about consciousness, the nature of humans, and epistemology play an important role in helping us understand the models that various theorists use when developing theories of personality. Philosophers have addressed many of these questions and have speculated about the answers, and they are worth reiterating to provide a foundation for the component disciplines of personology.

Mind-Body Dualism

One of the oldest debates in the behavioral sciences is the controversy between the mind and the body as the determining factor in the development of who we are and what we are capable of becoming. The fundamental question of whether humans are a product of genes or environment (nature vs. nurture) has sparked controversy in the field of psychology, and the fashion for one side of the debate or the other ebbs and flows, often with the sociopolitical fashions of the time. For example, in the 1930s, the eugenics movement assumed that there were "good genes" that should be preserved and carried on and offered "the perfect family" awards and prizes, suggesting that these families had a duty to repopulate the world with their superior genes. Looking at their representation of the ideal family left no doubt of the overt racism present in this movement, as with the similar movement advocated during the rise of the Third Reich in Germany that was responsible for the elimination of millions of Jews and other "less than ideal" individuals, according to Hitler's standard.

As you are aware from reading Chapter 2, the work of many philosophers has been seminal in the development of modern psychology. Rene Descartes (1596–1650) is generally considered to be the father of modern philosophical thinking. Descartes is noted for his attempt to discover what knowledge is, or the science of **epistemology;** by devising a method of doubt, he searched for subjective criteria for objectivity. His most noted conclusion is **cogito ergo sum—I**

think, therefore I am. This was one of the major developments in the struggle to understand humankind's capacity for consciousness.

Descartes was a major figure in the development of a system that separates the mind from the body and is referred to as the mechanistic viewpoint. Because, as he postulated, the mind and body are separate, the body should be studied as an automaton, or in other words, as a mechanical phenomenon. This theory of **Cartesian dualism** led to the establishment of many principles of the scientific approach. This was important to the understanding of humankind and especially the development of the field of physiology and physiological psychology (discussed in Chapter 2), the precursors to modern neuroscience. He also studied the emotions, the senses, and nerve conduction. He did recognize that in spite of his strong position, the mind did act on the body and the body on the mind. The natural sciences and social sciences have evolved considerably since then, and we are no longer afraid to delve into murky areas that convey mysticism, such as consciousness.

Consciousness

There have been a plethora of books on the topic of consciousness in the last decade of the twentieth century, which has been dubbed "the decade of the brain." Human consciousness remains one of the last great mysteries of science (Dennett, 1991). The study of consciousness has been taken up with fervor by neuroscientists and cognitive scientists. Damasio (1999) compares consciousness to the experience of "stepping into the light": "I have always been intrigued by the specific moment when, as we sit waiting in the audience, the door to the stage opens and a performer steps into the light; or, to take the other perspective, the moment when a performer who waits in semidarkness sees the same door open, revealing the lights, the stage, the audience" (p. 3).

Dennett (1991) compares consciousness, "just about the last surviving mystery," to "other great mysteries: the mystery of the origin of the universe, the mystery of life and reproduction, the mystery of the design to be found in nature, the mysteries of time, space, and gravity" (p. 21). Consciousness is the state of personal awareness that is derived from our ability to think, feel, perceive, sense, and dream and, one can readily see in this description the foundation of our unique personality. Many consider consciousness as that which separates us from the nonhuman animal kingdom, although others would challenge this notion as hominidcentric. Clearly, there are different levels of consciousness that are possessed by various animals, especially primates and dolphins, who demonstrate a capacity for consciousness similar to humans.

The Requirements for Consciousness

To contemplate and perceive ourselves as possessing a unique self or observable personality attributes, we require a high degree of consciousness. One could say that without the evolution of consciousness, there would be no such construct as personality. Many scientists believe this high level of consciousness serves as a line of demarcation between humans and other primates. C. Wynne (1999) reports on the findings of psychological researchers, summarizing three classes of evidence of consciousness:

1. *Language:* The mutual possession of language is one of the strongest indications used to determine consciousness.
2. *Self-awareness:* Being conscious requires one to be aware that there exists an "I" that is separate from other beings.
3. *Theory of mind:* Being conscious requires not only that one is aware of oneself but that others are conscious and can take this into account when relating.

Gaining a deeper understanding of the issue of our consciousness, Dennett (1991) in his book *Consciousness Explained* uses a "favorite thought experiment in the toolkit of many philosophers" (p. 3). The experiment goes like this. If an evil scientist were to put your brain in a vat and connect all the neuronal channels (if this were possible), could you be tricked into feeling alive? The evil scientist would have to provide the proper electrical/neurochemical input to stimulate the proper area of your brain to experience the sensations required for consciousness. Even if the technology were that advanced, the problems would be in calculating the proper feedback that would be required to, for example, experience the sensations of touching and feeding that back to the brain in the vat. Dennett believes this challenge would be impossible because the "evil scientist will be swamped by *combinatorial explosion* as soon as they give you any genuine exploratory powers in this imaginary world" (p. 5). The amount of information that would have to be processed and fed back to the brain in the vat is beyond anything imaginable. Although there have been many theories about consciousness and how it has evolved, Dennett writes: "With consciousness, however, we are still in a terrible muddle. Consciousness stands alone today as a topic that often leaves even the most sophisticated thinkers tongue-tied and confused. And, as with all the earlier mysteries, there are many who insist—and hope—that there will never be a demystification of consciousness" (p. 22).

Mind-Body Integration

The twentieth century saw the remarriage of the mind and body, which set the stage for the development of many new disciplines such as psychoimmunology, holistic medicine, and alternative medicine. But the significant factor was the attempt to reconnect the mind to the body: "Most scientists, however, have rejected dualism and generally champion some form of materialism" (Robins, Norem, & Cheek, 1999, p. 436).

Cognitive Science

Gardner's Cognitive Revolution

Howard Gardner (1985) defined "cognitive science as a contemporary, empirically based effort to answer long-standing epistemological questions—particularly those concerned with the nature of knowledge, its components, its sources, its development, and its deployment" (p. 6). Donald (1991) states that cognitive science and neuropsychology are concerned largely with the architecture or "structure of the modern human mind" (p. 5).

Cognitive science emerged from the radical behaviorism of the mid-twentieth century, exemplified by the work of Skinner (1953) and Hull (1943), who studied **drive** and **stimulus-response** (S-R) formulations (Lazarus, 1991; see Chapter 7). These simplified paradigms led to more complicated ones that included mediating mental structures: **stimulus-organism-response** (S-O-R) linkages. This "intellectual transition" from S-R theory to cognitive science was a conceptual leap that sparked an interdisciplinary dialogue among philosophy, linguistics, anthropology, neuroscience, artificial intelligence, and psychology. This interdisciplinary interaction is based on the assumption that "powerful insights" (Gardner, 1985, p. 42) can be achieved by blurring the interdisciplinary lines.

The Mind

In September 1948, the Hixon Fund sponsored a conference that led to a major conceptual leap in the development of this new discipline. Gardner (1985) writes of this event:

> *Lashley realized that before new insights about the brain, or about computers, could be brought to bear in the psychological sciences, it would be necessary to confront behaviorism directly. Therefore, in his opening remarks, Lashley voiced his conviction that any theory of human activity would have to account for complexly organized behaviors like playing tennis, performing on a musical instrument, and—above all—speaking. . . .*
>
> *In the topics he chose to address, and in the ways in which he addressed them, Lashley was adopting a radical position. Scientists concerned with human behavior had been reluctant to investigate human language, because of its complexity and its relative "invisibility" as a form of behavior; and when they did treat language, they typically sought analogies to simpler forms (like running a maze or pecking in a cage) in simpler organisms (like rats or pigeons). Not only did Lashley focus on language, but he reveled in its complexity and insisted that other motoric activities were equally intricate. . . .*
>
> *The scholars in attendance at the Hixon Symposium stood at a critical juncture of scientific history. They were keenly aware of the staggering advances of previous centuries in the physical sciences as well as of recent breakthroughs in the biological and neural sciences. Indeed, by the middle of the twentieth century, two major mysteries of ancient times—the nature of physical matter and the nature of living matter—were well on their way to being unraveled. At the same time, however, a third mystery that had also fascinated the ancients—the enigma of the human mind—had yet to achieve comparable clarification. (pp. 12–14)*

Reading Gardner's (1985) account of this major conceptual and scientific leap, one can sense the excitement. According to Gardner, one of the key features of this new field was the **emphasis on the**

computer as a model of human thought. If scientists could produce a computer that could think, they would have created artificial intelligence, which would serve as an analogue to human cognition. This was termed the Turin challenge. However, not all those who consider themselves cognitive scientists would agree. Anthropologists, who identify themselves as cognitive scientists, consider this model inadequate and believe the key to human cognition lies in cultural and historical forces. Donald (1991) also believes that cognitive scientists should not leave out the element of culture. He developed an evolutionary model of the development of human cognitive functioning that attributes cultural change as the major influence on the development of the mind. This computer metaphor has been a pervasive model in cognitive science, although it is giving way to the brain metaphor in neuroscience (Westen & Gabbard, 1999). It is interesting to note that other than a conference cosponsored in 1962 by Princeton University and Educational Testing Service (Tomkins & Messick, 1963) on the topic of computer simulation of personality, a similar trend failed to take hold in personality as it had in artificial intelligence.

Pinker (1997) envisions the mind differently in his book *How the Mind Works:* "The mind, I claim, is not a single organ but a system of organs, which we can think of as psychological faculties or mental modules" (p. 27). These modules are complex neural networks and probably look "like roadkill, sprawling messily over the bulges and crevasses of the brain" (p. 30). His concern here is not so much the complex neurocircuitry, the concern of neuroscientists, but rather the "special things they [1997] do with the information available to them, not necessarily by the kinds of information they have available" (p. 31). Pinker's model of the mind is based on principles of evolutionary psychology, discussed later in this chapter. Pinker's model does highlight the integrative and overlapping nature of the disciplines involved in understanding human nature.

Another feature of the cognitive science movement is the deemphasis on the affective realm. According to Gardner (1985), there is an attempt to minimize certain "phenomenalistic elements" (p. 41). Affective factors such as emotion and context are eliminated from the model to reduce what the critics view as "murky concepts" (p. 42). There is a belief among many that including these constructs would overly complicate the arena so they should be de-emphasized. Caine (1999) believes that reason has been overemphasized and that a richer approach and appreciation needs to couple reason with emotion. We will see shortly that this emphasis on cognition left a void that the discipline of affective science filled.

Advancements in cognitive science have assisted us in the quest for understanding personality. Cognitive science offered a new paradigm for how the mind works by using the analogy of a computer to understand how the brain is organized and functions. Human information processing became a topic of great interest. How the various systems of the mind worked was studied with sophisticated and innovative methods. The concept of **template matching** was introduced as a way of understanding how the brain recognizes certain patterns. There are some major areas of overlap among cognitive and neuroscience in the way computer analogies are used.

Neuroscience

Neuroscience is one of the most exciting new disciplines offering to reduce personality to its biochemical factors and build a theory of the mind and personality uncluttered by psychic functioning. Redfield Jamison (1999), an eloquent writer, describes this view: "Everywhere in the snarl of tissue that is the brain, chemicals whip down fibers, tear across cell divides, and continue pell-mell on their Gordian rounds. One hundred billion individual nerve cells—each reaching out in turn to as many as 200,000 others—diverge, reverberate and converge into a webwork of staggering complexity. The three-pound thicket of gray, with its thousands of distinct cell types and estimated one hundred trillion synapses, somehow pulls out order from chaos, lays down the shivery tracks of memory, gives rise to desire or terror, arranges for sleep, propels movement, imagines a symphony, or shapes a plan to annihilate itself" (p. 182).

One of the later arrivals on the scientific landscape is the field of neuroscience, which strives to understand how the brain, with its complex tangle of neurons, gives rise to consciousness. Neuroscience evolved from anatomy, physiological psychology, medicine, and neuropsychology. Redfield Jamison (1995) comments on the excitement she witnessed while attending conferences on this new arrival: "There is a wonderful kind of excitement in modern neuroscience, a romantic, moon-walk sense of exploring and setting out new frontiers. The science is elegant, the scientists dismayingly young, and the pace of discovery absolutely staggering. Like the molecular biologists, the brain-scanners are generally well aware of the extraordinary frontiers they are crossing, and it would take a mind that is on empty, or a heart made of stone, to be unmoved by their collective ventures and enthusiasms" (pp. 196–197).

Whereas cognitive scientists focus on how the mind works, the "software" of perceiving, organizing, and processing information, neuroscientists are primarily interested in how the "hardware" of the brain works. The human brain is a phenomenal evolutionary development whose complexity is just beginning to be understood. "What makes the brain unique among bodily organs is that its cells are arranged in a very specific manner—in delicate constellations that somehow reflect the knowledge gained from being alive" (Johnson, 1999, p. 1). Hundert (1990) writes: "Since the earliest days of philosophy and psychology, thinkers applying themselves in these disciplines have been aware that advances in our understanding of the brain could some day set limits on acceptable theories of the mind. Some have gone beyond this, anticipating that neuroscience will not merely set limits, but actually *direct* our theorizing about the mind. Some few have even believed that such scientific advances will eventually replace the idea of 'mind' altogether" (p. 189).

There are others who disagree with the boundless nature of neuroscience and believe that a physiological understanding of human consciousness is unattainable, especially without a psychological model. Hundert (1990) reminds us that neuroscience is still in its early stage of development. However, there has been an explosion of new findings that have added to our understanding of the structure of the brain. An understanding of how the mind works has to include how the brain functions to be taken seriously by other scientists. Although we have not yet evolved to the point of "perfect fit," Hundert suggests that a reasonable fit is acceptable.

The Brain and Its Functions

In 1979, an issue of *Scientific American* announced the excitement in the new field of neuroscience, examining the central problem of how the brain works. For new graduate students in physiological psychology, this was required reading. David Hubel (1979), one of the leading psychobiologists of the time, elegantly wrote about the progress and challenges: "The brain is a tissue. It is a complicated, intricately woven tissue, like nothing else we know of in the universe, but it is composed of cells, as any tissue is. They are to be sure highly specialized cells, but they function according to the laws that govern other cells" (p. 45). A brief review of the components of the brain follows.

Neurons—The Building Blocks of the Brain: Neurons are the essential building blocks of the brain. The human brain is thought to have 10^{11} neurons, about the number of stars in our galaxy (Stevens, 1979). "The important specializations of the neuron include a distinctive cell shape, an outer membrane capable of generating nerve impulses and a unique structure, the synapse, for transferring information from one neuron to the next" (Stevens, 1979, p. 55). "Synapses are among the most abundant structures in the brain—estimates suggest that a mammalian brain may contain 10^{15}" (National Institute of Mental Health, 1995, p. 56). Neurons are diverse and involve a substantial repertoire of transmitters. Typically, neurons can have between 1,000 and 10,000 synapses and can receive input from 1,000 other neurons. Nerve impulses are generated along the axon by a sodium and potassium exchange that creates an electrical charge.

Neuronal Systems: "Many neurobiologists believe that the unique character of individual human beings, their disposition to feel, think, learn and remember, will ultimately be shown to reside in the precise patterns of synaptic interconnections between the neurons of the brain" (Kandel, 1979, p. 67). Figuring these out is a daunting task. Neuronal systems are an elaborate interconnection of neurons that exchange electrical-chemical information at the synaptic gap.

Neurotransmitters: The synapse stores chemicals, which are released when a neuron is fired in a complex exchange of over 30 neurotransmitters, such as dopamine, monoamine oxidase, serotonin, and achetocholine. Various neurotransmitters have been implicated in neurological and mental disorders, as we will see in Chapter 5 on neurobiological theories of personality. As we shall see in that chapter, modern neurobiological theories of personality associate various of these neurotransmitters with behavioral-affective response tendencies that influence and shape personality configurations. For example, people with higher than average levels of dopamine may be more likely to be risk takers and require high levels of excitement and stimulation. Individuals with this tendency may be more likely to have antisocial personalities, of which thrill seeking can be a component.

Rivers of the Mind: Different types of cells secrete different neurotransmitters. Each brain chemical works in widely distinct but fairly specific locations and may have a different effect according to where it is activated. Some fifty different neurotransmitters have been identified, but most important seem to be the following:*

- *Dopamine:* Controls arousal levels in many parts of the brain and is vital for giving physical motivation. When levels are severely depleted, as in Parkinson's disease, people may find it impossible to move forward voluntarily. Low dopamine may also be implicated in mental stasis. Overly high levels seem to be implicated in schizophrenia and may give rise to hallucinations. Hallucinogenic drugs are thought to work on the dopamine system.

- *Serotonin:* The neurotransmitter that is enhanced by Prozac and has thus become known as the "feel-good" chemical. Serotonin certainly has a profound effect on mood and anxiety: High levels of it (or sensitivity to it) are associated with serenity and optimism. However, it also has effects in many other areas, including sleep, pain, appetite, and blood pressure.

- *Acetylcholine (ACh):* Controls activity in brain areas connected with attention, learning, and memory. People with Alzheimer's disease typically have low levels of ACh in the cerebral cortex, and drugs that boost its action may improve memory in such patients.

- *Noradrenaline:* Mainly an excitatory chemical that induces physical and mental arousal and heightens mood. Production is centered in an area of the brain called the locus coeruleus, which is one of several putative candidates for the brain's "pleasure" center.

- *Glutamate:* The brain's major excitatory neurotransmitter, vital for forging the links between neurons that are the basis of learning and long-term memory.

*Rita Carter, *Mapping the Mind*, © 1998. Published by University of California Press, Berkeley, California.

- *Enkephalins and Endorphins:* Endogenous opioids that, like the drugs, modulate pain, reduce stress, and promote a sensation of floaty, oceanic calm. They also depress physical functions like breathing and may produce physical dependence.

As we shall see, there often seems to be a chicken-and-egg debate: Did the neurotransmitters cause the depression, or did the psychological factors affect the neurotransmitters? For example, deficiencies in dopamine has been associated with Parkinson's disease (Iversen, 1979), and serotonin depletion has been shown to be a major mechanism for affective disorders such as major clinical depression and Bipolar Disorder.

Neuronal Networks: "The functioning of the brain depends on the flow of information through elaborate circuits consisting of networks of neurons. Information is transferred from one cell to another at specialized points of contact: the synapses" (Stevens, 1979, p. 55). Complex neuronal networks allow the range of functions in humans. The **voluntary nervous system** innervates skeletal musculature, and the **autonomic** innervates glands and the smooth musculature (Nauta & Feirtag, 1979).

Basic Brain Anatomy

The **limbic system,** connected by pathways of neurons, is a ring of structures. When functioning normally, the limbic system is thought to play a vital role in emotional responding. It is also likely to be a major component of learning complex tasks that require analysis and synthesis. The **cerebellum** is a rounded structure that is linked to the brain by thick bundles of nerve fibers. When functioning normally, it regulates signals involving movements, thoughts, and emotions from other parts of the brain. The **cerebral cortex** can be conceived of as a kind of mantle that envelops the cerebellum. It takes up a major portion of the brain and includes the temporal, parietal, and occipital lobes. Although there are other areas of the cerebral cortex, Broca's and Wernicke's are the best known for language (Damasio, 1999).

Specialization of the Brain

There is evidence that mapping of the brain was conceived of by Egyptians from 3000 to 2500 B.C.E. (R. Carter, 1998). The study of what occurs when various parts of the brain are damaged has helped neuroscientists understand how various portions of the brain function and what occurs when impinged upon. One of the distinguishing features of the brain is that it is not fully symmetrical in functioning (Geschwind, 1979). With advances in the practice of electrical stimulation of the brain and animal lesion experiments, "a craze for biological psychiatry took root in European universities" and helped cause the downfall of phrenology (R. Carter, 1998, p. 11). Brain regions were rapidly identified: Linguistic ability is primarily a left hemisphere function, and perception of nonverbal stimuli primarily the right; aptitude for music and recognition of complex visual patterns, for right-dominant individuals, resides in the right hemisphere, and recognition and expression of emotion in the left cortex.

Broca's Area: Early in the twentieth century, two neurophysiologists made landmark discoveries, providing evidence of how various brain regions influence function. Pierre Broca, a famous brain investigator, noticed that damage to a specific area of the left frontal lobe of the cortex resulted in aphasia or speech disorder. Speech was slow, labored, with impaired articulation. He went on to discover that damage on the right side left speech intact. What is striking is that patients with Broca's aphasia can speak with great difficulty, but they are able to sing with ease (Geschwind, 1979).

Wernicke's Area: Carl Wernicke, another eminent pioneer, studied another area of the cerebral cortex, the temporal lobe. Damage in this area of the brain also led to speech dysfunction but of a different sort. The speech of patients with Wernicke's aphasia is grammatically normal but demonstrates semantic deviations. The words chosen are often inappropriate or include nonsense syllables (Geschwind, 1979).

Emotion and Brain Regions: There is ample neuropsychiatric evidence that damage to various parts of the brain results in differential effects on emotional responding. For example, "lesions to the right hemisphere not only give rise to inappropriate emotional responses to the patient's own condition but also impair his recognition of emotion in others" (Geschwind, 1979, p. 192). Lesions in the left side of the brain are often accompanied by depression; in contrast, those with right cerebral damage sometimes seem unconcerned with their condition.

Plasticity of the Nervous System

The topic of the **plasticity** of the nervous system is a critical area of neuroscience that should inform us of the way the mind works, how brain structures are laid down, and whether personality is fixed or alterable. Plasticity has to do with the capacity of neuronal pathways to be modified. Experience affects both the structure and functions of the developing brain (Masten & Coatsworth, 1998).

Two Nobel prize-winning scientists, David Hubel and Torsten Wiesel, summarized 20 years of research in their Nobel lecture. The title of their lecture was "The Postnatal Development of the Visual Cortex and the Influence of Environment" (Wiesel, 1982). A number of influential experiments had demonstrated "the idea that early experience of the environment contributes to perceptual competence in adulthood" (Hundert, 1990, p. 228). Their findings demonstrated that the anatomical channels of the visual system, if deprived of stimulation, shrink. "Their decreased size is probably explained, however, by an actual decrease in the number of branches sent by each of these 'deprived' cells to the *cortex,* where there is an *actual shift of cells* from one 'ocular dominance column' to the other!" (p. 232). If findings from the visual system of cats can be generalized to human development, the findings are monumental in how they can be applied to developmental science, which we shall review shortly.

Reflecting on the developments in neuroscience, Hubel and Wiesel (1979) wrote, "There was a time, not so long ago, when one looked at the millions of neurons in the various layers of the cortex and wondered if anyone would ever have any idea of their function" (p. 162). These researchers demonstrated the plasticity of the visual system of the brain. There is other, equally compelling scientific evidence supporting plasticity; for example, children suffering from severe epilepsy who have had an entire hemisphere removed by and large develop normal brain functions.

The Neurobiology of Dreams: Was Freud All Wrong?

The Freudian notion of dreams as complex derivatives of unconscious process has experienced considerable scorn from most neurobiologists. Reiser (1990) proposes a neurobiological model of dreaming that attempts to understand the psychoanalytic concepts of dreams and their neurobiological underpinnings. Although this is preliminary work, it demonstrates how neuroscience has been strongly influential and has helped corroborate some of the findings that Freud postulated. The National Institute of Mental Health (1995) report on neuroscience summarizes: "Dreaming during rapid eye movement (REM) sleep is a normal human neurocognitive state with many of the formal features of mental illness, particularly delirium. For example, dreaming is characterized by visual hallucinations, memory loss, disorientation, and confabulation. Dreaming shares three other features with organic delirium, namely, loss of self-reflective awareness, emotional liability with high peak levels of anxiety, and poor social judgment. Thus dreaming can serve as a valid physiological model of major psychopathology" (p. 178).

Locating the Self in the Brain

Many scientists have dismissed the concept of the self as unworthy of empirical consideration. And yet, this concept continues to permeate many areas of psychology and has experienced resurgence, especially in the field of psychotherapy. William James (1890) referred to the self as psychology's "most puzzling puzzle" (p. 330). There is no consensual, accepted definition of the self because the construct is not a single entity, although Robins et al. (1999) boil down the definitions to two aspects: "(1) an ongoing sense of self-awareness and (2) stable mental representations" (p. 447). The authors write of the inherent problems and search for a solution: "Faced with this daunting level of pessimism, we propose the perhaps overly optimistic thesis that a scientific understanding of the self is not only possible but is in fact fundamental to a science of personality. . . . The complexities of the self-concept literature reflect the intrinsic complexity of the self as a construct. The complexity exists because self-processes operate at multiple levels, and different research camps have emerged to address the role of the self at different levels" (p. 444).

Mapping the Brain

In addition to the problem of defining the self, one of the great challenges of neuroscience is locating the self. "At the heart of the mind-body debate is the puzzle of how a mass of tissue and the firing of brain cells can possibly produce a mind that is aware of itself and that can experience the color orange, the feeling of pride, and a sense of agency" (Robins et al., 1999, p. 456). Robins and colleagues review the following specific methods of neuropsychological investigation that are being used to answer some of the questions.

Electrical Stimulation of the Brain: Electrical stimulation of the temporal lobe produces memory. This process of activation by neural stimulation is altering the content of self-awareness, but the implications are as yet unclear. Early neuroscientists demonstrated that stimulating certain regions of the brain would produce sensation, memory, and emotion, thus developing a map of the brain.

Single-Cell Recording: Various behavioral responses and stimulus patterns are provided and the activities of individual neurons are examined. Although not done on humans, this is a method for understanding whether self-recognition occurs in nonhuman primates.

Neuroanatomical Studies: "Neuroanatomical studies can also help by exploring how behavioral, cognitive, and affective deficits associated with neurological disorders map onto damage to particular brain regions" (Robins et al., 1999, p. 458). Cerebellar damage in patients is associated with impaired cognitive functioning in planning as well as in affect overregulation, evidenced by flat affect.

Brain Lesioning and Functional Neurosurgery: Earlier in the twentieth century, frontal lobotomies were performed on individuals with psychoses. This procedure dramatically altered the behavior of the individual and what we would describe as the self. It did, however, demonstrate also that destroying the frontal lobes of individuals resulted in a severe flattening of emotions and insensitivity (R. Carter, 1998).

Research on Neurological Disorders: The experimental study of neurological patients has provided fascinating information. In many neurological disorders, such as autism, Parkinson's, epilepsy, and Alzheimer's, there may be a complete loss of the self. Patients who have suffered strokes and accidents also experience changes in personality.

Studies of Neural Functioning in Healthy and Disordered Individuals: Various ways of measuring evoked potential and neuroimaging techniques have also proved to be useful tools in the neurosciences. Electrical signals can be measured with electroencephalography (EEG), which records electrical patterns from electrodes placed at various locations on the skull, as well as newer methods, such as (ERP) and magnetoencephalography (MEG). These newer methods permit the exact measurement of structural components of the brain as well as examination of the functional activation systems. These imaging techniques afford scientists a window into the living brain. Brain scientists use the following methods (R. Carter, 1998, p. 29):

- *Magnetic Resonance Imagining (MRI):* Also referred to as nuclear magnetic resonance (NMR), this technique magnetically aligns atomic particles in the body, shoots them with radio waves, and records the radio waves that return. Computer software, computerized tomography (CT), then converts this information into three-dimensional pictures.

- *Functional MRI (fMRI):* This procedure illuminates the basic anatomy by observing the activity of the brain. The activity of neurons is fueled by glucose and oxygen metabolization. When an area of the brain is active, increased oxygen is utilized and rapid scanning can show the flow of brain activity.

- *Positron Emission Topography (PET):* In this method of brain scanning, radioactive isotopes are injected into the bloodstream and, similar to fMRI, brain areas that are activated can be seen in vivid colors. Although beautiful, the resolution is not as fine-grained as in fMRI.

- *Near-Infrared Spectroscopy (NIRS):* This technique also records the fuel being used up when certain areas of the brain are activated. Low-level light waves are aimed at the brain and the light reflecting back is measured. Although no radioactive isotopes are used, this method cannot get to the deepest layers of the brain.

- *Magnetoencephalography (MEG):* This technique is similar to measuring the evoked electrical potential of the EEG but instead tunes into the magnetic pulse given off by neuronal oscillation.

Although prone to extraneous interference, it is fast and accurate in its representation of the brain.

Robins and colleagues (1999) sum up this line of research: "Although we still have a way to go before we truly understand the neural correlates of different forms of subjective experience and self-representation, new neuroimaging methods that allow us to delve into the mind have opened up a new frontier for self-researchers" (p. 460).

Chemical Alterations to Personality

Peter Kramer (1993), a clinical psychiatrist, wrote a controversial book that examined the impact of a new generation of antidepressant, Prozac. In his book *Listening to Prozac,* Kramer presents his clinical observations and some of the research concerning the impact of psychotrophic medication on personality. He describes many of the changes he observed in his patients as a result of antidepressant medication. Kramer wrote: "Prozac seemed to give social confidence to the habitually timid, to make the sensitive brash, to lend the introvert the social skills of a salesman. Prozac was transformative for patients in the way an inspirational minister or high-pressure group therapy can be—it made them want to talk about experience" (p. xv). He suggests that by taking medication and observing the changes in traits, mood, and personality, an individual can "come to see inborn, biologically determined temperament where before I had seen slowly acquired, history-laden character" (p. xv). He called this phenomenon "listening to Prozac." Kramer presents cases of individuals from his clinical practice that experienced "a quick alteration in ordinarily intractable problems of personality and social functioning" (p. 11). His controversial book explored the emerging trend for "cosmetic psychopharmacology" (p. 15); in other words, if you have a personality trait or quirk that you don't like, why not alter it with the use of pharmacological agents? The cultural preference for certain personality characteristics, it is thought, might now be modifiable with new chemical compounds. We will discuss the implications in a later section of the book.

Neuroscientists are challenging conceptions about personality, mood, temperament, and behavior. The place of emotion in personality and the clinical sciences is crucial to our understanding of personality. "Our understanding of psychopathology has changed tremendously since the early 1980s. Stunning advances in both molecular and systems neuroscience, on the one hand, and treatment modalities and diagnostic classification, on the other, have dramatically and positively changed the landscape for sufferers of mental illness in the twenty-first century" (National Institute of Mental Health, 1995, p. 159).

Affective Science

The father of affective science is Charles Darwin, who published *The Expression of the Emotions in Man and Animal* (1872/1998) and represents the first scientific examination of emotions. As mentioned, Descartes and others before were concerned with emotions, but these were never examined in such scope until Darwin. In this landmark volume, Darwin was one of the first scientists to use photographic illustrations (Ekman, 1998). Ekman comments: "In its wealth of fascinating observations about human and animal expressions this extraordinary book is unparalleled even today, more than one hundred years after it was written" (p. xxi). Ekman writes of the reaction to Darwin's work on emotions:

> *For most of the century after Darwin wrote about expression, his views were rejected or simply ignored. The intellectual and scientific world was dominated by those who saw culture as determining every important aspect of our behavior. As influential an anthropologist as Margaret Mead claimed that facial expressions differ from culture to culture as much as language, customs, attitudes and values. We may all have the same facial muscles, but they combine to form different expressions of emotions in each culture. Cultural relativists, such as Mead [1975], claimed that the same expression signifies different emotions in different cultures and some expressions, which might be unique to one culture, might never be shown in any other. So a smile could signify anger in one culture, joy in another, sadness in yet another, and there might be no smile in still another. Just as there are different words for happiness in each language there would be a different expression for happiness. A few scientists went so far as to claim that the very idea of emotions was an invention of Western culture. Emotions are a fiction (they said)—an explanatory device used in some cultures to explain what they do; emotions have no biological or psychological reality. (p. xxiii)*

The study of emotion was essentially ignored until the 1960s, when Silvan Tomkins (1962, 1963) reexamined them and opened up the study of *affect theory* (Nathanson, 1996). Paul Ekman, a major pioneer himself in affective science, discusses the relevance of Darwin's work as well as Tomkins and his own conceptual shift: "It is only in the last thirty years that systematic research using quantitative methods has tested Darwin's ideas about universality. I was one of the first to do such research, and I expected I would prove Darwin wrong. My findings caused me and many other social and behavioral scientists to change their mind" (p. xxiv). He believes that Darwin's assertion that the facial expression of emotion is a universal phenomenon has withstood the test of time.

The Universality of Emotion

Although still a controversial topic, the question of whether there are universal emotions has received much empirical support. Ekman (1998) summarized the debate between the cultural relativists, such as Margaret Mead, and the Darwinians, who believed that there were common emotional expressions for humankind. Ekman used pictures of individuals with various emotional expressions to test the universality of emotions. There are six primary emotions evident in the physiognomy of an individual: include anger, fear, sadness, disgust, happiness/joy, and surprise. Secondary emotions include guilt, shame, and pride and are referred to as "social emotions" (Damasio, 1999, p. 51).

"The topic of emotion was downplayed in psychology until the 1960s, a decade characterized by the advent of neobehaviorism and social learning theory, a movement toward cognitivism, and greater interest in systems theory" (Lazarus, 1991, p. 40). There has been a rapid growth in the study of emotion since the 1980s (Ekman & Davidson, 1994): "Psychology has rediscovered emotion" (Gross, 1999, p. 525).

Affective science is a relatively new branch of the behavioral sciences; its focus of study is emotion. Ekman and Davidson (1994), two pioneers in affective science, wrote: "For the first time in its history, the methodological sophistication of emotion research is on par with many other areas in the biobehavioral sciences. The combination of these new methods and novel conceptualizations bodes well for the future. Just as cognitive science took hold in the 1970s and 1980s, we expect that emotion research will witness a similar burgeoning of activity in the 1990s. No longer relegated to a subordinate position in the academy, a science of the emotions has arrived center stage" (p. 4).

Although emotions play a central role in the events of our lives (Lazarus, 1991), until recently, little attention has been given to emotions in psychological science. There has been a palpable resistance to the study of emotions, and the place of affective science has only recently been established as a credible area of scientific investigation. Lazarus writes:

> *Much of what we do and how we do it is influenced by emotions and the conditions that generate them. Pride and joy about our children revitalize our commitment to advance and protect the well-being of our family. Loss undermines our appreciation of life and may lead to withdrawal and depression. Anger at being wronged mobilizes and directs toward retribution. When "blinded by rage," our thinking is impaired, which places us at risk. It is even said with good reason that emotions contribute to physical and mental health and illness; positive emotions to health, negative to illness. Surely so powerful a process deserves careful study. From the time of my first contact with psychology, I was sure that we would not understand people unless we understood their emotions. (p. 3)*

Relevance of Emotion for the Study of Personality

Emotions constitute much of what we attribute to our human nature. Our fascination with individuals who do not respond emotionally can be seen in the popularity of Mr. Spock from *Star Trek*. Spock's inability to experience and understand the emotions of his human counterparts made for interesting interactions and conundrums. In the area of abnormal psychology, a condition was identified called Alexithymia, characterized by an individual who lacks the ability to put words to his or her emotional experience (Sifneos, 1988). Lazarus (1991) believes that emotions are crucial to the study of personality:

> *Although personality, too is said to be an organismic concept that encompasses adaptation, and indeed is so conceived traditionally, modern personality research has too often strayed from this ideal. Personality is seldom explored as a complex, integrated system—as a person struggling to manage transactions with the physical and social environment and being shaped and*

changed by this struggle. Instead, research in personality tends to be about one or a few traits with little or no attention paid to how they are organized within an individual.

If we are to speak of an organismic concept, one that best expresses the adaptational wholeness or integrity of persons rather than merely separate functions, emotion is surely it. Emotions are complex, patterned, organismic reactions to how we think we are doing in our lifelong efforts to survive and flourish and to achieve what we wish for ourselves. Emotions are like no other psychobiological construct in that they express the intimate personal meaning of what is happening in our social lives and combine motivational, cognitive, adaptational, and physiological processes into a single complex state that involves several levels of analysis. (p. 6)

What Is the Function of Emotions?

Emotions are necessary for survival: They allow us to attend to environmental cues and events that are potentially threatening to our survival. "Like rose-colored glasses, emotional states color one's perception of the world. Just about anything is judged more positively when one is happy and more negatively when one is sad. These are among the most reliable affective phenomena" (Clore, 1994, p. 105). Clore discusses the importance of emotion in judgment. Emotions influence our judgment: "They offer nature's best guess as to how to anticipate and respond to many of the vitally significant situations we face in everyday life" (Gross, 1999, p. 546). Strong emotions guide our attention to certain phenomena in our environment and influence how we problem-solve. Too high a level of emotion can easily cause an overreaction, resulting in a response that, in hindsight or to an unbiased observer, is considered inappropriate. Too low a level of emotional activation may reduce the possibility that an important event will be attended to in a suitable manner. Gross specifies two survival-related functions of emotion:

1. *Social communication:* "When we feel emotion, we often show how we feel through our verbal and nonverbal behavior" (p. 534).

2. *Activation and mobilization:* "Another [function] is to stimulate and sustain psychological and physiological mobilization in the face of essential biological needs that are not being met and challenges from the environment" (p. 26).

The Function of Emotional Responsivity: Frijda (1994) describes the function of emotion: "Personal loss produces sadness because it conflicts with one's attachment to the lost person, frustrations madden because we desire to complete progress toward our goals, and so on" (p. 113). "Emotions also provide *indispensable color* to our lives; we think of emotional experiences as hot, exciting, involving, or mobilizing, and distinguish them from experiences that are routine, cold, and detached" (Lazarus, 1991, p. 19).

The Affective System

Hebb's Assertion: Donald Hebb (1949) asserted that humans are the most emotional animal in the animal kingdom. "Hebb explained the paradox that the most rational primate, man, is also considered the most emotional by pointing to the effect of sociocultural control mechanisms that mask the high level of human emotionality" (Scherer, 1994, p. 127). "As one moves up the evolutionary scale, the following features appear to become more prominent: the ability to process more complex stimulus patterns in the environment, the simultaneous existence of a multitude of motivational tendencies, a highly flexible behavioral repertoire, and social interaction as the basis of social organization" (p. 127). There is an inverse relationship between emotional intensity and reaction time. This evolutionary feature of our affective system allows reappraisal of a situation before a less complex stimulus-response sequence is activated.

Variables Eliciting Emotional Response: Lazarus (1991) outlines four classes or conditions that activate an emotional response; she calls these conditions "observables":

- "*Actions,* such as attack, avoidance, moving toward or away from a place or person, weeping, making facial expressions, and assuming a particular body posture, constitute one class of observables" (Lazarus, 1991).

- "*Physiological reactions,* such as autonomic nervous system activity and its end-organ effects, brain activity, and hormonal secretions, constitute a second class of observables."

- "*What people say* about their emotions in reports of being angry, anxious, or proud, when they deny emotion, describe the conditions generating an experienced emotion, or indicate the goals at stake or the beliefs that underlie their reactions—all of these statements constitute a third class of observables."

- ■ "*Environmental events and contexts,* including the social, cultural, and physical events under which an emotion occurs, constitute a fourth category of observables." (pp. 43–44)

Mood versus Emotion: We all have a phenomenological understanding of what we feel and what our moods are and how they shift throughout our lives. We can observe that feelings are usually fleeting phenomena that suggest a course of action, such as when we are at a social gathering with our partner and notice he or she is involved in an eye-to-eye, intense, and animated conversation with another. As we shall discuss later, evolutionary psychologists believe that most of us are hardwired to experience jealousy in that situation. And that the jealousy provides the energy activating a reaction, whether a primitive one such as threatening the competitor, or a more civil tactic of asking our partner if he or she would like to see something of interest in another room. Mood, on the other hand, has a more lasting effect, as evident in the statements "I was in a lousy mood all day" and "I was feeling in a blue mood for a week." "Mood and emotion are two words that are used by psychologists and laypeople alike to refer to certain aspects of affect" (Davidson, 1994, p. 51). Lazarus (1991) writes about mood: "I suggest that moods have to do with the larger background of one's life, which feels either troubled or trouble free, negative or positive. When life seems good overall, the positive feeling is not necessarily connected with a specific event, though we sometimes point to one when asked. When life seems mostly bad, one feels bad or glum, which also is not necessarily connected with a specific event" (p. 48).

Davidson (1994) suggests that functional analysis can be useful in differentiating moods and emotions. Emotions, he contends, are used to bias actions and are elicited in situations where an adaptive response is required. Mood serves to alter information-processing priorities. Moods are much longer in duration than emotions: "For instance, whereas the full emotion of anger may last for only a few seconds or minutes, an annoyed or irritable mood may last for several hours or even a few days" (Panksepp, 1994, p. 90). Cognitive flexibility is facilitated by a positive mood, whereas a negative mood seems to reduce cognitive flexibility. Moods seem to follow events that occur over a longer period of time, whereas emotions are often a response to an immediate event and perceived as occurring without warning.

Damasio (1999) proposes that emotions be distinguished from feelings. He believes that feelings are private mental experiences of the sensations we know as feelings, and emotions are the publicly observable manifestations of feelings, such as facial expressions. He bases this distinction on the fact that no one can observe another's feelings, as these are entirely private experiences.

Conscious versus Unconscious Feeling: Neuroscientists now believe in the earlier, much discredited psychoanalytic concept of unconscious feeling. According to Damasio (1999), feeling can exist at an unconscious as well as a conscious level: "There is, however, no evidence that we are conscious of *all* our feelings, and much to suggest that we are not" (p. 36). "Moreover, for the sake of argument, the basic mechanisms underlying emotion do not require consciousness, even if they eventually use it: you can initiate the cascade of processes that lead to an emotional display without being conscious of the inducer of the emotion let alone intermediate steps leading to it" (pp. 42–43).

Affective Style and Temperament: Davidson (1994) uses "the term affective style to refer to the entire domain of individual differences that modulate a person's reactivity to emotional events" (p. 53). He views these differences as "trait-like constructs" that are consistently expressed over time. Mood is not included in this conceptualization: "However, certain personality traits might be considered to reflect affective style to the extent that they are associated with systematic differences in affective reactivity" (p. 53). Temperament, which is largely under genetic control, influences affective style. Both temperament and affective style are likely influenced by neurotransmitters, such as differences in receptor densities.

Emotional Development: "Emotional development consists of the processes whereby the emotions system achieves an increasingly complex matrix of functional links with the other sub-systems of the individual—the physiol.gcial/drive, perceptual, cognitive, and action systems" (Izard, 1994, p. 356). Greenspan (1997b) also emphasizes the critical role emotion plays in the growth of mind. Although his work straddles various domains, including affective, developmental, relational, and clinical science, his major contribution seems to fit best in the next section on developmental science. He is a strong believer in the ability of emotion to shape the self: "Our developmental observations suggest, however, that perhaps the most critical role for emotions is to create, organize, and orchestrate many of the mind's most important functions. In fact, intellect, academic abilities, sense of self, consciousness, and morality have common origins in our earliest and ongoing emotional experiences. . . . the emotions are in fact the architects of a vast array of cognitive operations throughout the life span. Indeed, they make possible all creative thought" (p. 7).

Silvan Tomkins—Affect Theory: Silvan Tomkins (1962, 1963, 1991), who originally worked with Henry Murray, published a major treatise on affective theory in a series of three volumes. Tomkin's primary affective theory stands alone in its comprehensive review of the place of affect in human evolution and adaptation. He believes that affects are all that is required for a primary motivational system in personality theory. He writes: "The human being is equipped with innate affective responses which bias him to want to remain alive and to resist death, to want to experience novelty and resist boredom, to want to communicate, to be close and in contact with others of his species, to experience sexual excitement and to resist the experience of head and face lowered in shame" (pp. 169–170). In his in-depth coverage, he elaborates the range of positive and negative affects and their placement in dominant theoretical systems.

Developmental Science

In a special issue of *American Psychologist*, guest editor E. Mavis Hetherington (1998) defines developmental science as "both the scientific and multidisciplinary foundations of the study of development and the recognition that development is not confined to childhood but extends across the life span" (p. 93). Developmental science arose out of the field of child development and is multidisciplinary in scope. Contemporary developmental science addresses a broad array of issues that influence the developmental processes. These include child care (Scarr, 1998), early intervention and experience

(Ramey & Ramey, 1998), consequences of abusive family relationships (Emery & Laumann-Billings, 1998), adolescent pregnancy and parenthood (Coley & Chase-Lansdale, 1998), marital transition and children's adjustment (Hetherington, Bridges, & Insabella, 1998), socioeconomic disadvantage and child development (McLoyd, 1998), competence in unfavorable environments (Masten & Coatsworth, 1998), and juvenile aggression and violence (Loeber & Stouthamer-Loeber, 1998).

Bowlby's Trilogy: Attachment, Separation, and Loss

In one of the most influential bodies of work in developmental science, John Bowlby (1969, 1973, 1980) presented his theory of attachment, separation, and loss and their relationship to human development in his three-volume series *Attachment and Loss*. Bowlby is such an influential developmental pioneer that his work is worth review by any student of psychology.

Attachment: The first human relationship is considered to be the foundation of personality. Bowlby (1969) proposed a theory of human attachment behavior and postulated that there are a number of behavioral systems that function to tie the infant to the mother and keep her in close proximity. He considers attachment behavior "a class of social behaviour of an importance equivalent to that of mating behavior and parental behavior" (p. 179). He disregards the Freudian concepts of needs and drives in this formulation. He describes how attachment develops: "The behavioural systems themselves are believed to develop within the infant as a result of his interaction with his environment, of evolutionary adaptedness, and especially of his interaction with the principal figure in that environment, namely his mother" (pp. 179–180). Unlike other theorists, he believed that food and eating are only minor elements in the attachment dance; clinging and sucking are the primary attachment propensities. Proximity-maintaining behavior can be seen when a mother leaves the room and the infant cries. Bowlby also emphasized the function of emotion in cementing the attachment bond: "No form of behaviour is accompanied by stronger feeling than is attachment behaviour. The figures towards whom it is directed are loved and their advent is greeted with joy" (p. 209). Bowlby cited research from, among others, Ainsworth (1967), who studied attachment behavior in naturalistic settings, Lorenz (1935/1957), who conducted experiments with imprinting (in the hours after young ducklings and goslings are hatched they prefer the first object they see), and Harlow (1961), who studied attachment in infant monkeys and the effects of maternal deprivation on development.

Separation: In Bowlby's (1973) work on separation, he drew from naturalistic observations of children and animals. He systematically examined data from a variety of sources on the effects of separation as the result of hospital stays, residential care, and substitute care. Bowlby proposed that "a period of separation, and also threats of separation and other forms of rejection are seen as arousing, in both

"Attachment Theory: The Ultimate Experiment" (Talbot, 1998)

"For every theory of human behavior, there is a diabolically perfect experiment that can never be performed—not, anyway, by ethical scientists in a democratic society. To test human tolerance of extreme cold, you cannot immerse a naked human subject in freezing water. To test the effects of maternal and sensory deprivation on infants, you cannot take a population of newborns and confine them to cribs in a gloomy, ill-heated orphanage with a small, rotating staff of caretakers who might spend an average of 10 minutes a day talking to them or holding them. But let's say that such an experiment has already occurred—in nature, as it were, far from the laboratory. And let's say that assessing its impact on the children who endured it would not only help them but might also shed light on an issue that has long intrigued developmental psychologists and tormented many working mothers" (p. 26).

   According to Talbot, this was the experiment that was carried out after the collapse of communism in 1989 in Eastern Europe, especially in Romania. Parents from the United States adopted approximately 18,000 of these children. She writes that a remark by one adoptive mother of a 9-year-old—" 'It's like the grooves were cut in the orphanage and that's music he's playing now,' . . . —made the tenets of attachment theory real in a way they had not quite been for me before" (p. 28).

child or adult, both anxious and angry behavior. Each is directed towards the attachment figure; anger is both reproach at what had happened and a deterrent against its happening again" (p. 253). Ahead of his time, Bowlby also observed that attachment-related disorders such as school phobia are related to four varieties of family patterns of interaction. He also found that in cases of agoraphobia in children, there were three categories of families: intact; intact with conflict, violence, and alcoholism, and lacking affection; and families broken by death or divorce, resulting in prolonged separations (p. 300). He goes on to discuss personality development: "We found that there is a strong case for believing that gnawing uncertainty about the accessibility and responsiveness of attachment figures is a principal condition for the development of unstable and anxious personality" (p. 322). "Similarly, the family experience of those who grow up to become relatively stable and self-reliant is characterized not only by unfailing parental support when called upon but also by a steady yet timely encouragement towards increasing autonomy, and by the frank communication by parents of working models—of themselves, of child, and of others—that are not only tolerably valid but are open to be questioned and revised" (pp. 322–323). He suggested that developmental pathways were fairly wide open at birth and that as development progresses, the number of pathways available diminishes.

Loss: "Loss of a loved person is one of the most intensely painful experiences any human being can suffer. And not only is it painful to experience but it is also painful to witness, if only because we are so impotent to help" (Bowlby, 1980). Prior to Bowlby's work, many believed that grief reactions in children were short-lived. As in his earlier works, Bowlby drew on some of the most profound research and observations of the time, and the volume on loss was no exception. Bowlby decided to use the term *mourning,* which had been used by Freud in the psychoanalytic literature, to describe the process that occurs when a child is separated from his or her attachment figure. He combined the analytic notion of defense with the cognitive view and concluded: "In the theory of defence proposed is that of the exclusion from further processing of information of certain specific types for relatively long periods or even permanently. Some of this information is already stored in long-term memory, in which case defensive exclusion results in some degree of amnesia" (p. 45). He outlined four phases of mourning in adults that the individual may oscillate among: (1) numbing, (2) yearning and anger, (3) disorganization and despair, and (4) reorganization.

Bowlby's work presages many of the contemporary issues in personality. He examines the vulnerability to pathological mourning:

> *Evidence at present strongly suggests that adults whose mourning takes a pathological course are likely before their bereavement to have been prone to make affectional relationships of certain special, albeit contrasting, kinds. In one such group affectional relationships tend to be marked by a high degree of anxious attachment, suffused with overt or covert ambivalence. In a second and related group there is a strong disposition to engage in compulsive caregiving. People in these groups are likely to be described as nervous, overdependent, clinging or temperamental, or else as neurotic. Some of them report having had a previous breakdown in which symptoms of anxiety or depression were prominent. In a third and contrasting group there are strenuous attempts to claim emotional self-sufficiency and interdependence of all affectional ties; though the very intensity with which the claims are made often reveals their precarious basis. (p. 202)*

Bowlby (1980) compared the differences between the adult and the child mourning process and emphasized that losses experienced in childhood are by nature more devastating. He also noted that children are more easily momentarily distracted from their grief, which may deceive those caring for the bereaved child. Bowlby also came to the conclusion that childhood loss influences the symptomatology of future psychiatric disturbance. These include: (1) serious suicidal ideation, (2) anxious attachment, and (3) severe depressive conditions, often with psychotic features (p. 301). Any student interested in grief and pathological mourning should read this volume.

Temperament

Thomas and Chess (1977), pioneers in developmental psychology, conducted studies of the temperamental variations in infants. Their efforts added much to the field of developmental psychology. They established 10 categories derived from their empirical investigation: (1) activity level, (2) rhythmicity (regularity), (3) approach or withdrawal, (4) adaptability, (5) threshold of responsiveness, (6) intensity of responsiveness, (7) intensity of reaction, (8) quality of mood, (9) distractibility, and (10) attention span and persistence

An Ongoing Controversy: Day Care versus Stay-at-Home Mothers

"That vital continuous one-to-one attention can rarely be achieved in group care, however excellent the facility may be. Babies in their first year need one primary adult each, and while that may be inconvenient, it is not very surprising. Human beings do not give birth to litters but almost always to single babies. Woman can only just feed two at a time (ask any mother of twins) and cannot singlehandedly care for more (ask any mother of triplets). No amount of "training" enables a nursery worker to do better. If one baby is sucking a bottle on her lap when another wakes from a nap and a third drops a toy from his highchair, she cannot respond adequately to them all. If one is unwell and one is tired, she cannot cuddle them both in a way that makes them feel she cares, let alone keep the third busy and safe. And that is three. How many day care centers really offer 1:3 adult-child ratio?" (p. 88)

Of course, the other side of the argument draws from the available research that fails to consistently demonstrate a significant difference in those children placed in day care compared to those who are at home with a caregiver. More research is required before this controversy can be adequately resolved, because questions remain concerning the impact of day care on the emotional, social, and personality development of those entrusted to its care.

SOURCE: Children First: What Our Society Must Do—And Is Not Doing—For Our Children Today *(Leach, 1994).*

(pp. 21–22). Three different constellations of temperament are derived from ratings on these factors.

Greenspan's Regulatory Patterns

Stanley Greenspan (1997a) has been an influential figure in the application of developmental styles and patterns to personality development and the field of psychotherapy. He also emphasizes the importance of the emotional bond between child and primary caregiver and implicates this relationship as the prime architect of the mind (Greenspan, 1997b). He has provided an important blend of empirically based research findings and astute observations from clinical practice to advance developmental science and psychotherapeutic processes.

One of Greenspan's (1997b) major contributions is his categorizing of behavior-regulating patterns in infants and children.

Type I—Hypersensitive Type: This behavioral pattern, manifested in early infancy, is characterized by overreactivity or hypersensitivity to environmental stimuli and has at its core two common patterns: fearful and cautious or negativistic and defiant. "The fearful and cautious person evidences excessive cautiousness, inhibition, or fearfulness. . . . The negative and defiant person evidences negativistic, stubborn, controlling, defiant behavior and often does the opposite of what is requested or expected" (pp. 90–91). According to Greenspan, each pattern is either exacerbated or enhanced by the caregiver's response. The fearful/cautious pattern will be intensified by a caregiver who is inconsistent (i.e., overindulgent and overprotective and then punitive and intrusive). Parenting that is overly demanding and punitive and overstimulating will exacerbate the negativistic/defiant pattern. Conversely, for the fearful/cautious individual, flexibility, empathy, and gradual encouragement to explore frightening areas will maximize the potential. The negativistic/defiant pattern will become more flexible if the parenting style is soothing and supportive and avoids power struggles.

Type II—Underreactive Type: There are various behavior manifestations of the underreactive regulatory pattern. Withdrawn/difficult-to-engage children seem disinterested in exploring relationships. They often appear apathetic and withdrawn and are easily exhausted. When infants, they are depressed, delayed, and unresponsive to interpersonal invitations. This type of individual requires a caregiver who reaches out and is engaging, sensitive, and wooing, inviting the individual out of isolation.

Self-absorbed individuals seem to "march to their own drummer" (Greenspan, 1997b, p. 93), tuning in to their own sensations and perceptions rather than those of others. Caretakers who are self-absorbed themselves or passive will naturally intensify this pattern, as will family systems with confusing communications. Conversely, caregivers who are interactive and collaborative will mitigate this pattern.

Type III—Stimulus-Seeking, Impulsive, Aggressive, Motor-Discharge Type: This pattern is characterized by impulsive, aggressive, and highly active behavior. There is an active interest in seeking stimulation and contact and a lack of caution. This can be seen in a tendency to destructive behavior, characterized by intruding into body space, hitting in an unprovoked manner, and breaking things. These individuals are often described as daredevils and risk-takers and have a preoccupation with aggressive play, using activity and stimulation to feel alive. When poor limits and boundaries are manifest in the parenting style, in the form of too much or too little stimulation and nurturing, this pattern will be exacerbated. Conversely, parenting styles "characterized by a great deal of consistent nurturing, firm structure and limits, opportunities for consistent, warm engagement, as well as modulation and regulation of activity, and opportunities for sensory and affective involvement with good modulation will enhance flexibility and adaptability" (Greenspan, 1997b, pp. 94–95).

Importance of Greenspan's Conceptualization: Greenspan's conceptualization of the innate regulatory processes has vital importance for contemporary personology. In his pioneering work, he emphasizes the importance of the temperamental or genetic predispositions and the caretaker's reaction as the crucible for personality development. For example, a child with an underreactive regulatory pattern who is parented by a withdrawn, unresponsive figure will tend to develop a personality that is introverted, avoidant, or schizoid, whereas the same child with an engaging caregiver will tend to be normalized in his or her orientation.

Relational Science

The field of relational science has experienced a "phenomenal growth" (Berscheid, 1994, p. 79). "Today, if you squint your eyes and cock your heads just so, you can see the greening of a new science of interpersonal relations" (Berscheid, 1999, p. 260). An even newer specialty than affective science in the evolution of the behavioral sciences is the branch of study termed relational science, which emphasizes the empirical study of relationships. "A relationship between two people resides in neither of the partners, but rather in the interaction that takes place between them. That interaction can be viewed as constituting the living organism, or dynamic system, we call an interpersonal 'relationship'" (Berscheid & Lopes, 1997, p. 136). In her seminal article in *American Psychologist*, Berscheid (1999) makes the case for "the potential of relationship science to change our disciplinary landscape" (p. 260). She believes that the elevation of the study of relationships to a new scientific discipline will provide an "integrating force within psychology" (p. 261). This movement is attempting to overcome the individualistic orientation in American psychology. In her article, Berscheid writes: "Psychology traditionally has been individualistic in at least two ways: First, psychologists usually search for laws that govern the behavior of a single individual, and second, in searching for the causes of an individual's behavior, psychologists typically look inside the individual. Attitudes, personality traits, skills, aptitudes, genes, and most other causes investigated by psychologists are located in the individual. Moreover, these causes are often assumed to have a physical, often neurophysiological, representation of some kind, whether or not that material representation explicitly figures into our theories, which it often does not" (p. 261). Relationship scholars, she adds, are more concerned with interactions and the influence that one person's behavior has on another. The relationship is the focus of study, as opposed to the individual. Relational science is directed toward analyzing the individual, dyad, or system (Berscheid & Reis, 1998). Thus, researchers are concerned with "the oscillating rhythm of influence observed in the interactions of two people" (Berscheid & Reis, 1998, p. 261) or in the triangular relationships that occur in unstable dyads.

The Relational Matrix

Representation of Self and Others and Relationship Schemas: There is accumulating evidence that the relationships we have with others influence the manner in which we perceive ourselves (Berscheid, 1994). Berscheid's review of Gergen (1991) and Ogilvie and Ashmore (1991) suggests that conceptions of the self may not be stable over situations and that any core identity or single conception may not be maintained. Thus, self-other representations may be a useful unit of analysis. She also reviews the term "relational schema" introduced by Planalp (1987), who wrote a series of papers discussing how individuals form schemas that represent their pattern of interaction in close relationships.

Berscheid (1994) also cites the increasing attention given to the topics of love, jealousy, social support, and relationship dissolution factors. Relational scientists also are examining how emotions are experienced in close relationships. Because close relationships are the main context in which individuals experience intense emotions, this is a fruitful line of investigation. The question often asked by theorists and clinicians is What does it mean to be close? As a first step, Berscheid and Ammazzalorso (2001) define relationship: "Two people are *interacting* when the behavior of one influences the behavior of the other and vice versa. As this implies, the essence of a relationship is the oscillating rhythm of influence that appears in the partners' interactions. If two people have never interacted, they do not have a relationship; if they seldom interact, they probably do not have much of a relationship; but if they often interact, and if each partner's behavior is influenced by the other partner's behavior, then, from the perspective of most relationship scholars, they are in a relationship with each other" (pp. 309–310).

Closeness and Intimacy : Closeness, or intimacy, as it is termed in the psychotherapeutic literature, is a cross-disciplinary construct. Intimacy has been discussed at great length in the clinical literature but has not been given much scientific consideration. Berscheid and Ammazzalorso (2001) define a close relationship as one in which the pattern of interaction, as reflected by each partner's behavior, is highly interdependent. Assessment of interdependence and closeness then considers the following: "First, the interaction pattern reveals that the partners *frequently* influence each other's behaviors; second, they influence a *diversity* of each other's behaviors (i.e., they influence many different kinds of their partner's activities, not simply their leisure activities, for example); third, the magnitude of influence they exert on their partner on each occasion observed is *strong*; and, finally, these three properties have characterized the couple's interaction pattern for relatively *long duration* of time" (p. 6).

The Emotion-in-Relationship Model: Berscheid (1983) and Berscheid and Ammazzalorso (in press) postulate an emotion-in-relationship model (ERM) to try to understand why intense emotions are more frequent in the setting of a close relationship and then attempt to predict when these "hot" emotions are likely to occur. The authors believe that close relationships are "fertile ground for the experience of intense emotion as contrasted to less close relationships" (Berscheid & Ammazzalorso, 2001, p. 317). When long-held expectancies about the relationship or partner are violated, this creates the condition for the experience of intense emotion. These expectancies held about those we are in close relationships with are based on relational schema. These are derived from past experiences and observations of other people's relationships. Sometimes, these expectancies are culturally instilled, such as when a husband imagines what a wife should be like. The authors go on to say that these expectancies are not always in our awareness, and many of us have difficulty articulating the expectations held in our relationships, even though we might react with strong emotion when these expectancies are violated. "In short, beneath the surface of every relationship is a web of expectancies the partners hold for each other's behavior. These expectancies allow the partners to coordinate their actions and plans to maximize their own and other's welfare" (Berscheid & Ammazzalorso, 2001, p. 319). Therefore, they conclude that the "greater the number of expectancies, and the stronger they are held, the greater the potential for emotion, although that potential may never be realized during the life of a relationship because those expectancies may never be disconfirmed" (p. 319).

This ERM model predicts that individuals in very close relationships, as compared to not-close relationships, are more likely to experience intense jealousy when threatened by a third party. Berscheid and Ammazzalorso (2001) cite several studies to support their theoretical predictions. Further, they predict that the likelihood of a jealous reaction is based on three factors: (1) degree of closeness in the relationship, (2) how available a substitute partner is, and (3) the level of threat to which the third party exposes the continuance of the relationship.

The Influence of General Systems Theory and the Development of Family Therapy

One of the most exciting developments in the history of twentieth-century science having application to the behavioral sciences was the development of general systems theory (von Bertalanffy, 1968), covered in greater depth in Chapter 10. Gregory Bateson applied general systems theory to the study of communication patterns in schizophrenic families in the early 1950s. Bateson, an eminent anthropologist who had wide-ranging interests and knowledge in communication theory, evolution, cybernetics, and ecology, received a grant from the Rockefeller Foundation to study the topic of communication. With a team of interdisciplinary scientists, including Jay Haley, who had been trained in communications, John Weakland, a chemical engineer with interests in cultural anthropology, and Don Jackson, a psychiatrist who had been supervised by Harry Stack Sullivan, Bateson developed the concept of the double-bind communication (Guerin & Chabot, 1992). As a result of their studies, they identified six basic characteristics of the double bind:

1. Two or more persons are involved in an important relationship.
2. The relationship is a repeated experience.
3. A primary negative injunction is given that conflicts with the first, but at a more abstract level. The injunction is also enforced by a perceived threat. This second injunction is often nonverbal and frequently involves one partner's negating the injunction of the other.
4. A second injunction is given that conflicts with the first, but at a more abstract level. This injunction is also enforced by a perceived threat. This second injunction is often nonverbal and frequently involves one partner's negating the injunction of the other.
5. A third-level negative injunction exists that prohibits escape from the field while also demanding a response.
6. Once the victim is conditioned to perceive the world in terms of a double bind, the necessity for every condition to be present disappears and almost any part is enough to precipitate panic or rage (Nichols, 1984).

Although the double-bind theory of schizophrenia has been discredited and modern-day psychiatry has established a neurobiological basis for this disorder, the work of Bateson and his research team launched the family therapy movement. Probably of greater importance is the fact that they began to develop and expand the notion that communication patterns play a part in family dysfunction

(Magnavita, 2000d). Bateson's belief that communication and behavior were synonymous included the concept of homeostasis, which, when applied to families, suggests that change is resisted and the status quo is often maintained at the cost of emotional suffering to certain members (Guerin & Chabot, 1992).

Dysfunctional Personologic Systems: Certain family systems seem to spawn high levels of personality disorders in their members and, indeed, transmit these through a multigenerational transmission process (Magnavita, 2000d). Greenspan (1997b) comments on his work with multiproblem families: "In these families, afflicted with almost every imaginable problem from child neglect and spouse abuse to alcoholism or drug addiction, the degree to which children fail to develop their cognitive and social skills matches the degree to which their families fail to meet their emotional needs at each stage of their growth" (p. 10).

Intersubjectivity: The study of intersubjectivity emerged along different developmental lines, primarily from psychoanalysis. It is mentioned here because there are many similarities to the developments and contributions of relational science. Intersubjectivity refers to the mutual making of meaning that occurs in a dyadic relationship, such as that of a therapist and a client. Thus, there is actually a third reality that emerges in the interpersonal field. This notion has challenged the "objectivity" of the analyst as scientific observer. Instead of one reality of the self, there are multiple realities and selves that are coconstructed in intimate relationships.

Sociobiology/Evolutionary Psychology

A recent and often controversial development in the field of psychology with application to the study of personality is the new subdiscipline of evolutionary psychology, which emerged from the field of sociobiology (Wilson, 1975). D. M. Buss (1984) proposes an evolutionary model for understanding personality based on Darwin's (1859) principles of **natural selection** and **survival of the fittest.** From an evolutionary perspective, Buss suggests, adaptations and their by-products can help us understand the core of human nature. He proposes that human nature can be described and explained and that "all psychological theories imply the existence of a human nature" (p. 36). Evolutionary psychologists believe that the mind can be understood and the "criteria for carving the mind at its joints" met by dividing the mind into evolved psychological mechanisms (see D. M. Buss, 1984, p. 1135). Buss (1999) writes: "This evolutionary analysis has profound implications for personality theories of human nature. It provides an incisive heuristic that guides theorists to the sorts of motives, goals, and strivings that commonly characterize humans. At the most general level, it suggests that, at some fundamental level of description, the *only* directional tendencies that can have evolved are those that historically contributed to the survival and reproduction of human ancestors" (p. 42).

The Evolutionary Process

It must be stated that evolutionary biology and its sister discipline sociobiology (Wilson, 1975) have engendered much polemic (Pinker, 1997). Earlier, we discussed the eugenics movement, based on genetic engineering of the perfect family. When sociobiology hit the scientific community, the prevailing model that emphasized nurture as opposed to nature attacked the sociobiologists with ferocity (Pinker, 1997). Although Pinker espouses intellectual freedom to pursue the truth, he writes: "My point is not that scientists should pursue the truth in their ivory tower, undistracted by moral and political thoughts. Every human act involving another living being is both the subject matter of psychology and the subject matter of moral philosophy, and both are important. But they are not the same thing. The debate over human nature has been muddied by an intellectual laziness, an unwillingness to make moral arguments when moral issues come up. Rather than reasoning from principles of rights and values, the tendency has been to buy an off-the-shelf moral package (generally New Left or Marxist) or to lobby for a feel-good picture of human nature that would spare us from having to argue moral issues at all" (p. 47).

The evolutionary model applied to psychology seemingly has engendered one controversy after another, so that it is hard to determine how well it will withstand the test of scientific scrutiny or will fall by the wayside, as did the "science" of phrenology. The use of this model to explain and account for various behavioral patterns such as mate selection and even rape has proved quite controversial.

For example, new theories by evolutionary psychologists attempt to overturn the widely held belief that rape is an act of power and aggression and not of sex (Goode, 2000).

Clinical Science

The evolution of clinical psychology and psychiatry has been extremely influential in the development and shaping of personality theory. In fact, the main theories of traditional and contemporary personality reviewed in this text were developed in the crucible of abnormal psychology, clinical psychology, and psychiatry. We have learned a great deal about personality by the study of disordered individuals.

The Disordered Mind/Brain

"Of all things we find in the world, *madness* has, through the ages, proven to be one of the most difficult to define. A variety of *political* and *sociological* explanations have been offered for the ambiguities and conflict inherent in defining madness" (Hundert, 1990, p. 157). The interest in and study of abnormal psychology laid the groundwork for the development of interest in personality. Emil Kraepelin (1904), a psychiatrist and classifier of mental disorders, **nosology,** made major advancements in his early categorization of psychopathology. His first effort was in the differentiation of schizophrenia from manic depressive illness and later personality disorders. His studies marked the first modern classification of mental disorders and the beginning of the field of psychopathology and abnormal psychology. Another objective-descriptive psychiatrist of the time, Bleuler (1911), "searched physical movements and streams of speech for evidence of specific psychotic illnesses . . . he introduced the term 'loosening of associations' to describe the speech of schizophrenic patients, suggesting that this reveals a 'vagueness of conceptual boundaries' in schizophrenia" (Hundert, 1990, p. 167).

Integrating the Components of Modern Personality Theory

I have presented, in an abbreviated form, a summary of the major related disciplines so the reader will have a context for the development of current theories of personality. Now it is necessary to understand how these component parts allow us to build contemporary models of personality (see Table 4.1). This will also allow us to trace the seminal developments that occurred early in the twentieth century and understand their place in the emergence of new theoretical models. It is important to note that the separation of the various scientific disciplines that have been reviewed at worst is overly simplistic but was done for heuristic purposes so that the reader can assimilate the necessary material. In reality, there are many overlapping and intersecting lines of study from one branch to another. For example, the study of emotion is not just relegated to the field of affective science; the reader has seen how relational science also uses the construct to further explain emotional aspects of relationships. Most of the fields, in fact, are interdisciplinary, and this integrative perspective has probably been another of the most useful advances in scientific theorizing. Berscheid and Reis (1998) comment from the perspective of relational science: "The science of interpersonal relationships is international in character, as well as multidisciplinary" (p. 194).

Table 4.1   **The Components of Modern Personality Theory: Interrelated Disciplines**

Primary Disciplines	Secondary Disciplines
Cognitive science	Anthropology
Affective science	Art/Literature
Neuroscience	Economics
Relational science	Sociology
Developmental science	Political science

Subdisciplines of Psychological Science
Evolutionary psychology
Clinical psychology and psychiatry
Abnormal psychology and psychopathology
Social psychology
Statistics

Toward Consilience in Personalty Theory and Understanding Human Nature

Wilson (1998) attempted to present a unified theory of knowledge, or consilience, in his groundbreaking book *Consilience*. His attempt, a grand one, was a useful intellectual and scientific endeavor to relate all areas of science in a cohesive whole. Personology is an area where such consilience now seems possible with the convergence of the various areas of inquiry reviewed in this chapter.

The Need for an Integrationist Perspective: Millon (1990) writes: "Integrative consonance . . . is not an aspiration limited to ostensibly diverse sciences, but is a worthy goal within the domains of each science" (p. 12). Pinker (1997) sums up what is required to understand humankind and the multitude of factors in operation: "In this scientific age, 'to understand' means to try to explain behavior as a complex interaction among (1) the genes, (2) the anatomy of the brain, (3) its biochemical state, (4) the person's family upbringing, (5) the way society has treated him or her, and (6) the stimuli that impinge upon the person. Sure enough, *every one* of these factors, not just the stars or the genes, has been inappropriately invoked as the source of our faults and a claim that we are not masters of our fates" (p. 53).

Summary

This chapter reviews the seminal developments and scientific endeavors that are shaping the field of personology. Descartes and other philosophers of science proposed a new philosophical perspective that engendered the scientific revolution. Descartes proposed a mind-body dualism that would serve as a model for science and separate it from theology. The study of consciousness has experienced a renewed interest in an effort to understand how the mind works and what it is that makes us self-aware to a degree unlike any other species. New disciplines and areas of investigation are adding much to our understanding of personality theory. A major revolution in cognitive science using computer models led to a paradigmatic shift from the stimulus-response model of behaviorism with the addition of the mediating aspect of cognition. New findings and techniques in neuroscience shed greater light on the workings of the brain and provided a map of brain functions not unlike the early one of phrenology. Stimulated by Darwin's work in the nineteenth century, a renewed interest in affective science has spawned much research about the emotional systems that guide and orient much of our behavior. Developmental science examines the importance of temperament, attachment, separation, and loss. A new discipline, relational science, is experiencing a phase of rapid growth in the emphasis on dyadic and triadic relationships, extending the individualistic model of personality to include interpersonal relations and complex systems. These new disciplines, with their many overlapping domains, are providing personality researchers and theorists with new fountains of knowledge in the quest to understand the nature of humankind and the individual differences that make each person unique. These component systems of personality are essential building blocks for modern comprehensive personality theory. Each perspective offers a window into the understanding of personality that enriches the theoretical models presented in the remainder of this text.

Suggested Reading

Damasio, A. (1999). *The feeling of what happens: Body and emotion in the making of consciousness* New York: Harcourt Brace.

Ekman, P., & Davidson, R. J. (Eds.). (1994). *The nature of emotion: Fundamental questions.* New York: Oxford University Press

National Institute of Mental Health. (1995). *The neuroscience of mental health: II. A report on neuroscience research: Status and potential for mental health and mental illness.* Rockville, MD: U.S. Department of Health and Human Services. (E-mail: nimhinfo@nih.gov).

Redfield Jamison, K. (1995). *An unquiet mind: Memoir of moods and madness.* New York: Alfred A. Knopf.

CONTEMPORARY MODELS
OF PERSONALITY

Psychobiological Models of Personality

5

Chapter

Introduction

This chapter begins the section of the text on contemporary models of personality. Because the **psychobiologic system** is basic to most of the contemporary models, it seems logical to begin this section with a presentation of it. Almost all contemporary models of personality explicitly recognize the biological substrate of behavior in temperamental variation and in biochemical-affect systems. Humankind, at its essence, is biological, and our behavior is in large part influenced by the evolutionarily shaped constraints of our central nervous system. The question is whether a neurobiological model in and of itself can make a reasonable accounting for the complex phenomena of personality or if this model will always have certain limited explanatory power and range. "At the heart of the mind-body debate is the puzzle of how a mass of tissue and the firing of brain cells can possibly produce a mind that is aware of itself and that can experience the color orange, the feeling of pride, and a sense of agency" (Robins, et al., 1999, p. 456). The continuum of emotions that we experience, the temperamental variation, our intellectual capacities, our social interactions are all shaped by the capacity of our nervous system. "In the broadest sense, then, the structure of behavior reflects the existence of neurobehavioral-emotional systems that elicit and motivate certain subjective emotional experiences and overt patterns of behavior to particular classes of stimulus" (Depue, 1996, pp. 348–349).

Although biological-based models of personality, as we have seen, are not novel but go back to the four humors of early Greeks, these models have experienced resurgence in the last few decades of the twentieth century with advances in neuroscience and biological psychiatry. This renewed interest, often controversial, has rekindled a zeal to pursue a psychobiological understanding of personality. Major advancements in the fields of biological psychiatry, genetics, and neuropsychology have begun to redefine and challenge many of our closest held notions about personality. In a highly popular book, *Listening to Prozac*, Peter Kramer (1993) challenges many of our assumptions about medications and their potential to alter personality. Kramer writes: "We are edging toward what might be called the 'medicalization of personality'" (p. 37). He believes that in the near future, the technology of brain science will allow us to pharmacologically alter our personality with various **psychotropic medications,** affecting mental activity—what he calls "cosmetic pharmacology." This development can be readily seen in the area of child psychology/psychiatry in the burgeoning area of attention-deficit disorders. More and more, an overreliance on psychostimulant medication to "improve" attention and learning is reported. In some cases, it seems that parents and teachers are too quick to request medications to sculpt behavior that previously might have been accepted as within normal range. If Kramer's prediction is correct, at some point, an individual with a passive, shy personality will be able to go to the local **psychopharmacologist**—a medical health professional with a specialization in the use of psychotropic medication—who will ask what kind of traits are desired and then prescribe the appropriate combination of medications to effect these traits. The necessity for self-discipline, relearning, and the existential angst of making changes in behavior and personality might be a thing of the past.

"Defining the basic structure of a general neurobehavioral-emotional system per se is of great importance if it is to guide an analogy to the structure of personality traits" (Depue, 1996, p. 350). Humans may have varying neurochemically predisposed sensitivities to environmental stimuli, expressed as differential experience and expression of emotions. As we have discussed, emotional systems are "major structural components of stable patterns of human behavior—or, put simply, of personality" (pp. 352–353). Individuals with unstable emotional systems prone to dysregulation or those with a predisposition to extreme shyness or anxiousness will lean toward various personality styles or, in more severe cases, prime the pump for a personality disorder.

Major Historical Figures

Ivan Petrovich Pavlov

Ivan Pavlov (1849–1936), a Russian physiologist, was one of the pioneers in attempting to understand the psychobiological correlates of personality "via the usual methods of natural science" (Pickering & Gray, 1999, p. 277). Pavlov advanced our understanding of some of the basic principles of the neurobiology of learning in his discovery and elucidation of the **classical conditioning** paradigm. Pavlov's (1927) experiments conducted on dogs showed that autonomic functions such as salivating can be conditioned. In this example, food is an **unconditioned stimulus** and the natural reaction of salivating is an **unconditioned response.** When a bell, a **neutral stimulus,** is temporally paired with food over a number of trials, the bell alone will produce the salivation response or **conditioned response.** His experiments clearly demonstrated how conditioning alters basic physiological response patterns through associative learning. His influence has exerted a major force on the development of behaviorism and the behavioral models of personality covered later.

Donald O. Hebb

The Canadian psychologist Donald Hebb (1949) developed a simple idea for how the brain learns. In his landmark book, *The Organization of Behavior: A Neuropsychological Theory,* Hebb laid the foundation for many current neurobiological models of personality. Hebb's learning rule postulated that memory is produced when two neurons are simultaneously activated in a manner that strengthens the synapse. Through this simple but elegant rule, Hebb was able to elucidate how memory is laid down and how learning takes places at a neuronal level. Others advancing this research demonstrated how the synaptic connections could be strengthened or weakened through the application of low levels of electrical stimulation.

Kramer's Stress-Kindling Model

Kramer (1993) approaches the neurobiology of personality through the lens of depression. He examines how pharmacological agents, particularly Prozac, can lead to changes in the personality of those who are depressed. An experienced clinical psychiatrist and astute observer of clinical phenomenon, Kramer was keenly aware of the suffering of his patients and their search for seemingly missing elements of their personality. His model is based on clinical data and extensive knowledge of the current research in neuroscience. The model has three important interconnected components for which he presents compelling evidence and research support. Kramer emphasizes research in the biology of separation, stress, and kindling.

Separation

Harry Harlow's (Harlow & Zimmerman, 1959) well-known studies of rhesus monkeys demonstrated that separation from their maternal figure caused more damage if surrogate mothers were made of wire mesh as opposed to a soft material to which they could cling. In further studies, Suomi (1991) demonstrated even subtler forms of separation stress by raising monkeys with their peers and then reuniting them with the troop. Although these monkeys look normal, they are more timid and less eager to explore, and biochemically, they show progressive deterioration. The peer-raised monkeys when separated show higher levels of cortisol and abnormal norepinephrine compared to monkeys raised by their mothers. These monkeys, Suomi suggested, showed signs of rejection sensitivity when social bonds were disrupted.

Stress

A number of studies have demonstrated the effects of stress: "Pain, isolation, confinement, and lack of control can lead to structural changes in the brain and can kindle progressively more autonomous acute symptoms" (Kramer, 1993, p. 117). For example, the effects of sexual abuse produce consistently higher levels of cortisol and easily triggered cortisol responses to stimulation. This has been associated with higher levels of depression. Psychological stress causes reductions in certain hormones such as beta-endorphin, glucocorticoid, and prolactin. Increased prolactin occurs when women are nursing. This may also explain why certain women who were having trouble conceiving became pregnant after relaxing on a vacation (Sapolsky, 1998).

Kindling

If rats or monkeys are given small electrical shocks to certain areas of the brain, nothing observable occurs at first. But if the stimulus is readministered, the animal will have a mild seizure. With successive application of the electric shock, less intensity will produce more seizure activity. This **kindling model** (Wada, 1976) of epilepsy has also been applied to understanding the progressive deterioration and rapid cycling observed in many bipolar disordered individuals. "Kindling has dramatic effects on nerve pathways" (Kramer, 1993, p. 112): Cells that have been kindled actually undergo anatomical change, and these changes can be observed quite early in the kindling process. Kramer describes how this occurs: "It looks as if a series of chemical reactions in the downstream cell reach right to the nucleus and affect the way the cell's DNA and RNA produce complex chemical substances. These substances include hormones that determine whether the cell makes new connections with other neurons or allows old connections to wither. Some cells die; others 'sprout,' or change shape. Kindling rewires the brain" (p. 112). Using this model, trauma can be translated into anatomical alteration of the brain. As we will see when we review the evidence from clinical science, psychotherapy may also rewire the brain anatomically.

Kramer (1993) sums up how these interconnected components form a model of depression: "The kindling model implies that at least one sort of depression is a progressive condition, biologically encoded long before it manifests itself in the form of overt episodes. The stress research in rats implies that a variety of psychosocial stressors can serve as triggers for this insidious encoding. And the monkey-separation studies show what animals look like early in the course of stress-induced kindling: except for transient, minor social inhibition (anxiety in the face of novelty), they appear normal in ordinary social circumstances; but they have heightened sensitivity to loss" (p. 122).

Although Kramer views personality through a very narrow lens of depression and patients' observed response to a newly developed antidepressant medication, this line of inquiry is compelling if not controversial. Kramer's book was in essence the mass-marketed version of the new biological psychiatry and the trend toward pharmacological approaches to human behavior. Aggression is another important dimension of personality that has a clear biological base.

The Biological Basis of Aggression

Hormones regulate the functioning of the brain. The endocrine system is responsible for the regulation of hormones by the hypothalamus, the master gland, and the pituitary gland, as well as peripheral glands. It is well established that there is a relationship between testosterone and aggression in men: As testosterone levels increase, so does aggression. Men have higher levels of testosterone than females and are more aggressive (Sapolsky, 1998). Castration decreases testosterone and results in a reduction of aggression that is well documented in various species. Men who take steroids are known for their hyperaggression because of the increase in testosterone. In spite of these findings, there is no way to predict level of aggressiveness in men with a range of testosterone levels. It may be that the aggression is caused by the increased spike in levels of testosterone released under stress or threat in some men and not in others. There are likely other mediating psychological factors in aggression, such as social learning.

The amygdala is also suspected of playing a role in aggression. When it is destroyed, aggression is significantly reduced; when the amygdala is electrically stimulated, there is a burst of aggression. At one time, psychosurgery to remove the amygdala of very violent patients was court-ordered but sadly did not significantly decrease aggression. This is a dark spot in the history of the neurobiological model (Sapolsky, 1998).

Temperament Models

The temperament models of personality can be viewed as the precursors of many of the current neurobiological models that are presented next. Temperament is influenced by a plethora of biological factors, such as genetic predisposition and prenatal influences such as maternal well-being, smoking, environmental toxins, and nutrition. Kramer (1993) states: "Studies from a variety of perspectives—

child development, animal ethnology, descriptive psychiatry, and sociobiology—point to temperament as a crucial factor influencing personality and overall psychological well-being in a large and recognizable slice of humanity: the inhibited, the vulnerable, the highly reactive, the mildly depressed" (p. 175). Stress hormones and neurotransmitters have a substantial impact on temperamental variation, and temperamental variations impact many other systems. Thomas and Chess (1977) write:

> The child's temperament influences his responses to parental practices and attitudes and helps to shape his parents' judgments and feelings toward him. Sib and peer group relationships, school functioning and academic achievement, behavioral responses to illness or other specific stress—all can be significantly affected by specific temperamental traits. Temperament plays a part in the ontogenesis and evolution of behavior disorders and in the developmental course of the brain-damaged, mentally retarded and physically handicapped child.
>
> For the adult, also, temperamental characteristics frequently play an important role in determining personal and social functioning, work patterns, and adaptation to change. For the mother who is led to believe that she is responsible for any deviation of her child's behavior from a conventional norm, the knowledge of the part played by temperament may relieve her of an oppressive burden of guilt and anxiety. (p. 183)

Thomas and Chess's Model

Thomas and Chess (Chess & Thomas, 1986; Thomas & Chess, 1977), briefly mentioned in the preceding chapter, produced landmark work in their observation and systematic rating of several hundred infants from birth into early adolescence. Nine categories of temperament were quantified and rated (Thomas & Chess, 1977; Thomas, Chess, & Birch, 1968):

1. *Activity level:* The motor component present in a given child's functioning and the diurnal proportion of active and inactive periods. Protocol data on motility during bathing, eating, playing, dressing, and handling, as well as information concerning the sleep-wake cycle, reaching, crawling, and walking, are used in scoring this category. [Scoring: High, Medium, Low]

2. *Rhythmicity (regularity):* The predictability and/or unpredictability in time of any function. It can be analyzed in relation to

sleep-wake cycle, hunger, feeding pattern, and elimination schedule. [Scoring: Regular, Variable, Irregular]

3. *Approach or withdrawal:* The nature of the initial response to a new stimulus, be it a new food, new toy, or a new person. Approach responses are positive, whether displayed by mood expression (smiling, verbalizations, etc.) or motor activity (swallowing a new food, reaching for a new toy, active play, etc.). Withdrawal reactions are negative, whether displayed by mood expression (crying, fussing, grimacing, verbalizations, etc.) or motor activity (moving away, spitting new food out, pushing a new toy away, etc.). [Scoring: Approach, Variable, Withdrawal]

4. *Adaptability:* Responses to new or altered situations. One is not concerned with the nature of the initial responses, but with the ease with which they are modified in desired directions. [Scoring: Adaptive, Variable, Non-adaptive]

5. *Threshold of responsiveness:* The intensity level of stimulation that is necessary to evoke a discernable response, irrespective of the specific form that the response may take, or the sensory modality affected. The behaviors utilized are those concerning reactions to sensory stimuli, environmental objects, and social contacts. [Scoring: High, Medium, Low]

6. *Intensity of reaction:* The energy level of response, irrespective of its quality or direction. [Scoring: Positive, Variable, Negative]

7. *Quality of mood:* The amount of pleasant, joyful, and friendly behavior, as contrasted with unpleasant, crying, and unfriendly behavior. [Scoring: Positive, Variable, Negative]

8. *Distractibility:* The effectiveness of extraneous environmental stimuli in interfering with or in altering the direction of the on going behavior. [Scoring: Yes (Distractible), Variable, No (Non-distractible)]

9. *Attention span and persistence:* Two categories, which are related. Attention span concerns the length of time a particular activity is pursued by the child. Persistence refers to the continuation of an activity in the face of obstacles to the maintenance of the activity direction. [Scoring: Yes (Persistent), Variable, No (Non-persistent)] (Thomas & Chess, 1977, pp. 21–22).

In their studies, they observed that infants demonstrated recognizable patterns even in the first few months. This was a critical finding that supported what most parents of multiple offspring knew: that children are not born equal; some children have very demanding, difficult to soothe temperaments from birth, whereas others are easily soothed and responsive to maternal input. Thomas and Chess were able to reduce their nine factors to two central ones: activity pattern and adaptability. **Activity** refers to whether a child is vigorous and continuously interactive with the environment or tends to be passive and wait for attention to come his or her way. **Adaptability** refers to a child's positive approach to new stimuli in the environment. Some children tend to approach new stimuli with a high degree of flexibility and are able to respond to the changing demands in their environment; others tend to withdraw, often expressing negative moods when exposed to novel situations. Thomas and Chess categorized three major temperamental variations: the easy child, the difficult child, and the slow-to-warm child.

The Goodness-of-Fit Model

In further refinement of their groundbreaking work, Chess and Thomas (1986) developed a deep appreciation for the systemic issues at play in personality development. They suggested that temperament variations in individual children could either have a goodness of fit or poorness of fit in terms of how compatible the parents are: "Basically, a psychologically determined behavior disorder in a child or adult develops out of a substantial incompatibility between the individual's capacities and coping abilities and the expectations and demands of the environment" (p. 9). This type of incompatibility may assume different forms; for example, "the slow-to-warm-up child who is pressured to adjust to a new group quickly, the highly active youngster who is expected to sit still without interruption for long periods of time, and so forth" (p. 9).

Although Chess and Thomas (1986) focus on the contribution of temperament, they remind the reader that "in no way do we advocate a temperament-based theory of personality. So many factors influence the course of normal and deviant psychologic development, that any theory based on one set of determinants, whether these are genes, neurochemical structures, instinctual drives, temperament, conditioned reflex patterns, early life experience, or the impact of the extra-familial social environment, is bound to be simplistic and inadequate" (p. 11).

Buss and Plomin's Model

Throughout this text, various factorial theories are presented. Some of the models are derived primarily from interpersonal models, others seem more behavioral, and yet others neurobiologic in their assumptions and roots. All of them attempt to distill the plethora of variables that they believe best account for personality variation, usually by statistical analysis. Buss and Plomin (1975, 1984) have posited a three-factor temperament model to explain the variation in personality.

1. *Activity:* Whether an individual tends to be tireless and constantly moving or lethargic and passive.
2. *Emotionality:* An individual's tendency to become easily emotionally aroused, displaying a temper, mood swings, and high expressiveness, or to be calm, nonreactive, and slow to emotional arousal.
3. *Sociability:* The need to be with others, finding social interaction gratifying, or appearing detached and uninterested in social discourse.

Various personality configurations can be described and explained by combinations of these factors. For example, an introvert is low on sociability and low on activity, and an extrovert is at the opposite pole on both continuums (Millon & Davis, 1996a). An individual with a hysterical personality is high in sociability, emotionality, and activity, and a depressive personality is low in sociability, emotionality, and activity. Each represents a unique combination of these dimensions in various configurations.

Depue's Three-Factor Model

"As appears to be the case for the general neurobehavioral systems, a limited number, typically varying between three and five, of higher-order personality superfactors have been repeatedly confirmed in recent years" (Depue, 1996, p. 353). Basically, these models attempt to correlate personality dimensions with underlying neurobiological systems and to correlate findings from neuroscience with brain behavior responses. Primarily, they explain the various neurotransmitters and their actions.

Depue (1996) accounts for personality by the underlying neurobiological systems that he associates with **three factors** that have consistently been reported in the research to explain the dimensions in personality. These three **superfactors** are positive emotionality, constraint, and negative emotionality. Depue offers the following caveat: "Models of personality traits based on only one neurotransmitter are clearly too simplistic and will require the addition of other modulating factors" (p. 372).

Positive Emotionality: Depue (1996) proposes that one of the major factors underlying personality structure is positive emotionality. This is the ability to "experience feelings of incentive, effectance motivation, excitement, ambition, potency, positive affect, and well-being" (pp. 353–354). He describes three core processes that are activated in various stimulus contexts: "(1) incentive-reward motivation, (2) forward locomotion as a means of supporting goal acquisition, and (3) cognitive processes" (p. 354). He relates this system to dopaminergic systems (DA) within the brain. There is a vast array of literature that he believes supports the importance of DA in motivation and emotional systems. Therefore, "individual differences in DA reactivity to incentive stimuli may have marked effects on the probability of behavioral facilitation" (p. 359).

Constraint: The second superfactor in this three-factor model is constraint. In other three-factor models, this is referred to as psychoticism (Eysenck, 1981). Constraint has a number of subfactors, including impulsivity, harm avoidance, and uneasiness with novelty. Depue (1996) focuses on the subfactor of impulsivity to explain this superfactor and its neurobiological correlate. He proposes that the neurotransmitter serotonin (5-HT) provides a widespread pattern of innervation in the brain. In an interesting study that confirmed the correlation between 5-HT and impulsivity, Brown, Goodwin, Ballenger, Goyer, and Mason (1979) found that men who were characteristically explosive and impulsive and had an aggressive life history were likely to have a higher level of a major metabolite of 5-HT in their cerebrospinal fluid (CSF). Those with higher levels, it is suspected, need much more stimulation to react aggressively. "Numerous studies have since documented a strong relationship between irritable, assaultive aggression and various indicators of low 5-HT" (Depue, 1996, p. 263). Low 5-HT is also associated with violent suicidal behavior. He proposes that aggression and suicidal behavior are two indices of a central biochemical/behavioral trait of having a low emotional threshold. In his review of both the animal behavior research and human studies, he proposes three characteristics of low 5-HT functioning: (1) emotional instability, (2) exaggerated response to stimulus, and (3) irritability-hypersensitivity.

Negative Emotionality: The third superfactor is negative emotionality, which includes subjective experience of various negative emotions such as depression, hostility, anxiety, alienation, and sensitivity to distress. Depue (1996) hypothesizes that the locus ceruleus (LC) and the neurotransmitter norepinephrine (NE) modulate this affective system. A number of other neurotransmitters feed this system, including "5-HT, enkephalins, substance P, acetylcholine, neurotesin, corticotropin-releasing hormone, somatostatin, and epinephrine as a neurotransmitter" (p. 367). This LC system modulates various global functions, including behavioral orientation and alertness, fear-alarm responses, and selective attention

Cloninger's Unified Biosocial Theory of Personality

Cloninger (1986a, 1986b) also developed a well-articulated neurobiological model of personality. He published two seminal papers in the mid-1980s that describe his unified biosocial theory of personality. Kramer (1993) believes that "Cloninger's is a true spectrum theory of personality" (p. 188). Cloninger proposes a series of characteristics, which are heritable. These are novelty seeking, harm avoidance, and reward dependence. These characteristics or dispositions are associated with three behavioral-brain systems.

1. *Novelty seeking:* Novelty-seeking individuals actively pursue novel situations because of the excitement and feeling of exhilaration that result in these activities. This behavioral trait is related to the DA system. Individuals with high levels of dopamine may be more likely to demonstrate this trait. Individuals with lower levels of this neurotransmitter are likely to be slow, passive, and preoccupied with details.

2. *Harm avoidance:* Harm-avoidant individuals respond strongly to aversive stimuli and will therefore do what they can to minimize behaviors that might result in punishment. This behavioral

trait is associated with the 5-HT system. Individuals with this trait are more likely to be inhibited.

3. *Reward dependence:* Reward dependence is the tendency to respond to stimuli that suggest a reward is forthcoming. This trait is associated with the noradrenergic system.

These three neurobehavioral systems then set the parameters for the development of personality. Cloninger's system is highly developed and quite complex. "The three axes—reward dependence, harm avoidance, and novelty seeking—allow Cloninger to cover vast territory" (Kramer, 1993, p. 187). Combining these predispositions, a number of second- and third-order personality characteristics can be postulated. Millon and Davis (1996a) describe how combining these systems can describe various personality configurations: "For example, the histrionic personality is seen as exhibiting high novelty seeking, low harm avoidance, and high reward dependence; these derive from second-order trait patterns of being impulsive, emotionally vulnerable, and narcissistic" (p. 65).

Siever's Dimensional Model

Siever's (Siever & Davis, 1991; Siever, Klar, & Coccaro, 1985) neurobiological model of personality is dimensional, with general clinical syndromes situated at one end and personality configurations at the other. He proposes four neurobiological dispositions.

1. *Cognitive/perceptual organization:* Individuals with inadequate neurobiological systems are likely to display schizophrenic spectrum disorders manifest in disorders of thought and other psychotic symptoms. When there is a heavy loading on this factor, schizoid and schizotypal personality is more likely to develop.

2. *Impulsivity/aggression:* Individuals with faulty neurobiological systems will manifest on this dimension poor impulse control and aggressive acting-out. These individuals will tend toward borderline and antisocial personality.

3. *Affective instability:* Individuals with inadequate neurobiological systems will demonstrate affective instability and dysregulation of emotions. This can become an obstacle to stable interpersonal

relationships. Most likely, these individuals develop borderline or histrionic personalities.

4. *Anxiety/inhibition:* Individuals with faulty neurobiological systems will manifest on this dimension an extreme state of anxiety that, if left unchecked, may develop into personality disorders such as avoidant and compulsive.

Summary of the Neurobiologic Factor and Dimensional Models

The models presented share much in their efforts to explain what the theorists see as the main factors or dimensions that account for the variation in personality. Much is being discovered about the complexity of neurotransmitters, but the complexity is daunting. These models can be considered preliminary attempts to explain how neurotransmitter action will be expressed and how these neurobiologic-affect/cognitive systems create various developmental pathways to personality expression when shaped by the environment.

Klein's Chemical Dissection Model

D. F. Klein (1967, 1970), a predecessor of Kramer, uses pharmacological agents to dissect and analyze personality. He attempts to understand personality by observing the response an individual has to a pharmacological agent, seeing which symptom complexes respond to medication. Using various medications to test his theory, Klein developed different groupings of personality. He is most known for his description of the hysteroid-dysphoric, emotionally unstable, and phobic-anxious types.

The Neurobiology of Trauma and Affective Stimulation

Another very interesting and important line of research has to do with the impact of trauma on personality from a neurobiological perspective. Personality development is influenced by a number of factors, including genetic predisposition and neonatal development, but traumatic events can kindle certain neuronal pathways that then become sensitized to react in evocative situations. Herman (1992) describes what occurs:

Traumatic reactions occur when action is of no avail. When neither resistance nor escape is possible, the human system of self-defense becomes overwhelmed and disorganized. Each component of the ordinary response to danger, having lost its utility, tends to persist in an altered and exaggerated state long after the actual danger is over. Traumatic events produce profound and lasting changes in physiological arousal, emotion, cognition, and memory. Moreover, traumatic events may sever these normally integrated functions from one another. The traumatized person may experience intense emotion but without clear memory of the event, or may remember everything in detail but without emotion. She may find herself in a constant state of vigilance and irritability without knowing why. Traumatic symptoms have a tendency to become disconnected from their source and to take on a life of their own. (p. 34)

Too much emotional arousal associated with traumatic experience has been found to be a consistent element of many severe personality disorders and major depression (Levitan et al., 1998). Conversely, too little emotional activation can also have a profound effect on various aspects of personality. The National Institute of Mental Health's (1995) report summarizes the neurobiological findings:

Based on a variety of experimental and clinical studies, it appears that posttraumatic stress disorder (PTSD) may involve dysfunction of a neural system comprising the amygdala, locus ceruleus, and hippocampus and including norepinephrine, opioid, and CRF [cortico-tropin-releasing factor] systems. The recent findings that stress increases norepinephrine release and that fear conditioning and behavioral sensitization are related to alterations in noradrenergic neuronal activity may have important clinical implications. Such stress-induced increases in noradrenergic neuronal activity may contribute to frequent abuse of alcohol, opiates and benzodiazepines by PTSD patients to relieve their symptoms; all three drugs attenuate stress-induced norepinephrine activity to some degree. (p. 169)

Affective Experience and Structure of the Brain

Greenspan (1997b) believes that there are substantive empirical evidence and observational data to suggest that emotions play a critical part in the creation and organization of the mind's most crucial structures. When an individual is the victim of early trauma, the level of emotional arousal may overwhelm the developing mind and "influence the very structure of the brain itself" (p. 7). He writes: "In fact, intellect, academic abilities, sense of self, consciousness, and morality have common origins in our earliest and ongoing emotional experiences. Unlikely as the scenario may seem, the emotions are in fact the architects of a vast array of cognitive operations throughout the life span. Indeed, they make possible all creative thought" (p. 7).

As we have seen, hormones have a profound effect on behavior. Greenspan (1997b) describes how the hormonal system is activated by interpersonal experience and stress: "Recently it has been found that in order for neurons to make connections through the use of a neurotropic factor, they must be activated through experience. Experience can stimulate hormonal changes; for example, soothing touch appears to foster growth hormones, and hormones such as oxytocin appear to foster critical emotional processes such as affiliation and closeness. Furthermore, emotional stress is associated with changes in brain physiology" (p. 8). Greenspan emphasizes the affective component as critical to the structural development and growth of the brain. Other current theorists emphasize the importance of interpersonal experience.

Interpersonal Experience

According to Siegel (1999), "Relationship experiences have a dominant influence on the brain because the circuits responsible for social perception are the same as or tightly linked to those that integrate the important functions controlling the creation of meaning, the regulation of bodily states, the modulation of emotion, the organization of memory, and the capacity for interpersonal communication" (p. 21). Highly emotional experiences, as William James (1890) pointed out, may scar the cerebral tissue and create lasting changes in the activity of neuronal systems. The quality of attachments in childhood may have a profound effect on personality in adulthood. Insecure attachment may create an increased risk for psychological and social impairment. Siegel emphasizes "that a delicate interplay exists between nature and nurture" (p. 85).

Neurodynamics of Personality

Grigsby and Stevens (2000) published a compelling integration of neuroscientific findings and propose a modular theory to account for individual differences in personality. They summarize their findings:

> The brain has a structure, although this structure changes considerably over the course of life, and subtly from moment to moment. Yet, while the brain's structure is not unimportant, it is the brain's dynamic processes that give minds their distinctive properties. In contrast to the brain, the mind has no structure, and it makes no sense to discuss it as though it did. Mind is an emergent property of complex transactions among the environment, hierarchically organized neurophysiological processes, and other physiological properties of the organism (e.g., endocrinological processes). Mind is not a substance, something with an existence apart from neural processes. All psychological processes necessarily have a neural substrate and cannot be separated from neural processes. (p. 226)

One of the interesting conclusions made by Grigsby and Stevens (2000) is that Ferenczi's active therapy, presented in Chapter 3, seems consistent with their findings about how character can be altered. They emphasize the need to continually call attention to actions in interpersonal process, which tend to disrupt habitual patterns that have been "procedurally learned" (p. 325). They also suggest that high levels of emotional arousal may be required for relearning new characterological patterns. As we have reviewed, traumatic events that cause a high level of emotion can produce very rapid learning and effectively reorganize neural networks. Undoing patterns may also require high levels of emotional arousal.

Behavioral Genetics

The foundation of any neurobiological model of personality rests on the nature versus nurture controversy (Plomin & Caspi, 1999): "Joining these two words created a fission that exploded into the longest controversy in science" (p. 251). The manner in which genes are expressed, or **phenotypes,** is an ongoing matter of controversy. Certainly, genetic predisposition sets the stage for personality development, but to what extent is where the controversy lies. Millon and Davis (1996a) state: "Despite these ambiguities and complications, there can be little question that genetic factors do play some dispositional role in shaping the morphological and biochemical substrate of certain traits. However, these factors are by no means necessary to the development of personality pathology, nor are they likely to be sufficient in themselves to elicit pathological behaviors. They may serve, however, as a physiological base that makes the person susceptible to dysfunction under stress or inclined to learn behaviors that prove socially troublesome" (p. 88).

Heritability

Studies of twins have been the standard method to determine heritability of various factors, and personality is no exception. "Heritability is a statistic that describes the effect size of genetic influence and refers to the proportion of observed (phenotypic) variance that can be explained by genetic variance" (Plomin & Caspi, 1999, p. 252). The results of twin studies have consistently assessed that genetic contribution or heritability can explain 50% of the variance in personality. "Explaining 50% of the variance is an astounding achievement in personality research, which has been pushing against a glass ceiling of explaining more than 10% of the variance, as indexed by correlations of .30. Because behavior is multiply determined, it is unlikely that any single factor can explain more than 10% of the variance" (p. 252). These findings come from various studies that compare personality factors in identical twins, fraternal twins, and siblings. Identical twins share 100% of their genetic material, so comparing their personalities is an excellent way to tease out the nature versus nurture components of personality. According to Plomin and Caspi, "Across dozens of self-report personality questionnaires, twin correlations are consistently greater for identical twins than for fraternal twins for other traits in addition to Extraversion and Neuroticism" (p. 252). Citing a study by Loehlin (1992), the authors write that of the Big Five factors, "Agreeableness, Conscientiousness, and Openness to Experience showed identical twin correlations of about .45 and fraternal twin correlations of about .20, suggesting heritability estimates of about 40%" (pp. 252–253).

Environmental Factors and Personality

Genetic studies help researchers understand how the environment contributes to the shaping of personality. Because the heritability of personality is generally in the 50% range, environmental factors

The Search for the Male Leadership Gene

In the book *Darkness in El Dorado: How Scientists and Journalists Devastated the Amazon*, Tierney (2000) writes of Napoleon Chagnon, a popular professor of anthropology who, in the 1960s, studied the Yanomami Indians, a very isolated group in the Amazon. Proposing an evolutionary theory to explain his belief that the Yanomami pursued warfare to gain access to women, Chagnon named them the "fierce people." He believed that the men who were the fiercest and killed the most attained the most women and contributed disproportionately to the gene pool. Tierney suggests that the researcher was biased and raises doubts about the claim that the Yanomami are more aggressive than other preindustrial peoples. In a review of the book entitled, "The Other Side of Science," Weiss (2001) writes: "Arguably the most explosive charge is that Chagnon and renowned geneticist James V. Neel either deliberately—or through benign neglect—administered a form of measles vaccine that was inappropriate for an immunologically naive population and, in doing so, were substantially responsible for a 1968 measles epidemic that ravaged the Yanomami" (p. 78). Neel was searching for confirmation of the "male leadership" gene, which, according to Weiss, was an attempt to prove a "dubious bit of neo-eugenic theory" (p. 78). "The book raises disturbing questions about how social science research is—or should be—conducted, and the obligations of researchers who work with the few remaining isolated populations" (p. 78).

---

contribute the remaining 50% (Plomin & Caspi, 1999). Plomin and Caspi describe the current thinking:

> *From Freud onward, most theorists about how the environment works in personality development implicitly assume that offspring resemble their parents because parents provide the family environment for their offspring. Similarly, siblings resemble each other because they share that family environment. Twin and adoption research during the past two decades has dramatically altered this view. The reason why genetic designs, such as twin and adoption methods, were devised was to address the possibility that some of the widespread resemblance between family members may be due to shared heredity rather than to shared environment. The surprise is that genetic research consistently shows that family resemblance for personality is almost*

entirely due to shared heredity rather than to shared family environment. The environment is important, but it is not shared by family members. This remarkable finding means that environmental influences that affect personality development operate to make children growing up in the same family no more similar than children growing up in different families. (p. 256)

These environmental factors have been termed **nonshared environmental factors** because even children growing up in the same family experience major milestones, such as parental treatment, differently. Also, a number of studies in the area of birth order and the space between siblings consistently demonstrate "that first-borns are more conforming and traditional, more conscientious, and more neurotic than later-borns" (Plomin & Caspi, 1999, p. 257). **Shared environmental factors** refer to loss, social class, and parenting style, although even these range from child to child, often based on genetic factors. Research on twins has determined that parental loss, for example, is a shared factor that makes children from the same family similar, because there is an increased likelihood of anxiety and depression as a result of parental death and divorce. The authors summarize this exciting field: "These findings support a current shift from thinking about passive models of how the environment affects individuals toward models that recognize the active role we play in selecting, modifying, and creating our own environment" (p. 261).

Identifying Specific Genes Associated with Personality

A current direction of research is to use techniques of molecular genetics to identify genes that are responsible for certain personality characteristics (Plomin & Caspi, 1999). Plomin and Caspi believe this will revolutionize the field of personality. They believe that this technique will ultimately focus on causal processes, starting with the cells and proceeding to social systems. The search for genes will be challenging because a single gene is unlikely to account for a specific personality attribute. "For quantitative traits like personality, genetic influence is much more likely to involve multiple genes of varying but small effect size, which greatly increases the difficulty of detecting such genes. Genes for complex traits influenced by multiple genes and multiple environmental factors are known as **quantitative trait loci** (QTLs)" (p. 262). They believe that the goal of this line of research is to find the combinations of genes that contribute various effect sizes to the variance of personality traits. They describe this endeavor: "Perhaps one gene will be found that accounts for 5% of the variance, 5 other genes might each account for 1% of the variance, and many other genes might have effects so small that we can never detect them. If the effects of these QTLs are independent, together these QTLs would account for 25% of the variance, or half of the heritable variance for the trait. All of the genes that contribute to the heritability of the trait may never be identified if some of their effect sizes are very small" (p. 262).

A Breakthrough in Genetic Research in Personality

In 1996, according to Plomin and Caspi (1999), a major advancement in genetic research on personality was achieved. Two independent studies (Cloninger, Adolfsson, & Svrakic, 1996) published in the prestigious journal *Nature Genetics* identified the gene (DRD4) for the dopamine receptor that is expressed primarily in the brain's limbic system. This cutting-edge research brings together various aspects of personality theory. It demonstrated that individuals high in novelty seeking, "characterized as impulsive, exploratory, fickle, excitable, quick-tempered, and extravagant" (p. 263), measured on Cloninger's Tridimensional Theory of Personality Questionnaire (Cloninger, Svrakic, & Przybeck, 1993), have genetically predisposed differences in the manner in which dopamine is transmitted. Newly developed genetic techniques such as DNA pooling allow researchers to combine DNA markers for a group of individuals who are high or low on a particular personality trait. A second technical advance, DNA chip technology, combines the circuitry of electronic chips with DNA analysis; this allows small chips the size of a credit card to genotype in minutes thousands of DNA markers using a few drops of blood. This "means that an entire genome scan for allelic association can be conducted for a particular personality trait in a few minutes" (Plomin & Caspi, 1999, p. 265). **Allelic association** is the "correlation between alleles of a DNA marker and trait scores across unrelated individuals" (p. 262).

The Human Genome

The Nobel prize winners J. D. Watson and Crick (1953) discovered the structure of DNA. The hereditary factors, which were a mystery until then, were found to be discrete and digital. Over the past decade, scientists have been attempting to read the entirety of the human genome and place it in the proper order. There are approximately three billion characters of text in DNA molecules (Ridley, 2000). Recently, the human genome has been read and reported by two separate research groups in simultaneously published issues of *Science* and *Nature* (Jasny & Kennedy, 2000). Jasny and Kennedy remark on this advancement in biological science:

> *Humanity has been given a great gift. With the completion of the human genome sequence, we have received a powerful tool for unlocking the secrets of our genetic heritage and for finding our place among the other participants in the adventure of life.*
>
> *This week's issue of* Science *contains the report of the sequencing of the human genome from a group of authors led by Craig Venter of Celera Genomics. The report of the sequencing of the human genome from the publicly funded consortium of laboratories led by Francis Collins appears in this week's* Nature.
>
> *. . . This has been a massive project, on a scale unparalleled in the history of biology, but of course it has built on the scientific insights of investigators. By coincidence, this landmark announcement falls during the week of the anniversary of the birth of Charles Darwin.*
>
> *. . . The human genome has been called the Book of Life. Rather, it is a library, in which, with rules that encourage exploration and reward creativity, we can find many of the books that will help define us and our place in the great tapestry of life.* (p. 1153)

Altering Genetic Endowment

The scientific understanding of molecular components of learning and memory has advanced the technology to modify genetic structure. This has resulted in the development of smart mice that are capable of learning much more efficiently then their non-genetically altered counterparts (Tsien, 2000). According to Tsien, the possibility that this technology will be applied to humans exists, although there are ethical and safety barriers. The ethical challenges that the biopsychosocial field faces are very complex and will require a close alliance between researchers and ethicists. For example, if someday it is possible to create your own "designer child" by specifying the physical and personality traits you deem most desirable, how will society handle this technology? It will probably be possible within this century to alter genetic material enough to do so!

Interaction between Genetics and Environment

What is apparent from a century of converging research is the fact that nerve fibers grow with repeated stimulation. There is ample evidence to demonstrate that early stimulus deprivation has dire consequences. If certain neurotransmitters and neuronal pathways are not stimulated, "the biological substrate for a variety of psychological functions may be impaired irrevocably" (Millon & Davis, 1996a). Furthermore, early intense levels of stimulation result in changes in neurophysiology and brain weight.

Understanding the interaction between genetics and environment will be an important line of investigation. Genetic differences create different sensitivities to experiences (Plomin & Caspi, 1999). Plomin and Caspi predict that "tracing the developmental pathways between specific genes and personality through environmental mechanisms is likely to be one of the most important advances that emerges from application of specific genes associated with personality" (p. 268). They discuss this topic: "Using DRD4 [dopamine receptor] and Novelty Seeking as an example, drug-experimenting peers might be at a greater risk for drug abuse for individuals who have a long-repeat DRD4 allele. This is the general form of interactions suggested by the diathesis-stress model of psychopathology: Individuals who are at genetic risk (diathesis) are most sensitive to environmental risk (stress), and to environmental opportunities as well, as suggested in the . . . example of the possible influences of peers who use drugs" (p. 267).

The Contribution of Neuroscience

According to Pickering and Gray (1999), modern personality research is poised for a "scientific makeover" influenced by the past 15 years of developments in neuroscience. There have been only a few studies investigating the relation between brain functions and personality using the technology of neuroimaging. Using single photon emission tomography (SPET), Gray, Pickering, and Gray (1994) found significant negative correlations between impulsive sensation seeking and dopamine systems.

Selected Research Findings

- *"A study of temperament and personality in anorexia and bulimia nervosa"* (Diaz-Marsa, Carrasco, & Saiz, 2000). *Establishing a link between neurobiological correlates and their behavioral expression is an important task of the neurobiological model.* Dimensions of personality and personality disorder were evaluated using Cloninger's and Eysenck's dimensions (see Chapter 7 for review of Eysenck) and their relationship to eating disorders. The findings suggest that impulsivity is a key factor in the temperament of bulimic patients, and anorectics displayed higher scores in persistence, a contrasting trait.

- *"Menstrual cycle influences on mood and behavior in women with borderline personality disorder"* (Ziv, Russ, Moline, Hurt, & Zendell, 1995). *The relationship among neurobiological component systems such as the endocrine system and psychological correlates such as mood is important to understand.* Although patients with Borderline Personality Disorder tend to report a worsening of affective instability and impulsivity premenstrually, when investigators examined this association it was not supported. This was a limited pilot study of 14 patients, so caution in generalizing the results is urged.

- *"Heritability of personality disorders in childhood: A preliminary investigation"* (Coolidge, Thede, & Jang, 2001). *The controversy (nature vs. nurture) between those who emphasize biology and genetics and those who emphasize socialization and environment as primary influences in personality development is ongoing and often investigated with twin studies.* Personality disorders of 112 children ages 4 to 15 consisting of 70 pairs of identical (monozygotic) and 42 fraternal (dizygotic) twins were assessed and heritability coefficients calculated. The researchers concluded that there is a substantial genetic component to childhood personality disorders, with the median estimate of heritability reported to be .81 for all personality disorders.

- *"Neural correlates of memories of childhood sexual abuse in women with and without posttraumatic stress disorder"* (Bremner et al., 1999). A key challenge in neurobiological research is to find measurable correlates of the effects of various experiences such as trauma. Researchers completed positive emission tomography imaging of the brains of 22 women with a history of sexual abuse with and without a diagnosis of Posttraumatic Stress Disorder (PTSD) while listening to personalized tapes of abuse or neutral tapes. The memories of abuse were associated with increased flow of blood to regions of the brain in the PTSD trauma survivors. The investigators concluded that brain dysfunction may underlie PTSD symptoms.

- *"A multidimensional twin study of mental health in women"* (Kendler, Myers, & Neale, 2000). A sample of 794 pairs of female twins was examined on six dimensions of mental health to provide insight into the genetic and environmental factors in healthy psychological functioning. The "best-fit model" to explain the findings suggested that although genetic factors are important, ranging from 16% to 49% heritability coefficients, family environment strongly influences substance abuse, interpersonal relations, and social support. Individuals with a high index of mental health, functioning well across multiple domains, had a lucky combination of genetic factors, but family environment also was a significant contributor to mental health in women.

There has been increased media attention in the area of developmental neurosciences (Tompson & Nelson, 2001). These accounts have been somewhat exaggerated. Tompson and Nelson write: "Despite the excitement over the 'new' brain development research, much of the knowledge reported in media accounts is based on studies that have been around for a long time" (p. 8). How this information is reported to the public requires a "constructive dialogue between scientists and journalists" (p. 14).

Principles of the Biopsychosocial Models

Philosophical Underpinnings and Assumptions

The philosophical underpinnings of the neurobiological approach assume that knowledge is amassed from a logical deductive approach. This is essentially a Lockean scientific style of explanation, which assumes that we can account for personality by the underlying physiological substratum. There may be limitations with this type of scientific reductionism that may fail to account for the unique complexity of human personality functioning. The challenge of the field to define consciousness, covered in Chapter 4, is an example of the difficulty in moving from the biological substrate to higher psychological processes, the most challenging to explain being consciousness. The rapid advances are compelling and will certainly shape the landscape for future theories of personality.

Notions of Normal versus Abnormal

There are some well-defined criteria of what represents normal versus pathological. Certainly, normal personality functioning requires an intact neurobiological system. Abnormal functioning is related to compromise in the neurobiological system. From a neurobiological perspective, it is clear that severe brain injury and other physical conditions alter personality. However, many stroke patients retain a core sense of themselves that sometimes defies explanation. The complexity of understanding the neurochemical, neuroanatomical, and interactive environmental aspects of this model will require major research effort and time. Theoretically, as the science advances, notions of normality could be keyed directly to levels of neurotransmitters that are present in the nervous system. Too little dopamine or too much serotonin could indicate abnormal states. We are beginning to understand the complexity of these systems and the difficulty of reducing behavior to various neurotransmitters alone. This model challenges current systems of understanding the continuum of normal-abnormal personality by measuring and observing the various manifestations of behavior, affect, and interpersonal relationships using neurobiological correlates.

Assessment Strategies and Tools

Although the tools and techniques of neuroscience, such as MRIs, CT scans, and PET scans, are exciting, there are those who believe that merely mapping the brain is not necessarily an effective use of these expensive technologies. Merely mapping areas of the brain that "light up" when subjects are performing various tasks may not be far from the earlier attempts of phrenology in adding meaningful knowledge to our understanding of brain function and personality. Although these tools offer great promise for the future, currently there is little direct application of these for assessing personality.

In the foreseeable future, however, it is likely that advances in genetics will reach the point where various personality vulnerabilities can be assessed and thus remediation and prevention can occur. Also, there are likely to be neurobiological tests that can assay the metabolites of various neurotransmitters so that profiles can be developed and chemical alterations suggested.

Application of Model

The therapeutic approaches that emanate from the neurobiological model emphasize neurochemical alteration of brain deficiencies. Therefore, individuals with personality problems such as chronic shyness or rejection sensitivity are likely candidates for receiving psychotropic agents aimed at enhancing the functioning of the dopamine system. Major advances in the field of psychopharmacology have enabled clinicians to treat catastrophic conditions such as Bipolar Disorder, other major affective disorders, and Schizophrenia, for which individuals were often relegated to lifelong hospitalization.

Modern-day psychiatric treatment relies on many of the advances in neuroscience to treat a variety of clinical conditions. Many of these advances have been remarkable breakthroughs, especially in the treatment of chronic mental disorders such as forms of psychosis and major mood disorders. For other, seemingly less debilitating disorders, such as social phobia, anxiety, and personality disorders, the advances are also substantial. For example, an individual with a history of shyness, social anxiety, and avoidant personality would be treated using pharmacological agents by a mental health professional who ascribes to this model. A combination of drugs may be prescribed that target the symptom patterns expressed. A typical treatment approach might incorporate an antianxiety agent to reduce the anxiety and thus reduce the social discomfort. An antidepressant medication may also be used to augment the effect of the anxiety medication and thus reduce the underlying rejection sensitivity often seen in these individuals. Sophisticated psychopharmacologists attempt to understand the underlying temperamental vulnerability, which can be mended with the proper medication to allow development to proceed in a less compromised fashion.

Although at this time, prescribing medication is based on some research, much is left to clinical experience in terms of suggesting a medication or combination of medications. Often, more than one medication is prescribed, and some combinations augment the actions of others. Typically, in addition to medication management, many patients are encouraged to engage in psychotherapy to further aid in changing maladaptive behavioral patterns. However, this is not always the case, and as more primary care physicians have taken on the role of first-line clinicians for mental health problems, many patients do not receive the psychotherapeutic component.

Strengths and Limitations of Model

The *strengths* of this model lie in the promise of understanding personality from the complex cellular processes to the social systems and how these interrelate. This is a daunting task. At this time, there is much excitement, but researchers and theorists are at the early stage in the development of comprehensive neurobiological models. The strength of this model can be seen in the advances that have been made in the treatment of chronic mental illness. At no time during the evolution of humans has there ever been so much hope that debilitating mental illness is being more effectively treated with medications. Pharmaceutical companies expend a large share of their resources in attempts to come up with new and more effective pharmacological agents with fewer side effects and greater potency.

Probably the main strength of this model is not as a stand-alone theory of personality but in how it informs the other models that are presented in this text. An understanding of the neurobiological substrates of personality provides a much richer foundation for theoretical models. Models that are not firmly anchored in a biopsychosocial matrix will not accurately reflect the complex array of variable sets that determine personality.

One *limitation* of this model has to do with the question of whether personality and consciousness can ever be entirely explained by the neurochemical processes of the brain. "With the exception of a few well-circumscribed lesions that are directly associated with specific organic syndromes, the data relating neurological damage to psychopathology [are] equivocal" (Millon & Davis, 1996a).

Another limitation is that cultural differences are not directly addressed in this model. With the addition of evolutionary perspective, cultural differences in personality reflect the interaction between neurobiological factors and environmental demands.

Additionally, there are major ethical issues that have been raised by those in the field and others who are critical of this line of investigation. It is inevitable that the genetic factors that predispose us to certain personality traits will be determined. When the technology is available, it then becomes a question of how this information is used by society. We are reaching a point where confidential information is no longer sacrosanct. Insurance companies routinely ask medical professionals to provide detailed accounts of both physical and mental health treatments when individuals apply for medical, life, and disability insurance. It is not a stretch to imagine the day when an individual's genetic profile is requested. Other "big brother" issues are emerging more rapidly than ethics and religion can handle. There may come a day when the technology is available to provide an army of clones that match a certain predetermined personality profile. In the past, certain cultures promoted the development of superior warriors, such as during the Roman Empire where the Spartans were socialized from childhood to be fierce warriors. Soon, we may have the technology to develop designer citizens or children based on one's preference. One could theoretically develop a whole country based on a sociopathic personality; probably no other model of personality presents the inherent dangers that exist in this one. It will be a challenge for society and all of us to keep pace by developing ethical guidelines for the use of this rapidly advancing technology of personality. Kramer (1993) sums up both the hope and danger for the future: "The research that yields these results will not be targeted at changing personality. But once we believe that temperament is ruled by the neurohumors, there is no separating progress in treating mental illness from progress in altering temperament. Necessarily, research of the treatment of major illness will also be research into cosmetic psychopharmacology. The better we are at changing specific transmission patterns in the brain, the better we will be at recasting the foundations of normal variants in personality. New drugs should be able to modify inborn predispositions and to repair traumatic damage to personality that had become functionally autonomous on a physiological basis" (p. 184).

Summary

The neurobiological models of personality hearken back to the Greeks' formulations of the four humors. The basis of many models can be seen in early temperament variation. Current neurobiologic models attempt to link biologically based variation to psychological factors to account for personality expression. Certain neurotransmitters are associated with various personality traits and may predispose the individual toward a certain configuration. For example, those prone to emotional dysregulation based on deficiencies in neurotransmitters may develop borderline personality.

Dimensions of temperament can be measured and infants can be rated on their variation. This is considered to be one of the foundations of personality for the neurobiologic models. How temperament expresses itself and its compatibility with parenting style is called goodness of fit. Buss and Plomin propose a three-factor model of temperament that includes activity, emotionality, and sociability. Depue also proposes a three-factor model of underlying neurobehavioral dimensions that include positive emotionality, constraint, and negative emotionality. Cloninger's unified theory of personality includes novelty seeking, harm avoidance, and reward dependence. Siever's dimensional model includes cognitive/perceptual organization, impulsivity/aggression, affective instability, and anxiety/inhibition. These models attempt to link these factors and dimensions to underlying neurobiological structures and neurotransmitter function. The neurobiological effects of trauma on altering personality are well documented. Behavioral geneticists are interested in isolating the underlying genetic mechanisms for certain personality traits, although the way they are expressed, termed phenotype, is influenced by the environment. A moderate degree of variance in personality of approximately 30% may be attributed to genetic factors. The ethical issues are rapidly becoming very complex in the field of psychobiology and will require ethicists to assist in dealing with the advances that are on the horizon with the mapping of the human genome

Suggested Reading and Tapes

Kramer, P. D. (1993). *Listening to Prozac: A psychiatrist explores antidepressant drugs and the remaking of the self.* New York: Viking/Penguin Books.

National Institute of Mental Health. (1995). *The neuroscience of mental health II: A report on neuroscience research: Status and potential for mental health and mental illness.* Rockville, MD: U.S. Department of Health and Human Services.

Sapolsky, R. M. (1998). *Biology and human behavior: The neurological origins of individuality.* Springfield, VA: The Great Courses on Tape, The Teaching Company Limited Partnership. (1-800-832-2412).

Contemporary Psychodynamic Models of Personality

Chapter

Introduction

Contemporary psychodynamic models of personality have evolved significantly since Freud's psychosexual model of personality that was so influential in the early development of psychoanalysis and personality theory. Conceptual developments have substantially broadened the original psychoanalytic model to include conceptions of the **self** and establish the importance of **attachment** as a basic aspect of human development.

Contemporary psychodynamic theory emerged after World War II, or about the second half of the twentieth century. Valuable concepts and theoretical systems that seemed to more fully characterize the modern human condition were advanced. The influence of sociocultural factors seemed to have profound influence on the human experience. The rapidly changing cultural, scientific, and political landscape of the twentieth century seemed to engender a loss of or fragmentation of the self. Psychoanalytic theory, developing out of the cultural influence of Victorian society, no longer seemed to adequately account for what was being witnessed in clinical practice as well as in society. Personality disorders seemed to be more prominent in this ever-changing industrialized context. Cushman (1992) describes this societal influence: "First, the absence of ongoing communal experiences, meaningful traditions, and religious or philosophical certainty is experienced interiorly. Second, in order to avoid economic stagnation or depression, contemporary capitalism had to devise a way to ensure the continual purchase of nonessential and quickly obsolete consumer products. It accomplished this through the economic development of easy credit and the construction of a gnawing emotional hunger within the self that could not be satisfied" (p. 54).

Major Historical Figures

Many of the important contributors to contemporary psychodynamic models of personality were reviewed in Chapter 3. There are many who also contributed to the development of object-relations theory, including Melaine Klein, W. R. D. Fairbairn, Margaret Mahler, and Annie Reich (Buckley, 1986). The object-relations movement was stimulated by attachment theorists who were beginning to emphasize the importance of the relational matrix in both psychotherapy and individual development. Klein may very well be considered the mother of object relations as a result of the pioneering work that she conducted in child therapy. Mahler was also influential in understanding how the processes of symbiosis and individuation are essential aspects of identity development (Mahler, Pine, & Bergman, 1975). **Symbiosis** refers to the mother-infant unit where the child remains undifferentiated; **individuation** is the process by which the infant becomes increasingly separate. Separation that is too rapid causes too much anxiety and thus can lead to a disruption in the normal **separation-individuation phase.**

Object-Relations and Self Psychological Theories

Winnicott: Primacy of Attachment

D. W. Winnicott (1896–1971) is considered to be the father of **object relations.** Winnicott was a pediatrician who was exposed to the work of Melaine Klein and Anna Freud, becoming a student at the Institute of Psycho-Analysis (D. W. Winnicott, 1988). As a child analyst, Winnicott intensively studied children and, later, psychotic patients. He believed he could learn much about the psychology of early infancy by studying these regressed adult patients. Object-relations theory departed from classical structural drive theory, in which aggression was assumed to be part of the instinctual organization of humans. Winnicott viewed aggression as a result of attachment disruption. His theoretical constructs were developed after World War II. "The overriding issues relate to how to live independently without feeling lonely; how to cooperate and give without being used; and how to live with others, receive from them, and rely on them without being engulfed or stunted" (Cushman, 1992, p. 51). "Winnicott's debts to Freud (especially the concepts of the unconscious, early childhood development, and transference) and Klein (the concept of internal objects, primitive infant feelings, and the value of fantasy) are obvious, but what is most striking about Winnicott is his divergence from them both" (p. 50).

Winnicott did not believe that the infant could be viewed outside the context of the maternal-infant dyad. He conceptualized the beginning of the child's life as a mother-baby unit. He was noted to have said "There is no such thing as a baby" and suggested that when you describe a baby you are describing the dyad (Rayner, 1991, p. 60). He believed that the self developed in the context of or relationship between child and parent. He believed that there was a core struggle between intimacy and striving for separation.

D. W. Winnicott understood the multiplicity of factors that determine human development and personality but nevertheless attempted to find the commonalties from multiple perspectives. In the introduction to his work *Human Nature* (1988), he wrote about the multidisciplinary search for the child:

The child's body belongs to the pediatrician.

The soul belongs to the minister of religion.

The psyche belongs to the dynamic psychologist.

The intellect belongs to the psychologist.

The mind belongs to the philosopher.

Psychiatry claims mental disorder.

Heredity belongs to the geneticist.

Ecology claims an interest in the social milieu.

Social science studies the family setting and its relation to society as well as to the child.

Economics examines the strains and stresses due to conflicting needs.

The law steps in to regularize and humanize public revenge on account of antisocial behavior. (p. 7)

As we have reviewed, a comprehensive theory of personality requires a multidisciplinary perspective, and Winnicott was a forerunner in his belief in multiple perspectives. He provided an important contribution to this endeavor with some universally explanatory constructs. D. W. Winnicott (1988) understood the importance of developing an integrative theory: "In the formulation of psychological theory it is only too easy to take integration for granted, but in a study of the early stages of the developing human individual it is necessary to think of integration as an achievement. No doubt there is a biological tendency towards integration, but in psychological studies of human nature it is never satisfactory to lean too heavily on the biological aspect of growth" (p. 116).

The "Good-Enough Mother": One of Winnicott's best-known concepts is the **good-enough mother,** which is a very useful concept in understanding the development of healthy and unhealthy selves. He describes this:

> *This term is used in description of the dependence that belongs to earliest infancy. The implication is that mental health has to be founded in every case by the mother who, in health, has it in her to meet the minute-to-minute needs of her infant. What is needed and absolutely needed by the infant is not some kind of perfection of mothering, but a good enough adaptation, that which is part of a living partnership in which the mother temporarily identifies herself with her infant. To be able to identify herself with her infant to the necessary degree the mother needs to be protected from external reality so that she may enjoy a period of preoccupation, the baby being the object of her preoccupation. To be able to lose this high degree of identification at the rate of the infant's journey from dependence to independence the mother needs to be healthy in the sense of not being liable to morbid preoccupation. (C. Winnicott, Shepherd, & Davis, 1989a, p. 44)*

The concept of the good-enough mother seemed to have a ring of truth to it for many clinicians and theorists. It is not necessary to be a "perfect" parent to have healthy children; it is important to be available at a critical level of parental functioning, although this is not something that can be measured, to fulfill the basic needs of un-complicated developmental progression. What was important was not the precise measurement of what is good enough, but rather the idea that at a certain level of insufficiency, development will be compromised.

The Experience of Emptiness: Winnicott (C. Winnicott et al., 1989a) was able to articulate certain clinical phenomena that were reported by his patients and better understand them using his ideas about object relations. Some patients reported experience of a deep empti-ness. Winnicott understood this as an event, probably before the person developed language, when there was no response from the primary attachment object/figure. "It is easier for a patient to re-member trauma than to remember nothing happening when it might have happened. At the time the patient did not know what might have happened, and so could not experience anything to note that something might have been" (pp. 93–94). What was important in the development of object relations was that it offered a new lens with which to view pre-Oedipal insufficiency that might better account for clinical phenomena than was previously offered. Michael Balint (1968) also drew attention to this problem, which he de-scribed as the **basic fault,** referring to the failure of parent-child at-tunement. This, he believed, led to a chronic sense that there is something wrong or defective about oneself.

Psychoneurosis and Normal Development: Winnicott's conceptions of normal and neurotic aspects in the development of personality are clearly stated in his writings: "The question arises, what is normal-ity? Well—we can say that in health the individual has been able to organise his or her defenses against the intolerable conflicts of the personal psychic reality—but in contrast to the person ill with psycho-neurosis the healthy person is relatively free from massive repression and inhibition of instinct. Also in health the individual can employ all manner of defences, and can shift around from one kind to another, and in fact he or she does not display that rigidity of defence organisation which characterises the ill person" (C. Winni-cott et al., 1989a, p. 71). One can see that Winnicott's boundary be-tween the healthy and the unhealthy individual is delineated by how the defenses are organized. The healthy person does not employ massive repression or denial, as would an unhealthy one. Similar to

The Squiggle Game

Winnicott was a well-respected clinician who developed many innovations in theory and clinical practice. One of these innovations is a common game that children and often adults play. Winnicott termed this the Squiggle Game. He describes this as "one method for making contact with a child patient" (C. Winnicott et al., 1989b, p. 300). He believed it was a nonthreatening way to explore aspects of a child's personality. Winnicott describes this procedure:

"At a suitable moment after the arrival of the patient, usually after asking the parent to go to the waiting room, I say to the child: 'Let's play something. I know what I would like to play and I'll show you.' I have a table between the child and myself, with paper and two pencils. First I take some of the paper and tear the sheets in half, giving the impression that what we are doing is not frantically important, and then I begin to explain. I say: 'This game that I like playing has no rules. I just take my pencil and go like that . . . ,' and I probably screw up my eyes and so squiggle blind. I go on with my explanation and say: 'You show me if that looks like anything to you or if you can make it into anything, and afterwards you do the same for me and I will see if I can make something of yours.'" (C. Winnicott et al., 1989b, pp. 301–302; originally published in 1968)

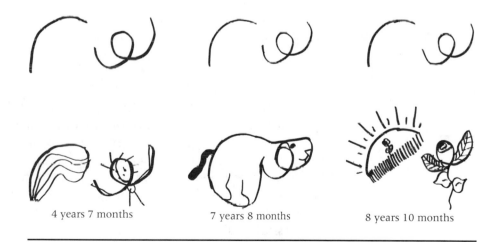

4 years 7 months   7 years 8 months   8 years 10 months

Freud, he believed that the flexibility of one's system of defenses, as opposed to a more rigid defense system, characterizes the healthier individual. The healthy person can tolerate the conflicts inherent in life and maintain contact with the emotional self: "Having said all this I want to suggest that *clinically* the really healthy individual is nearer to depression and to madness than to psycho-neurosis. Psycho-neurosis is boring. It is a relief when an individual is able to be mad and to be serious and to enjoy the relief afforded by a sense of humour, and to be able, so to speak, to flirt with the psychoses. Through modern art we experience the undoing of the processes that constitute sanity and psycho-neurotic defence organisations and the safety-first principle" (p. 71).

Good and Bad Objects: Object-relations theorists use the terms "good" and "bad" objects. My 4-year-old daughter nicely demonstrated these concepts to me as I was writing this section. When I reminded her that she needed to have her teeth brushed and get her pajamas on before bed, she declared, "I hate you." After this mission was completed, in spite of her hateful feelings toward me, I read her a book before bed, at which time she now declared, "I love you." How does one go from being hated to loved in about 15 minutes? Children who have not differentiated and are not autonomous easily make this shift. As an individual develops and begins to integrate both positive and negative aspects of the other, this kind of shift is not so apparent. In some personality disorders, especially borderline, this shift, called splitting, continues into adulthood.

Kohut: Narcissism and the Self

Heinz Kohut (1913–1981) developed a model similar to Winnicott's in some respects, with some important new ways of understanding personality development, especially in a class of disorders of human personality known as **narcissism** (Ornstein, 1978b). According to Millon and Davis (1996a), "Kohut's primary focus was on the development of the self from its infantile state of fragility and fragmentation to that of a stable and cohesive adult structure. Disagreeing with classical analytic views concerning the role of conflicts as central to pathology, Kohut asserted that most disorders stemmed from deficits in the structure of the self" (p. 52). Freud's conceptualization of psychosexual development as being the formative factor in the development of personality was also rejected. Instead, Kohut felt that the drive toward maturation was fueled by an innate potential that he called narcissism. As Winnicott had also discussed, the attachment to the primary caretaker was crucial in this aspect of development.

As with many other psychoanalytic concepts, the concept of narcissism is derived from Greek mythology, as is the story of Oedipus, on which Freud modeled his Oedipal complex. Narcissus was a young man transfixed by his own image, who fell in love with his reflection and died of starvation, staring at his image.

Kohut's formulation, following Freud's early conceptualization, described narcissism as the libidinal investment (in pathological states, too much sexual energy is invested in the form of self-love at the cost of investment in other relationships). The early experience of the child is merged with the mother and is a precursor to the "I-you" differentiation that occurs in normal development but does not occur in pathological forms of narcissism (Kohut, 1986). Kohut believed that **exhibitionism** was the narcissistic manifestation of all drives. In other words, the drives for intimacy and sexual gratification are directed toward the self, instead of toward others, with the primary goal of re-creating the wished-for parental response. Children, normally exhibitionistic, are seeking the approval of the parent. As development proceeds, this normal need is frustrated in increasingly greater doses. Yet, the older child still looks for the "gleam in the mother's eye" (p. 69) to maintain the drive toward mastery and maturational functions. When the healthy narcissistic needs of an individual are chronically thwarted, a narcissistic personality can develop. "If the pressures from the narcissistic self are intense and the ego is unable to control them, the personality will respond with shame to failures of any kind, whether its ambitions concern moral perfection or external success (or, which is frequently the case, alternatingly the one or the other, since the personality possesses neither a firm structure of goals nor of ideals)" (Kohut, 1986, p. 73). Kohut (1971) believed that a healthy individual was autonomous, with good self-esteem and self-confidence. Individuals suffering from narcissism, on the other hand, have fluctuations in self-esteem, often triggered by perceived slights or disapproval. To maintain consistency in their esteem, they need continual external validation. "The interplay between the narcissistic self, the ego, and the superego determines the characteristic flavor of the personality and is thus, more than other building blocks or attributes of the personality, instinctively regarded as the touchstone of a person's individuality or identity" (p. 72).

The Importance of Mirroring: An essential aspect in the development of a healthy **self system** includes a relationship with a **mirroring** figure. Mirroring refers to the process by which the primary attachment figure provides feedback in the form of reflection and affirmation of the positive qualities and experiences that a child demonstrates. All children have a need for affirmation and admiration for achievements and excitement over their experiences, most commonly provided by the maternal figure. The experience of mirroring is key to development. Kohut and Wolf (1986) explain the process:

> *In view of the fact that the disorders of the self are, by and large, the results of miscarriages in the normal development of the self, we shall first present an outline of the normal development of the self. It is difficult to pinpoint the age at which the baby or small child may be said to have acquired a self. To begin with, it seems safe to assume that, strictly speaking, the neonate is still without a self. The new-born infant arrives physiologically pre-adapted for a specific physical environment—the presence of oxygen, of food, of a certain range of temperature—outside of which he cannot survive. Similarly, psychological survival requires a specific psychological environment—the presence of responsive-empathic selfobjects. It is in the matrix of a particular selfobject environment that, via a specific process of psychological structure formation called* transmuting internalization, *the* nuclear self *of the child will crystallize. Without going into the details of this structure-building process, we can say (1) that it cannot occur without a previous stage in which the child's mirroring and idealizing needs had been sufficiently responded to; (2) that it takes place in consequence of the minor, non-traumatic failures in the responses of the mirroring and the idealized selfobjects; and (3) that these failures lead to the gradual replacement of the selfobjects and their functions by a self and its functions."* (p. 181)

Kohut is emphasizing the central importance in healthy personality development of a responsive attachment figure that can provide emotional attunement. This type of emotional responsiveness on the part of the parent may in fact be necessary for the development of healthy brain functions. There is mounting evidence to suggest that the biology of humiliation may be toxic to the brain and actually influence brain structure and function (Siegel, 1999). We will return to this theme and explore current speculations of interpersonal theory in Chapter 9.

Transmuting Internalization: "The concept of transmuting internalization is thus crucial to Kohut's theory and treatment of narcissistic personality disorders" (Ornstein, 1978a, p. 64). Transmuting internalization is a key aspect in the formation of psychic structures. The main elements of this process are: (1) The psychic structure is receptive to absorb introjects; (2) due to frustration, these internalized objects are broken up as part of the energy is withdrawn, which is similar to mourning; and (3) the introject is slowly depersonalized so that it does not provide a total identification figure. This represents a gradual developmental process wherein the adult caretaker is absorbed and metabolized bit by bit until an internal psychic structure is formed. Thus, the gradual absorbing of the introjects provides

---

Ancient Spiritual Perspective on the Danger of Narcissism

It is interesting to compare Kohut's ideas to other perspectives, in this case, a spiritual one. In the book *The Four Agreements,* Don Miguel Ruiz (1997), a Toltec *nagual* (ancient Mexican spiritual healer), shares the traditions of this ancestral wisdom. Among other things, he discusses the importance of not taking things personally to attain personal happiness. He writes: "Personal importance, or taking things personally, is the maximum expression of selfishness because we make the assumption everything is about 'me' . . . Me, me, me, always me" (p. 48). This requires one to be thick-skinned; the individual with severe narcissism has been described as "thin-skinned." We all have had the experience of waiting in a crowed checkout line when a new cashier is being introduced to the register. Many of us have also witnessed the extreme reaction that one person in the line occasionally has to this event; the individual may become agitated and begin making hostile comments. Kohut would describe this as an example of narcissistic rage. Ruiz would say that the individual has not mastered the ability not to take things personally, believing that even such random "slights" are about himself or herself.

---

the matrix for the development of the psychic structures. If this seems difficult to grasp, you're not alone: one of the criticisms leveled at Kohut was his esoteric use of language. What seems essential to me is that a child will gradually take in the features of a parent. At first, the entire parental matrix will be taken in either as "good" or "bad," and then slowly, over time, the good and bad parts will be integrated into a coherent picture of the parent. In this process, the child develops his or her internal structure, such as the ability to regulate affect when good parts are withdrawn and maintain consistent self-esteem.

Core Affects: Shame and Rage: Kohut's formulation of narcissism emphasized the matrix of shame and rage that are manifestations of disequilibrium of the intrapsychic system. These two affects are key components to understanding narcissism. **Shame** arises when the parental figures—selfobjects—do not provide the needed mirroring, admiration, and approval of the emergent self of the child. Mirroring, as we have discussed, is the ability to respond to the affective state of another person; in this way, the minds of the two individuals are connected. It is the way that we learn emotional differentiation, which fuels positive attachments. The child desires the **idealized parental image** to sustain himself or herself. Evident in therapeutic and other significant relationships, adults may attempt to re-create this matrix by idealizing other important attachment figures. Some of this, as we shall see, is an important part of identification, but if overly used, is often a sign of narcissism. The child is filled with what Kohut termed "boundless exhibitionism," which is manifested in the **grandiose self.** If there is a lack of response from the parent, an effort to inhibit the exhibitionistic urge will occur (Ornstein, 1978b); this leads to blushing, which is a painful expression of the shame as opposed to the warm glow that occurs in reaction to admiration and acceptance. Thus, shame is the binding up of the unadmired exhibitionistic impulses and the repression of this desire of the grandiose self.

Rage, the other core affect in narcissism, is a reaction to the range of narcissistic injuries. In childhood, the lack of phase-appropriate response by the parent results in a deflation of the grandiose self. When this type of injury is reoccurring, the frustration may result in a fixation. The self-esteem is chronically unstable. This fixation can last into adulthood, where what was an age- and phase-appropriate response—frustration and anger to injury—is no longer phase appropriate. Kohut refers to this as narcissistic rage and likens it to the fight component of the flight-or-fight response.

Narcissistic Rage: Kohut writes: "In its undistinguished form, narcissistic rage is a familiar experience which is in general easily identified by the empathic observer of human behavior" (quoted in Ornstein, 1978b, p. 636). For example, in one case from clinical practice, a narcissistic male, when his wife did not serve dinner precisely at 5:30, responded with rage, during which he threw his plate of food on the floor and later expected her to clean up. He was incensed by his wife's failure to provide for him in the way he demanded, experiencing it as a major injury that she was late. Kohut writes: "Strictly speaking, the term narcissistic rage refers to only one specific band in the wide spectrum of experiences that reaches from such trivial occurrences as a fleeting annoyance when someone fails to reciprocate our greeting or does not respond to our joke to such ominous derangements as the furor of the catatonic and the grudges of the paranoiac" (quoted in Ornstein, 1978b, p. 636). If the narcissistic rage does not subside, it can turn into **chronic narcissistic rage,** whereby the individual increasingly tries to establish control over the perceived injurious external world.

The Empty Self in Modern Society

Winnicott's and Kohut's theoretical formulations have broader implications than personality theory and psychotherapy. They also are useful in explaining some of the societal trends that occurred in the twentieth century: "Both Winnicott's and Kohut's theories describe a self that is bounded, masterful, subjective—a continuation of the late modern and post-World War II self in the West" (Cushman, 1992, p. 52). Cushman describes how this conception of human personality differs from the Freudian in that the internal psychic space is not so much filled with drives and conflict but is a hidden or empty self. He makes the case that this notion of the self was influenced by the postwar portrait of middle-class Americans as suffering from empty selves that need to be filled up with commodities: "Several prominent psychiatric symptoms today feature an empty self that yearns to be filled up: overeating, addictions, interpersonal loneliness, compulsive shopping" (p. 53). The emphasis on consumerism in our society seems to imply that if one purchases and consumes products there will be a transformation of the self. "Commodities, then, have become the transformational object of our time, and consuming has become the ultimate transformational process" (p. 53).

Erikson: Identity Development

Erik Erikson (1902–1994) was an educator, intellectual, and clinician who had vast influence on both theoretical and practical developments in contemporary psychoanalysis (Erik Erikson, 1970). Erikson was analyzed and mentored by Anna Freud, who greatly influenced his decision to become a lay analyst. Although he never received a doctoral degree in either medicine or psychology, he made a major contribution to psychoanalysis in 1950 with the publication of his first landmark book, *Childhood and Society.*

Erikson believed that cultural forces were a vital aspect of an individual's growth and development. He postulated the **epigenetic principle,** by which the individual progresses through eight stages of development, each needing to be mastered before proceeding to the next. He viewed personality development and formation as taking a lifetime and each stage as offering a different set of challenges to master. The human personality moving through these stages reconfigures itself with aspects of positive and negative identities. The stages of life as Erikson (1959) outlined them and the corresponding Freudian psychosexual stages of development are depicted in Table 6.1.

Success at one stage of development and the manner in which the life crises are resolved will necessarily affect the following stages. The number of positive versus negative outcomes will determine the long-term impact of experiences. In each stage are embedded developmental challenges, such as separating from parents, establishing a career path, leaving home, and selecting a mate, that will set the stage for others to come.

Erikson's schema seemed to fit most individuals' sense of their developmental challenges. This was widely accepted as a major advancement in understanding personality development beyond the psychosexual aspects that Freud depicted earlier in the twentieth

Table 6.1   **Erikson's Eight Stages of Personality Development and the Corresponding Freudian Psychosexual Stages**

	Erikson	**Freud**
Infancy	Trust versus Mistrust	Oral stage
	Autonomy versus Shame and doubt	Anal stage
Childhood	Initiative versus Guilt	Phallic stage
	Industry versus Inferiority	Latency stage
Adolescence stage	Identity versus Confusion	Early genital
Adulthood	Intimacy versus Isolation	Later genital stage
	Generativity versus Stagnation	
	Ego integrity versus Despair	

century. Erikson's work had a much more contemporary feel for the post-World War II Western mind, seemingly depicting the ongoing developmental struggles faced at various stages in one's life.

The Significance of Identity and Identity Crisis: Erikson (1968) attempted to clarify the meaning of the concept of identity. He broke with the deterministic thinking of Freud, who thought that personality takes final shape during infancy. He was very interested in the role of culture in the shaping of identity, as well as in the role of identity crises in the shaping of personality. He believed that the identity crisis often seen in individuals in their late teens and early twenties were formative experiences. Erikson also had a special interest in the way identity crises shaped the personality development of great and infamous men such as Gandhi, George Bernard Shaw, Adolph Hitler, and Martin Luther (1958, 1970); he was interested in understanding how these men's identities meshed with cultural forces to produce radical turning points for humankind (*Newsweek,* 1970). He believed that identity is characterized by a "self-sameness and continuity to the ego's synthesizing methods" (p. 50). He also included the *"style of one's individuality,* and that this style coincides with the sameness and continuity of one's *meaning for significant others* in the immediate community" (p. 50).

Fame and Identity—A Daughter's Perspective

Erik Erikson attained the status of a cult figure to many people who admired his work. In an article in *The Atlantic Monthly* (Erikson Bloland, 1999) titled "Fame: The Power and Cost of a Fantasy," Erikson's daughter discusses the impact that her father's celebrity status had on her and members of the family. She talks about her father's emotional underdevelopment and his fame, and the difficulty she had reconciling the two: "How was I to reconcile my experience of that emotionally fragile man (who understood so little about his public feelings or mine and was terrified by both) with the public image of the intellectual pioneer who had challenged the authority of the great Sigmund Freud, daring to revise some of Freud's basic assumptions about human nature?" (p. 54). She goes on to explore the relationship between the private and public self, utilizing some of the conceptualizations of self we have discussed: "In the relationship between the public image of a famous person and the private human being there is *inherently* something profoundly paradoxical. The public image is the reverse of the private person as experienced by him or her self and by intimate others. It might be accurate to say that the public image reflects what the private person most longs to be. It represents the ideal self" (p. 54). Those interested in further understanding the life of Erikson should read *Identity's Architect: A Biography of Erik H. Erikson* by Lawrence J. Friedman.

Hartmann: Ego Psychology

Heinz Hartmann (1913–1981) elaborated another important contemporary development in the psychodynamic understanding of personality: ego psychology (1958, 1964). Hartmann attributed greater significance to the ego and its role in adaptation than Freud had originally posited. Remember that the ego is the intrapsychic agency that mediates between the instinctual forces of the id and the value system and conscience of the superego. He was concerned with presenting a conceptualization that would describe not only pathology but healthy personality functioning as well. This was one of the earliest calls for a psychology of healthy functioning as opposed to neurotic adjustment. Previously, it was thought that the main criterion of health was freedom from symptoms. Hartmann (1964) described problems with the conceptions of health and illness at the time:

> The objections which I felt obliged to raise against the definitions of mental health and illness last mentioned (in connection with the problems of defense, regression, etc.) may be summarized as follows: these conceptions of health approach the problem too exclusively from the angle of the neurosis, or rather they are formulated in terms of contrast with the neuroses. Mechanisms, developmental stages, modes of reaction, with which we have become familiar for the part they play in the development of the neurosis, are automatically relegated to the realm of the pathological—health is characterized as a condition in which these elements are absent. But the contrast thus established with the neuroses can have no meaning so long as we fail to appreciate how much of these mechanisms, developmental stages, and modes of reaction is active in healthy individuals or in the development of those who later become so, i.e., so long as an analytic "normal psychology" is still very largely nonexistent. (pp. 13–14)

Modes of Normal Functioning: Hartmann made an effort to outline a normal psychology, with emphasis on the problems of adaptation. The ego was seen as the portion of the intrapsychic system that was concerned with self-preservation. Hartmann (1958) wrote: "I want to stress that it is the functions of the ego, developed by learning and maturation—the ego's aspect of regulating the relations with the environment and its organizing capacity in finding solutions, fitting the environmental situation and the psychic systems at the same time— which become of primary importance for self-preservation in man" (p. 84).

Ego Adaptive Capacity: Hartmann (1958) wrote: "Generally speaking, we call a man well adapted if his productivity, his ability to enjoy life, and his mental equilibrium are undisturbed" (p. 23). He viewed adaptation as "primarily a reciprocal relationship between the organism and environment" (p. 24). But this was not specific enough, and Hartmann sought to elaborate the various aspects of **ego functions.** Ego psychology provided a description of the various aspects of healthy functioning, termed **ego adaptive capacity.** Ego functions are essentially what we would describe as coping mechanisms and capacities in various areas. Someone with good ego functions or high ego adaptive capacity is able to maintain a balance between demands of the outer world and inner impulses. Good ego functions include the capacity to tolerate frustration, disappointment, and other forms of stress; defenses are not excessively used and there is a high capacity to tolerate anxiety without calling on defenses.

Kernberg: Object-Relations Theory

Otto Kernberg (1928–) is considered by many to be one of the most prolific contemporary psychodynamic theorists whose work has shed substantial light on understanding personality. Kernberg has always been interested in viewing personality from the perspective of severe personality disorders, which he has spent much of his professional career treating and for which he has refined systems of intervention.

Controversy over Systems of Classification: Kernberg believes that there are major problems with research and theoretical formulations based on the traditional classification of personality using the traditional **dimensional** or newer **categorical** models for personality disorders. He believes that both have inherent problems. O. F. Kernberg (1996, p. 107) writes of the Five-Factor Model: "To develop factorial profiles for each personality disorder on the basis of those five factors has an eerie quality of unreality for the experienced clinician" (p. 107). Although he believes the categorical model has been somewhat useful in that it has better acquainted mental health professionals with personality disorders, he is also critical of this system: "This approach has been plagued . . . by the high degree of comorbidity of the severe types of personality disorders, and by the unfortunate politicization of decision making, by committee, of what personality disorders to include and exclude in the official *DSM* system and under what labels" (p. 108). Kernberg instead espouses a theoretical system based on the psychoanalytic model. In his system, disordered personality is arranged on a continuum from psychotic, to borderline, to neurotic

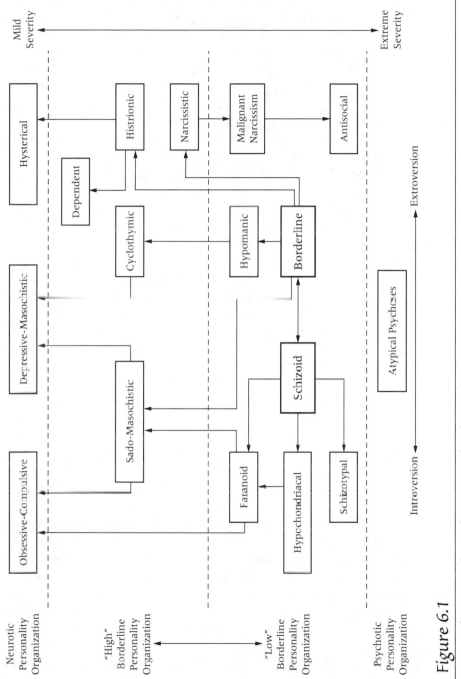

Figure 6.1

Personality Disorders: Their Mutual Relationships. *Major Theories of Personality Disorder* by J. F. Clarkin and M. F. Lenzenweger, © 1996. Reprinted by permission of The Guilford Press.

(see Figure 6.1). His classification system combines these categorical and dimensional structural categories and developmental concepts of the object-relations school but clearly grounds them on a solid theoretical foundation. Kernberg does offer his readers a caveat: "It is far from my intention to suggest that a psychoanalytic exploration will resolve existing problems. I cannot, at this point, present a satisfactory, integrated psychoanalytic model of classification of personality disorders" (p. 108).

O. F. Kernberg (1996) characterizes **psychotic personality organization** "by lack of integration of the concept of self and significant others, that is, identity diffusion, a predominance of primitive defensive operations centering around splitting and loss of reality testing" (p. 118). He also emphasizes the importance of various defenses that are incorporated by the individual and organized at the psychotic level. These include "projective identification, denial, primitive idealization, omnipotence, omnipotent control, [and] devaluation" (p. 118). There is a concomitant loss of reality testing: "Reality testing refers to the capacity to differentiate self from nonself, intrapsychic from external stimuli, and to maintain empathy with ordinary social criteria of reality, all of which are typically lost in the psychoses and manifested particularly in hallucinations and delusions" (p. 120).

Borderline personality organization "is also characterized by identity diffusion and the same predominance of primitive defensive operations centering on splitting, but distinguished by the presence of good reality testing, reflecting the differentiation between self and object representations in the idealized and persecutory sector, characteristic of the separation-individuation phase" (O. F. Kernberg, 1996, p. 120). In severe cases, there is ego weakness that makes anxiety tolerance and impulse control very low. This makes it difficult to persist in work and long-term commitments. Consistency and creativity are impaired due to this lack of tolerance for anxiety, which seeks discharge almost immediately in action, called acting-out.

Neurotic personality organization "is characterized by normal ego identity and the related capacity for object relations in depth, ego strength reflected in anxiety tolerance, impulse control, sublimatory functioning, effectiveness and creativity in work, a capacity for sexual love and emotional intimacy disrupted only by unconscious guilt feelings reflected in specific pathological patterns of interaction in relation to sexual intimacy" (O. F. Kernberg, 1996, p. 121).

The Importance of Temperament and Character: O. F. Kernberg's (1996) system attempts to delineate the essential building blocks of personality using many of the concepts that we have previously reviewed. Kernberg is a very thoughtful and scholarly worker who bases much of this material on a solid knowledge of theoretical advancements, as well as his substantial experience in clinical practice. Even though his works are challenging even for the advanced reader, they are well formulated and worth the effort to understand. Kernberg does not artificially attempt to simplify what he views as very complex phenomena. He writes:

> *To begin, I shall refer to temperament and character as crucial aspects of personality. Temperament refers to the constitutionally given and largely genetically determined, inborn disposition to particular reactions to environmental stimuli, particularly to the intensity, rhythm, and thresholds of affective responses. I consider affective responses, particularly under conditions of peak affect states, crucial determinants of the organization of the personality. Inborn thresholds regarding the activation of both positive, pleasurable, rewarding, and negative, painful, aggressive affects represent, I believe, the most important bridge between biological and psychological determinants of the personality (Kernberg, 1994). Temperament also includes inborn dispositions to cognitive organization and to motor behavior, such as, for example, the hormonal-, particularly testosterone-derived differences in cognitive functions and aspects of gender role identity that differentiate male and female behavior patterns. Regarding the etiology of personality disorders, however, the affective aspects of temperament appear as of fundamental importance. (pp. 109–110)*

Character, another important element of personality, refers to ego identity, including how the self-concept and conception of significant others are integrated. For example, a person may see himself as "wronged" by others and believe that other people are to be used in whatever manner is required to get what he needs. This type of character, termed antisocial, is noted for a lack of conscience or reduced capacity to experience guilt when harming others. Character, therefore, includes ego functions and structures such as the ability to regulate affect, defense functioning, and level of object relatedness.

From O. F. Kernberg's (1996) point of view, personality is "codetermined by temperament and character, but also by an additional intrapsychic structure, the superego" (p. 110). This is how the value system is integrated into one's personality. Thus, the internalized value system of the previously described individual does not include not harming others, but values taking what he needs when he needs it regardless of the harm.

Conception of Normal Personality Functioning: Kernberg describes normal personality functioning as having several essential features. First, there is an integrated sense and conception of the self and significant others. This requires a balance between mature dependency and autonomy. The normal individual is capable of empathy for others, as well as a capacity for emotional investment. This stable sense of self ensures that one's long-range goals and desires can be met because interests and drive work in the same direction to provide motivation and gratification in activities and relationships. Ego strength is sufficient to allow the individual to tolerate the vicissitudes of life and still function effectively, without quitting when the going gets tough or losing sight of the goal. A mature superego is also necessary, allowing for a stable value system, which includes a sense of responsibility, flexible, ethical decision making, and a commitment to certain values and standards of behavior. Last, there is a full capacity to experience sexual and sensual needs in a committed relationship, characterized by tenderness and emotional involvement with one's partner.

Kernberg's Treatment Model for Severe Personality Disorders: Kernberg is well known for his willingness to tackle the most challenging cases of personality disorders, about which he has written extensively (O. F. Kernberg, 1976, 1984; O. F. Kernberg, Selzer, Koenigsberg, Carr, & Appelbaum, 1989). He has developed an approach to treating borderline patients that emphasizes the transference relationship that develops between patient and therapist. He believes that the major therapeutic action occurs in the analysis of this transference relationship. This is an intensive form of treatment that requires much advanced training and supervision. He describes the objective of his treatment approach as "the diagnosis and psychotherapeutic resolution of the syndrome of identity diffusion, and, in the process, resolution of (1) primitive defensive operations characteristic of these patients and (2) transformation of their primitive internalized 'part-object' relationships into 'total' object relationships characteristic of more advanced, neurotic and normal functioning individuals" (O. F. Kernberg, 1996, p. 133).

Kernberg's approach requires the therapist to remain **technically neutral,** which, like classic psychoanalysis, requires the therapist to withhold support, guidance, advice giving, and direct intervention in the environment, with the exception of limit setting that is necessary to preserve the treatment frame. This approach is not for the fainthearted. He describes some of the clinical challenges that the therapist must contend with that result from the tendency to act out conflict and discharge anxiety: "Given the strong tendencies toward acting out on the part of the borderline patients, dangerous complications in their treatment may derive from their characterological based 'nondepressive' suicidal attempts, drug abuse, self-mutilation and other self-destructive behaviors, and aggressive behaviors that may be life threatening to themselves or others" (1996, p. 136).

More recently, Clarkin, Yeomans, and Kernberg (1999) published Kernberg's work in the form of a treatment manual that details the issues and technical interventions in his evolving approach to borderline pathology.

Multiperspective Theory of Personality

A number of current personality and clinical theorists have been influenced by the **integrative movement** (Norcross & Goldfried, 1992) in the field of psychotherapy and emphasize using multiple theoretical lenses through which to examine personality and the process of psychotherapeutic intervention aimed at personality modification. Pine (1990) proposed that the main branches of psychoanalytic development during the twentieth century are all vital in understanding clinical phenomena. Pine presented a synthesis of drive, ego, object, and self psychological models, emphasizing the way each perspective provides a valid view of the different types of pathology seen in clinical practice.

Short-Term Dynamic Models of Treatment for Character and Personality Disorders

Another important trend in contemporary psychodynamic theory and treatment that evolved in waves over the past century is short-term dynamic therapy or brief dynamic therapy (Magnavita, 1993a). Although the validity of psychoanalytic constructs was challenged many times, they remained vital to clinical practice for most clinicians (Magnavita, 1993b). Short-term dynamic workers of many generations began to challenge the dogma that personality change took years or decades (Magnavita, 2000c). Beginning with Ferenczi (Ferenczi & Rank, 1925), who is considered the father of the movement, various pioneers have experimented with the methods and techniques of this approach, directly applying this to the treatment of personality disturbance (F. G. Alexander & French, 1946; Davanloo, 1978, 1980; Malan, 1963, 1976, 1979). Contemporary workers have expanded the theoretical domain, integrating other models of treatment for personality change (Fosha, 2000; Horner, 1994; Horowitz et al., 1984; Magnavita, 1997; McCullough Vaillant, 1997). This movement has enabled clinical theorists to investigate within a circumscribed period (usually between 20 and 80 sessions) the transformation of personality. Numerous case reports have been published demonstrating some of the techniques and methods as well as outcomes of this intensive approach.

In addition to the publication of cases highlighting personality change, another critical component of this movement is to use audiovisual technology to record therapy sessions. Although considered an intrusion into the therapeutic process by traditional analysts (some long-term analytic treatments were recorded for research, but as a rule this practice was eschewed), the use of audiovisual technology was likened to the discovery of the microscope in biology (Sifneos, 1990). Never before had the technology been available to study the therapeutic process in depth and with low-cost equipment. This enabled researchers, clinicians, and theorists to study the process and to do microanalysis of the factors that seem to be responsible for change, providing a convergence in theory, technique, and research. As opposed to classic psychoanalysis, which lasts for many years and has proved enormously difficult to study, brief psychodynamic treatment offers an encapsulated period of change and growth more accessible to clinical and empirical study.

Contemporary Psychodynamic Model of Integrative Theory

Malan's Theoretical Advance

Essential constructs to simplify our understanding of personality and the contemporary psychodynamic model of treatment were brought together by a pioneering worker in Britain, David Malan (1979, p. 80), and used by Habib Davanloo (1980) in Montreal. These two constructs, developed by separate theorists, have the advantage of being visually depicted as triangles. The first of these two triangles was depicted by Menninger (1958). The **triangle of insight** demonstrated how the relationships of the past, current relationships, and the therapeutic relationship parallel one another in terms of core relational themes. Malan renamed this more appropriately the **triangle of persons.** The second triangle in this schematic representation was borrowed from Ezriel (1952) and termed the **triangle of conflict.** This triangle depicts the intrapsychic interplay among underlying emotions, anxiety, and defensive operations that serve to contain affects and modulate the derivative anxiety (see Figure 6.2). Malan's (1979) genius was to bring these two constructs together, applying them to clinical treatment called short-term dynamic psychotherapy (STDP). These constructs allow for a parsimonious explanation of the complex interplay that occurs in the intrapsychic and interpersonal matrix (Magnavita, 1997; McCullough Vaillant, 1997).

Triangle of Conflict: The Intrapsychic Matrix

One can understand visually the way these two constructs operate. The triangle of conflict represents the intrapsychic functions or the affective and defensive system described by Freud and others that, you will recall, is termed structural-drive theory. This configuration of **feelings** in the lower corner, **anxiety** in the upper right corner, and **defense** in the left corner are in constant motion within all of us. An individual who has experienced an episode of painful emotional arousal will tend to reexperience this emotion in

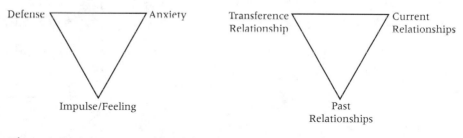

Figure 6.2

Triangle of Conflict and Triangle of Persons.

similar situations. For example, someone who has experienced traumatic treatment, such as physical or sexual abuse, would naturally have a complex of reactive emotions such as anger, fear, shame, and sadness when confronted with stimuli that are reminiscent of the abuse. As this complex of feeling threatens to surface into conscious awareness in a painful and possibly disorganizing manner, anxiety is triggered to signal the intrapsychic system to call forth defense to protect the integrity of the system. "Defenses (typically) not only keep thoughts, images, and instinctual drives our of consciousness, but they also prevent their assimilation by means of thinking. When defenses break down, the mental elements defended against and certain connections of these elements become amenable to recollection and reconstruction" (Hartmann, 1958, p. 63). Thus, if the system is working, the conscious experience can be controlled and feelings kept at bay (see Figure 6.3).

Referring back to the defenses in Chapter 3 and in Figure 6.3, we can place the array of defenses in the upper left corner of the triangle. In this way, we can begin to illustrate both the individuality in

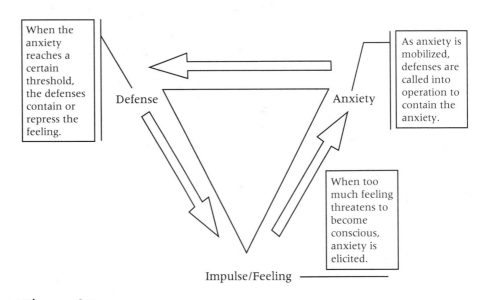

Figure 6.3

The Depiction of the Intrapsychic Forces That Regulate the Emotional System.

personality and some of the personality types that various authors and researchers have documented. The array of defenses allows for infinite variation, accounting for individual differences. We can also look at types of personality when we look at certain constellations or clusters of defenses (Magnavita, 1997). For example, individuals described as having obsessive personality traits or, if extreme, an obsessive-compulsive personality will generally utilize a certain array of defenses such as intellectualization, isolation of affect, rumination, repression, compulsiveness, and others identified with this type of personality. However, there will be great variation in the blend of defenses different individuals' utilize, which can account for differences at a micro level of analysis, but at the macro level, the similarities will make overall traits recognizable.

Defense Categorization

Cramer (1998a), a researcher in the area of defenses, offered a contemporary working definition of defense: "The term 'defense mechanism' refers to a mental operation that occurs outside of awareness. The function of the defense mechanism is to protect the individual from experiencing excessive anxiety. According to the older, classical psychoanalytic theory, such anxiety would occur if the individual became aware of unacceptable thoughts, impulses, or wishes. In contemporary thinking about defenses, an additional function is seen to be the protection of the self—or self-esteem and, in more extreme cases, protection of the self" (p. 885). This definition effectively and concisely combines the important elements of both classical and contemporary psychodynamic thinking. Anxiety is seen as generating from both internal conflict between psychic agencies and preservation of self functions and object relatedness. Using this definition, we can explore the defenses from the models presented.

Primary Defense Categories: Various authors have placed the defense mechanisms into categories (Meissner, 1981; Perry, 1992; Vaillant, 1992). Doing so gives us another way to understand and measure the variability in personality. Most authors place defenses along a continuum, from psychotic, to immature, to neurotic, to mature (see Table 6.2). These categories of defenses are not precisely defined and categorized, and there is some overlap among them. However, the general schema does have some empirical validation

Table 6.2   **Categories of Defenses**

Psychotic defenses: delusional projection, severe denial, distortion (cognitive/perceptual)

Immature defenses: projection, schizoid fantasy, hypochondriasis, passive-aggression, acting-out, dissociation, blocking, introjection, regression, externalization, splitting, projective identification, devaluation, idealization, omnipotence, withdrawal, explosiveness of affect, weepiness, depression

---

Neurotic defenses: repression, displacement, reaction formation, intellectualization, somatization, controlling, isolation of affect, rationalization, sexualization, undoing, detachment, avoidance, compartmentalization, complaining

---

Mature defenses: altruism, humor, suppression, anticipation, sublimation

---

(Vaillant, 1992). Table 6.2 represents a compilation of defenses from various sources (Magnavita, 1997).

Ancillary/Tactical Defense Categories: Another category of defenses that was elaborated by Davanloo (1980) is **tactical defenses.** These might be considered "microdefenses" in that they are epiphenomena as opposed to major defenses (Magnavita, 1997). Magnavita further elaborated these and terms them **ancillary defenses,** which seems like a more fitting name in that these tend not to be cornerstone defenses an individual uses, but minor defenses that most of us use at least some of the time. Davanloo (1980), however, deserves credit for their identification and use in clinical practice. These are presented in Table 6.3.

Defense Constellation Recognition: All humans incorporate a variety of defenses in everyday life to function effectively. It is clear that defenses allow us to function without unnecessary loss of overall coping. For example, if we were not able to incorporate some level of healthy denial, how many of us would daily subject ourselves to the experience of speeding in an automobile at 55 or more miles per hour with only a few feet separating us from the oncoming traffic in the opposite lane? We need defenses to live effectively, but they need to be calibrated to the situation or else they can

Table 6.3 **Categories of Ancillary Defenses Developed by Habib Davanloo (1980) and Recategorized by Magnavita (1997)**

Interpersonal category defenses: smiling, sarcasm, argumentativeness, negativity, compliance, submission, blaming, poor eye contact, criticizing, defiance, stubbornness, seductiveness, complaining, provocation, teasing, distancing

Cognitive category defenses: rumination, tentativeness, vagueness, retraction, generalization, ambivalence, equivocation

Anxiety-siphoning: gum chewing, cursing, fidgetiness, pacing, smoking, eating/drinking, rocking

become a liability. Each of us has a specific constellation of defenses and no two of us are alike. This is like our personal psychological fingerprint. That is not to imply that our defenses are fixed; in fact, for most of us, they shift under various circumstances. We all have had the experience of being under prolonged stress and noticed that our defenses became more primitive. We might, for example, begin to feel aches or pains that we usually don't have, or have a tension headache or backache (somaticizing our feelings); we might more easily lose our temper and explode (explosive discharge of affect). As the stress is reduced, our defenses might then regain their hold at a more mature level of operation.

Defense Constellation Properties: Generally speaking, when doing a defense constellation analysis, we can observe or measure the defensive operation and how it shifts under stress. The general rule is that the fewer defenses individuals use, the more they will be coping overall at a lower level of effectiveness; conversely, those with a wider array of defenses are often more flexible in their pattern of adaptation. Another feature of defenses analysis is that the more primitive the defenses in the constellation, the more difficulty individuals will have in functioning.

Evidence of Empirical Validation of Defenses: Although clearly relevant to many practicing clinicians, researchers have not always shared the same affinity for the concept of defense, nor have they held this subject in the same high regard. However, there has been somewhat of a resurgence in the empirical study and validation of these mechanisms. In an introduction to the *Journal of Personality*'s special issue on the topic of defenses, Cramer (1998a) suggests that this topic was overlooked in personality research due to an "aversion to psychoanalysis and its concepts and a mistaken belief that defenses only belong to the realm of psychopathology" (p. 880). George Vaillant from Harvard and Phebe Cramer from Williams College have been influential in stimulating empirical investigation into this topic. Vaillant conducted longitudinal studies and Cramer numerous empirical studies on defenses. Vaillant (1977) proposed that defenses exist in a hierarchy, as we have discussed. In one study of 42 children, using Thematic Apperception Test (TAT) stories, Cramer (1987) demonstrated that there is validity to this hierarchical organization. Her findings suggested that the youngest group of subjects most often used denial, and that identification, considered the most mature defense, was used by the oldest subjects; projection, an intermediate defense, was used most often by the middle group. In a subsequent study, Cramer and Gaul (1988) studied 64 children from the second and sixth grades. The subjects who experienced failure used more primitive defenses (denial and projection) as opposed to those who experienced success, who relied on higher-level defense (identification). The investigators used this evidence to support the hypothesis "that the use of mature defenses is related to favorable life experiences, while the use of immature defenses is related to unfavorable experiences" (p. 739). The developmental continuum hypothesis of defenses was again supported using a group of 90 hospitalized men and women ranging from 18 to 29 years of age (Cramer, Blatt, & Ford, 1988). The idea that increased anxiety would enhance defensive responding was also supported (Cramer, 1991). Students who had their feelings experimentally manipulated to arouse anger made the greatest use of defenses.

In a series of other studies, Cramer (1995, 1997, 1998b) investigated the relationship among narcissism, identity development, and defensive functioning. Consistent with the theoretical tenets of defense mechanisms, "the results showed the expected pattern for late adolescents of greater use of the age-appropriate defenses of Projection and Identification and less use of Denial" (1998b, p. 169).

Anxiety: A Ubiquitous Aspect of Human Existence

We are still concerned with understanding the triangle of conflict, but will now diverge from the defense corner of the triangle and move to the anxiety corner. As you recall, in this theory anxiety comes from affect that is not experienced fully and that emanates from the feelings that result from conflict areas. What is anxiety? As we have reviewed in previous chapters, anxiety as a subject has taken up many volumes. For our purposes, it is important to understand the basic construct of anxiety and its function in this theoretical system.

Anxiety, something that we all experience, is a necessary aspect of our adaptation to our surroundings. Anxiety is thought to be a neurobiologically wired affect that alerts and orients an individual to what needs to be attended to in the environment. Too much anxiety and we can be flooded and paralyzed, like a deer caught in headlights. Too little anxiety and the motivational system is not lubricated enough to accomplish what we need to. Anxiety regulation (McCullough Vaillant, 1997) is considered to be an **ego function;** those who cannot tolerate anxiety are lower and those with higher tolerance are higher on the scale of ego adaptive capacity. For our purposes, we will anchor anxiety to physiology as the subjective sense of distress that can include autonomic arousal such as increased heart rate, palpitations, sweating, need to urinate, sweaty palms, dry mouth, tension in muscles, nausea, tightness in the chest, and restlessness. Most of us can recognize when we are in an increased state of anxiety and are familiar with our own constellation of physiological experiences. Imagine being asked to stand up in front of your class to give an extemporaneous talk; this fear of public speaking is the most common phobia that creates instant dread and concomitant anxiety in most people.

Feelings: Our Interpersonal Survival System

Finally, if we move to the lower corner of the triangle of conflict, we explore the nature of impulses and feeling. Referring to Chapter 4, you will recall that researchers in affective science have identified six probable basic emotions (**anger, fear, sadness, disgust, happiness/joy,** and **surprise**) and three secondary or social emotions (**guilt, shame,** and **pride**). Also, as we have reviewed, neuroscientific findings have supported the observation that feelings can exist at the unconscious level. Feelings orient us to what needs to be attended to in our life and give meaning and importance to various activities necessary for survival and growth. In this sense, they are our personal navigational system. When individuals are out of contact with their feelings, we often experience them as emotionally flat or wooden. Think of Mr. Spock in *Star Trek;* he could only process his experience at an intellectual level and often missed much of what transpired in his social interactions.

The Importance of Emotional Development

Emotional development begins with early attachment experience and proceeds throughout the stages of development. Individuals who do not experience good-enough mothering or have disturbed attachments will not enjoy the full emotional development necessary for healthy maturity. Humans learn about emotions through their experiences with primary attachment figures. Recall the example of the children from the Romanian orphanages; many of these children, without sufficient emotional stimulation that occurs in positive attachments, became extremely stunted in their personality development. Traumatic experiences, losses, and developmental insults may compromise the integrity of individuals' emotional system. Too much emotional stimulation may overwhelm a child's emotional system and not enough stimulation may create a failure-to-thrive syndrome. Healthier individuals tend to have a greater level of emotional differentiation and experience. They are able to fully experience the range of human emotions, label them appropriately, and express them to others when indicated. Thus, the affective system and how it is managed by defenses is an important component system of personality.

All of us can be placed on an emotional continuum with regard to how well our emotional system functions; this is evident even to the untrained individual. We might describe certain people as being emotionally reactive, suggesting that they are having trouble regulating their emotional system. In fact, extreme **emotional dysregulation** is a central feature of some forms of severe personality disorders. Other people appear emotionless and in fact are emotionally overregulated.

Triangle of Persons: The Interpersonal Matrix

Returning to the triangle of persons, we can view the interpersonal matrix in its complexity (see Figure 6.4). At the lower corner of the triangle, we are in the zone of past relationships from an adult's vantage point. This represents the core relational experiences that shape our ideas about trust, intimacy, and attachment to others. If an individual has positive attachments that are growth-promoting, the emotional matrix will develop without the need for defensive functioning. If, however, the early relational matrix is disturbed in any of the ways we have discussed, defenses will be developed in an attempt to protect the self in the most adaptive way possible. As an individual matures, the early components of the relational matrix in which he or she was immersed will be retained and re-created in relationships with others. These then become characteristic traits and relational patterns that in part demarcate and define our personality. Dynamic therapists also note that this pattern of defensive operation and personality patterns of interpersonal relationships are brought to the therapeutic relationship in a cyclical relational dynamic (Luborsky & Crits-Christoph, 1997). In Chapter 7 we expand on the interpersonal component of this theoretical model in greater detail.

Figure 6.4

The Expression of Personality in Three Corners of the Triangle of Persons.

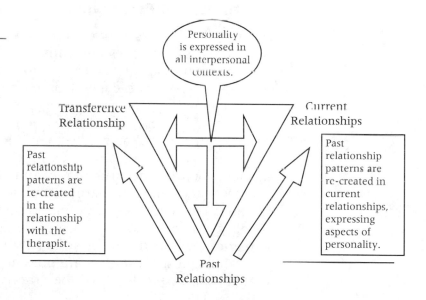

Personality is expressed in all interpersonal contexts.

Transference Relationship

Current Relationships

Past relationship patterns are re-created in the relationship with the therapist.

Past relationship patterns are re-created in current relationships, expressing aspects of personality.

Past Relationships

Using the Triangles to Explain Personality Development and Organization

Personality is shaped and consolidated by our positive and negative experiences and in the interpersonal matrix depicted by the triangle of persons. These interpersonal experiences interacting with temperament variation leads to the building of an intrapsychic matrix, depicted by the triangle of conflict. Our personality is expressed in both our interpersonal patterns and our intrapsychic matrix and how it is organized. For example, a father who tends to be authoritarian and controlling may create reactive angry-hostile feelings in his son. To protect himself, the son may learn ways of expressing this hostility that are not open to direct attack. Possibly, the son will adopt a passive defense system where, on the surface, he appears compliant and pleasing but may express his hostility by resisting his father's control in passive-aggressive ways; he may forget to do something his father has asked him or sabotage his performance in a sport his father values. If this type of personality pattern is consolidated over time, the son might become an individual who uses these passive-aggressive traits to deal with conflict he is now ill-equipped to deal with more openly or constructively.

Structural, Categorical, and Developmental Continuum of Personality

As we have discussed, contemporary psychodynamic classification of personality takes into consideration structural components (psychotic, borderline, neurotic, normal), categorical aspects of personality (avoidant, dependent, obsessive-compulsive, etc.), and a developmental perspective (stages of identity development).

Examining the various dimensions and categories of personality in Figure 6.5, we can see the range of flexibility and diversity that this systems affords and its utility for clinicians. Everyone functions at some point on the structural continuum, from psychotic (out of contact with reality, primarily primitive defenses, primitive object relations are good/bad) to normal. There are various types of personality disorders, which seem to cluster into three categories (American Psychiatric Association [APA], 1994). See Table 6.4.

Although the disorders are presented in *DSM-IV* as categorical (either you have enough of the criteria to qualify or you don't),

Figure 6.5

Combination of Structural, Categorical, and Developmental Perspectives of Personality.

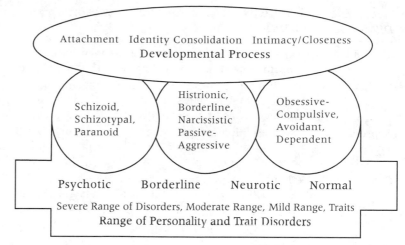

more likely they are best understood as a prototypal system, which is better able to account for the variation in personality. Various types of personality disorders exist on a continuum, ranging from those who have fully diagnosable (according to *DSM* criteria) personality disorders to those who have aspects or traits from the various categories. These categories do seem to be intuitively useful in classifying personality. Most of these types have their roots in the systematic observations of the early psychoanalytic theorists and clinicians. Even "normals" will have a proclivity to various aspects of these. Millon, Davis, Millon, Escovar, and Meagher (2000) describe the characteristics of the 14 personality disorders in the various editions of the *DSM* (see Table 6.5). Additionally, at each point on the structural continuum, there are corresponding developmental issues, such as attachment, necessary for trust, identity consolidation, and intimacy and closeness.

Table 6.4   **Three Clusters of Personality Disorders from *DSM-IV***

Cluster A: (eccentric) schizoid, schizotypal, paranoid

Cluster B: (emotionally unstable) borderline, narcissistic, histrionic

Cluster C: (emotionally constrained) avoidant, dependent, obsessive-compulsive, dependent

Table 6.5 **Brief Descriptions of the 14 Personality Disorders of *DSM-III*, *DSM-III-R*, and *DSM-IV*.**

Schizoid	Apathetic, indifferent, remote, solitary. Neither desires nor needs human attachments. Minimal awareness of feelings of self or others. Few drives or ambitions, if any.
Avoidant	Hesitant, self-conscious, embarrassed, anxious. Tense in social situations due to fear of rejection. Plagued by constant performance anxiety. Sees self as inept, inferior, or unappealing. Feels alone and empty.
Depressive[1]	Somber, discouraged, pessimistic, brooding, fatalistic. Presents self as vulnerable and abandoned. Feels valueless, guilty, and impotent. Judges self as worthy only of criticism and contempt.
Dependent	Helpless, incompetent, submissive, immature. Withdraws from adult responsibilities. Sees self as weak or fragile. Seeks constant reassurance from stronger figures.
Histrionic	Dramatic, seductive, shallow, stimulus-seeking, vain. Overreacts to minor events. Exhibitionistic as a means of securing attention and favors. Sees self as attractive and charming.
Narcissistic	Egotistical, arrogant, grandiose, insouciant. Preoccupied with fantasies of success, beauty, or achievement. Sees self as admirable and superior, and therefore entitled to special treatment.
Antisocial	Impulsive, irresponsible, deviant, unruly. Acts without due consideration. Meets social obligations only when self-serving. Disrespects societal customs, rules, and standards. Sees self as free and independent.
Sadistic[2]	Explosively hostile, abrasive, cruel, dogmatic. Liable to sudden outbursts of rage. Feels self-satisfied through dominating, intimidating, and humiliating others. Is opinionated and close-minded.
Compulsive	Restrained, conscientious, respectful, rigid. Maintains a rule-bound lifestyle. Adheres closely to social conventions. Sees the world in terms of regulations and hierarchies. Sees self as devoted, reliable, efficient, and productive.
Negativistic[1]	Resentful, contrary, skeptical, discontented. Resists fulfilling others' expectations. Deliberately inefficient. Vents anger indirectly by undermining others' goals. Alternately moody and irritable, then sullen and withdrawn.
Masochistic[3]	Deferential, pleasure-phobic, servile, blameful, self-effacing. Encourages others to take advantage. Deliberately defeats own achievements. Seeks condemning or mistreatful partners.
Paranoid	Guarded, defensive, distrustful, and suspicious. Hypervigilant to the motives of others to undermine or do harm. Always seeking confirmatory evidence of hidden schemes. Feels righteous but persecuted.
Schizotypal	Eccentric, self-estranged, bizarre, absent. Exhibits peculiar mannerisms and behaviors. Reads thoughts of others. Preoccupied with odd daydreams and beliefs. Blurs line between reality and fantasy.
Borderline	Unpredictable, manipulative, unstable. Frantically fears abandonment and isolation. Experiences rapidly fluctuating moods. Shifts rapidly between loving and hating. Sees self and others alternately as all-good and all-bad.

Source: Personality Disorders in Modern Life by T. Millon and R. Davis, © 2000. Reprinted by permission of John Wiley & Sons, Inc.
[1] Listed as a provisional disorder in *DSM-IV.*
[2] From the appendix of *DSM-III-R.*
[3] Called Self-Defeating in *DSM-III-R* appendix.

Character Diagnosis

How do we know where a person is on the structural continuum and the person's type of personality? Knowing where to approximately place an individual on the structural continuum is as much a clinical art as a science. Reviewing an essential point of what has been discussed about contemporary psychodynamic theory of personality, McWilliams (1994) summarizes:

> *Classical psychoanalytic conceptualization approached the study of character or personality in two very different ways, each deriving from an early theoretical model of individual development. In the era of Freud's original* drive theory, *an attempt was made to understand personality on the basis of fixation (at what developmental phase is this person stuck?). Later, with the development of* ego psychology, *character was conceived as expressing the operation of particular styles of defense (what are this person's typical ways of avoiding anxiety?). This second way of understanding character was not in conflict with the first; it provided a different set of ideas and metaphors for comprehending what was meant by a type of personality, and it added to the concepts of drive theory assumptions about how we develop our characteristic adaptive defensive patterns. (p. 19)*

McWilliams (1994) depicts the typologies of personality and the developmental dimensions in Figure 6.6. She emphasizes this point in her work: *"The essential character structure of any human being cannot be understood without an appreciation of two distinct and interacting dimensions: developmental level of personality organization and defensive style within that level"* (p. 40; italics in original). One can again see in her schema the structural levels of organization of the personality and the types.

Horner (1995) states: "Character structure refers to the overall organization of the personality—the specifics of that organization for a given individual" (p. 104). There are useful theoretical constructs from the structural-drive, ego, object-relations, and self psychological perspective that we have reviewed for making this type of assessment (Horner, 1994). Horner (1995) has made a very practical and useful summary of the various aspects of establishing "a picture of how the individual's psyche is organized (i.e., structured)" (p. 103), which she describes as "more like an x-ray than a photograph" (p. 104). An assessment of personality includes ego and superego functions and is made through a combination of clinical

Developmental Dimension	Typological Dimension									
	Psychopathic	Narcissistic	Schizoid	Paranoid	Depressive	Masochistic	Obsessive Compulsive	Hysterical	Dissociative	Other
Neurotic-to-Healthy Level										
Identity integration and object constancy										
Freudian oedipal										
Eriksonian initiative versus guilt										
Borderline Level										
Separation–individuation										
Freudian anal										
Eriksonian autonomy versus shame and doubt										
Psychotic Level										
Symbiosis										
Freudian oral										
Eriksonian basic trust versus mistrust										

Figure 6.6

Developmental and Typological Dimensions of Personality.
Psychoanalytic Diagnosis by N. McWilliams, © 1994. Reprinted by permission of The Guilford Press.

interviewing and projective and standardized testing. Horner reminds the reader that "ego is not a synonym for 'self' or 'self-esteem' (as in the vernacular, 'He sure has a big ego!')" (p. 104). The **ego functions** as described by Horner (1995, pp. 104–114) include:

- *Relation to reality:* **Reality testing** is the ability to distinguish between external and internal states such as emotions, fears, and wishes; the **sense of self as real** over time and in various contexts; and the ability to **look at the self objectively** or stand back and view oneself with some perspective.

- *Regulation and control of drives and impulses:* There is a **capacity to delay acting** on wishes, which requires a tolerance for frustration. **Impulse control** is the capacity to talk about sexual and aggressive impulses without the need to discharge by acting on them. There is a capacity for **adaptive expression** so that in reality these drives can be appropriately expressed.

- *Quality of thought processes:* This is the ability to **use logical thought** and think in abstract concepts, and not have one's thoughts disrupted from emotional/psychological causes.

- *Integrity and maturity of defenses:* This describes **adequacy of defenses** to tolerate both negative and positive emotions and recoverability when an emotional outbreak results in regression; and **flexible defenses** that can shift when appropriate and can be self-observed or acknowledged when pointed out by another person. **Mature defenses** predominate the defense constellation (see categories discussed in the defense constellation section).

- *Autonomous functioning:* This concerns relative **freedom from conflict** in various spheres of functioning, such as perception, speech, cognition, and motoric behavior expression; the **ability to recover** responsive functioning after periods of stress; and **integrity of neuropsychological system** indicative of no major organic deficits.

- *Synthetic functioning:* **Psychological mindedness** entails one's ability to see psychological relationships and connections. The **capacity for insight** entails making inferences about the behavior of self and others based on thoughts, feelings, and actions.

- *Quality of object relations:* This describes the **capacity to establish basic trust,** evident in at least one trusting relationship, and the **capacity for establishing relatedness** or be emotionally available and present with others. **Differentiation between self and others** includes the ability to experience oneself as separate, as opposed to fused or merged with another. **Stable object relations** means that the person can consistently experience the other as separate from self. The **integration of object relations** means that one can hold both the positives and negatives (good/bad objects) of others without dichotomous splitting. The **maturity of object relations** is demonstrated by the capacity for maintaining peer relationships and altruism.

Selected Research Findings

- *"Borderline personality disorder symptoms as predictors of 4-year romantic relationship dysfunction in young women: Addressing issues of specificity"* (Daley, Burge, & Hammen, 2000). The relationship between borderline personality and relationships is an area of interest to contemporary psychodynamic theorists and researches. In a sample of 142 older adolescents, BPD symptom constellation was associated with romantic chronic stress, conflicts, partner satisfaction, abuse, and unwanted pregnancy. The results support the view that BPD is associated with relationship dysfunction.

- *"Borderline personality disorder exists in India"* (Pinto, Dhavale, Nair, & Patil, 2000). The prevalence of borderline personality disorder was evaluated in India by focusing on 75 individuals who made suicide attempts. Using a variety of questionnaires and a semi-structured interview, it was found that BPD is underdiagnosed in India. These patients also had a high incidence of sexual and physical abuse, thought to be one of the main contributing factors in the development of this disorder.

- *"Measuring overall defensive functioning with the defense style questionnaire: A comparison of different scoring methods"* (Trijsburg, Van T' Spijker, Van, & Hesselink, 2000). Empirical validation of the construct of defense has been important to psychodynamic theorists and researchers. In a study on this topic, the researchers provided empirical validation of the usefulness of the Defense Style Questionnaire for measuring overall defensive functioning and correlated scores with the Global Assessment of Functioning commonly used in clinical practice to rate overall functioning.

- *"Construct validity of the Rorschach Oral Dependency (ROD) Scale: Relationship of ROD scores to WAIS-R scores in a psychiatric inpatient sample"* (Bornstein & O'Neill, 2000). The Rorschach Inkblot Test has been a major development in psychoanalytic theory for measuring personality, but there is continuing debate about its validity. In this study, the Rorschach Oral Dependency Scale was a valid measure of interpersonal dependency (suggestibility, conformity, and interpersonal yielding).

- *"The early relationship of drug abusing mothers and their infants: An assessment at eight to twelve months of age"* (Burns, Chethik, Burns, &

Clark, 1997). The researchers compared 10 mother-infant dyads in which mothers were abusing drugs during pregnancy to 10 dyads that were drug-free. Interactions between mother and infant were later studied. Significant differences were found on two variables of maternal mood (enjoyment and pleasure) in structured play, and mutual arousal, enthusiasm, and enjoyment in unstructured play situations. The importance of the maternal-child dyad was demonstrated.

The superego functions include (Horner, 1995, pp. 114–115):

- *Functioning conscience:* This entails clear standards of right and wrong, with the person desiring to live up to these; and the capacity to experience guilt when one transgresses or doesn't live up to these standards. The standards are realistic, based on capacity and ability, but not overly moralistic or perfectionistic.
- *Reasonable ego ideal.* The person exhibits a sense of self-worth that is well ingrained. The ego ideal is realistically based in reality and not overly exaggerated or grandiose.

Using the above theoretical lenses and criteria, we can attain a picture of an individual's personality structure, traits, defense constellation, and areas of developmental vulnerability.

Principles of the Contemporary Psychodynamic Models

Philosophical Underpinnings and Assumptions

The philosophical underpinnings of contemporary psychodynamic models of personality share much in common with classic psychoanalytic theory, where the introspective model is emphasized. Although introspection can never be a substitute for more empirical methods of validation, we cannot dismiss it, as it is an important form of knowing. This introspective model of philosophy was founded by an Egyptian philosopher from about the second century A.D. and also revitalized by St. Augustine (A.D. 354–430) (Rychlak, 1968). According to Rychlak, even though these theories often lack empirical validation, they nevertheless hold meaning about various aspects of human nature: "The clinical methods of interview, projective testing, and psychotherapy are often cited as contemporary examples of introspection" (p. 203).

Notions of Normal versus Abnormal

Personality is conceptualized as multidimensional, relating to both the structure of and maturity of an individual's intrapsychic system, including defenses, emotional capacity, and the degree of capacity achieved for interpersonal connections and intimacy, termed quality of object relations. There is no clear differentiation between normal and abnormal personality, as the lines of distinction can be somewhat fuzzy. Most important is an individual's adaptive capacity and flexibility in responding to environmental demands of both work and family. Normal behavior is adaptive and flexible across a variety of contexts and situations. Individuals can be generally classified into normal, neurotic, borderline, or psychotic categories; within each of these, they can be placed on a dimension. Individuals may move from one "category" to another under times of stress, called regression. In addition, each person has a unique configuration of traits and characteristics that we come to know as his or her personality. When extreme variants are present, self-defeating patterns of behavior are often seen; in severe personality disorders, disturbance occurs in almost all spheres of functioning.

Assessment Strategies and Tools

Contemporary models of psychodynamic personality theory utilize a wide array of assessment strategies and tools. However, clearly, the psychodynamic model is most noted for introspective strategies such as **depth interviewing** and **projective techniques,** which have emanated from this theoretical perspective.

Depth interviewing originated with the psychoanalytic model, where the process of free association was used to access unconscious material. Later methods of in-depth interviewing were developed that attempt to accelerate the pace by providing some degree of stress, which is said to increase defenses and allow access to deeper feelings and unconscious material as well as provide a manner of conducting an assessment. This is a **structural interview** and was pioneered by Kernberg and Davanloo. Various other semistructured interviews have been developed to attain comprehensive information about various aspects of an individual's life and functioning. For example, Masters and Johnson (1966), the famous sex researchers, developed one for taking a sexual history.

Projective techniques have individuals project their own perceptions, thoughts, and feelings onto ambiguous stimuli, like looking at clouds and describing what you see. "Psychology has produced few more popular icons than the Rorschach inkblot test" (Goode, 2001, p. F1). Probably the most famous of these is the **Rorschach Inkblot Test,** which although criticized by many, still holds an important position in both psychodynamic assessment and research. Developed in the 1920s by Swiss psychiatrist Hermann Rorschach (1942/1951), the test was based on a popular European parlor game that involved making inkblots and then telling a story about them. Rorschach devised the test by spilling ink on paper and folding it in half, creating symmetrical inkblots, 10 of which were selected for the test. There are a variety of ways to score the responses: form features, color, shading, content, texture, movement, and many others. Although first scored by clinical impression, later attempts were made to standardize scoring and validate the response profiles with substantial normative data. This assessment instrument is utilized in the assessment of personality "several hundred thousand times a year, by conservative estimates, to both children and adults" (Goode, 2001, p. F1). Although academic psychologists have often attacked the scientific basis and usefulness of this test, it remains a mainstay of clinical personality assessment.

Another famous test, developed by Christine Morgan (who drew most of the pictures) and Henry Murray, is the Thematic Apperception Test (TAT), which also has been widely used in research and clinical practice. The TAT is based on the interpersonal model and is covered in Chapter 9.

Application of Model

The psychodynamic model has had many applications over the century, most notably in treating mental illness. However, another interesting application of this model is to create psychological profiles of both historical and living figures, which was pioneered by Freud and the early disciplines. A very interesting and compelling application of the psychodynamic model was demonstrated during World

War II in an attempt to profile Adolf Hitler for use by the Allied forces; a secret psychological report written in 1943 for the Office of Strategic Services was declassified 25 years later (Langer, 1972). This psychohistorical reconstruction based on psychoanalytic theory provided insight and in-depth description of Hitler's motivation and personality functioning. Interestingly, the report suggested that Hitler might commit suicide: "This is the most plausible outcome. Not only has he frequently threatened to commit suicide, but from what we know of his psychology it is the most likely possibility" (pp. 211–212). Hitler did indeed commit suicide as Berlin was falling to the Allied forces.

Cultural Influences and Differences

The psychodynamic model originated in Freud's seminal work in the early twentieth century in upper-middle-class European society. Although he touted it as a metapsychology, Freud could not escape the perspective of his sociocultural and historical period. Clearly, many of his original formulations are outdated and probably have limited cross-cultural application. Psychodynamic theory was primarily an individualistic orientation that is limited by its own narrow frame of reference. Primarily conceived of as a male-oriented psychological system, vestiges of this early perspective still can be seen in the evolution of psychodynamic theory. Unfortunately, because it remained a closed system for such an extended time, there was little chance for cross-cultural fertilization. However, this seems to be changing recently, as more women and minorities are extending the parameters and stimulating the creative process that this model was once known for.

Strengths and Limitations of Model

The contemporary psychodynamic model of personality is very popular, particularly with clinical practitioners, and offers much that is useful for conceptualizing personality and mental disorders. The *strength* of this model seems to lie in the power of many of its fundamental constructs, such as the unconscious, defense systems, and the relation among component personality structures. It is hard to imagine a psychology of personality without some reference to these and other constructs. Many who read contemporary

psychodynamic theory are surprised at the resonance these conceptualizations have for understanding human nature and motivation.
This system is often rich with deep insight gleaned from extensive attention to human behavior that can be attained only by endless hours
in the consulting room, listening day after day to the struggles of
patients attempting to overcome obstacles that seem derived from
past experiences.

The *limitations* of this model are many. Unfortunately, after
years of perpetuating itself in a closed system, a crisis developed
about the viability of this model. Contemporary psychodynamic
theory seems to have emerged from the storm and is gaining increasing acceptance by students looking for a system that seems to
provide deep insight into human nature and psychopathology. Another drawback is the tendency to eschew empirical research, which
would have established wider scientific acceptance. For many, the
conceptualizations and esoteric language make it difficult to immerse oneself in what seems a dogmatic intellectualized system for
those who hide behind language.

Summary

This chapter presents a synopsis of contemporary psychodynamic
theory along with some of the seminal developments that later psychodynamic theorists pioneered in their efforts to expand the parameters of the structural-drive theory of Freud's psychoanalytic
perspective. Object-relations theory emerged from the fertile soil of
Freud's theory, and the primacy of attachment was emphasized by
Winnicott, Klein, Fairbairn, Mahler, and A. Reich. Object relations
describe the process by which significant attachment figures are internalized and their representation (objects) are carried around inside of us. This is not dissimilar to cognitive theory and its emphasis
on internalized schema (see Chapter 8). Winnicott developed the
concept of the good-enough mother to explain how most mothering
does not need to be perfect to produce satisfactory adjustment, but
if not good enough, produces psychopathology. Self psychology was
pioneered by Kohut, who expanded Freud's notion of narcissism to
explain how development is derailed when insufficient mirroring
for and responsiveness to the child by the caretaker cause narcissistic disorders. When narcissistic needs are satisfied, development of a

healthy self often is ensured; when these needs are not met, the core affects of shame and rage are engendered. Cultural factors may have promoted the development of a high incidence of narcissistic disorders in Western society. Erikson proposed one of the first models of adult personality development, with various stages that need to be mastered before progression to the next (the epignenetic principle). Identity crises may occur at the various developmental transition points. Ego psychology focused on the role of the ego in adaptation to the world and the defenses used to protect the personality. Kernberg developed a theoretical model of personality through his studies of those with severe personality disorders. A multiperspective approach combines various psychodynamic theories, such as object relations, self psychology, structural-drive, and ego psychology. Two foundation constructs, the triangle of conflict and triangle of persons, can be used to depict the dynamic process of both the intrapsychic operation that occurs among feelings, anxiety, and defense and interpersonal patterns.

Suggested Reading

Langer, W. C. (1972). *The secret wartime report: The mind of Adolf Hitler.* New York: Basic Books.

Behavioral Models of Personality

7

Chapter

Introduction

Behavioral models of personality represented a major departure from the "depth" model of understanding human psychic and personality functioning postulated by philosophers and psychoanalytic thinkers. "During the heyday of behaviorism, respectable scientists avoided talk of unconscious functioning at all costs" (Grigsby & Stevens, 2000, p. 245). Behaviorism has its roots in empiricism and animal behavior and was enormously popular because of "its claim to be the first truly scientific psychology" (Hunt, 1993, p. 262). In this chapter on behavioral "theories of personality," the reader will justifiably ask Where are the theories? This is a useful question to consider. Behaviorism, as you shall see throughout this chapter, in many ways has eschewed the overly theoretical, speculative thinking of other theoretical models.

To develop a comprehensive theory of personality, speculation and moving beyond empirical and clinical data are required. However, not everyone would agree that this endeavor is worthwhile; certainly many would not consider it relevant scientific investigation. The primary **inductive thinking** of behaviorism starts from the point of data and elementary relationships, from which should emerge laws of human behavior. As you shall see, many times this has occurred, and important laws of behavior have been discovered. Much of the seminal clinical and academic research has explored various component systems of personality, such as learning, anxiety acquisition, learned helplessness, and conditioning paradigms, that continue to influence our understanding of how personality is formed, shaped, and maintained as well as how it is modified by various external factors. Behaviorism is a crucial part of the dialectic process that has occurred between wildly speculative theory with little scientific basis, such as phrenology (and many would include psychoanalysis as well) and empirical investigation using the scientific method. "One important feature of this theoretical revolution

---

ETHICAL GUIDELINES FOR ANIMAL RESEARCH

It should be noted that the type of animal research reviewed in this chapter is no longer acceptable under the ethical guidelines for animal research. Much of this research would be considered subjecting animals to unnecessary levels of suffering. Animal rights groups have become very active in the United States and especially in Great Britain, where they have been known to espouse violent retribution toward scientists they believe are sadistically torturing and neglecting laboratory animals.

---

was a decided preference for subject populations that would yield data to meet stringent standards for scientific purity. For this purpose, animals were much more appropriate than human beings" (Goldfried & Merbaum, 1973, p. 8).

We begin our review of this perspective by discussing some of the major historical figures who shaped the field for many decades and who many believe forced the study of personality into a period of quiescence. The first, Edward L. Thorndike, was a student of William James, considered the founder of psychology, who, interestingly, used introspective techniques to understand psychological principles. Thorndike made a radical departure from his mentor at Harvard, where he chose to study the principles of learning using animals—in this case, baby chickens in the basement of James's beloved house, which he built for his family while he was a professor at Harvard.

Major Events in the Development of the Behavioral Movement

Thorndike's Elemental Laws of Learning

One of the major influential figures in the development of behaviorism was Edward Lee Thorndike (1874–1947). He had a prodigious career in psychology as a professor at Teachers College, Columbia University, writing 50 books and publishing 450 research articles

(Hunt, 1993). Thorndike was a student of William James and chose to study animals, which he may have found easier to work with than people. Because of a lack of laboratory space at Harvard, James offered the basement of his residence for Thorndike's work with chickens. Thorndike created mazes of stacked books and studied how the chicks found their way to reinforcement of food, water, and other chicks. The chicks' performance improved on repeated trials, when they often were stuck in blind alleys or occasionally reinforced when they blundered to the enclosure. He later did research at Columbia, building puzzle boxes from vegetable crates to study the escape patterns of cats and some dogs. From these animal experiments, Thorndike formulated two laws of learning, which "became the basis of behaviorist psychology, human as well as animal" (Hunt, 1993, p. 248).

The Law of Effect: The puzzle boxes offered a number of alternatives to the animals. The two classes of responses were what he termed "annoyers" and "satisfiers." These responses either "stamp in" or "reinforce" certain stimulus-response connections, while others are eliminated or weakened. Therefore, any action has the effect of determining whether a response will occur to a stimulus (Hunt, 1993).

The Law of Exercise: The number of times a response has been connected with a stimulus, as well as the duration of the connection, will strengthen that response.

In January 1898, Thorndike was asked to discuss his results at a meeting of the New York Academy of Sciences, and the following June a monograph supplement of his findings was published in the *Psychological Review.* In December, he was invited to present at the annual American Psychological Association meeting. According to Hunt (1993) in *The Story of Psychology,* this was a major breakthrough in the field: "Thorndike's monograph had an immediate effect on psychological thinking. It lent new, research-based meaning to old philosophic notions of associationism; it provided convincing support for C. Lloyd Morgan's dictum against assuming higher mental functions if lower ones could explain behavior; and it established animal experimentation as the pattern for most learning research for the next half century" (p. 248).

Pavlov's Conditioned Reflex

One of the most influential figures of modern behaviorism was the Russian physiologist Ivan Pavlov (1849–1936), also presented in Chapter 2. Pavlov was transformed by reading Darwin's *Origin of Species* and Sechenov's *Reflexes of the Brain*. Pavlov, who studied medicine and became an expert surgeon, was interested in unraveling the mysteries of the digestive system and gastric reflex. He surgically created little pouches in the stomach of laboratory dogs and implanted fistulas to observe the gastric reflexes. In the course of his experimentation, he became aware of an annoying phenomenon that was disrupting his experiments: Dogs would secrete gastric juices at other than their feeding times when seeing an assistant prior to feeding. In 1902, he began to study this occurrence, which he spent the rest of his life focusing on. In his next phase of experimentation, he implanted a fistula in one of the salivary glands, then connected this to a measuring and recording device. The dog was held in a harness, facing a window, in which was housed a bowl into which food could be dropped mechanically. When the food was delivered, the dog would automatically begin to salivate. He termed this behavior **unconditioned reflex** because it was a natural response wired into the animal's physiological system (Pavlov, 1927). He then applied a neutral stimulus, one that would not create salivation in and of itself, such as a bell or buzzer. When presented alone, the neutral stimulus would produce only a raising of the dog's ears. When paired on several occasions with the delivery of food, a conditioning process occurred. The sound alone now produced salivation, which Pavlov termed **conditioned reflex.** He experimented with a number of other neutral stimuli, turning them into conditioned stimuli. In 1904, Pavlov was awarded a Nobel prize in medicine for his work.

According to Hilgard and Bower (1975), in attempting to make his investigation empirically based, Pavlov anticipated American behaviorism: "While he remained strictly within physiology, as he understood it, he was not unaware that he was dealing with essentially psychological problems, and in his Wednesday seminars he made a good many references to those psychologists he had read. He thought particularly well of E. L. Thorndike, and felt in some respects Thorndike's work had anticipated his own" (p. 88).

Watson's Popular Behaviorism

Behaviorism owes much of its acceptance by American psychology and the public to the efforts of John B. Watson (1878–1958): "No one did more to sell behaviorism to American psychologists than Professor John B. Watson of Johns Hopkins University" (Hunt, 1993, p. 253). Watson, who rose to the top of his profession but was then expelled from academic circles due to a sexual scandal, spent the rest of his career applying his behavioral knowledge to advertising.

Watson began studying conditioned reflexes in infants in 1916. Working at the Harriet Lane Hospital in Baltimore, he observed over 200 babies searching for innate responses (Hillner, 1984). He catalogued a number of infant reflexes, including sneezing, sucking, grasping, and reaching. He also noted some emotional responses, such as fear, rage, and love, that had associated observable behavioral components, such as crying and cooing. The experiment that brought him the greatest attention was the one he conducted with Rosalie Rayner, in which they attempted to produce a conditioned fear response in an 11-month-old boy named **Albert B.** (J. B. Watson & Rayner, 1920). They placed a white rat near Albert when he was 9 months of age and he showed no fear. Then they hit a steel bar with a hammer behind his ear, which produced the fear response. In the next phase of the experiment, they put the white rat near Albert, and when he touched it, the steel bar was banged behind his head. He responded with the expected terror of a child exposed to this noise. To avoid disturbing the child too much, the researchers did nothing more until a week later, when they continued with about a dozen more paired learning experiences between the sound and the rat. Needless to say, Albert developed a strong fear response after the trials to the sight of the rat alone.

Continued experiments demonstrated that Albert had developed **conditioned fear** to a number of other furry things, such as a rabbit and a seal coat, as well as Watson wearing a Santa Claus mask. Thus, they had created experimentally induced "neurosis," demonstrating the principles of learning in the shaping of human neurosis. Rilling (2000) summarizes this work and its impact: "It has been 80 years since Little Albert, one lone subject, shed his tears in a sacrifice for science on the altar of John Watson's behaviorism" (p. 310). He goes on to say: "The larger issues that concerned Watson, the validity and relevance of psychological concepts and the use of the data from research by practitioners, are still issues today" (pp. 310–311). Watson and Rayner made no effort to extinguish the experimentally produced neurosis they had created. By today's ethical standards for human experimentation, this type of behavior would not be condoned, but during this era much more was tolerated (compare this to the Chapter 1 discussion about Murray's experimentation on Theodore Kaczynski). Now all institutions that conduct human as well as animal research must have research proposals approved by a committee of peers, ensuring that harmful treatment is avoided or at least minimized.

Another element of historical importance was Watson's challenge to mainstream psychology to jettison methods and ideas that dealt with mental processes, which he considered unscientific. He urged psychology to develop a new scientific attitude by focusing only on observable behavior. He coined the term **behaviorist** at the same time James R. Angell did, so they both are due credit for it. Watson published his "radical" ideas and challenge to psychology in the *Psychological Review* in 1913 as "Psychology as the Behaviorist Views It," which became "a declaration of independence from all schools of psychology that dealt with mental processes" (Hunt, 1993, p. 256). This article, later known as behaviorism's "manifesto," had three important aspects, according to Hunt (1993): "In three sentences, he had proclaimed three revolutionary principles: first, the content of psychology should be behavior, not consciousness; second, its method should be objective rather than introspective; and third, its purpose should be 'prediction and control of behavior' rather than fundamental understanding of mental events" (p. 256). Watson (1913) wrote in his manifesto: "Psychology as the behaviorist views it is a purely objective branch of natural science. Its theoretical goal is the prediction and control of behavior. Introspection forms no essential part of its methods, nor is the scientific value of its data dependent upon the readiness with which they lend themselves to interpretation in terms of consciousness. The behaviorist, in his efforts to get a unitary scheme of animal response,

Watson and Freud—Similar Construct Different Theoretical Lenses

Mark Rilling (2000) in the *American Psychologist* wrote: "Sigmund Freud and John Watson are two of the most important individuals in twentieth-century psychology; yet, they rarely have been considered together. Freud's ideas were increasingly penetrating American culture at the time, roughly between 1909 and the mid-1920s" (p. 301). Rilling suggests that Watson borrowed Freudian concepts such as transference in an attempt to compete with Freud's psychoanalytic concepts. In fact, the experiment with classical conditioning of Little Albert may have been Watson's attempt to verify this concept in a laboratory setting. Watson enjoyed attacking psychoanalysis and predicted that it would fall by the wayside in the same fashion phrenology had. In his classic article on Little Albert's conditioning, he even went so far as to mock psychoanalysis. In their paper, J. B. Watson and Rayner (1920) wrote: "The Freudians twenty years from now, unless their hypotheses change, when they come to analyze Albert's fear of a seal skin coat—assuming that he comes to analysis at that age—will probably tease from him the recital of a dream which upon their analysis will show that Albert at three years of age attempted to play with the pubic hair of the mother and was scolded violently for it" (p. 14).

Rilling writes of the impact of this work: "Despite the weakness identified by historians, Watson and Rayner's (1920) study remains a classic, a benchmark against which theoretical questions, methods, and psychological limitations of the past anchor us to the same psychological questions about emotional learning and psychopathology that we are considering today with better methods and theories than were available to Watson and Rayner" (p. 310).

recognizes no dividing line between man and brute. The behavior of man, with all of its refinement and complexity, forms only a part of the behaviorist's total scheme of investigation" (p. 158).

Watson rallied against the study of consciousness and speculation concerning the mind and mental states. Hunt (1993) writes of Watson's impact: "Watson's manifesto was actually less original than it seemed; it presented ideas that had been germinating for fifteen years. But it did so in an audacious, forceful, crystallizing way; it was, in short, a sales pitch. Watson's ideas did not sweep the field overnight, but over the next half-dozen years behaviorism became an important topic at meetings and a formative influence on the thinking of psychologists. By the 1920s it had begun to dominate psychology, and was the ruling paradigm in American psychology and an important one in Europe for well over four decades" (p. 257).

Watson should be credited with, among other things, bringing the work of Pavlov to American psychology and the concepts of behaviorism to the theoretical landscape. His influence was substantial and, according to Hunt (1993), in "his popular writings, he waxed messianic: behaviorism could create a better world by scientifically engineering the development of personality" (p. 260). J. B. Watson's (1924, 1930) most often quoted statement from his book *Behaviorism* sums up this quality: "Give me a dozen healthy infants, well-formed, and my own specified world to bring them up in and I'll guarantee to take any one at random and train him to become any type of specialist I might select—doctor, lawyer, artist, merchant-chief and, yes, even beggar-man and thief, regardless of his talents, penchants, tendencies, abilities, vocations, and race of ancestors" (p. 104).

"To Watson, personality was a straightforward summation of activities, neither mysterious nor necessitating concepts other than those used before" (R. I. Watson, 1963, p. 442). Personality is the sum of an individual's habit systems, which include potential and actual manual, visceral, and verbal reactions (J. B. Watson, 1924, 1930). Watson used the term "habit system" to refer to various categories or clusters of individual habits, the building blocks of personality. He believed that personality was malleable and that no individual's personality remained consistent over time. "Watson asserted that concepts from normal psychology or experimental psychology could be extrapolated to explain abnormal behavior" (Rilling, 2000, p. 303). His belief was that behaviorism could stimulate these changes in adults and that raising children in a scientific way would lead to the betterment of humankind.

Watson received the gold medal for his contribution to psychology from the American Psychological Association in 1957, after almost four decades of exile from psychology. Although he went to

New York to receive the medal, he was concerned that he would become overwhelmed with emotion and sent one of his sons to receive the award instead. His gold medal citation read: "To John B. Watson, whose work has been one of the vital determinants of the form and substance of modern psychology. He initiated a revolution in psychological thought and his writings have been the point of departure for continuing lines of fruitful research" (Hunt, 1993, p. 261). He died the year after receiving this prestigious award at age 80.

The Neobehaviorists

More complex versions of behaviorism evolved from the 1920s to the 1960s and gained ascendancy in American academic psychology, which was also reported to the rest of the world (Hunt, 1993). The majority of research during these three decades "dealt with minute, undeniably objective but not very enlightened topics" (p. 263). Much of the research used animals as the subjects, but even when humans were used, the subject matter was rather dry.

Skinner's Radical Behaviorism

One of the most well-known psychologists of the twentieth century was B. F. Skinner (1904–1990). Consistent throughout his prolific career was his belief in radical behaviorism. Hunt (1993, p. 268) writes, "He held fast to his extreme behaviorist view that 'subjective entities' such as mind, thought, memory, and reasoning do not exist but are only 'verbal constructs, grammatical traps into which the human race in the development of language has fallen,' 'explanatory entities' that themselves are unexplainable" (Skinner, 1953, pp. 19–21; 1979, p. 117). Skinner had no interest in the human psyche; he was concerned with the external, observable, and measurable causes of behavior. Nor did he have a theory of psychology or personality, which concept was illusory and a distraction to the scientific study of behavior. His radical departure from introspective models of the mind was quite dramatic. Skinner (1972) wrote, "We do not need to try to discover what personalities, states of mind, feelings, traits of character, plans, purposes, intentions, or other perquisites of autonomous man really are in order to get on with a scientific analysis of behavior" (pp. 12–13). He eschewed allocating behavior to some mental functioning and believed that thinking is behaving.

Skinner made numerous discoveries and advancements in our knowledge of learning. He had great mechanical aptitude and designed and constructed an experimental box that much improved the ones designed by Thorndike. This is known as the **Skinner box,** and any student in a behavioral-oriented program in the 1960s and 1970s will remember experimenting with rats using this apparatus. The box, which was basically a cage with a lever that administered pellets of food or water, generally to white rats, was an efficient way of gathering data, which Skinner and his followers did much of. Rates of reinforcement and their impact on acquisition or extinction of behavior could be brought under experimental control, creating a true empirical science.

Skinner discovered that various schedules of reinforcement either increase the probability of a behavior occurring or reduce it (see Table 7.1). He realized that certain schedules of reinforcement

Table 7.1   **Various Types of Reinforcement Schedules**

Fixed interval	After a specific interval of time has passed, reinforcement is given.	After every class, a child receives stars for his or her effort at school.
Fixed ratio	After a specific number of responses, reinforcement is given.	After every five completed assignments, the child receives a toy.
Variable interval	After a variable period of time, reinforcement is given.	The teacher verbally reinforces a child for effort during class.
Variable ratio	After a variable ratio of responses, reinforcement is given.	The teacher intermittently reinforces a child, on the average of every five responses.

are very resistant to extinction, such as an intermittent one where only occasional rewards are provided. An example is casino slot machines: The hope of getting the reward keeps the individual pulling the lever and, when out of money, borrowing more to continue.

One of Skinner's other contributions to behaviorism was his explication of the paradigm of operant conditioning. Hunt (1993) writes of this development: "Any random movement the animal makes, for whatever reason, can be thought of as 'operating' on the environment in some way and therefore, in Skinner's terms, is an 'operant'; rewarding the movement produces operant conditioning. By rewarding a series of little random movements, one by one, the experimenter can 'shape' the behavior of the animal until it acts in ways that were not part of its original repertoire" (p. 272).

Using operant conditioning, Skinner demonstrated that complex behavioral sequences can be taught to animals; thus, he had pigeons playing Ping-Pong and a pig putting dirty clothes in a hamper. He also applied these techniques to education, developing "programmed instruction." His students applied his techniques to emotional disorders. He used reinforcement principles to treat a severely depressed woman who was in danger of dying from not eating; using reinforcement contingencies, her behavior was modified. This approach spread to mental institutions, many of which established token economies. Skinner (1948) published *Walden Two*, describing a utopian community based on behavioral principles. A real community based on these principles, called Twin Oaks, still survives, although its residents do not much adhere to Skinnerian principles of shaping one another's behavior.

Skinner's View on Personality: As we have seen, the psychodynamic model that was prevalent at the time looked for underlying traits and motives. Hilgard and Bower (1975) sum up Skinner's position on personality. "Skinner (1953 and elsewhere) specifically rejects this psychodynamic interpretation. For him, motives, wishes, or desires are not explanations of behavior. To explain that a man spends an excessive amount of time cleaning and grooming himself neatly because he 'has a compulsive need or wish for cleanliness' is to explain nothing at all. It merely moves the question back a step: *Why* does he have it? *What* determines that wish? To go beyond such useless 'motive explanations,' Skinner proposes that we analyze the observable events, conditions, situational variables, and past history to regulate the behavior in question" (p. 238). Skinner did not classify individuals as emotionally or mentally sick, nor described and categorized by personality traits. He considered these social judgments and not within the realm of scientific activity.

Explaining Personality Using Behavioral Principles: Behavioral principles can readily be applied to the construct of personality. Even though Skinner (1953) did not officially recognize the need for the construct of personality in his writings, he incorporated aspects of trait psychology:

> *Another generalized reinforcer is the* submissiveness *of others. When someone has been coerced into supplying various reinforcement, any indication of his acquiescence becomes a generalized reinforcer. The bully is reinforced by signs of cowardice and members of the ruling class by signs of deference. Prestige and esteem are generalized reinforcers only insofar as they guarantee that other people will act in certain ways. That "having one's own way" is reinforcing is shown by the behavior of those who control for the sake of control. The physical dimensions of submissiveness are usually not so subtle as those of attention, approval, or affection. The bully may insist upon a clear-cut sign of his dominance, and ritualistic practices emphasize deference and respect. (p. 79)*

Hull's Mathematical Psychology

Another influential figure was Clark L. Hull (1884–1952), who attempted to develop behaviorism into an exact science modeled after Newtonian physics. He believed that in his grand theory all human behavior could be reduced to primary laws using quantitative methods and equations (Hull, 1943). He is probably most remembered for his complex equations that he used to quantitatively depict his principles. Many students of Hull struggled to understand the complex formulations, and many of us who were students of learning theory wondered why we did so. An example is one that depicts reaction potential (Hull, 1952, p. 7):

$$sEr = sHr \times D \times V \times K$$

Hull attempted to bring psychology up to par with the physical sciences, which he thought would give psychology more credibility. His attempt to turn psychology into a more "rigorous" scientific discipline gained credibility, but the overelaborate nature of his system led to its downfall.

A Brief Review of Foundation Concepts

As we have briefly discussed, there are a number of fundamental behavioral concepts that have altered our understanding of how learning occurs and is maintained in both animals and humans. Readers who want an in-depth presentation of learning should review Hilgard and Bower's (1975) classic text on this topic, *Theories of Learning*. A comprehensive review of the major developments in learning theory is beyond the scope of this text. The most commonly used terms are reviewed for those who want to refresh their memory and for those who have not taken a course on this topic.

Classical Conditioning

Pavlov's famous experiment is common knowledge for most students of psychology: "When meat powder is placed in a dog's mouth, salivation takes place; the food is the unconditioned stimulus and the salivation the unconditioned reflex. Then some arbitrary stimulus, such as a light, is combined with the presentation of the food. Eventually, after repetition and if time relationships are correct, the light will evoke salivation independently of the food; the light then becomes the conditioned stimulus and the response to it is the conditioned reflex, on the ground that all that gets conditioned is not reflex, but the difference in terms is not very important" (Hilgard & Bower, 1975, p. 62).

Using Little Albert's conditioning paradigm as another example, the **unconditioned stimulus (US)** is the loud noise and the **unconditioned response (UR)** is the fear reaction. A neutral stimulus is one that does not elicit the US, in this case, the infamous white rat, who was probably also startled by the loud noise (there are no reports of whether he was conditioned to fear Albert or, more likely, the experimenters). The **conditioned stimulus (CS)** is one that was previously neutral but, when paired with the US over a number of paired associative learning trials, will elicit the response. The fear then becomes a **conditioned response (CR),** which can be elicited by the **conditioned stimulus.**

Stimulus-Response (S-R) Psychology

The Skinnerian description of the association between stimulus and response forms the basic unit of his psychology of learning. In

instrumental conditioning, a response followed by a reward will increase the chance of the response occurring again. **Habits** are stimulus-response connections strengthened by rewards. **Generalization** occurs when stimuli bearing some resemblance to the CS produce the response. This was evident in Watson and Rayner's experiment with Little Albert when his fear response was elicited by furry objects that had some stimulus features of the white rat.

Some stimuli act as cues for certain behavioral responses but do not necessarily have complete control over the behavior. A **discriminative stimulus,** such as a shrill sound from a smoke detector, is a cue that if you do not vacate the premises, harm might result. The piercing sound is a cue for escape behavior.

Skinner's conception of **operant conditioning** has two essential components: **operants** and **respondents.** Respondents are behaviors that have a high likelihood of following a stimulus, such as ducking when someone throws a punch. Operants are behaviors acquired as a result of the environment acting on the respondent behavior. Behavior is emitted and whether the behavior will occur again is based on the consequences that follow. If a hungry rat presses a bar and receives a pellet of food, the environmental response has been instrumental in strengthening the association between the bar press and the pellet of food. Anything that increases the probability of a behavior occurring when it follows that behavior is a **reinforcer.** Money, food, sex, attention (positive and sometimes negative) are common reinforcers of behavior. Reinforcers may be species-specific so that one may need to search for one that will increase the probability of a response. "In **punishment,** a negative reinforcer is made contingent upon a response which typically had some prior source of strength" (Hilgard & Bower, 1975, p. 223). "The effect of punishment was a temporary suppression of the behavior, not a reduction in the total number of responses" (Skinner, 1953, p. 184). When a response is not reinforced over time, the emission of that response will weaken and disappear in a process called **extinction.** Usually during extinction phases, there is an increase in responding before the behavior is eliminated.

Shaping is a procedure by which behavior is gradually molded from component or smaller parts. This creates chains or sequences of behavior that form complex patterns. Skinner used shaping to teach complex tasks to animals, such as training rats to dance, which was not normally part of their repertoire. **Response chains** are sequences of behavior that have been reinforced through successive approximation. To achieve complex tasks, initially, behavior similar to the desired behavior is reinforced, bringing the subject closer and closer to the desired behavior by reinforcement. Various learning and extinction curves can be explained using **schedules of reinforcement.** For example, Skinner discovered that a variable ratio response schedule, where the individual is rewarded randomly within an average time period, creates behavior that is much more resistant to extinction than behavior created by a fixed schedule of response.

Theoretical Models

Overall, the behaviorists eschewed any formalized theory of human behavior, and many academics were even more adamant about the construct of personality as a viable area of empirical research. Therefore, in this section, the reader will not find a cohesive explanation of personality. However, this in no way diminishes the importance of these "atheoretical" approaches to understanding human behavior. Behavioral psychologists often express their deeply held sentiment that if behavior changes, "personality" is sure to follow; in other words, if an individual changes his or her habits or sequences of behavior, it is not important whether or not we believe some ephemeral construct such as personality changes. The behavioral approach emphasizes the pragmatics of learning and the principles by which the laws of learning can be used to modify behavior. The dialectic process that occurred primarily between the overly elaborate theoretical system of psychoanalysis and the pragmatic science of behaviorism created much controversy that propelled the entire field of psychology forward.

Salter's Conditioned Reflex Theory

A little-known figure in the field of behavioral personality is Robert Salter, who wrote *Conditioned Reflex Theory of Personality: The Direct Approach to the Reconstruction of Personality* (1949). Although Salter's work is not ordinarily mentioned in personality theories texts, his work, published the year before Dollard and Miller's (1950) *Personality and Psychotherapy* (see following), represents a very interesting theoretical attempt to explain personality from the viewpoint of

Pavlovian psychology. In this volume, Salter explains the excitatory personality, inhibitory personality, psychopathic personality, and various related topics such as shyness, stuttering, addictions, anxiety, inhibition, masochism, and homosexuality. Salter challenges psychoanalysis and espouses naturalistic science instead of the "supernatural" (p. 1). He describes the empiricists' perspective: "It uses as few concepts as possible. The simplest available explanation should be preferred, that is, the one which involves the fewest or least complexly related concepts that are adequate" (p. 1). Salter (1949) gives us the example of General Eisenhower for the **excitatory personality,** which he describes thus: "The excitatory person is direct. He responds outwardly to his environment. When he is confronted with a problem, he takes immediate constructive action. He is energetic, but there is nothing hyperthyroid about it. He sincerely likes people, yet he does not care what they may think. He talks of himself in an unaffected fashion, and is invariably underestimated by the inhibitory. He makes rapid decisions and likes responsibility. Above all, the excitatory person is free of anxiety. He is truly happy" (pp. 45–46).

Salter believes most people have an **inhibitory personality,** which he describes as "living death" (1949, p. 54): "The inhibitory have developed the brake habit. They have collided with too many automobiles on the highway of life, and have learned to drive with the brakes on" (p. 54). In addition to Salter's colorful way of describing his personality types, he is innovative in his use of principles of conditioning to describe complex behavior. He also recognizes the importance of affect when he writes: "Fundamentally, the inhibitory person suffers from constipation of the emotions. Good physical condition requires that internal generatings be passed regularly from the body. Similar generatings in the feelings need to be vented continually, otherwise psychological accumulation, toxicity, and ulceration will result" (p. 47).

Salter clearly recognizes the importance of affect in the construction of personality theory, believing that those who conceal their emotions and find relationships "irksome or not too comfortable" are suffering from faulty conditioning. What is interesting about Salter's use of the conditioned reflex as the basic construct on which to explain human conditioning is that he acknowledges the relevance of emotion and interpersonal relations as important aspects of personality adjustment. Dollard and Miller (1950) achieved a less tongue-in-cheek and more accepted translation of learning theory the following year.

Dollard and Miller's Learning Theory

Probably the most systematic effort to produce a comprehensive behavioral theory of personality was attempted by John Dollard and Neil Miller (1950). Dollard and Miller bridged the gap between psychoanalytic theory and learning theory when they published their groundbreaking book *Personality and Psychotherapy*. Based on Hull's learning theory and their knowledge of psychoanalysis, as well as Dollard's knowledge of anthropology, they developed an explanation of personality. Dollard and Miller proposed four essential components to learning: **drive, cue, response,** and **reinforcement.** These components shape learning and, in so doing, shape our behavior and personality:

1. *Drives:* "Strong stimuli which impel action are drives" (Dollard & Miller, 1950, p. 30). Drives may be **primary,** such as hunger, thirst, sex, fatigue, and pain. The strength of the primary drives is related to the degree of deprivation. Drives may be acquired, or **secondary,** such as fear and the need for approval. Secondary or learned drives are acquired through relationships to primary drives. Regardless of whether they are primary or secondary, drives propel behavior by energizing the individual. The notion of secondary drive was a brilliant extrapolation by Dollard and Miller that enabled them to have far greater explanatory power than derived from the concept of primary drive alone. This was especially important in their attempt to provide a comprehensive explanation of human personality and the development of neurosis.

2. *Cues:* "Cues determine when he will respond, where he will respond, and which response he will make" (p. 32). These are the stimuli that determine or direct attention to certain aspects of the environment. "Usually a change in an external source of stimulation is a more distinctive cue than the absolute value of that source" (p. 34). They describe this phenomenon with an example: If an individual is reading and someone increases the intensity of a light by six levels of illumination, it is easier for

the reader to notice the change than to say at which level the light is burning. Cues can be internal, such as hunger, or external, such as a flashing sign in front of a diner.

3. *Response:* "Drive impels the individual to respond to certain cues" (p. 35). A behavior that occurs after a stimulus is a response. Responses can be weak at first but strengthen under conditions of reinforcement. There are hierarchies of responses: "The ease with which a response can be learned in a certain situation depends upon the probability that the cues present can be made to elicit that response" (p. 36). The most likely response is the "dominant response," and the least likely the "weakest response" (p. 36).

   There are various manners in which habits are acquired: "The least efficient of these is trial and error" (p. 37). Imitation is another way habits are learned: "After a person has learned to attach appropriate responses to the cue of seeing another person perform an act, imitation can help the person to limit the range of trial and error" (p. 37)

4. *Reinforcement:* "Repetition does not always strengthen the tendency for a response to occur" (p. 39). Any stimulus (S) that increases the probability of a response (R) occurring or reduces the strength of a drive is reinforcing. When an S-R connection is not rewarded, **extinction** occurs. The following relationships are observed between drive and reinforcement: "(1) A prompt reduction in the strength of the drive acts as a reinforcement; (2) reinforcement is impossible in the absence of drive because the strength of stimulation cannot be reduced when it is already at zero; and (3) the drive must inevitably be lower after the reinforcement so that unless something is done to increase it, it will eventually be reduced to zero, at which point further reinforcement is impossible" (p. 40).

Another important construct of Dollard and Miller's theory, used to explain complex behavior, is **learned drives.** Learned or secondary drives develop because of the reinforcement they receive in complex social systems. The manner in which individuals' early drives are satisfied or not determines the power of secondary drives. For example, higher-level reinforcers such as money and achievement can be linked to the early satisfaction of primary drives and have associated power. When not reinforced, these secondary drives, unlike primary drives, will weaken. There are exceptions; however, secondary drives can become extremely resistant to extinction. Take, for instance, a prisoner during the Vietnam War who maintains his patriotism in spite of repeated torture.

If a stimulus is similar to one that has produced reinforcement in the past, a certain degree of **stimulus generalization** will occur. Generalization is one of the mechanisms of prejudice: Individuals who have characteristics of the disliked group will be responded to in a similar manner. Language can facilitate generalizations in very powerful ways and is a mediator of many responses. Humans do not have to learn everything on a trial-by-trial basis but can use language and thought to anticipate and play with responses.

Another remarkable aspect of Dollard and Miller's (1950) work was their translation of Freudian defense mechanisms into behavioral terms (see Table 7.2).

One can begin to see in the unfolding of Dollard and Miller's (1950) work how the beginnings of cognitive psychology were being incorporated into the theoretical model. However, it still remained a whisper that would explode on the clinical landscape a few decades after Dollard and Miller's groundbreaking work.

Development of Personality: Dollard and Miller (1950) were not much interested in traits, structure, or characteristics. Like the behaviorists, they were concerned with habits and how these are acquired. Humans are born with reflexes that are shaped by the environment and learning conditions. These innate reflexes shape behavior by various response hierarchies. Humans have specific reflexes, innate hierarchies, and primary drives. Using the construct of drive reduction, various behavioral repertoires are strengthened or extinguished. Various development experiences, such as feeding, toilet training, learning about sex, and conflict resolution, offer highly charged learning experiences in which behavior will be shaped and strengthened into individual habit patterns or personality traits.

Mowrer's Two-Factor Theory

Mowrer (1947, 1950) modified the theory of classical conditioning, proposing a two-factor theory. He believed that if an individual avoids a feared stimulus, extinction will not take place. In other

Table 7.2   Freudian Defenses Explained Using Behavioral Constructs

Repression: "Drives, cues, and responses that have never been labeled will necessarily be unconscious" (p. 198).

Suppression: The changing of an anxiety-provoking topic by a group of people talking about something unpleasant reinforces the avoidance by reducing anxiety.

Regression: "When the dominant habit is blocked by conflict or extinguished through nonreward, the next strongest response will be expected to occur" (p. 171). This habit is often reinforced, such as the secondary gain that a temper tantrum elicits for a child.

Displacement: When a dominant response is blocked, the next strongest is likely to occur. The response then will generalize to another stimulus. A woman in love with a rejecting man might generalize these feelings to other men with similar characteristics.

Rationalization: When a true explanation of an event causes anxiety, the individual is motivated to construct an alternative explanation that will reduce anxiety. Thus, if a loved one is dying of cancer, a less anxiety-provoking explanation for the symptoms might be offered.

Projection: This defense depends on the principle of generalization: Each individual expects others to react in a certain manner. Although not a unitary phenomenon, various biologically based reactions that occur tend to reinforce this defense. Acting in a friendly manner is likely to elicit friendly behavior; conversely, a hostile manner elicits a hostile reaction. People tend to assume that others react in the way they do and use this to judge others.

Reaction formation: "A person who is motivated to do something he had learned to disapprove or fear may respond with thoughts, statements, or behavior of the opposite kind" (p. 184).

Source: Dollard and Miller, 1950.

words, if someone is traumatized and develops a phobia of rats, as in Little Albert's case, not exposing him to the rat in the future will maintain the phobic response. Mowrer was keenly interested in the study of conditioned anxiety and reinforcement. "The two-factor theory had not fared particularly well, although it undoubtedly makes a contribution to understanding anxiety disorders, particularly when modified" (Barlow, 1988, p. 224). Mowrer believed two principles of reinforcement were required: "(1) Instrumental responses involving the skeletal musculature mediated by the central nervous system are reinforced and strengthened by drive reduction; (2) such emotions as fear, nausea, and so forth involving the smooth musculature (glands, viscera, vascular tissue) mediated by the autonomic nervous system are learned by sheer temporal contiguity of a CS to the elicitation of the emotional response" (Hilgard & Bower, 1975).

Wolpe's Systematic Desensitization

Joseph Wolpe (1915–1997) was a psychiatrist who published a seminal book, *Psychotherapy by Reciprocal Inhibition* (1958). He extensively studied the role of counterconditioning in cats who had conditioned experimental neurosis. Wolpe's view of behavior was similar to Watson's and Hull's: Behavior is elicited, not emitted, as Skinner believed. Wolpe developed a system of psychotherapy called reciprocal inhibition based on a technique called systematic desensitization. "Now, at long last, an alternative to psychodynamic therapy became available, an alternative which could be meaningfully and efficiently applied for treatment of complex problems" (Fishman & Franks, 1992, p. 168).

A most important concept of Wolpe's system is **anxiety.** He does not distinguish between anxiety and fear. He defines anxiety as the automatic response patterns that occur in reaction to noxious stimuli. In his experiments, Wolpe placed cats in a cage and shocked them after they were exposed to a "hooting sound" of two to three seconds duration. The cats developed signs of extreme anxiety, as noted by heavy breathing, crouching, and trembling. When the escape route was blocked, signs of extreme terror were evident; the cats urinated and defecated. As we would predict from classical conditioning, these reactions were brought on by the hooting sound before the shock was administered. Wolpe noticed that the cats developed a "neurotic" pattern. In other situations, they would respond to other noises that would disrupt their eating pattern. In behavior terminology, they had generalized this response to other similar stimuli. Wolpe noticed that when a response was caused to cease by a competing response, the stimulus associated with the cessation acted as a conditioned inhibitor. In other words, when the cat had acquired the conditioned anxiety response, the eating response was inhibited.

Wolpe discovered that these conditioned anxiety reactions could also be experimentally inhibited. He started by feeding the animal in a less anxiety-provoking environment where the eating response would be more likely to result. Thus, the cat would be fed outside of the experimental room, where the tendency to have a generalized response was less likely to occur. After the animal had shown that it could eat in this situation, it would be brought successively closer to the room where the experiment had occurred; with each step in the gradient, the animal would eat before being moved closer to the feared stimulus of the experimental room. In this manner, Wolpe demonstrated that he could "cure" the experimentally created neurosis by his method of systematically desensitizing the animal to anxiety-provoking stimuli.

Assertiveness: Wolpe (1958) proposed the concept of **assertive responding,** which includes the expression of both aggressive and affectionate feelings. This is a form of reciprocal inhibition in that **assertive responding** countermands the free-floating anxiety. He also developed the method of behavioral rehearsal, whereby the client would role-play with him so that when confronted with an anxiety-provoking relationship, the client has practiced what to say to maintain an advantage.

Aversion Therapy: Wolpe (1958) also used aversive techniques by pairing punishment such as electroshock with a response that he wanted to eliminate. The treatment of an alcoholic, for example, might include giving the client a nausea-producing drug followed by an alcoholic beverage. Wolpe was not the only behavior therapist who used these techniques, but he gave considerable attention to this topic in his book. In the past, this technique has been used to try to countercondition homosexuals by pairing electric shock with pictures of nude members of the same sex. It has also been used to attempt to countercondition pedophiles, those sexually attracted to children. Ethical issues aside, these methods had limited usefulness for these populations.

Wolpe (1969) did not consider his system superficial or secondary. One could say that behavior therapy changes personality, if what is meant by personality is the sum of an individual's habits. He also believed that the model of reciprocal inhibition could explain cures, even those induced by drugs (Wolpe, 1960). Many behaviorists would agree with his claim that changing habits is the critical step in altering one's "personality."

Thomas Stampfl (1966), who speculated that neurotic symptom complexes were the result of learning to avoid anxiety, similar to many other behaviorists, elaborated another interesting development, a specialized therapeutic technique he termed **flooding.** In implosive therapy, Stampfl exposed the patient in fantasy to anxiety-provoking stimuli as a way of extinguishing the response.

Eysenck's Empiricism in Personality Research and Theory Building

Hans J. Eysenck (1916–1997) was one of the most controversial figures in academic psychology. Born in Germany, he left in protest of the Nazi regime in 1934, spending most of his career at the University of London in the Institute of Psychiatry (Bischof, 1970). According to Bischof, Eysenck scorned "nonempirical research and invite[d] controversy in his outspoken statements" (p. 488). He was a prolific researcher, innovator, and theorist whose wide-ranging interests cover a multitude of psychological topics.

Psychostatistical Theory of Personality: Eysenck never claimed to have a well-articulated theory of personality, which he believed would have been premature (Bischof, 1970). In his study of personality, he thought that it was essential to have as many variables as possible, as well as a control group. He favored work that centered on dichotomous groupings, such as honest versus dishonest. Personality is the sum of cognition, character, affect, and somatic components. He very strongly believed that the study of personality should be concerned with discovering the general laws of the group (nomothetic approach) as opposed to studying the individual (idiographic), as is the emphasis in psychoanalysis. He favored statistical techniques of **factor analysis,** which entails reducing many variables to their essential factors through multiple correlation, and **discriminant function analysis,** which develops equations to predict group membership.

Three-Factor Model of Personality: Eysenck (1982) used the technique of factor analysis to search for the main personality types. He dates his factors to ancient Greeks' melancholic, choleric, sanguine, and phlegmatic temperaments (Chapter 2). He rearranges these on a dimensional continuum for which he credits Wilhelm Wundt (1874), "the first man who can be called a psychologist without qualifying the statement by a reference to another perhaps stronger interest" (R. I. Watson, 1971, p. 267). Eysenck translates these formulations into two personality dimensions, **introverted-extroverted** and **unstable-stable,** arranging the first dimension on a horizontal axis and the second on an intersecting vertical axis (see Figure 7.1). To these two factors, Eysenck (Eysenck & Eysenck, 1985) adds **psychoticism.** According to Bischof (1970), "Eysenck is extremely inventive in the methods with which he studies personality. Whatever they are, and they are numerous, all of his methods are directed to studying the relationship of behavior to introversion-extroversion, and neuroticism and psychoticism" (p. 493).

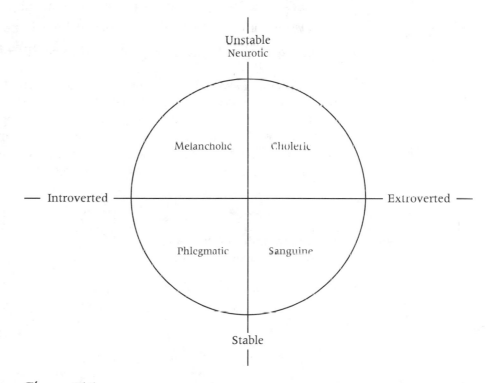

Figure 7.1

Eysenck's Two Major Dimensions and Placement of Four Greek Temperaments.

Eysenck (1952b) organizes the variation among individual personality in another way. He places the various categories from normal to psychotic in quadrants, instead of arranging them on a normal or bell-shaped curve or dichotomizing them, whereby the neurotic and psychotic deviate in two separate paths from normal. Eysenck depicts these possibilities in a novel way (see Figure 7.2). In this schema, an individual can be placed at any point in the quadrants, eliminating the need for classification and so fitting clinical observations more comfortably (Bischof, 1970). Bischof lists some of Eysenck's research findings on the neurotic factor:

1. Neuroticism is a primary structure and not merely a syndrome.
2. Derived from excitation of autonomic system.
3. Behavior not as readily apparent to others as is extraversion.
4. Less able to see in the dark than normal subjects.
5. When blindfolded will sway forward more than normals.
6. Seem to have higher drive than normals (p. 498).

Eysenck (1947, 1953, 1960) believed that neurotic patterns are learned and become unadaptive and that it is possible to uncondition neurotic symptoms. He emphasized learning theory in his quest to understand and predict human personality dynamics. Personality could be restructured according to the same learning principles on which it was structured. He espouses Mowrer's two-factor theory

Figure 7.2

Eysenck's Depiction of the Proximity of Psychotic, Mixed Neurotic/Psychotic, Normal, and Neurotic.

Psychotic Behavior	Mixed Type Psychotic and Neurotic Behavior
Normal Behavior	Neurotic Behavior

Eysenck's Attack on the Effectiveness of Psychotherapy

Probably one of the most controversial aspects of Eysenck's (1952) work was his attack on the effectiveness of psychotherapy. In an article titled "The Effects of Psychotherapy: An Evaluation" (1952), he stated that approximately two-thirds of psychotherapy clients recover within two years regardless of whether they received psychotherapy or not. His article is generally credited with initiating the "modern era of outcome research" with his "broadside attack on all forms of psychotherapy" (Strupp & Howard, 1992, p. 312). Strupp and Howard, preeminent psychotherapy researchers, comment on this attack: "Ironically, his results supported the efficacy of psychotherapy, but his conclusions—to abandon the training of psychotherapists—was very damning" (p. 312). In his provocative style, Eysenck challenged the field of psychotherapy to strive for higher levels of accountability. Another, equally famous study published some 30 years later by Smith, Glass, and Miller (1980) finally refuted Eysenck's attack. In a meta-analysis of psychotherapy outcome, they determined that psychotherapy was highly effective, reporting an effect size of .85, which they equated to 80% of psychotherapy clients showing improvement rate compared to 20% of nontreated individuals. Without Eysenck, the field of psychotherapy may not have achieved its current level of scientific rigor.

for changing behavior. "His interest in utilizing learning theory for restructuring personality is indicated by Eysenck's helping to create a new journal, *Behavior, Research, and Therapy,* begun in 1963 as an international multidisciplinary periodical" (Bischof, 1970, p. 501).

Component Subsystems of Behavioral Theory

Many of the developments in the evolution of the behavioral model entail the investigation and elaboration of component subsystems of personality. Thus, many researchers and clinical scientists did not strive to develop a comprehensive model of personality, although, as we have seen, there were a few. What can be seen is the development of many theoretically useful component subsystems of personality. Although not explaining personality as we have reviewed, instead there was an emphasis on thoroughly understanding a narrower aspect of personality functioning. Extrapolating from these constructs, one can see their expression in various clinical phenomena as well as in various abnormal personality configurations (see Table 7.3).

Seligman's Concept of Learned Helplessness

Martin Seligman (1975), a past president of the American Psychological Association, developed the concept of **learned helplessness.** Working in the laboratory, Seligman studied the reactions of dogs that were shocked and allowed to jump over a barrier to escape, which they learned very quickly. When he modified the experimental conditions and shocked the dogs without allowing an escape route, he induced a state of helplessness in them: Instead of trying various maneuvers to escape the aversive conditions, the dogs stood or crouched and shook, seemingly with anxiety. Even more compelling to Seligman was that when the barrier was subsequently removed, affording the dogs the opportunity to escape, they did not. He labeled this state learned helplessness, suggesting that this animal model could be applied to humans to explain how individuals with depression seem to view the world in negative terms and don't believe any response they make will make matters better. In a sense, he believed they had undergone similar conditioning, whereby they

Table 7.3 **Subcomponent Systems and Their Relationship to Clinical Phenomena and Personality**

Construct	Clinical Application	Application to Personality Disorder
Learned helplessness	Depression	Depressive personality development
Self-control	Impulse disorders	Antisocial personality
Anxiety	Agoraphobia	Avoidant personality

learned that no behavior they could perform was linked to the possibility of escape or reward. This type of environment might be evident in severely dysfunctional families where chaos rules and expectancies of having any impact are kept to a minimum.

Seligman (1996) believed that this state of helplessness was a reaction to uncontrollable events where the individual gave up without trying. He comments on this period in his research:

> *My coworkers, Steve Maier and Bruce Overmier, and I spent the next five years working on the cause, cure, and prevention of helplessness. We found that we could cure helplessness by teaching animals that their actions had effects, and we could prevent helplessness by providing early experience with mastery.*
>
> *The discovery of learned helplessness created a stir. Learning psychologists were upset. As behaviorists they maintained that animals and people were stimulus-response machines and could not learn abstractions—whereas learned helplessness required learning that "nothing I do matters," an abstraction too cognitive for stimulus-response theory. Clinical psychologists were intrigued because learned helplessness looked so much like depression. (p. 3)*

It is an interesting aside, given the animal rights movement, when looking back on the experimentation taking place during the 1960s, that Seligman (1996) states, "Producing animal suffering is wrong, it can be justified only if the experiments promise to help alleviate much more suffering in humans (or animals), and only if there is no other feasible method" (p. 3). More recently, Seligman (1990) has turned his attention to the study of optimism.

Goldfried and Merbaum: Changing Behavior through Self-Control

Self-control is an important feature of personality functioning. In abnormal personality, self-control often is an obvious impaired functional capacity. Behavioral theorists have provided much empirical evidence and elaboration of this construct, described by Goldfried and Merbaum (1973): "Self-control can be viewed as a process through which an individual becomes the principal agent in guiding, directing, and regulating those features of his own behavior that might eventually lead to desired positive consequences. Typically, the emphasis in self-control is placed on those variables *beneath the skin* which determine the motivation for change. It is equally important to realize, however, that environmental influences have played a vital role in developing the unique behavioral properties of the self-control sequence. . . . One might best characterize this aspect of self-control as an exercise in discrimination and problem solving" (p. 11).

Barlow: The Nature of Anxiety

One of the most prolific contemporary workers in psychology is David H. Barlow, who continues to use the behavioral paradigm and has developed treatment interventions based on these principles. Barlow's (1988) conceptualization of anxiety and its various subdivisions, such as panic and phobias, represents a more sophisticated, inclusive model than that of the radical behaviorists. Barlow's model maintains its allegiance to behaviorism but is multidimensional. By including much of what is current in neuroscience, his work demonstrates the power of a well-formulated behavioral model.

Anxiety is such a ubiquitous clinical phenomenon and an important component of any major theory of personality that it is essential to understand its place in human personality. Barlow (1988) has done much to deepen and broaden our understanding of this central issue. His book *Anxiety and Its Disorders: The Nature and Treatment of Anxiety and Panic* offers a major treatise on this topic. Barlow is a preeminent clinical scientist who has conducted extensive clinical research as well as having a broad knowledge of the clinical literature. Even though he is not considered a personality theorist, he is a behavioral investigator in the best sense, assisting in building a substantial database on anxiety that is a critical component system of personality.

Some of Barlow's findings demonstrate the power of the explanatory value of the behavioral model. For example, he presents evidence that there is a relationship between the development of agoraphobia, which is a fear of venturing into a strange place or into crowded areas. Agoraphobia is "basically a complication of anxiety about a fear of panic is supported by reasonably strong evidence" (1988, p. 357). Barlow suggests a number of behavioral methods to treat the spectrum of anxiety disorders. Many of these have substantial empirical documentation of effectiveness. One can see in Barlow's work how anxiety can be crucial in the development of certain personality types and disorders. For example, a highly anxious individual, who is reinforced by avoiding new situations, may develop an avoidant personality over the course of a lifetime of reinforcement. An avoidant personality is characterized by the need for substantial reassurance when entering new situations; although such individuals are interested in human contact, the thought of such intimacy makes them highly anxious and thus avoidant.

Barlow (1988) incorporates various learning theories into his conceptual framework. He writes: "An early modification to classical fear conditioning theory was the avoidance learning model (Mowrer, 1947), which hypothesized that fears or phobias will fail to extinguish if one successfully learns to avoid the feared stimulus. The idea here was that substantial avoidance prevents the individual from 'reality testing' or learning that there is no longer any reason to be afraid. This notion, known as the 'two-factor theory,' was popular for decades, since it seemed to explain why phobias do not extinguish: Fear is originally learned through classical conditioning and is subsequently maintained due to avoidance" (p. 223). The place of anxiety in both human and animal learning paradigms parallels what we have seen in the psychoanalytic model.

Paradigmatic Behaviorism

The development of "paradigmatic behaviorism" (Eifert & Evans, 1990), a derivative of "social behaviorism" (Staats, 1975, 1981), offers a more integrative, behaviorally based model. Fishman and Franks (1992) sum up this view:

> *Paradigmatic behaviorism emphasizes the integration of conditioning theory with traditional concepts in personality, clinical, and social psychology. Staats sees the foundational elements of personality as formed by conditioning. He views the principles of contiguity and reinforcement as always present and interacting, with operant conditioning affecting overt behavior patterns and classical conditioning affecting emotional and cognitive response patterns. Staats' concept of "cumulative-hierarchical learning and development" explains how complex combinations of simple behaviors*

Selected Research Findings

- *"The role of parental fearfulness and modeling in children's fear"* (Muris, Steerneman, Merckelbach, & Meesters, 1996). Researchers investigated the contribution of parental modeling to fearfulness. The results, based on 40 children ranging in age from 9 to 12, indicated that fearfulness was correlated with the mother's fearfulness. They suggest that modeling played a crucial role in this relationship.

- *"The effectiveness of behavioral parent training to modify antisocial behavior in children: A meta-analysis"* (Serketich & Dumas, 1996). The authors conducted a meta-analysis of 26 studies on the outcome of behavioral parent training on modifying children's antisocial behavior at home and school. The findings indicate that training the parents to modify behavior improves preschool and elementary school children's behavior.

- *"Acquisition and maintenance of dental anxiety: The role of conditioning experiences and cognitive factors"* (de Jongh, Muris, ter Horst, & Duyx, 1995). The investigators studied 224 undergraduate students to determine what factors are involved in the development and maintenance of dental anxiety. Their findings suggest that when treatment is perceived as traumatic and painful, individuals are likely to develop dental anxiety. When a number of relatively painless procedures are experienced, individuals are less likely to develop dental anxiety. They suggest that this supports a conditioning paradigm for dental fear and anxiety reactions.

- *"Assertiveness, submissive behaviour and social comparison"* (Gilbert & Steven, 1994). The researchers explored the relationship among assertiveness, social comparison, and submissive behavior in a cohort of 75 mental health workers. They completed a number of scales, including Eysenck's Personality Questionnaire. The findings suggest that submissive behavior is not the mirror opposite of assertiveness; submissive behavior is associated with introversion and neuroticism.

- *"Behavioral treatment of child stutterers: Replication and extension"* (Gagnon & Ladouceur, 1992). The efficacy of behavioral treatment was supported using a group of 11 male stutterers ranging from 6 to 11 years old. Results showed significant changes, with improvement maintained at six-month follow-up.

learned by basic conditioning can, over time, evolve into three complex "personality repertoires" of responses: sensory-motor, emotional-motivational, and language-cognitive. Taken together, these ideas provide the conceptual tools for Staats to apply the principles of conditioning to all areas of traditional psychology, including such clinically relevant domains as personality assessment, psychopathology, and psychotherapy and behavior change. (p. 171)

As has occurred in many of the models presented in this text, a move toward integration has taken place that generally broadens the explanatory value of a theory. Behavioral principles offer a powerful perspective in understanding how patterns of behavior are elicited and shaped.

Principles of the Behavioral Models

Philosophical Underpinnings and Assumptions

The philosophical underpinnings of the behavioral model are seen in patterns of thought developed during the Enlightenment of the seventeenth and eighteenth centuries and later twentieth-century modernism (Fishman & Franks, 1992, p. 161). Four main principles are emphasized by early empiricists:

1. That knowledge comes from experience with the world rather than introspective rumination or divine inspiration.
2. That scientific procedures have to be based upon observation rather than opinion, intuition, or authority.
3. That the mind of the child is a blank slate (tabula rosa) upon which experience writes, so that adult mental life is primarily a recording and unfolding of the previous history of the person concerned.
4. That consciousness is best viewed in terms of "mental chemistry," in which all thoughts can be broken down into basic elements which have become connected into more complex ideas through various laws, such as continuity, similarity, contrast, vividness, frequency, and recovery (Kimble, 1985).

Notions of Normal versus Abnormal

The behavioral "theory" of personality has generally not been too concerned with the issue of what is normal versus what is abnormal. "Abnormal" manifestations of behavior are generally viewed as existing within faulty learning environments. Unlike many other theoretical perspectives, behaviorism has not attempted to classify and categorize aberrant forms of human behavior. This represented a refreshing change from the pathology-oriented language of the psychoanalytic theorists and continues to be a point of demarcation.

Assessment Strategies and Tools

The major assessment strategy of the behavioral model is the analysis of behavioral sequences, termed **applied behavioral analysis.** This procedure is used to understand how certain behavioral repertories are shaped and maintained. Behavior analysis is a powerful methodology that has many uses. Essentially, behavior is observed and the sequences of positive and negative reinforcement and punishment are observed. The major tool is in the application of empirical observation that this model is so strongly associated with. This type of assessment is suitable for the laboratory as well as clinical settings. It is best used in a naturalistic setting, such as observing children in day care or in the classroom.

Application of Model

The behavioral model has many applications covering a variety of areas, including school psychology, education, advertising, learning, clinical treatment, and social policy and planning. One of the most interesting applications was Skinner's model of the utopian community he wrote about in *Walden Two.* A group of people applied his ideas, developing a community based on his learning principles. Although it has gone through many changes, the community still exits.

More widespread application has been in using these principles to shape social behavior in children by observing how asocial behavior is reinforced in the environment and changing the contingencies. For example, a child who is acting like a bully and disrupting class might be placed on a reinforcement schedule that reinforces him when he displays prosocial behavior.

Cultural Influences

Cultural differences are understood as reflecting different learning environments. Various cultures are exposed to different environmental variables that will have some effect in the shaping of behavior: Cultural preferences are reinforced and nonpreferred behavior punished or extinguished through a lack of reinforcement. In this model, cultural differences are understood as is any other behavior, via the nature of the reinforcement and punishment that follows the behaviors. For example, in certain Eastern cultures, women are more likely to be seen as submissive in their behavior; a behavioral analysis would demonstrate how subjugation occurs by reinforcing behaviors that are consistent with the broader cultural values.

Strengths and Limitations of the Behavioral Model

One could say that both the *strength* and *limitation* of this model is its emphasis on empiricism. Even though there have been many breakthrough concepts that have emerged out of the data, in particular, classical and instrumental conditioning, the emphasis on what often seems like the minutiae of learning has resulted in decades of research effort be spent with, in many cases, no appreciable gain in knowledge.

Behaviorism began to lose its hold on psychology during the 1960s when, as described in Chapter 3, "research in a number of other fields was beginning to cast new light on the workings of the mind. From anthropology came studies of how preliterate peoples think; from psycholinguistics came accounts of how human beings acquire language; and from computer science came a wholly new way to conceive of thinking—as information processing, proceeding step by step like a computer program" (Hunt, 1993, p. 278). "With the advent of cognitive science, behaviorism rapidly lost its commanding position in psychology and its claim to be a sufficient explanation of all behavior" (p. 278). Behavior theory as a stand-alone model has limitations in explaining the complex phenomenon we call personality. However, behaviorists would say that this was never their stated goal, as behaviorism isn't really science. However, the subcomponents of behavior theory, some of which have been presented in this chapter, provide a critical aspect of understanding personality.

Summary

The development of behaviorism heralded a major departure from the psychodynamic models of personality. Eschewing the concepts of psychoanalysis, such as the unconscious, behaviorists attempted to develop an empirical foundation for the study of behavior. Unlike other models presented in this text, behaviorism espouses no grand theories. One of the seminal workers in the field who pioneered behaviorism as a scientific discipline was Thorndike, who discovered the law of effect and the law of exercise. The field was strongly influenced by Pavlov's discovery of the conditioned reflex. Watson popularized behaviorism in a remarkable way in his experiment on Little Albert, in whom he and his associate induced an experimental neurosis, demonstrating the explanatory power of conditioning. He also brought behavioral principles to the public with his application to child psychology and parenting. Watson's manifesto emphasizing the prediction and control of behavior changed the theoretical landscape of psychology for over 50 years.

Radical behaviorism, introduced by Skinner, held firmly to the notion that constructs of the mind, cognition, and reasoning, are not worthy topics because they are too subject to introspection. Skinner outlined the major schedules of reinforcement that can be used to shape complex behavior using operant conditioning. Others, such as Hull, attempted to follow in the path of Newtonian physics and develop a mathematical model of behavior. Dollard and Miller published a major work in their translation of psychodynamic theory into learning theory. Many Freudian concepts were explained using principles discovered by learning theorists. Wolpe also studied conditioning in animals but then applied his findings to humans to understand how anxiety is caused and extinguished using his principles of systematic desensitization. Seligman investigated learned helplessness, which could be demonstrated in animal experiments as a reaction to uncontrollable events; this was used as a model for depression in humans. Principles of the behavioral model can be used to understand how personality is shaped and formed by environmental contingencies.

Suggested Reading

Dollard, J., & Miller, N. E. (1950). *Personality and psychotherapy: An analysis in terms of learning, thinking, and culture*. New York: McGraw-Hill.

Rilling, M. (2000). John Watson's paradoxical struggle to explain Freud. *American Psychologist, 55*(3), 301–312.

Skinner, B. F. (1948). *Walden two*. New York: Macmillan.

Cognitive and Cognitive-Behavioral Models of Personality

8

Chapter

Introduction

Cognitive science was a revolutionary development in the field of psychology that budded in the 1950s (see Figure 8.1). This movement had a major impact on the field of psychology and continues to have tremendous impact on current personality theory. Exploding out of radical behaviorism, with its emphasis on empiricism and learning paradigms, which tended to avoid any notion about what occurs in the mind, cognitive science challenged the ascendancy of behaviorism. As you will recall from the previous chapter on behavioral theory, this avoidance of speculation about the mind was what fueled behavioral psychology's break from what was then the mainstream. "To behaviorists, the mind, invisible, nonmaterial, and conjectural, was an obsolete metaphysical concept that no experimental psychologist concerned about his career and reputation would talk about, much less devote himself to" (Hunt, 1993, p. 513). By the mid-1960s, cognitive psychology had grown exponentially. According to J. R. Anderson (1990), the major text by Ulric Neisser titled *Cognitive Psychology* (1967) gave the field "a new legitimacy" (p. 10). This book gave an overview of the important topics in the field, with six chapters on perception and attention and

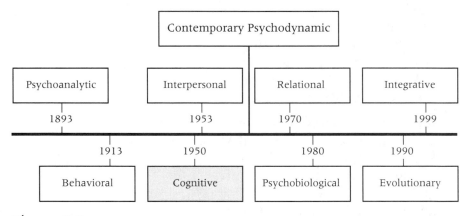

Figure 8.1

Timeline from the Beginning of Psychoanalytic Theory at the Turn of the Twentieth Century to Current Integrative Models.

the remaining four on thinking, memory, and language. In 1977, Mahoney used the term "cognitive revolution" in describing this shift in the field of psychology. The developments in computer science were seminal in advancing cognitive psychology.

Major Historical Figures

Miller: The Cognitive Revolution

George Miller was a Harvard-trained experimental psychologist who was discontent with the prospect of spending his career studying rat-based learning (Hunt, 1993). A professor of psychology at Harvard and Massachusetts Institute of Technology, Miller began to shift his interest to mentalism. He attended a summer program run by the famous linguist Noam Chomsky (1965), who was analyzing the structure of language. Chomsky believed that the prevailing behavioral model was unable to explain the complexities of language. Miller was influential in bringing this new understanding to psychology (J. R. Anderson, 1990). Also influential was his sabbatical year at the Center for Advanced Study in the Behavioral Sciences at Palo Alto, which exposed him to new thinking based on the application of computer programs to simulate thought processes. This caused a major transformation in Miller's own thinking. Miller returned to Harvard and, with the support of the provost of Harvard, attained approval to found the Harvard Center for Cognitive Studies. According to Hunt (1993): "George Miller's coming-out typifies what was happening to experimental psychologists in the 1960's. At first a few, then many, and soon a majority abandoned rats, mazes, electric grids, and food-dispensing levers in favor of research on the higher mental processes of human beings. Within the decade, the movement had assumed such proportions as to earn the name 'the cognitive revolution'" (p. 513).

Miller's work focused on human memory. In a thought-provoking article, Miller (1956) suggested that immediate memory is limited in terms of chunks of elements to seven. He discovered that these chunks were not limited to the retention of numbers but also included two-syllable words and single letters. He found that they were all treated in memory as single units. "Learning, then, was to be viewed as a matter of segregating, classifying, and grouping the elementary units into a smaller number of richer, more densely packed chunks" (Hilgard & Bower, 1975, p. 585). We can see in this article the emerging cognitive perspective. What occurs in our mind is no longer meaningless armchair speculation but the realm of the scientific method. This article was a harbinger of the explosion of new ways of viewing human behavior and mental functioning.

Relevance of Memory Research to Personality

Research in memory adds to our understanding of how the mind works, with major implications for the field of personality and psychotherapy. One controversy regards the degree to which "false memories" are implanted in vulnerable patients (Loftus & Ketcham, 1994). The controversy about child sexual abuse that Freud struggled with continues to emerge (as controversial as ever, many believe) in a different guise.

"The Most Dangerous Book You May Already Be Reading": Elizabeth Loftus versus Marlene Steinberg

In a recent issue of *Psychology Today* (Loftus, 2000; Steinberg, 2000b), the controversy over the therapy aimed at recalling repressed memories of sexual abuse is heatedly debated between two experts. Loftus, a major researcher in the field of memory, writes: "When you look into a mirror, who looks back? If you sometimes have the eerie feeling that you don't know who that is in the looking glass, then you may be one of the 30 million Americans who suffer from Dissociative Identity Disorder (DID). Such is the extraordinary claim of psychiatrist Marlene Steinberg" (p. 32).

Steinberg (2000a) defends her position in her rebuttal: "Elizabeth Loftus' commentary on *Stranger in the Mirror: Dissociation: The Hidden Epidemic* illustrates the elaborate mythology and misrepresentations surrounding the field of dissociation. As many people are aware, Loftus is not a licensed clinical psychologist and has never diagnosed or treated a single person through psychotherapy" (p. 34).

Von Neumann and McCulloch: A Conceptual Leap from Computers to the Mind

The impact of discoveries in computer science was crucial in the cognitive revolution. Hunt (1993) comments on the importance of these developments:

> *Computer science had by far the greatest impact on psychology. This new field was the product of intense research during World War II, when Allied forces urgently needed calculating machines that could rapidly handle large sets of numbers to direct antiaircraft guns, operate navigation equipment, and the like. But even very high-speed calculating machines needed to be told by a human operator, after each calculation, what to do next, which severely limited their speed and introduced inaccuracies. By the late 1940s, mathematicians and engineers were starting to provide the machines with sets of instructions (programs) stored in their electronic memories. Now the machines could swiftly and accurately guide their own operations, carry out lengthy sequences of operations, and make decisions about what needed to be done next. The calculating machines had become computers. (Hunt, 1993, p. 514)*

Mathematicians such as John von Neumann and Claude Shannon reasoned that symbols such as numbers could be substituted for letters and mathematical computations could be used to express relationships among these symbols. With a set of rules, words can be turned into numbers, and through algebraic equations can express abstract verbal relationships (Newell & Simon, 1972). At a seminal conference in 1948 of Cerebral Mechanisms in Behavior, von Neumann and Warren McCulloch suggested that the computer might function like the mind (Simon, 1969, 1991). Herbert Simon, a professor of political science, was at this conference and became fascinated by this development. Simon and a young graduate student, Allen Newell, took up the challenge of developing a computer that could reason. They developed simple computer programs that were capable of basic logic (Newell, Shaw, & Simon, 1963). Their first computer programs were capable of solving mathematical problems by using logic to prove theorems; later, they developed a program that could play chess. According to Hunt (1993), these programs had two basic features that were responsible for a "metamorphosis in cognitive psychology," represented by the information-processing or computational model of psychology that has been a guiding metaphor since the 1960s.

Foundation Concepts

Information Processing

Emerging from the use of the computer as a potential model for how the mind works was an ever-expanding field termed **information processing.** Hunt (1993) writes of this development: "To be sure, the finding is an inference from results, not a direct observation of the process. But contrary to behaviorist dogma, inference of an unseen process from results is considered legitimate in the 'hard' sciences. Geologists infer the events of the past from sediment layers, cosmologists the formation and development of the universe from the ancient light of distant galaxies, physicists the characteristics of short-lived atomic particles from tracks they leave in a cloud chamber or emulsion, and biologists the evolutionary path that led to *Homo sapiens* from fossils. So, too, with the interior universe of the mind: psychologists cannot voyage into it, but they can deduce how it works from the track, so to speak, made by an invisible thought process" (p. 518). The two basic features of the information-processing model, according to Hunt, are representation and information processing.

Representation is using symbols to depict or signify other symbols or occurrences. "By analogy, cognitive psychologists could conceive of the images, words, and other symbols stored in the mind as representations of external events, and of the brain's neural responses as representations of those images, symbols, and thoughts" (Hunt, 1993, p. 516). **Information processing** is one way cognitive psychologists attempt to depict what actually occurs in the mind "and has enabled researchers and theorists to explore the inner universe of the mind as never before" (p. 516). Thus, models of information processing are conducted by inference. Information processing is a way of depicting the sequences of problem solving that are performed on incoming sensory information. J. R. Anderson (1990) uses an analogy: "Suppose we followed a letter in a successful passage through the postal system. First, the letter would be put in a mailbox; the mailbox would be emptied and its contents brought to a central station. The letters would be sorted according to region, and the letters for a particular region shipped off to their destination. There they would be sorted again as to area within the postal district. Letters having the same destination would be given to a carrier, and the carrier would deliver the letter to the correct address" (p. 12). He then follows information through the human mind in a similar fashion. He asks the question "Where does your grandmother live?" The first thing that must be done is to retrieve the meaning of each word and then the meaning of how the words are configured. This requires understanding of the question. Memory must then be searched until the correct answer is found. This information must be transformed into an answer.

In this model, information signifies various mental objects or representations, which follow a sequence in which the information is serially ordered. "The important characteristic of an information-processing analysis, then, is that it involves a tracing of a sequence of mental operations and their products (information) in the performance of a particular cognitive task" (Anderson, 1990, p. 13).

Pattern Recognition

One way of understanding how information is processed is by recognizing patterns. "Perhaps the most obvious way to recognize a pattern is by means of template matching" (J. R. Anderson, 1990, p. 58). It is hypothesized that the brain stores patterns, called templates, and that the perceptual system compares these stored templates with incoming information to find a correspondence.

Feature Analysis

Another model that has been proposed for perceiving and processing information recognizes certain features. Features combine basic elements of stimulus configurations. This represents an advance over templates, in that feature analysis represents a simpler way to notice the differences in stimuli and the necessity of storing large numbers of templates is reduced.

Reasoning and Logic

Our current understanding of human behavior is that "a large portion of human thought is not logical reasoning in any useful sense" (J. R. Anderson, 1990, p. 291). However, reasoning remains important to the cognitive model. Reasoning is the process by which individuals generate and evaluate the logic of arguments (J. R. Anderson, 1990). Logic refers to the process of attempting to deduce what is logical and correct by the use of reason. There are two kinds of logic that we have identified in philosophy and that are discussed in the philosophy of science and epistemology. **Deductive reasoning** is the process by which certain conclusions are reached with a degree of certainty from the facts, although the conclusion might not be true. For example, the following is deductive thinking:

> All dogs are animals.
>
> This is a dog.
>
> Therefore, this is an animal.

The truth is dependent on the method used. If, for example, the facts are wrong, even though the reasoning is logically consistent the conclusion may be wrong:

> All men are morally inferior.
>
> Morally inferior individuals should not run major corporations.
>
> Men shouldn't run major corporations.

Inductive reasoning is a process by which all observations are based on experience and the conclusion extrapolated. For example:

> Every crow that has been observed is black.
>
> All crows are black.

However unlikely, at some future time a crow of a different color may be observed. Thus, the conclusion is not guaranteed to be true.

Memory

The study of memory has been a major area of investigation and has produced many insights. The manner in which memory functions is crucial to understanding behavior. It has been well documented in various clinical cases and empirical studies that change in memory leads to changes in personality. George Miller, who made it a topic of importance, stimulated much of this trend. Experimentation during the 1960s and 1970s provided a model of three types of memory (J. R. Anderson, 1990; Hunt, 1993):

1. Sensory buffers that receive and hold sensations.
2. Short-term memory, which fades in a matter of seconds without rehearsal.
3. Long-term memory, in which memory is retained for months or up to a lifetime.

Later, we will see that the research in memory has taken on prodigious importance because of the danger inherent in an individual's using memory to reconstruct past experiences as well as remember facts in criminal investigation and forensic settings. A controversial question has to do with the veracity of memories "recovered" in therapy. In forensic settings, in cases relying on memory, which is notoriously inaccurate and prone to schematic modification, many individuals have been found guilty and have served time for crimes they did not commit. With the advent of DNA sampling, which offers much more accurate data, many who were convicted from faulty recounting or identification have been exonerated.

Schema

Memory is an imaginative reconstruction based on an individual's mass of experience (Bartlett, 1932). Bartlett told non-Western folktales to Westerners and found that the subjects inadvertently filled in the blanks and omitted details that did not make sense to the Western mind. Bartlett termed this organized mass of experiential memory schemata or schema. Hunt (1993) comments on this important discovery: "Bartlett's idea has been revived and elaborated in recent years. Schemas—also known as 'frames' and 'scripts'—are now thought of as packages of integrated information on various topics, retained in memory, on which we rely to interpret the allusive and fragmentary information that ordinary conversation—and even most narrative writing—consists of" (pp. 530–531).

This construct of schema was later used by cognitive theorists as a cornerstone of their model of how depression is influenced by thoughts and beliefs and how personality is indeed influenced by the schematic representations that are learned from our environment.

Cognitive, Social Cognitive, and Cognitive-Behavioral Theoretical Models

As discussed earlier, the development of systems of psychotherapy and personality theory often occurred simultaneously. "Opinions differ whether cognitive therapy should be considered as an evolution within modern behavior therapy or as a revolution leading to a new point of view" (Arnkoff & Glass, 1992, p. 658). The theoretical models presented in this chapter clearly led to a new point of view. We can see how the dialectic process has led to the rejection and then reintegration of seminal concepts that have broadened our understanding of personality.

Differentiation of Models

There is considerable overlap in current cognitive and cognitive-behavioral models of personality (see Figure 8.2). As we have discussed, the evolution of psychology and personality theories include myriad phases and subphases. One way to conceptualize the differences in these sister theories is to look at the way they were influenced by various other disciplines. Cognitive theory was highly influenced by the advancements in computer models, along with linguistics and anthropology. Cognitive-behavioral models seem to have emerged out of the behavioral tradition and may feel more loyalty to that system, combining aspects of cognitive theory within the behavioral tradition. "The fundamental assumption of cognitive behaviorism is that response output is not a simple linear or automatic product of the stimulus input" (Hillner, 1984, p. 181).

Figure 8.2

The Influence of Various Disciplines in the Evolution of Cognitive and Cognitive-Behavioral Theories.

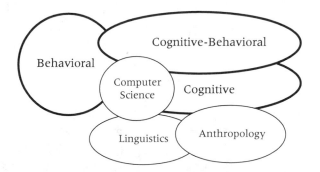

Ellis's Rational-Emotive Therapy

One of the earliest applications of the cognitive model to psychotherapy emerged in the mid-1950s with Albert Ellis's (Ellis & Harper, 1961) development of **rational-emotive therapy** (RET). Although Ellis (1974) did not attempt to develop a comprehensive theory of personality, RET "has an implicit theory of personality" (p. 309). He rediscovered and applied the cognitive model to human psychopathology and outlined a system to treat those disturbances. However, as with many other theories of psychotherapy, one can ascertain the basic elements about personality by viewing the process and method of change that is promulgated. Ellis writes: "A theory of personality tends to have one basic postulate and several subsidiary theorems derived from this postulate, or else it simply has several major theories or hypotheses, without any special unifying core. In some ways, the RET theory of personality falls more within the second than the first of these classes, since it is a cognitive-emotive-behavioral theory and practice, and it liberally borrows from many disciplines, ranging from the phenomenological-existential to the operant conditioning schools of thinking" (p. 310).

Ellis was a staunch proponent of his system; it paved the way for other cognitive models but is especially responsible for translating these concepts to the pragmatic world of clinical psychology. It must be remembered that cognitive therapy did not become a major force in psychotherapy until the mid-1970s. Arnkoff and Glass (1992) explain the hunger for cognitive methods: "At that time *Beck's Cognitive Therapy and the Emotional Disorders* (1976), Mahoney's *Cognition and Behavior Modification* (1974), and Meichenbaum's *Cognitive-Behavior Modification* (1977) appeared when clinicians were increasingly looking for a way of conceptualizing and changing inner experience" (p. 659).

Ellis's basic tenet is that irrational thinking causes human suffering. His theory is in part derived from the work of Alfred Adler (1924), who believed that humans constantly evaluate and give meaning to events in their lives. Ellis acknowledges the influence of Karen Horney (1950), who talked about the "tyranny of shoulds." He also was influenced by the work of Julian Rotter (1954), who emphasized the cognitive aspects of learning theory and theories of personality (Arnkoff & Glass, 1992). More specifically, he believes that it is not the actions of others, the defeats we experience, the problems of the external world, or other events that cause suffering but the way we think about or interpret these events:

> *This theory states that when you have either an appropriate or an inappropriate emotional reaction, at point C (the emotional Consequence), after some Activating Event or Activating Experience, especially of an obnoxious nature, has occurred at point A, A definitely does* not *cause C. Instead, B, your Belief System about A, directly causes you to react emotionally at C.*
>
> *More specifically, if you feel depressed or suicidal at point C, after you have been rejected for a job or a love relationship at point A, your rejection does* not *cause your depression. Rather, it is your* beliefs *about this rejection, at point B. And normally, you are first strongly holding a rational Belief (rB)—e.g., "I don't like being rejected; how unfortunate that I have been; it is really a drag!"—that results in an appropriate feeling of sorrow, irritation, and annoyance. But you are also holding an irrational Belief (iB)— e.g., "It's* awful *to be rejected; I* should not *have got myself in this position; what a worthless slob I am for arranging this!"—that results in your inappropriate feeling of depression, anxiety, and perhaps rage at your rejector. (A. Ellis, 1974, p. 312)*

Ellis describes human responses as a combination of thinking, feeling, and interacting. Thus, when individuals respond emotionally, they also react and think. Ellis believes that conditioning shapes personality.

A. Ellis (1974) only minimally addresses the issues of personality development or even personality disorders directly. He believes "there is an enormous amount of evidence that shows that the tendency of an individual to be severely emotionally disturbed is at least in part biological" (p. 328). He believes in the innate nature of human conditioning: "Because even if psychoanalytic and behavioristic theories are correct, and early environment is an important influence on personality development (as is almost certainly true), it seems obvious that human conditionability or suggestibility must be innate *for* conditioning to occur, and it is most likely that all of us are born equally conditionable" (p. 329). Instead of focusing on the biological influences, he focuses his energy on cognitive misrepresentations. Millon and Davis (1996a) write: "He does state clearly that personality difficulties reflect an individual's unrealistic and self-defeating assumptions about him- or herself and others" (p. 55).

If we apply the ABCs of RET to personality development, we can derive a basic understanding of how personality patterns develop. Based on variations in biologically based affective-emotional response tendencies, an individual is going to be shaped by the conditioning patterns present in his or her social-cultural environment. An individual who is sensitive to rejection might, along the developmental path, begin to interpret minor rejections as "too awful" to bear and develop a conditioned response pattern of avoiding situations in which there is a potential for rejection. This system will continue to be shaped by the internal belief system, which is reinforced interpersonally into patterns of behavior that become entrenched and which might later be described in terms of the individual's being extremely shy, withdrawn, and prone to patterns of avoidance.

Bandura's Social Learning Theory

Another influential theorist, Albert Bandura, developed a hybrid social cognitive theory combining notions about behavior, cognition, and neurobiological functioning. Bandura emphasizes the influence of emotions and feelings on behavior. He believes that individuals learn in a variety of ways, such as modeling others or symbolically turning information into models by forming inner representations of them, such as when we read of characters we admire and then try to emulate them. An important construct developed by Bandura (1997) is **self-efficacy,** which is simply the belief that you have in yourself the ability to succeed. For example, those with high levels of self-efficacy are more likely to stop smoking. People with high self-efficacy expect to be successful, thus bolstering their self-efficacy. You might compare this to the concept of learned helplessness in Chapter 7, whereby individuals believe that they have no control over outcomes.

Beck's Cognitive Theory and Therapy

Aaron Beck, said to be the father of cognitive therapy, was a psychoanalytically trained psychiatrist who was originally interested in validating psychoanalytic concepts of depression and then discerning the constellation of features of depression to build a model of brief treatment. Some of the hypotheses that were believed to be psychodynamic factors responsible for depression, such as anger turned

against the self and a need to suffer to punish one-self, were later refuted in his research. This led him to reappraise psychoanalytic theory. He became disenchanted with the analytic model and began to utilize aspects of the information-processing model. His evidence suggested that depressed patients' view of the world is distorted by negative thinking. Further, he began to use the rules of evidence and logical argument to alter the depressed patient's cognitive distortions (Beck, Rush, Shaw, & Emery, 1979).

It is interesting to note that there are elements of the cognitive approach in the work of Karen Horney, Otto Rank, and Alfred Adler, all of whom influenced Beck (Sperry, 1999). In 1976, Beck published *Cognitive Therapy and the Emotional Disorders*, which articulated the application of cognitive theory. Beck "presented a broad extension of the specific cognitive aberrations in each of the neuroses, a detailed description of the general principles of cognitive therapy, and a more comprehensive outline of the cognitive therapy of depression" (Beck et al., 1979, preface-1).

Beck's Model of Depression: Beck's (Beck et al., 1979) interest in the clinical phenomenon of depression culminated in the publication of what many consider a paradigm-shifting book entitled *Cognitive Therapy of Depression.* This work on depression was an important prelude to the expansion of Beck's work a decade later, when he tackled the personality disorders, developing the cognitive theory of personality (Beck & Freeman, 1990). The relationship between personality and depression has been a fruitful area of theoretical development and a challenging clinical concern; personality factors may play a role in the development of depression, and there are numerous theoretical explanations for this link (M. H. Klein, Kupfer, & Shea, 1993). We will review these later. At this time, it is important to emphasize that in the cognitive model of depression, there may be multiple links among overlapping cognitive schema that link depression to personality. Personality features may also make one more vulnerable to the loss that can precipitate depression; for example, a highly provocative and demanding individual may have trouble maintaining functional attachments and may have to deal with the resultant relational disruptions the behavior promotes.

Beck et al. (1979) presented a clear and compelling information-processing model of depression: "The cognitive model offers a hypothesis about predisposition to depression. Briefly, the theory proposes that early experiences provide the basis for forming negative concepts about one's self, the future, and the external world. These negative concepts (schema) may be latent but can be activated by specific circumstances which are analogous to experiences initially responsible for embedding the negative attitude" (p. 16). Cognitive distortions at work in those suffering from depression were described as a primitive as opposed to a mature way of thinking (see Table 8.1).

Beck's success and the popularity of his approach increased the confidence and excitement of those theorists, clinicians, and researchers who found this model pragmatic and effective. This led to the expansion of clinical syndromes and populations to whom it was

Table 8.1   Application of the Information-Processing Model to the Thinking of the Depressed Individual

1. *Arbitrary inference* (a response set) refers to the process of drawing a specific conclusion in the absence of evidence to support the conclusion or when the evidence is contrary to the conclusion.

2. *Selective abstraction* (a stimulus set) consists of focusing on a detail taken out of context, ignoring other more salient features of the situation and conceptualizing the whole experience on the basis of the fragment.

3. *Overgeneralization* (a response set) refers to the pattern of drawing a general rule or conclusion on the basis of one or more isolated incidents and applying the concept across the board to related and unrelated situations.

4. *Magnification and minimization* (a response set) are reflected in errors in evaluating the significance or magnitude of an event that are so gross as to constitute a distortion.

5. *Personalization* (a response set) refers to the patient's proclivity to relate external events to himself when there is no basis for making such a conception.

6. *Absolutistic, dichotomous thinking* (a response set) is manifested in the tendency to place all experiences in one or two opposite categories; for example, flawless or defective, immaculate or filthy, saint or sinner. In describing himself, the patient selects the extreme negative categorization.

Source: Beck, Rush, Shaw, and Emery, 1979, p. 14.

applied among others, individuals suffering from anxiety, pain, and substance abuse. These factors seem to have readied the cognitive wave to again crest with a major effort to conceptualize and treat individuals with personality disorders, an increasingly compelling area because of their prevalence in society and the difficulty of effectively treating them.

Expansion of the Model to Personality Theory: The next wave of development of the cognitive model was presented in 1990 with the publication of *Cognitive Therapy of Personality Disorders* (Beck & Freeman, 1990). The model is an expansion of the information-processing model of depression. Beck and Freeman describe their model: "A broad range of a patient's difficulties may be subsumed under one class, and can be influenced by changes in a single schema or a few schemas. This formulation is consistent with the principal contemporary theories of cognitive structure and cognitive development, all of which stress the function of schemas as determinants of rule-guided behavior" (p. 4). The schemas are anchored in the individual's "behavioral, cognitive, and affective elements" (p. 10).

Evolutionary-Based Strategies: Beck's theory takes into consideration "the role of our evolutionary history in our patterns of thinking, feeling, and acting" (Beck & Freeman, 1990, p. 23). Beck assumes that both animal and human behavior are programmed and "that these programs frequently depend on the interaction between genetically determined structures and experience" (p. 24). Beck and Freeman write, "It is reasonable to consider the notion that long-standing cognitive-affective-motivational programs influence our automatic processes: the way we construe events, what we feel, and how we are disposed to act. The programs involved in cognitive processing (affect, arousal, and motivation) may have evolved as a result of their ability to sustain life and promote reproduction" (p. 24). Individuals may, in fact, have various personality types that are genetically determined: Some people are predisposed to attack when threatened, others might freeze, and yet others go out of their way to avoid danger. Each of these patterns may have a certain adaptive survival value (Beck & Emery, 1985).

Strategies may be likened to personality traits or patterns of behavior in that they "may be regarded as forms of programmed behavior that are designed to serve biological goals" (Beck & Freeman,

1990, p. 25). These are not necessarily conscious in the individual. These strategies can be either maladaptive or adaptive, depending on the circumstances in which they are expressed. "Egocentricity, competitiveness, exhibitionism, and avoidance of unpleasantness may all be adaptive in certain situations but grossly maladaptive in others" (p. 25).

Applying the Information-Processing Model: Beck's theory of personality is based on the information-processing model (Pretzer & Beck, 1996). Individuals process data about themselves based on their beliefs and other elements of their cognitive organization (i.e., memory, perception, and the like). The manner in which information is interpreted shapes an individual response pattern. Therefore, inferred cognitive structures determine how information is acted on. Beck and Freeman (1990) write, "Although phenomena such as thoughts, feelings, and wishes may flash only briefly into our consciousness, the underlying structures responsible for these subjective experiences are relatively stable and durable. Furthermore, these structures are not in themselves conscious, although we can, through introspection, identify their content" (p. 31).

One of the most important elements of Beck's theoretical model is the emphasis on schema. He traces this concept to others before him, such as Bartlett (1932), Kelly (1955), and Piaget (1926), the famous developmental psychologist. Schema may include information about relationships, such as attitudes toward self and others, as well as concrete or abstract impersonal categories. They can be narrow or wide in scope and flexible or rigid. They have a certain potential for emotional valence that can be latent or hypervalent. Thus, an individual might have a schema about large dogs being aggressive, perhaps resulting from past negative experiences. When the schema for dogs is hypervalent, loaded with emotion, behavior will be guided more powerfully by this schema than in an individual whose latent schema is not so loaded.

Different types of schema serve various functions:

1. *Cognitive schemas* "are concerned with abstraction, interpretation, and recall."
2. *Affective schemas* "are responsible for the generation of feelings."
3. *Motivational schemas* "deal with wishes and desires."

4. *Instrumental schemas* "prepare for action."
5. *Control schemas* "are involved in self-monitoring and inhibiting or directing action" (Beck & Freeman, 1990, p. 33).

Components of Personality Organization: Cognitive structures may be viewed in a linear and logical manner. For example, in a situation of imminent danger, the "danger schema" is activated. Then, in sequence, "the effective, motivational, action, and control schemas are activated" (Beck & Freeman, 1990, p. 34). In the presence of danger, the system might function as follows: (1) the **cognitive schema** assesses the situation; (2) anxiety ensues when the **affective schema** is activated, calling for action: flight or fight; (3) action (**instrumental schema**) is taken as the motivational system responds; and (4) further assessment may inhibit (**control schema**) the response if it is judged to be counterproductive.

Internal Control System: An essential aspect of this theoretical model is how impulses are controlled or inhibited. Impulses may be thought of as wants and are inhibited by beliefs. Beliefs are the "should" and "should nots" that inhabit our schema; thus, they exert a counterforce on our impulses and wishes: *I **wish to punch** someone who hurts me but do not because of **the belief that it is wrong** to act in violence.* In a sense, this system represents how individuals communicate with themselves. "The internal communication consists of self-monitoring, self-appraisal and self-evaluation, self-warnings, and self-instructions" (Beck & Freeman, 1990, p. 35). This self-talk is an important aspect of determining whether one is "on course." In depression, the self-evaluations are generally negative. "In normal functioning, this system of self-evaluations and self-directions operates more or less automatically" (p. 36).

SELF-CONCEPT: An individual's self-schemas or self-concept is the deeper structure from which self-evaluations and self-instructions emanate. "In the course of maturation, we develop a medley of rules that provide the substrate for our self-evaluations and self-directions. These rules form the basis for setting standards, expectations, and plans of actions for ourselves" (p. 36). When these self-schemas are exaggerated, the person may cross the threshold from a personality type to a disorder. For example, if normal dependency persists and becomes exaggerated in adulthood, it might reflect a maladaptive schema: *"I must be dependent on others, whatever the cost, to survive."*

FUNCTIONAL VERSUS DYSFUNCTIONAL BELIEFS: As we can see, all humans, according to Beck's model, are guided in life by internal beliefs that can be organized into various schemas and constitute a self-concept. If one's internal beliefs (also called automatic thoughts) are generally positive, one can function without significant difficulty. For example, if while reading this book you are challenged by the material and experience some frustration with the concepts and say to yourself, *"I believe I have sufficient intelligence to master this material, although difficult and frustrating at times,"* you are probably a person with positive self-concept. Compare that response to these: *"I am not smart enough to master this material"* and *"This material is really stupid and I am too smart to concern myself with exerting much effort."* You might expect the person in the first case to become despondent and in the second artificially puffed up. In both cases, there is evidence of dysfunctional beliefs ("I am not smart enough" and "I am too smart") perhaps based on maladaptive schema.

Linehan's Cognitive-Behavioral Model

Various individuals have combined cognitive and behavioral approaches and constructs (Meichenbaum, 1977). Taking the therapeutic community by storm, Marsha Linehan (1993) developed a cognitive-behavioral model of personality based on her work with individuals suffering from severe personality disorders. A researcher at the University of Washington, Linehan developed her model based on clinical need: "In recent years, interest in borderline personality disorder (BPD) had exploded. This interest is related to at least two factors. First, individuals meeting criteria for BPD are flooding mental health centers and practitioners' offices. Eleven percent of all psychiatric outpatients and 19% of psychiatric inpatients are estimated to meet criteria for BPD; of patients with some form of a personality disorder, 33% of outpatients and 63% of inpatients appear to meet BPD criteria. Second, available treatment modalities appear to be woefully inadequate" (p. 3). As such, her model emerged out of her interest in working with patients having a Borderline Personality Disorder.

Table 8.2   Typical Overdeveloped and Underdeveloped Strategies

Personality Disorder	Overdeveloped	Underdeveloped
Obsessive-compulsive	Control Responsibility Systematization	Spontaneity Playfulness
Dependent	Help seeking Clinging	Self-sufficiency Mobility
Passive-aggressive	Autonomy Resistance Passivity Sabotage	Intimacy Assertiveness Activity Cooperativeness
Paranoid	Vigilance Mistrust Suspiciousness	Serenity Trust Acceptance
Narcissistic	Self-aggrandizement Competitiveness	Sharing Group identification
Antisocial	Combativeness Exploitativeness Predation	Empathy Reciprocity Social sensitivity
Schizoid	Autonomy Isolation	Intimacy Reciprocity
Avoidant	Social vulnerability Avoidance Inhibition	Self-assertion Gregariousness
Histrionic	Exhibitionism Expressiveness Impressionism	Reflectiveness Control Systematization

Source: Cognitive Therapy of Personality Disorders by A. T. Beck and A. Freeman, © 1990. Reprinted by permission of The Guilford Press.

Linehan's (1993) model of personality is **biosocial,** as she considers both the genetic-emotional predispositions for emotional dysregulation and the invalidating environment as responsible for the creation of this disorder. Her theory of personality is based on the "fundamental world view" of "dialectics" (p. 28). She writes of

Brief Description of Borderline Personality Disorder

"Unpredictable, manipulative, unstable. Frantically fears abandonment and isolation. Experiences rapidly fluctuating moods. Shifts rapidly between loving and hating. Sees self and other alternatively as all-good and all-bad" (Millon & Davis, 2000, p. 4; also see Chapter 12).

this view: "First, dialectics stresses interrelatedness and wholeness. Dialectics assumes a systems perspective on reality. The analysis of parts of a system is of limited value unless the analysis clearly relates the part to the whole. Thus, identity itself is relational, and boundaries between parts are temporary and exist only in relation to the whole; indeed, it is the whole that determines the boundaries" (p. 31).

Linehan's model is primarily a treatment model, so it is not a grand theory of personality, as in Freud's attempt at theorizing. However, by developing a treatment model that has shown preliminary empirical support, she has demonstrated that cognitive-behavioral methods are effective. This provides some level of validation for the theory. Another important consideration is the blending of theoretical elements that include biological, relational, cognitive, behavioral, and systemic components. This trend toward integrative models of personality, discussed in later chapters, represents a shift from monolithic models of the past to the more flexible ones of current-day theorists. Millon (1999) comments: "What makes the approach of Linehan so significant is the exhaustive and systematic nature of her analysis and treatment of one specific personality disorder, the so-called borderline patient" (p. 86).

Linehan (1993) believes attempting to categorize behavior into the various modes traditionally used by cognitive-behaviorists—"motoric, cognitive-verbal, and physiological"—is artificial (p. 37). She describes the component systems: "Motor behaviors are what most people think of as behavior; they include overt and covert actions and movements of the skeletal muscular system. Cognitive-verbal behavior includes such activities as thinking, problem solving, perceiving, imaging, speaking, writing, and gestural communication,

The Need for Classifying Mental Disorders and the Controversy in Diagnostic Labeling

The advance of any scientific discipline requires that the phenomena observed be classified into groups and labeled. This is an elementary step in any natural science. Phenomena, such as flora and fauna in botany are sorted by various similar features. In psychological science, the same need exists: Various signs and symptoms must be catalogued. This has culminated in the current system of psychiatric classification of mental disorders in a manual used by most mental health professionals, the *Diagnostic and Statistical Manual of Mental Disorders-Revised (DSM-IV-R)* of the American Psychiatric Association (APA, 1994), which has gone through a number of editions. As we shall explore in greater depth later, the advancement of the field was accelerated by this manual, which has operationalized various mental disorders so that there is some degree of consistency among those who diagnosis them. This is essential for research in the field and has spawned much scientific study, particularly in the area of personality disorders.

This manual and some of the diagnostic categories listed have not been without controversy. In fact, the diagnostic category Borderline Personality Disorder is one of the more controversial. Some believe this disorder, predominantly diagnosed in women, is an example of pejorative psychiatric labeling. Many therapists and clinical researchers have suggested that the symptoms are better described as Posttraumatic Stress Disorder (PTSD) because the majority of those with this diagnosis have a history of early sexual and physical abuse. There is a movement to relabel this disorder "affective deregulation syndrome."

as well as observable behavior (e.g., attending, orienting, recalling, and reviewing). Physiological behaviors include activities of the nervous system, glands, and smooth muscles. Although usually covert (e.g., heartbeat), physiological behaviors can also be overt (e.g., blushing and crying)" (p. 37). One can see in the comprehensive

Selected Research Findings

- *"Effects of optimism on psychological and physical well-being: Theoretical overview and empirical update"* (Scheier & Carver, 1992). The authors reviewed research that examined the beneficial effects of optimism on well-being. The evidence suggests that optimists are more likely than pessimists to engage in positive health habits and cope more adaptively with stress. This construct has some similarity to self-efficacy.

- *"Dysfunctional attitudes and vulnerability to depressive symptoms: A 14-week longitudinal study"* (Dykman & Johll, 1998). The researchers conducted a longitudinal study with 275 subjects, during which they found that under conditions of high stress, those who were asymptomatic and had high levels of dysfunctional beliefs had greater increases in depressive symptoms. This interaction was specific to the female subjects.

- *"The relation of early abuse to cognition and coping in depression"* (Kuyken & Brewin, 1999). The researchers investigated cognitive factors that are related to a history of sexual abuse in 58 women. The findings showed that abuse history and intrusive memories are associated with lower levels of self-esteem.

- *"The efficacy of dialectical behavior therapy for borderline personality disorder"* (Westen, 2000). After reviewing the literature, the author states that the most scientific conclusion to draw from the empirical evidence is that DBT does produce initial improvement on multiple variables, especially on reducing parasuicidal behavior. However, he also concludes that there is a major gap in the literature concerning long-term impact.

- *"Gender differences in pain and pain behavior: The role of catastrophizing"* (M. J. Sullivan, Tripp, & Santor, 2000). The researchers evaluated 80 subjects in an experimental pain procedure. The results showed women reported more intense pain and pain behavior. For women, the helplessness scale contributed to the prediction of pain.

description of the subcomponents of personality the influence of the information-processing behavioral orientation.

Principles of the Cognitive and Cognitive-Behavioral Models

Philosophical Underpinnings and Assumptions

"The roots of the cognitive model date back to the Phrygian philosopher Epictetus (ca. A.D. 55–ca. 135) who said, 'People are disturbed not by things, but the view they take of them'" (Arnkoff & Glass, 1992, p. 658). The philosophical foundation for cognitive models of personality include "Cartesian philosophy, British empiricism, Kantian philosophy and nineteenth century Scottish school of philosophy" (Hillner, 1984, p. 186). Descartes's emphasis on dualism and rationalism can be seen in this model of human personality. Kant postulated that humans have innate categories that structure the manner in which the world is perceived.

Notions of Normal versus Abnormal

Notions about what constitutes normal as opposed to abnormal are given more attention in the cognitive model than in the behavioral model that was its predecessor. The level and degree to which maladaptive behavior is manifest determine abnormality. Abnormal behavioral responses are directly traced to dysfunctional schematic representations. Individuals who have negative internal beliefs that are deeply ingrained will act in a manner consistent with these. People who believe they are unlovable may adopt various "adaptive" strategies as a way of confirming their internal schematic representation; they may then act in ways that demand love from others in a hostile way and reinforce their schema when people pull away and do not respond in the way they desire.

Assessment Strategies and Tools

Cognitive theorists have a strong foundation in empiricism and therefore value objective assessment instruments. Beck (Beck et al., 1979) developed one of the most widely used instruments, the Beck Depression Inventory, to assess depression; many consider this tool equivalent to taking a patient's temperature. He also developed the Scale for Suicide Ideation. Both of these instruments are quickly taken and easily scored. Assessment of personality in the cognitive model relies on the assumption that various personality configurations have common schematic representations that can be identified (Beck & Freeman, 1990; Young, 1994). Most assessment tools are self-administered scales that are then scored by a clinician. For example, Young has developed a schema-focused questionnaire that is used to identify various schematic representations associated with various patterns of personality. Beck and Freeman (1990) also "include those that directly evaluate the patient's schemas with the clinically acknowledged schematic structures seen in the various disorders" (p. 351).

Application of Model

The cognitive model of personality has had major impact on the field of psychotherapy over the past quarter century, becoming the dominant approach used by mental health professionals and quickly gaining prominence in the treatment of personality disorders. The cognitive model has not only been applied to psychopathological conditions but is also highly influential in various approaches for those seeking self-improvement and enhancement of self-esteem and relationships. Many self-help books base their premise on the "power of positive thinking," which has become trivialized in certain self-help spheres. The cognitive model is also, as we saw in Chapter 4, a major discipline that is being applied to the study of consciousness.

Cultural Influences and Differences

There is not much formal attention given to cultural differences, although the basic model takes into consideration the environmental factors that influence and shape schema. For example, those raised in a culture in which women are expected to be submissive would understand this as a reflection of cultural demands. Because of its flexibility, there is probably good generalizability to other cultures of the basic tenets of this model. An interesting question is whether those raised in other cultures learn to process information differentially and what impact this might have on personality development and consolidation.

Strengths and Limitations of Model

The cognitive model has many strengths, which has fed the continual growth of this model in a variety of psychological arenas. First, the fact that, to a large degree, the cognitive model stayed committed to research support has led to a number of advances in many systems of human functioning, including perception, memory, and problem solving. Second, the cognitive model demonstrates a level of parsimony that is very attractive to the student of personality as well as the clinical practitioner. At this point in the development of this model, it is hard to point out the limitations. Certainly, a pure cognitive model does not take into account the range of factors that influence and shape personality. However, to the credit of the cognitive model, much flexibility has been demonstrated in incorporating metaphors and findings from other disciplines, which has tended to strengthen and broaden its application and explanatory value. As the cognitive theorists have expanded to personality theory, one limitation has become somewhat more apparent: Much of the terminology seems to reinvent psychoanalytic concepts that were rejected when this model was developing. One sees many points of convergence that in the long term will lead to a comprehensive theory of personality.

Summary

Cognitive science represents a revolutionary advance in the field of psychology. It emerged from radical behaviorism but went a step beyond, giving the field a new legitimacy that has spawned many new theoretical developments. Miller, who believed the behavioral model lacked sufficient complexity, engendered this cognitive revolution. Miller was interested in memory, a highly relevant topic for psychology and personality. Another conceptual leap occurred when the computer was used as a tool for developing a model of how the mind works, an area of great interest to neuroscientists. The computer offered an analogue to how the mind might process information and form connections. Information-processing led to the conceptualization of seminal constructs such as schema, which are cognitive templates we use to process information. Various blends of cognitive models have been developed with slightly different emphases; cognitive, social cognitive, and cognitive-behavioral are the most prominent. Many of these developed out of cognitive theories and models of psychotherapy. Each has contributed to our understanding of personality. Constructs such as self-efficacy are useful in understanding how our perceptions and self-beliefs affect our behavior. Personality is not just a reaction to external events and conditioning but is strongly affected by the manner in which we cognitively process our world and form schematic inner representations of our relational experiences.

Suggested Reading

Beck, A. T., & Freeman, A. (1990). *Cognitive therapy of personality disorders*. New York: Guilford Press.

Meichenbaum, D. H. (1977). *Cognitive-behavior modification*. New York: Plenum Press.

Young, J. E. (1994). *Cognitive therapy for personality disorders: A schema-focused approach* (Rev. ed.). Sarasota, FL: Professional Resource Exchange.

Interpersonal and Factorial
Models of Personality

9

Chapter

Introduction

The interpersonal model of personality represented a major departure from previous models. Moving away from the emphasis on the intrapsychic system, interpersonal theorists viewed personality from the perspective of dyadic relationships. There were a few seemingly separate lines of development in the evolutionary process of this model. The main branches, the interpersonal-psychodynamic and the interpersonal-factorial models, use the interpersonal circumplex. However, the cross-fertilization of conceptual systems links many of the major progenitors of this approach through interpersonal relationships. In this chapter, the interpersonal theory of Harry Stack Sullivan is presented and then some of the models that have both direct and indirect lineage are discussed. As the reader will have already surmised, the history and evolution of personality theory is a rather convoluted and sometimes confusing trail. To preview, there is an important theoretical lineage between Sullivanian interpersonally based theoretical models presented in this chapter and the two main branches of relational theory presented in Chapter 10.

Major Historical Figures

Sullivan's Theory of Interpersonal Relations

Harry Stack Sullivan (1892–1949) is considered the father of interpersonal theory (Millon et al., 2000). Sullivan, a psychiatrist, developed his own theory, which he called **the theory of interpersonal**

relations. Sullivan conducted research in schizophrenia early in his career at the Pratt Hospital in Maryland (Bischof, 1970). He helped found and direct the Washington School of Psychiatry and was a social activist who gave much time and financial resources working to attain peace.

Sullivan strongly believed that interpersonal relationships were the foundation of personality. Clara Thompson (1952) described Sullivan's perspective: "He holds that, given a biological substrate, the human is the product of interaction with other human beings, that it is out of the personal and social forces acting upon one from the day of birth that the personality emerges" (p. 211). This was a radical departure from the intrapsychic emphasis of classical structural drive theory and the empiricist emphasis of the behavioral model.

Sullivan was not much concerned with what transpired inside people; what was compelling was the evolving relational patterns (Chrzanowski, 1977). His emphasis on adaptation, in Chrzanowski's view, qualifies including this model in the ego psychology framework.

Sullivan believed all needs are essentially interpersonal and that satisfaction seeking inevitably involves others. Our survival, in fact, is dependent on **cooperation** and **complementary** transactions, as well as need satisfaction. He was much more compelled to understand what transpires between people as opposed to inside them. He coined the term **participant-observer** to describe what occurs between therapist and patient. This is a major innovative development, differing from Freud's concept of neutrality of the therapist (see Chapter 4) and Kohut's mirroring relationship (see Chapter 6). The participant-observer relationship is nonauthoritarian, concerned with the evolving relational matrix between therapist and client. In other words, the analyst cannot be a blank screen but, by the very nature of the relationship, was a participant in the meaning making. In Sullivan's model, the individual is managing his or her own needs and trying to attain approval from those whose approval is desired (Hazell, 1994). Interpersonal communications are essential to shaping and maintaining personality. It is noteworthy that Sullivan's development set the stage for relational models of personality (covered in Chapter 10).

There are many who believe that Sullivan contributed much to our current understanding of personality. Sullivan did lack a well-articulated theoretical system. Although his basic notion about the centrality of interpersonal relationships was a major advance, many of his constructs are esoteric and he is difficult to read. Some concepts are relevant to contemporary theory, others are interesting because of their somewhat idiosyncratic language. Some of the formulations tend to be fuzzy; for example, main constructs such as self and self-system are contradictory in nature. "The distinction between the term Self and Self-system is highly complicated in Sullivan's terminology, and we cannot find a clear-cut line of demarcation. Both terms refer to the organization of experiences triggered off by the intervention of anxiety, and both represent a process rather than an entity" (Chrzanowski, 1977, p. 99). According to Millon et al. (2000):

Despite his many interesting and brilliant contributions, Sullivan is not regarded as a systematic thinker. Many of his books, in fact, represent past lecture series organized for publication by dedicated followers. Moreover, the personality constructs he proposed are not notably interpersonal, at least by contemporary standards. These include, for example, the stammerer and the homosexual personality. Nevertheless, Sullivan is regarded as one of the most important theorists of the twentieth century. His ideas spawned diverse lines of research, including work that led to the famous "double-bind" theory of schizophrenia (Bateson, Jackson, Haley, & Weakland, 1956), the study of family communications patterns, and even studies of nonverbal gestural communications, called kinesics. (p. 41)

H. S. Sullivan (1953) coined the term **self-system** to account for how the interpersonal experiences affect the manner in which personality is formed. He believed the self-system was organized around gaining satisfaction and avoiding anxiety. Insecurity and organic needs generate tension or anxiety. Humans attempt to reduce anxiety, present from the moment of birth, by striving for security. An optimum level of anxiety is sought; too little, and there will be a lack of drive; too much means paralysis. Conformity results in approval but at the cost of the true self, which creates anxiety. Anxiety interferes with intimacy and hinders creativity (Chrzanowski, 1977). Individuals need to learn how to function in the presence of anxiety without taking refuge in self-defeating operations for security. "The interpersonal tenet of anxiety refers directly to formative relational experiences and their present-day emotional and cognitive extensions" and "is viewed as the most powerful barrier to meaningful integration" (pp. 53, 65).

The Function of Anger and Its Relation to Anxiety: Personality problems are evident in those who are unable to experience anger as well as those who are chronically reacting with irritation. Anger is a natural response to an interpersonal injury or mistreatment. Fear of interpersonal aggression and of loss of control can inhibit the experience of anger; fear of anger in others can induce anxiety (Chrzanowski, 1977).

One does not have to be in relationship with a real person in Sullivan's model. The interpersonal context is present in relation to fictional characters as well as dreams. Bischof (1970) describes the central theme of Sullivan's theory revolving around anxiety as a primary force responsible for building the self-system, as well as providing an education about life. Sullivan depicted developmental progression through seven states and their associated pertinent interpersonal experiences.

He divided cognitive experience into three forms of thinking: prototaxic, parataxic, and syntaxic. **Prototaxic** refers to the beginning of conscious processes, where sensations and perceptions are fragmentary. **Parataxic** refers to cognition, which is capable of discerning causal relationships. **Syntaxic** refers to the ability to use symbolic thinking; the most advanced level, it allows for the highest level of communication with others.

Sullivan did not view personality as an entity for investigation; instead, he emphasized the relationship between personalities (Bischof, 1970). According to Benjamin (1993): "Most important is his explicit marking of connections between the patient's adult personality and the patient's *perceptions* of early social education experiences" (p. 17). Sullivan believed that interpersonal patterns learned early in life are major determinants of adult personality. He also emphasized the importance of the environment; those immersed in an unstable environment will likely have an unstable personality.

Murray's Unified Theory of Personality

Henry A. Murray (1893–1988) was originally trained as a medical doctor and then attained a PhD in biochemistry. Later, he developed a passion for the field of psychology, particularly personality theory. This was stimulated by meeting Freud and further fueled by meeting Jung, which he described as transformational. Jung had a major influence on his professional and personal life. Murray later assisted Morton Prince in founding the Harvard Psychological Clinic, which he later directed. According to Hunt (1993), his "most significant contribution to personality research was a three-year project that he and some two dozen other psychologists conducted at the clinic" (p. 325). The results of this landmark study were published in 1938 in *Explorations in Personality*. Never before had so much personality data been amassed. Fifty-one male students from Harvard were extensively tested and interviewed. Although there were some mixed reviews when this was published, most workers in the field believed

that Murray had succeeded in strengthening the position of psychoanalytic theory by bridging the gap between research and analytic
constructions (Winter & Barenbaum, 1999).

Murray attempted to build a comprehensive system of personology using a multidisciplinary approach (Shneidman, 1981). Although Murray was highly influenced by both Freud and Jung,
Sullivan's interpersonal perspective also shaped him. The interpersonal influence is deeply etched in his writing and formulations. He
wrote of the interpersonal system or **dyadic relationship:** "The notion came and stuck that a dyadic (two-person) relationship,
whether transient or enduring, should be formulated as a single system, equal analytic attention being devoted to each participant. Although I have never been inclined to accept Harry Stack Sullivan's
restriction of the domain of psychology to the sphere of interpersonal relations, I use dyadic interactions as a test of every formulation or theoretical system I encounter in the literature" (Shneidman,
1981, p. 29)

Murray's interest in the dyad led him to the idea that in interpersonal transaction, themes are expressed and can be categorized
as a simple microtheme or a simple macrotheme. He also proposed
that these themes were expressed and received in a complementary
way between the two participants. For example, an individual who
needs to inform (relate facts, rumors), the **transmitter,** will require
a **receptor** who needs the information (state of curiosity, interest).
Other types of dyadic themes include (1) reciprocation, (2) cooperation, (3) competition, and (4) opposition. He wrote: "It has become
more and more apparent to me that the energetic components of
personality can be better defined as thematic dispositions than as
general actional dispositions" (quoted in Shneidman, 1981, p. 32).
He describes this perspective in an example: "Instead of saying that
X possesses the trait of aggressivity, or that he has a ready and intense need for aggression, one should, if possible, specify . . . that
two properties of his personality . . . are supersensitive dispositions
to react with resentment and aggressive words (1) to apperceived
insults to his self-respect and (2) to apperceived vainglorious boast-
ings by an alter" (p. 32). Murray's acknowledged grandiose vision
for personology was a very compelling force in his own personality.
Shneidman (1981) describes his vision: "Although I was educated
on the principle that limitation of aim is the secret of success in science, and that the scientist is responsible for particulars, it must be

only too apparent to you that I have been tempted to depart from the wisdom of this strategy by the dream of an all-embracing scheme, a unified science, not, of course, to be achieved in my own lifetime but in the distant future, if there is to be a future for our species" (p. 45). Later, Murray wrote: "Personology, if it is ever developed, will rest upon an organized collection of facts pertaining relevantly to the long course of complex events from human conception to human death" (Shneidman, 1981, p. 115).

Murray hoped that the study of personality would develop basic concepts, such as energy and laws in physics. His innovative thinking could also be seen in his early embracing of **general systems theory** (von Bertalanffy, 1952) and the application of this to the "system of personality" (Shneidman, 1981, p. 48). We shall go into greater depth on this topic in a later chapter, when we talk about integrative models. Clearly, Murray was an innovative thinker and a synthesizer. His knowledge of other disciplines kept him from myopic theoretical formulations or scientific fact finding. He was truly interested in achieving a comprehensive grasp of personality functioning from which he could develop an integrative theory.

Emerging from Murray's interest in interpersonal relationships and dynamics and having a need to measure his constructs, in collaboration with Christina Morgan he developed the **Thematic Apperception Test (TAT)** (Murray, 1943). Current historical research suggests that, in fact, Morgan was the main force in the TAT's development. In any case, the TAT was a novel projective technique based on the fact that when individuals interpret a social situation, they are saying more about themselves than about what they are observing (Murray & Morgan, 1935). Murray and Morgan describe their approach: "The procedure which suggested itself was this: to present subjects with a series of pictures, each of which depicts a different dramatic event, with the instructions to interpret the action in each picture and give an imaginary reconstruction of the preceding events and the final outcome. It was anticipated that in the performance of this task a subject would necessarily be forced to project some of his own fantasies into the material and so reveal some of his more pressing underlying needs" (quoted in Shneidman, 1981, p. 391). Although the TAT is still very popular and used extensively in clinical practice, and to a much lesser degree in research (see Chapter 8 on Cramer's work on the empirical validity of defenses), according to Benjamin (1993), "The scientific status of the

TAT has remained equivocal, largely because subjective judgment is required to assess the meaning of the stories told in response to the TAT pictures" (p. 19). Cramer (1982) has developed a manual for scoring defenses, which was subsequently validated by Hibbard et al. (1994) and further validated in another study by Hibbard and Porcerelli (1998). Regardless of the quibbles over the empirical validation of the TAT, there is no doubt that this was a major innovation in personality assessment and continues to be relevant in clinical practice and research 65 years after it was published.

Importance of Murray's Efforts: Although Murray's efforts at developing a comprehensive theory of personality were not successful to the degree he might have desired, and the system that he developed is too cumbersome, many of his efforts and predictions are bearing fruit. Murray displayed an enormous level of openness to developments in various disciplines that he thought might be useful to building a scaffold for his theory. This required much grit in a time when most workers were chauvinistically committed to one theory or another. Murray attempted theoretical integration that would broaden the range of the theoretical system. He was able to see the useful elements of many of the current systems and incorporate them into his thinking. Murray was prolific in spawning the research interests of the many professional collaborations and students that he developed along the way. Most noteworthy in the evolution of Murray's conceptualization was the development of the **Interpersonal Circle (IPC).** According to Benjamin (1993), "His categories of need provided the basic building blocks of the Interpersonal Circle (IPC), a monumentally important development that began with Freedman, Leary, Ossorio, and Coffey" (1951, p. 20). A second article published by LaForge, Leary, Naboisek, Coffey, and Freedman (1954) further advanced this conceptualization. In a landmark monograph, Leary (1957) created a complete interpersonal diagnostic system using the IPC.

Leary's Interpersonal Circle

Timothy Leary (1920–1996) was another important figure in the development of the interpersonal model. Working under the auspices of the Kaiser Foundation Research Project, Leary, the principal investigator, built on the previous work of Murray and his colleagues. He took the basic IPC and expanded it in a significant fashion. Leary became quite a controversial figure in the 1960s, when he began experimenting with and encouraging others to use mind-altering drugs to expand their consciousness.

Guttman (1966) renamed Leary's (1957) Interpersonal Circle the **circumplex** (see Figure 9.1). The circumplex model had a number of interesting features. Murray's (1938) list of needs was reduced and reorganized; these were arranged so their relationships would be obvious. The basic dimensions of the IPC were used as the foundation. There are two basic axes: The horizontal axis has at the left point "hate" and the right "love"; the vertical axis has at the top point "submissive" and at the bottom "dominant" (see Figure 9.2).

According to Benjamin (1993), Leary's conceptual leap was based on Sullivan's formulations about the importance of interpersonal behavior as the basis for diagnosing psychiatric conditions. Interpersonal behavior, rather than character traits or symptom constellations, was a reflection of personality. Using the new conceptual framework, Leary offered an interpersonal diagnostic system for personality disorders, being "the first to make explicit connections between medical diagnostic nomenclature and the interpersonal descriptions offered by the IPC" (p. 21). Benjamin (1993, p. 20) lists the interpersonal descriptions in Leary's circumplex and their corresponding personality disorder from Kraepelin's (1904) psychiatric diagnostic system:

Octant AP: Managerial-Autocratic = Compulsive personality.

Octant BC: Competitive-Narcissistic = Narcissistic, exploitative personality.

Octant DE: Aggressive Sadistic = Psychopathic personality.

Octant FG: Rebellious-Distrustful = Schizoid personality.

Octant HI: Self-effacing–Masochistic = Masochistic or obsessive personality.

Octant JK: Docile-Dependent = Anxiety neurosis.

Octant LM: Cooperative-Overconventional = Hysterical personality.

Octant NO: Responsible-Hypernormal = Psychosomatic personality.

However, according to Benjamin (1993), Leary was not persistent in his efforts to develop this line of thinking, although he was

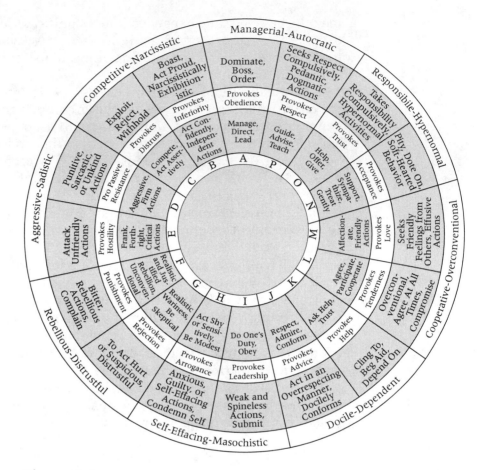

Figure 9.1

Leary's Interpersonal Circle (IPC). Art and text are from Leary (1957, p. 65). This is the classification of interpersonal behavior into sixteen mechanisms or reflexes. Each of the sixteen interpersonal variables is illustrated by sample behaviors. The inner circle presents illustrations of adaptive reflexes (e.g., for the variable A, *manage*). The center ring indicates the type of behavior that this interpersonal reflex tends to "pull" from the other one. Thus we see that the person who uses the reflex *A* tends to provoke others to *obedience*, and so on. These findings involve two-way interpersonal phenomena (what the subject does and what the "Other" does back) and are therefore less reliable than the other interpersonal codes presented in this figure. The next circle illustrates extreme or rigid reflexes (e.g., *dominates*). The perimeter of the circle is divided into eight general categories employed in *interpersonal diagnosis*. Each category has a moderate (adaptive) and an extreme (pathological) intensity (e.g., *Managerial-Autocratic*).

Figure 9.2

**The Two Dimensions Represented in Leary's
Interpersonal Circle.**

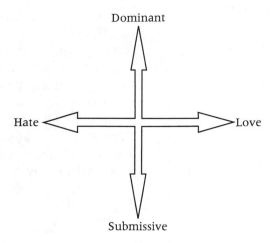

clearly a "brilliant and systematic" (Millon et al., 2000) theory builder. This is clearly an elegant model that captures much of human interaction. Unlike the major categorical system for arranging personality disorders used by *DSM*, the circumplex model is organized like a clock, with various personalities merging with other, similar ones. Greater flexibility exists in this system because it can account in a dimensional way for the variation from normal to abnormal personality. According to Millon and Davis (2000), Leary noted the similarities the four quadrants of this model have to the four humors of temperament of the early Greeks. Along the horizontal and vertical axes one can also superimpose sexual and aggressive drives from psychodynamic theory. This model spawned two separate lines of investigation and theoretical development: a continuation of Sullivan and Leary's work by Lorna Benjamin, a major theorist, clinician, educator, and researcher; and the Five-Factor Model (Wiggins, 1979, 1996), which, in a narrow sense, is not considered a theory of personality.

Historical Note on Theoretical Developments: Although Benjamin's interpersonal model and the Five-Factor Model share some common roots in Murray's work, they diverge in important ways. Benjamin's model is closer to contemporary psychodynamic theory, sharing many of the elements of depth psychology; however, because of the importance of the conceptual advances made by interpersonal theorists, it is desirable to present this work in this chapter and not with psychodynamic models. Benjamin's model is a more clinically based model, although combining a strong research orientation, unlike many of the other models presented in this volume. As the reader shall see, the Five-Factor Model, although sharing some of Murray's ideas, makes a radical departure, in that it is much more concerned with topography or determining the landscape of personality using traits. This model shares much in common with Eysenck's *Behavioral Models of Personality*, presented in Chapter 7. The Five-Factor Model and other similar factorial models have more affinity with the statistical models of academic psychology and have strong roots in the lexical model originated by Allport (Allport & Odbert, 1936).

Contemporary Theoretical Models

Benjamin's Structural Analysis of Social Behavior

One of the most empirically based models of contemporary personality theory is Lorna Smith Benjamin's structural analysis of social behavior (SASB; Benjamin, 1974, 1986, 1993, 1996). Benjamin believes that biology and social behavior are inextricably linked, evolving together, and urged that the intrapsychic and social factors not be neglected in favor of trait descriptions (1986). Her original training as a primatologist, as a student of Harry Harlowe, and later training with Carl Rogers and experience as a clinical psychologist provided her with strong scientific, psychotherapeutic, and investigative skills. Her interest in social behavior, stimulated by her early experiences with primates, may have drawn her to Sullivan's ideas. SASB combines aspects of both Leary's model and Schaefer (1965), who emphasized the autonomy-giving component of parental behavior (Millon et al., 2000). This added dimension depicts the "fundamental tension between controlling children and eventually giving up control, thereby allowing them to develop into responsible adults, masters of their own destiny" (Millon & Davis, 2000, p. 45).

Benjamin (1986) was interested in relating social variables to psychiatric diagnostic categories. In an effort to provide empirical validation, she conducted a study using a variety of measures, including the Minnesota Multiphasic Personality Inventory, with an initial sample of 108 psychiatric inpatients.

SASB is a tri-circumplex model of personality that strives for empirical replication. It was developed as an objective measure of interpersonal processes; therefore, it can be used to code both videotapes and audiotapes of social interactions in such formats as psychotherapy or family and group encounters. Benjamin (1986) describes her theoretical system: "SASB is a model that classifies social interactions and intrapsychic events in terms of three basic underlying dimensions. By assigning a value to each of the three dimensions, the logic of the model then yields 108 qualitatively different classifications. In other words, by making only three judgments, 108 different social and intrapsychic descriptions can be generated. Categories in the model can be collapsed to reduce the system to as few as 12 categories (quadrants) if a simpler description is desired" (p. 606).

Most interpersonal patterns can be expressed in three ways: (1) **recapitulated** simply by continuing them; (2) **copied** through identification with past figures; and (3) **introjected,** when individuals treat themselves as they were previously treated. These patterns can be traced using the SASB coding. For example, Benjamin (1993) describes the process in the case of a paranoid husband:

*Suppose the husband's father used hostile **control** and **blame** on the husband's mother. The husband now does the same with his wife. This is an example of identification of imitation. Suppose the wife of the jealous husband had a controlling, demeaning mother (CONTROL, BLAME). As a child, it was natural and adaptive for her to complement her mother with SUBMIT, SULK. As she internalized the messages from her mother, her self-concept came to include SELF-CONTROL and SELF-BLAME. As an adult, her self-concept and hostile compliance hold her in the marriage to the jealous husband and complement or reinforce his pattern of hostile control. Her patterns illustrate the principle of recapitulation. Their respective interpersonal histories have prepared them for a miserable but stable marriage. (p. 71)*

Benjamin depicts the SASB model in Figures 9.3 and 9.4.

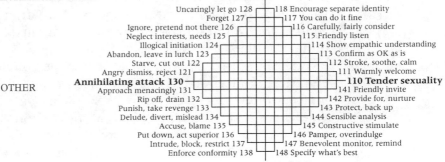

INTERPERSONAL

120 Endorse freedom

Uncaringly let go 128 — 118 Encourage separate identity
Forget 127 — 117 You can do it fine
Ignore, pretend not there 126 — 116 Carefully, fairly consider
Neglect interests, needs 125 — 115 Friendly listen
Illogical initiation 124 — 114 Show empathic understanding
Abandon, leave in lurch 123 — 113 Confirm as OK as is
Starve, cut out 122 — 112 Stroke, soothe, calm
Angry dismiss, reject 121 — 111 Warmly welcome

OTHER   **Annihilating attack 130** — **110 Tender sexuality**

Approach menacingly 131 — 141 Friendly invite
Rip off, drain 132 — 142 Provide for, nurture
Punish, take revenge 133 — 143 Protect, back up
Delude, divert, mislead 134 — 144 Sensible analysis
Accuse, blame 135 — 145 Constructive stimulate
Put down, act superior 136 — 146 Pamper, overindulge
Intrude, block, restrict 137 — 147 Benevolent monitor, remind
Enforce conformity 138 — 148 Specify what's best

Manage, control 140

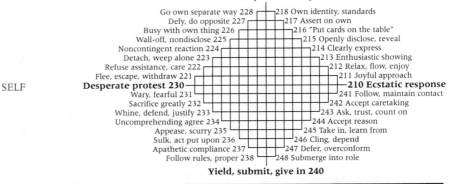

220 Freely come and go

Go own separate way 228 — 218 Own identity, standards
Defy, do opposite 227 — 217 Assert on own
Busy with own thing 226 — 216 "Put cards on the table"
Wall-off, nondisclose 225 — 215 Openly disclose, reveal
Noncontingent reaction 224 — 214 Clearly express
Detach, weep alone 223 — 213 Enthusiastic showing
Refuse assistance, care 222 — 212 Relax, flow, enjoy
Flee, escape, withdraw 221 — 211 Joyful approach

SELF   **Desperate protest 230** — **210 Ecstatic response**

Wary, fearful 231 — 241 Follow, maintain contact
Sacrifice greatly 232 — 242 Accept caretaking
Whine, defend, justify 233 — 243 Ask, trust, count on
Uncomprehending agree 234 — 244 Accept reason
Appease, scurry 235 — 245 Take in, learn from
Sulk, act put upon 236 — 246 Cling, depend
Apathetic compliance 237 — 247 Defer, overconform
Follow rules, proper 238 — 248 Submerge into role

Yield, submit, give in 240

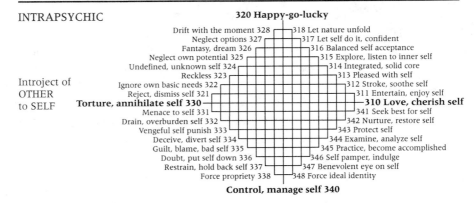

INTRAPSYCHIC

320 Happy-go-lucky

Drift with the moment 328 — 318 Let nature unfold
Neglect options 327 — 317 Let self do it, confident
Fantasy, dream 326 — 316 Balanced self acceptance
Neglect own potential 325 — 315 Explore, listen to inner self
Undefined, unknown self 324 — 314 Integrated, solid core
Reckless 323 — 313 Pleased with self
Ignore own basic needs 322 — 312 Stroke, soothe self
Reject, dismiss self 321 — 311 Entertain, enjoy self

Introject of
OTHER   **Torture, annihilate self 330** — **310 Love, cherish self**
to SELF

Menace to self 331 — 341 Seek best for self
Drain, overburden self 332 — 342 Nurture, restore self
Vengeful self punish 333 — 343 Protect self
Deceive, divert self 334 — 344 Examine, analyze self
Guilt, blame, bad self 335 — 345 Practice, become accomplished
Doubt, put self down 336 — 346 Self pamper, indulge
Restrain, hold back self 337 — 347 Benevolent eye on self
Force propriety 338 — 348 Force ideal identity

Control, manage self 340

Figure 9.3

The Full SASB Model. The space defined by the primitive axes can be divided up into infinitely many components. The full model is the most detailed version available. From Benjamin (1979). Copyright 1979 by the William Alanson White Psychiatric Foundation. Reprinted by permission.

Figure 9.4

The Simplified Cluster SASB Model.   The points shown on the full model in Figure 9.3 can be grouped to provide a simpler version. The horizontal axis runs from hate to love, and the vertical axis from enmeshment to differentiation. The three types of focus are represented by different styles of print. Complementarity is shown by adjacent **BOLD** and <u>UNDERLINED</u> points. Introjection is shown by adjacent **BOLD** and *ITALICIZED* points. From Benjamin (1993). Copyright 1993 by the Guilford Press. Reprinted by permission.

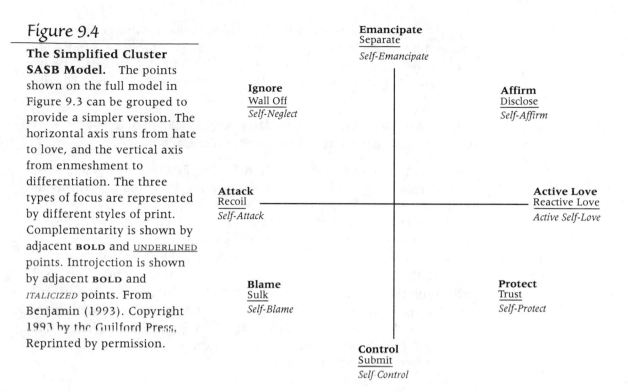

Benjamin uses five predictive principles to determine what may have happened before or after an interpersonal event:

1. *Complementarity:* A dyadic unit in which each participant in the interaction is in the same position in terms of interdependence and affiliation.

2. *Introjection:* Individuals treating themselves as they have been previously treated by significant figures.

3. *Similarity:* A person acting like or copying another through a desire to identify with him or her.

4. *Opposition:* A person desires the opposite interpersonal pattern that another is exhibiting; for example, seeking affirmation from someone who is blaming.

5. *Antithesis:* Pulling for the opposite interpersonal response; for example, wanting to protect someone who is neglected.

Although Benjamin (1994) includes the construct of defenses in her system, this element is not given major emphasis to classify and understand personality, as in other psychodynamic models. She believes that defenses can support both normal and disturbed behavior.

Klerman and Weissman's Interpersonal Model of Depression and the Link to Personality

Husband and wife Gerald Klerman (1928–1992) and Myrna Weissman (Klerman & Weissman, 1986; Klerman, Weissman, Rounsaville, & Chevron, 1984) developed an interpersonal model of depression based on Sullivan's work. A greatly expanded volume was published more recently, extending their model to other clinical syndromes and personality disorders (Weissman, Markowitz, & Klerman, 2000). Although their model is not considered a personality theory, it deals with important components seen through an interpersonal lens, underscoring the developments of Sullivan and others presented in this chapter and elsewhere in this text. They ground their model on Bowlby's (1969) attachment theory (discussed in Chapter 4). To recapitulate: Attachment theory posits that humans have an innate tendency to seek and maintain attachments. Attachments lead to the formation and expression of intense human emotions, which strengthen and renew these bonds. Furthermore, these attachments serve as a major source of human survival and security in relations with caretakers when young. When major attachments are disrupted, anxiety and sadness often result and, for some, pathological grief can later predispose one to depression.

The Emphasis on Social Roles in Defining the Self: Roles within the family, workplace, community, and friendships are the major point of interest in this model (Klerman et al., 1984). "These relationships between the individual and others, the self and others, have a structure, and this structure is provided by the position of the individual within the social system—most precisely by the specific roles the individual plays" (p. 48). Again, as emphasized by Sullivan, disturbed interpersonal relationships are responsible for human dysfunction.

The emphasis of this model is on understanding and treating depression in an interpersonal context. Critical to our theme is the relationship between personality traits and depression. The current installment of this theoretical and treatment approach attempts to understand three components of the personality matrix:

1. *Symptom function:* The development of depressive affect and the neurovegetative signs and symptoms (sleep and appetite disturbance, low energy, diurnal mood variation, etc.). These are presumed to have both biological and psychological precipitants.
2. *Social and interpersonal relations:* Interactions in social roles with other persons derived from learning based on childhood experiences, concurrent social reinforcement, and personal mastery and competence.
3. *Personality and character problems:* Enduring traits such as inhibited expression of anger or guilt, poor psychological communication with significant others, and difficulty with self-esteem. These traits determine a person's reactions to interpersonal experience. Personality patterns form part of the person's predisposition to depressive symptom formation (Klerman et al., 1984, p. 8).

The Primacy of Relationships to Healthy Functioning: One of the assumptions of this model is that humans are social beings and that healthy functioning requires interpersonal connections. Interpersonal aspects of depression include deficits related to insufficient relational skills or social impoverishment. There may be a limited number of sustaining relationships, or sufficient numbers lacking in fulfillment. The individual may also have symptoms either present or insufficiently resolved from the past that reduce the satisfaction from relationships. Positive intimacy and closeness facilitate emotional responding, the presence of which seems to provide some level of inoculation against stress and mental disorder. Marital discord has been linked in many studies to depression. Marital disputes may lead to symptoms of depression, although there is some question as to whether this relationship works conversely, that is, if depression leads to marital disputes. Probably, both hold true to some extent. Within intimate relations, those who have a proclivity for dependency also seem to be more likely to become depressed.

Kiesler's Interpersonal Force Field

Kiesler (1983) developed a two-dimensional model based on the work of Leary (1957) that differs from Benjamin's three dimensions. Kiesler (1986, p. 573) uses these two dimensions, "affiliation (love-hate, friendliness-hostility) and control (dominance-submission, higher-lower status)," to account for interpersonal behavior. He explains: "At an early developmental stage, a person settles on a distinctive interpersonal style, role, and/or self-definition which leads the person repeatedly to make interpersonal claims on others in terms of how close or intimate and how much in charge or dominant the person wants to be with others. In subsequent interaction, this relatively constant self-presentation is reciprocally reinforced or validated by responses the person pulls from interactants. In short, interpersonal theory asserts that each of us continually exudes a 'force field' which pushes others to respond to us with constricted classes of control and affiliation actions; thereby we pull from others 'complementary' responses designed to affirm and validate our chosen style of living and being" (p. 573). Kiesler's use of the term **interpersonal force field** is significant in the elegant manner in which it describes the interpersonal pushes and pulls that occur in all of our relationships. Kiesler's (1986) Interpersonal Circle is depicted (as adapted by Millon et al., 2000) in Figure 9.5. Kiesler's emphasis is clearly spelled out in this model and consistent with the way relationships and personalities are continually in synergy. If you behave in a certain way in your relationships, others will react to this style and respond accordingly. If someone treats you in a hostile and suspicious manner, you are likely to become defensive in return, further increasing the other's suspiciousness and hostility. Another phenomenon that can occur is **transactional escalation,** wherein the pattern of the interpersonal response style becomes more rigid, as in the suspicious man who becomes more and more so, to the point of paranoia.

Wiggins's Interpersonal-Factorial Model

Wiggins (Wiggins & Trobst, 1999) combined an interpersonal circumplex model with a factorial model. Wiggins (1982) proposed that the majority of diagnostic categories for personality disorders emphasize interpersonal behavior. He selected adjectives from the

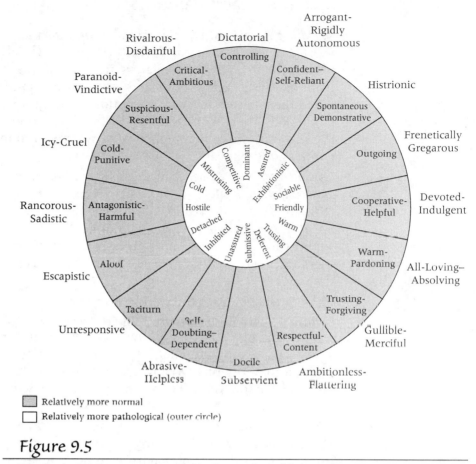

Figure 9.5

Kiesler's 1982 Interpersonal Circle.   Adapted from Millon & Klerman, 1986.

interpersonal domain and derived a scale that describes the traits and the interpersonal representation.

Principles of the Interpersonal Models

Philosophical Underpinnings and Assumptions

The interpersonal model combines both deductive and inductive forms of reasoning. Sullivan's interpersonal model is certainly similar in its origins to Freud's theory in terms of its introspective methods.

Selected Research Findings

- *"Relation of mothers' affective development history and parenting behavior: Effects on infant medical risk"* (Hammond, Landry, Swank, & Smith, 2000). The investigators used a sample of 311 mothers from diverse ethnic groups and low socioeconomic status and divided them based on their perception of acceptance or rejection in childhood. The results indicated that those who recalled having the highest level of acceptance were warmer and more flexible regardless of the level of infant medical risk.

- *"An interpersonal model of psychotherapy: Linking patient and therapist developmental history, therapeutic process, and types of outcome"* (Hilliard, Henry, & Strupp, 2000). The researchers used Benjamin's SASB model to code 64 psychodynamic therapies. The findings lend support for the model and suggest a direct effect of patient's and therapist's early parental relations on the outcome and process of therapy.

- *"Risk factors for depressive symptoms in late adolescence: A longitudinal community study"* (Frost, Reinherz, Pakiz-Camras, & Gianconia, 1999). The investigators followed a sample of 386 children from age 5 and examined them at age 18. For females, the findings showed that low birthweight and the death of a parent were risk factors for depression. For males, risk factors were emotional dependency and internalizing behavior.

- *"Demand-withdraw interaction in couples with a violent husband"* (Berns, Jacobson, & Gottman, 1999). Researchers videotaped the interaction of 47 couples with a violent husband, 28 distressed but nonviolent couples, and 16 well-adjusted couples. The battering couples showed less positive and more negative communication than the other two groups. Batterers were more likely to alternate between demand and withdraw interpersonal styles, and their spouses tended to be more demanding of change and less likely to withdraw.

- *"Codependency as a mediator between stressful events and eating disorders"* (Meyer, 1997). Researchers using a sample of 95 women ages 18 to 35 assessed for codependency, level of self-differentiation, and eating disorder. The results showed that women who experienced a significant relationship with an alcoholic figure or a chronic stressful situation had a higher level of eating disorder behavior. Also, women higher on codependency were higher on eating disorder behavior.

There is a dramatic shift to viewing the individual as a gestalt in a complex interpersonal field. Rychlak (1968) writes: "H. S. Sullivan's (1953) concept of personality as a system of interlacing dynamisms (roughly, 'habits') within a field of interpersonal relations also reflects this organismic influence. By viewing the individual as an independent organism within the social group, theorists of a gestalt persuasion have been reviving the 'one and the many' thesis of Socrates and Plato" (p. 395). Humans are viewed not as a higher-order animal with primitive drives but as essentially good, not striving for sexual and aggressive dominance but for interpersonal connection. However, others, such as Benjamin, have added a more inductive component by emphasizing empirically based research methods to modify and advance the theory. Leary also used an empirical approach in his development of the interpersonal circumplex model that has spawned generations of research. The purer factorial models definitely follow the rationalist philosophers and have allegiance to Cartesian dualism.

Notions of Normal versus Abnormal

The interpersonal model does address the dilemma of what constitutes normal and abnormal behavior. This model uses the notion of alienation (Rychlak, 1968) to explain the various manifestations of pathology and normality. Disturbances in interpersonal relationships alter patterns of relationships and behavior expression from symptom complexes to personality disturbance. There are various statistically based methods for determining what is normal and abnormal based on response patterns and normative behavior.

Assessment Strategies and Tools

The interpersonal model has produced an array of assessment strategies and tools. Probably the best-known is the projective TAT developed by Murray and Morgan for use in determining interpersonal themes. The TAT is a widely administered assessment tool that has been used extensively in clinical settings as well as in numerous research studies; although, as with the Rorschach and the use of drawings as projective devices, there has been much controversy about the empirical validity and accuracy of the findings produced. The TAT consists of a number of drawings in black and white that show various characters in ambiguous situations. Generally, they tend to elicit emotional responses as they tend to pull for themes of aggression, sexual feelings, competition, and many others. It is interesting to note that although Henry Murray has been given much credit for the development and acceptance of the TAT, Christine Morgan, with whom he worked for decades, is probably the creative force behind this instrument.

Another major assessment tool, developed by Benjamin (1996), includes a coding system that provides ratings by self and others based on her interpersonal circumplex model. This system is rather complex, but, according to Benjamin, the predictive principles may be useful in determining antecedents and what follows an interpersonal event. Benjamin has developed both long and short forms, called the Intrex questionnaire; the long form provides detailed information about interpersonal functioning. Software has been developed to summarize the data generated for research and clinical purposes.

Application of Model

The major applications of the interpersonal model have been in the areas of psychotherapy and assessment. The developments in the interpersonal school have led to many new lines of development in systems of psychotherapy and personality theory. Almost all models of personality have been influenced by developments in the interpersonal school. The interpersonal approach was a necessary step in the development of relational approaches. The emphasis on the interpersonal aspects of personality moved the field beyond the narrow focus on the intrapsychic and behavioral. Factor models have spawned much research and provided a means to use statistical techniques to investigate component aspects of personality and then relate them to other areas to investigate relationships and predict behavior.

Cultural Influences

Cultural influences are not a specific focus of the interpersonal model, yet the theory is consistent with one that allows for diversity and a variety of ways of expressing one's values and preferences. Many of the early workers in the interpersonal school were very interested in working with severely disturbed individuals. A greater acceptance of and emphasis on working with the most disturbed individuals has demonstrated that many of the pioneering individuals were sensitive to the plight of the marginalized members of society, those suffering from severe mental illness. The cross-cultural application of this model has not been demonstrated through research, but there are no inherent reasons why this system could not accommodate this type of investigation.

Strengths and Limitations of Model

There are many strengths of the interpersonal model, but the major one is the emphasis on the interpersonal field and the value placed on the influence of relationships. Much research from a variety of areas of investigation demonstrates the importance of attachment in the development of both animals and humans. Until the interpersonal model was developed, there was a lack of understanding about the power of the interpersonal field in shaping development. Many of the theoretical assumptions made by interpersonal theorists have been empirically demonstrated. Current theoretical formulations have gone beyond the somewhat vague and esoteric system of Sullivan, who was never known for his clarity of writing and, as a clinician, had little interest in empirical evidence to support his constructs. The blending of the introspective models of many theorists with the more rational-empirical models is another strength of this system.

Probably the major limitation of contemporary interpersonal models is the difficulty most readers have in understanding the complexity of the system. Also, many clinicians who use the theory are often frustrated in trying to translate the theoretical constructs to actual practice. Many of the concepts are well accepted, but reliance on them alone may limit a more comprehensive understanding. For the nonpsychologist, the concepts are often foreign and, with the exception of the fundamental ideas, hard to digest and identify with.

Summary

The interpersonal model represented a remarkable departure from previous theoretical systems. Many workers were involved in making the transition from the intrapsychic and behavioral predecessors to the interpersonal. Interpersonal theory diverged along two primary lines: those more closely aligned with Sullivan's interpersonal model and those with Cattell's factor theory. There is considerable cross-fertilization that makes easy classification difficult.

Clearly, the father of the interpersonal model is Sullivan, a practicing clinician who was interested in severe emotional disturbances. He developed a loosely arranged theory that emphasized the survival and adaptation functions of interpersonal relations. He coined the term participant-observer to account for the fact that a dyad is greater than the two individuals with its own dynamics and processes. Mostly, he was concerned with transactions that occur in dyadic relationships and, as you shall see in the following chapter, presaged the advances made in triadic theory to come. He also coined the term self-esteem system to account for the manner by which personality is formed by modulating interpersonal anxiety through attachments. Murray, another influential pioneer, was influenced by Sullivan, Jung, and Freud, but was particularly interested in the dyad. He attempted to operationalize his system and published a major work that spelled out his system and vision for the field he termed personology. A major integrative thinker and systemizer, Murray acknowledged the importance of the newly developed general systems theory that he believed was essential for a comprehensive system of personality. He and his associate developed the Thematic Apperception Test (TAT), one of the most widely used projective instruments in clinical practice and in many research studies. Leary, expanding on the work of Sullivan, made a major contribution with his model, the Interpersonal Circle, which he used to characterize the dimensional aspects of interpersonal relationships as a reflection of personality. Leary's work spawned many theoretical advances and research studies. Most notable is Benjamin's structural analysis of social behavior, a widely cited, empirically derived application and integration of Sullivan's and Leary's work. This model is the most influential of the current interpersonal lines. Other interpersonal models have been developed that have supported the theoretical emphasis of this model. Klerman and Weissman developed an interpersonal model that was used to understand and treat depression. They emphasized the importance of roles and interpersonal relations in the development of depression and personality. Kiesler developed a two-dimensional model using

Leary's Interpersonal Circle; he emphasized how relationships shape and define who we are and how we act, coining terms such as transactional escalation to show how traits can be exaggerated in interpersonal transactions. Factor models such as developed by Wiggins and others have also evolved as these theories cross-fertilized, emphasizing the use of statistical methods to find the structure of personality.

Suggested Reading

Benjamin, L. S. (1993). *Interpersonal diagnosis and treatment of personality disorder.* New York: Guilford Press.

Bowlby, J. (1969). *Attachment and loss. Volume I: Attachment.* London: Hogarth Press.

Relational Models of Personality

Introduction

The developments in relational theories have not been systematically applied to the field of personality theory although they have much to offer (Berscheid, 1994; Berscheid & Lopes, 1997; Berscheid & Ammazzalorso, 2001). However, the emergence of relational models based on systems theory and cultural/relational theory based on a feminist model of female development offers a valuable perspective to the field of personality. The two main branches of relational theory relevant to the topic of this text, although they are termed "relational," have very different origins (Magnavita, 2000b). The earlier development is the family systems model or **relational-systems theory,** used in this chapter to demarcate the new developments; it emerged from research on schizophrenia in the 1950s (see Figure 10.1). "The family has long been recognized as an important factor in the physical, spiritual, and emotional well-being of its individual members. Research and clinical work on emotional dysfunction in families dates back at least as far as Freud" (Guerin & Chabot, 1992, p. 225). However, not until some essential theoretical leaps, now described as **paradigmatic shifts,** took place did relational theories take hold in psychology.

Early Development and the Challenge of Understanding Schizophrenia

Most of the early work in family systems theory was based on research with families with a member diagnosed with schizophrenia. "Bateson, Jackson, Weakland, and Haley in California; Bowen in Topeka and Washington; Lidz in Baltimore and then in New Haven; Whitaker and Malone in Atlanta; Scheflen and Birdwhistle in Philadelphia" (Guerin, 1976, p. 3) were some of the early investigators working in parallel at different centers. A breakthrough occurred when a classic article, "The Family of the Schizophrenic: A

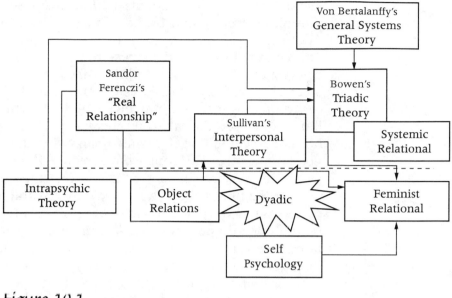

Figure 10.1

The Multiple Pathways and Influences of Relational Theory.

Model System," published by Jay Haley (1959), showed evidence of complex and contradictory communications in these systems, termed the **double-bind communication.** Although later somewhat discredited on the grounds that the etiology (cause) of schizophrenia has been shown to have a strong genetic basis, this article remains seminal in that it opened the door to a new way of thinking about family process.

It is interesting to note that new lines of research have provided some support for the communication dysfunction in families with schizophrenic members (Miklowitz, 1995). This style of communication is termed **communication deviance (CD)** (L. C. Wynne & Singer, 1963). Miklowitz (1995), who has done some fascinating research on this topic of **expressed emotion (EE)** (G. W. Brown, Birley, & Wing, 1972), states: "A common thread in the early clinical observations about families of schizophrenic patients was that family-wide transactions seemed to be unfocused, unclear, and contradictory" (p. 184). EE research has shown that high levels of "criticism, hostility, or environmental overinvolvement" (p. 187) is a risk factor for relapse for patients with schizophrenia. Clearly, schizophrenia is predisposed by hereditary factors, yet stress caused by dysfunctional family dynamics can trigger the onset of the illness. This concept is termed the **stress-diathesis model.** Each individual has certain genetic vulnerabilities that can be set into motion when a certain threshold of stress is experienced; therefore, both biological and family factors are involved, and it is artificial to attribute the illness to one or the other (J. Alexander & Barton, 1995). Research has documented that if one identical twin has the illness, the likelihood of the other suffering from it is only 50%. This leaves room for psychosocial variables such as family communication process.

At the time, many clinicians were frustrated with the reliance on the intrapsychic model and were primed for a new model that would open up new ways of working with disturbed patients. The family movement was helped along to some degree by Sullivan's interpersonal theory, which allowed "the focus of therapy to shift away from purely intrapsychic toward interpersonal examination" (Guerin, 1976, p. 5). Great innovators, such as Frieda Fromm-Reichmann, the therapist of the author of *I Never Promised You a Rose Garden* (Green, 1964), worked at Chestnut Lodge, a renowned private psychiatric hospital in Rockville, Maryland. Fromm-Reichmann was an icon who pushed the parameters of who could be treated with intensive analytic psychotherapy. She was influential in developing methods for treating schizophrenics and coined the term **schizophrenigenic** to describe mothers of preschizophrenic children who combined both subtle rejection and overprotectiveness (Fromm-Reichmann, 1950). Although the use of this term "has a long and rather unfortunate history" because of the blame inherent in it (Miklowitz, 1995, p. 183), Fromm-Reichmann and others influenced Don Jackson and Don Bloch, who worked at Chestnut Lodge and later moved to California to form Gregory Bateson's research team.

The Second Branch of the Relational Tree: A New Model of Women's Development

The second major theoretical advance was a new model of psychology for women. Many clinicians and theorists became frustrated with the male-dominated psychology that had been ascendant since Freud. It is true that various influential pioneers along the way, such as Karen Horney, who rejected the notion of penis envy as a ludicrous male speculation, attempted to remedy this situation, but most did not substantially affect mainstream psychology. Advances were made in the general direction of a **feminist relational theory** when Kohut (1984; see Chapter 6) developed his model stressing empathic attunement in the treatment of narcissistic disorders. Carl Rogers (1951), the founder of client-centered therapy, and H. S. Sullivan (1953) were, according to Jordan (2000, p. 1006), "explicitly relationally oriented theorists," as were a branch of current psychoanalysts, the "intersubjective theorists" (Mitchell, 1988; Stolorow & Atwood, 1992).

Major Historical Figures

von Bertalanffy's General Systems Theory

As described by Thomas Kuhn (1970), the philosopher of science, scientific revolutions are the result of a sudden jump that represents a paradigmatic shift not derived from previous theoretical formulations. Skynner (1976) writes, "General systems theory represents such a conceptual leap. One might say of it that it is not so much a science, as a point of view, for essentially it is a way of looking at phenomena in their total relationships rather than in isolation from one another" (p. 382). Skynner describes this development: "Following close on the end of the Second World War, and no doubt stimulated by the development of weapons and other military hardware which utilized computers, guidance systems, automatic pilots, radar and other mechanical or electronic devices designed to take the place of a human intelligence, increasing interest was shown in the correspondence between the structure of these machines and of living organisms. Complex mathematics and logical systems were called upon to provide theories applicable to both, and this juxtaposition of machine and man led to strange and startling viewpoints and new concepts as each was seen from the standpoint of the other" (p. 381).

A number of theoretical systems were developed in this rich milieu. Von Neuman and Morgenstern (1944) formulated **game theory,** Wiener (1948) and Shannon and Weiner (1949) **cybernetics,** and von Bertalanffy (1942, 1948) **general systems theory.**

General systems theory was von Bertalanffy's "attempt to bring together in an integrated way the common principles underlying these new perspectives" (Skynner, 1976, p. 381). This perspective emphasized the need to look at the world as a complex mixture of interrelated variables affecting one another in a way that made the system greater than the sum of its parts. No piece of any complex system could be viewed at in isolation without losing something important in the **interrelationships** between the part and the rest of the system. It was assumed that all systems functioned by the same laws. Humankind's neurological system is a good example of how one cannot understand a complex system by examining the parts. As we saw in Chapter 4, the system works using complex feedback systems. For example, the hormonal system affects the conductivity of the neurotransmitters: Premenstrual syndrome is a group of symptoms that are affected by the interrelationship of cultural, hormonal, and personality variables and neurotransmitters such as serotonin.

We can also apply the principles to the field of ecology. One cannot just look at the output of a particular factory, the regulatory laws, the biological effects, or the behavior of humans and their beliefs about the environment. There exist multiple positive and negative feedback loops that propel the process in a certain direction at a certain rate. One feedback loop might exist in the relationship between economic factors and the value of conservation: Purchasing large volumes of disposable packaging might financially reward a fast-food company; a positive feedback loop exists where the more the company makes, the more it seeks out cheap disposable packaging, which has a dire effect on the environment because it takes an exorbitant amount of time to decompose. In this loop, the problem gets worse for the environment and the corporation increases profits for its shareholders; the effect is damage to the environment and the public. If, however, as has happened, environmentally conscious consumers raise a certain threshold of discomfort, the balance can shift, and the loss of business and the bad public relations of being labeled environmentally unfriendly will begin to turn the system in another direction.

General systems theory was concerned with identifying and establishing the laws of systems. In any discipline, there are component elements and the laws and forces that govern how these relate to one another. Applying this model to the field of family functioning, communication and family therapy engendered a search for the laws of the family system. The development of this cross-disciplinary theoretical model had the result of bringing together scientists from unrelated disciplines to study these forces (Skynner, 1976). Many of the concepts presented in the systemic relational model presented in this chapter have developed out of this scientific crucible. "The concepts of family homeostasis, of feedback, of double-bind and of symptoms as nonverbal messages are well-known consequences of this new interest" (p. 283). Not everyone in the family movement agrees with the importance of the development of general systems theory in the development of this model. Bowen (1976) rejects the notion that family systems theory is synonymous with general systems theory; he did acknowledge attending a lecture by von Bertalanffy in the 1940s "which I did not understand" (p. 63). Other investigators, such as Murray, were interested and used general systems theory, but were somewhat "wary" and did not apply it to the context of families to understand how personality is shaped. As with many of the paradigmatic shifts discussed in this text, there is a palpable level of tremendous excitement conveyed in the original writing of these scientific investigators and theorizers, which I attempt to convey by including excerpts from their original works. I recommend that the interested reader go back to these and relive the excitement of scientific discovery!

Bateson's Communication Theory and the Double Bind Theory

Gregory Bateson (1904–1980) was an anthropologist who was married for 13 years to another famous anthropologist, Margaret Mead, with whom he had a productive professional collaboration. His interests were wide-ranging, and he was the consummate natural scientist, seeking to understand the object of his study from a new perspective. An enigmatic man, he studied social relations in Bali with Mead, where they developed methods of ethnographic fieldwork using photography and cinematography in an attempt to preserve the images they were studying (Lipset, 1980). He also studied cybernetics—the study of systems—and communication theory, as well as learning patterns in dolphins. He remained on the frontier of social science, looking for patterns and the interconnections of all

life (Lipset, 1980). Although not trained as a psychologist, he was invited to spend two years at the University of California Medical School in collaboration with Jurgen Ruesch, a psychiatrist, to study human communication in psychotherapy. "Simultaneously, they were looking into the nature of communication among 'a tribe called psychiatrists' " (Lipset, 1980, p. 187). In the early 1950s, Bateson gathered a multidisciplinary team in California, the members of which went on to have very productive careers in family systems theory and therapy. His initial interest was to study the nature of communications and later communication patterns in families with a schizophrenic member (Guerin & Chabot, 1992). Bateson is a good example of how an interdisciplinary approach to the study of human behavior and personality can be extremely fruitful. His introduction to clinical psychiatry along with his training in anthropology and interest in cybernetics prepared the ground for novel theoretical formulations. Bateson's work, funded by grants from the Rockefeller Foundation and then the Macy Foundation, afforded him the opportunity to intensively engage in the study of communication. His research team included Jay Haley, who had just attained his graduate degree in communications, and John Weakland, a chemical engineer by training who also had a keen interest in cultural anthropology. Later, Don Jackson, a psychiatrist who, as a resident, had been supervised by Harry Stack Sullivan, joined the team.

Their research efforts focused on the communication patterns in families with a schizophrenic member. Interviewing hospitalized patients confirmed their hypothesis that contradictory levels of communication occur in these families. This type of contradictory communication was termed the **double bind** (Bateson, Jackson, Haley, & Weakland, 1956). Nichols (1984) summarizes the basic characteristics of the double bind: (1) more than one person in a relationship; (2) the relationship is ongoing; (3) negative injunctions are given with a threat of punishment; (4) another injunction, usually nonverbal, is given that negates the first one; (5) a third-level injunction prevents the individual from leaving and demands a response; and (6) the target becomes conditioned to see the world in terms of a double bind; any part of the conditions are then sufficient to trigger rage or panic. When contradictory communications are given and there is no attempt to make the communication explicit, concomitant with the lack of opportunity to escape, symptomatic behavior often results.

Bateson believed that all forms of behavior are communication. Even when an adolescent sits in a family therapy session and refuses to talk, he is communicating much about his feelings and his family pattern. Bateson brought to awareness the fact that humans "can't not communicate." Guerin and Chabot (1992) summarize his contribution: "What began as Bateson's interest in culture, communication, and the mysteries of schizophrenia has become a clinical methodology for dealing with a wide spectrum of psychological disturbances within the individual and in relationships" (p. 236).

Ackerman's Relational Diagnostic System

Nathan Ackerman was a psychiatrist with broad interests who wrote prolifically on many topics (Guerin & Chabot, 1992). He came to the family relational model from psychoanalysis. At the age of 28, Ackerman (1937) published a seminal article, "The Family as a Social and Emotional Unit," while he was working in the children's division of the Menninger Clinic. Although only five pages in length, it succinctly described his view that the social impact of the family in development is substantial. Another article, "The Emergence of Family Diagnosis and Treatment: A Personal View" (Ackerman, 1967), marked the "beginning of the family movement" (Guerin, 1976, p. 4).

Ackerman's work was not as revolutionary as Bateson's and Bowen's; instead, he adopted a more integrative blend of analytic and family theory. The importance of his work to the topic of personality centers on his contribution of a preliminary diagnostic system of family typology (Ackerman, 1958). In his book *The Psychodynamics of Family Life: Diagnosis and Treatment of Family Relationships*, Ackerman catalogued the following relational diagnoses: (1) disturbances of marital pairs, (2) disturbances of parental pairs, (3) disturbances of childhood, (4) disturbances of adolescence, and (5) psychosomatic illness and family disturbance. He describes some of his views: "The special problems of marital and parental pairs can best be understood

The Underground Movement

Murray Bowen (1976), one of the pioneering figures in the development of the family movement, describes the secrecy that prevailed as early workers began to break taboos: "The psychoanalytic principle of protecting the privacy of the patient-therapist relationship may account for the family movement's remaining underground for some years. There were strict rules against the therapist's contaminating the transference by seeing other members of the same family: the early family work was done privately, probably to avoid critical colleagues who might consider this irresponsible until it was legitimized in the name of research" (p. 54).

in terms of the mutuality and interdependence of the respective family role adaptations, the complementarity of sexual behavior, the reciprocity of emotional and social companionship, the sharing of authority, and the division of labor" (p. 148). This preliminary formulation was counter to the evolving individual diagnostic model of the time.

Bowen's Triadic Theory

Murray Bowen was one of the most innovative and prolific theorists and investigators of an exciting new development in social sciences in the last half of the twentieth century. A psychiatrist and professor of psychiatry at Georgetown University Medical Center, Bowen was one of the early founders of the family movement. He was fueled by his interest in advancing formulations about symbiotic mother-child dyads. In the early 1950s, Bowen made a radical theoretical departure "from previous theories of human emotional functioning, by conceptualizing the family as an emotional unit and the individual as part of that unit rather than as an autonomous psychological entity" (Kerr, 1988, p. 35). Bowen (1976) began formulating his concept of triangle in the late 1950s. This discovery was a major theoretical advance. "Intensive Family Therapy" was a seminal paper in which he outlined his concept of **triangulation**, which he later referred to as the interdependent triad. As discussed in previous chapters, models of personality evolved from the **intrapsychic** to the **dyadic** or interpersonal; this development presented a conceptual leap to the **triadic.** Bowen's work represents the most comprehensive theory of family systems and adds a dimension to personality theory that had not been formulated.

Bowen was interested in theoretical parsimony. Guerin and Chabot (1992) describe this quest: "Bowen (1978) believed that the task of the theorist was to find the smallest number of congruent concepts that could fit together and serve as a working blueprint for understanding that part of the human experience under observation" (p. 241). Bowen was unusual in that he was very interested in theory building, as opposed to clinical practice, and in the "belief that his observations and ideas could form the beginning of a new theory of human emotional functioning" (Guerin & Chabot, 1992, p. 241). He conducted some groundbreaking research in an attempt to understand schizophrenia. At the National Institute of Mental Health, he developed a "landmark" (Guerin, 1976, p. 9) project where schizophrenics and their family were hospitalized and observed, stimulating his ideas about triangulation. Some of the families stayed for as long as a year and allowed for the careful study of their patterns of interaction. Bowen (1976) comments: "For me, 1955 to 1956 was a period of elation and enthusiasm. Observing entire families living together on a research ward provided a completely new order of clinical data never before recorded in the literature" (p. 54). One fact that emerged among the plethora of data was that the relationship between schizophrenic and mother was intensely strong; a second was that this emotional intensity was characteristic of the whole nuclear family (Kerr, 1988). Bowen (1976) believed that what allowed his radical new theory was "a shift in the observing lens from the individual to the family" (p. 54).

Bowenian Theory

Known as family systems theory and later Bowenian theory, this model "is based on the assumption that the human being is a product of evolution and that human behavior is regulated by the same natural processes that regulate the behavior of all other living things" (Kerr, 1988, p. 36). Borrowing from biology, Bowen believed that families, like other organic systems, are resistant to change and invested in maintaining **homeostasis,** or stability, often at the cost of more flexible adaptation. Bowen noticed that **reciprocal relationships** in families were predominant. Kerr describes this finding:

> *Examples include overadequate and inadequate (one did everything right and could cope, and the other did everything wrong and could not cope), decisive and indecisive (one made all the decisions and the other felt incapable of making any decisions), dominant and submissive (one led and the other followed), hysterical and obsessive (one was a fountain of feelings and the other inexpressive). The degree of polarization that these reciprocal traits reached was influenced by the degree to which family members defined the differences between them as a problem and anxiously focused on "correcting" these differences. In the process of this focusing, each family member would be driven to become a certain way in relationship to another family member which was different from the way he or she was with people outside the family. (p. 37)*

One can see some of the vestiges of interpersonal theory in this description, but systems theory did not stop here but added many novel observations. With regard to personality functioning, systems theory posits that when a significant personality characteristic exists in one family member, the mirror opposite will be seen in another: One trait reinforces the other and cannot be expressed without the other. Therefore, **personality has to do with the relationship,** not the individual, as in most other prominent theories. Families as well as larger social groups are **emotional systems.**

Triangles: The Molecules of Triadic Theory

Bowen is "considered by many to be the originator of the concept of triangulation" (Gurein & Chabot, 1992, p. 244). Triangulation is the dynamic process that occurs among three people. The "molecule or basic building block of any emotional system" (Bowen, 1976, p. 76) is the relational triangle. The instability inherent in dyadic relationships is what produces triangles. "A triangle is an abstract way of thinking about a structure in human relationships, and triangulation is the reactive emotional process that goes on within that triangle" (Guerin & Chabot, 1992, p. 244). "Bowen postulated that the driving force in triangles was an anxious attachment carried to an extreme" (Guerin, Fogarty, Fay, & Kautto, 1996, p. 10). Especially when tension exists in a dyad there will be a move toward a vulnerable third party to stabilize the dyad and form a new configuration: a triangular one (see Figure 10.2). According to systems theorists, life can be "a maze of triangular shoals and reefs to be navigated around" (Guerin et al., 1996, p. 1). Guerin et al. describe how this occurs before an individual is born: "At the very beginning—of your life, as soon as your conception became known, either your father, your mother, or both may have experienced you as an intruder. The fact of your existence may have overjoyed your father and presented a threat to your mother's career, making your father too eager for your arrival and your mother too anxious. Even before your conception, not-so-subtle pressure from your maternal grandmother may have led the campaign for your existence. At your birth, whatever genetic map was on your face was probably the stimulus for all kinds of loyalty-driven distinctions by well-meaning relatives. 'He looks just like George's mother,' says George's sister" (p. 1).

When the tension of a triadic relationship becomes too great, "series of interlocking triangles" are developed. The emotional currents within triangles are continually in motion, even in periods of calm. When there is relative calm, the favored position is in the dyad, where "togetherness" is preserved. However, in periods of stress, the favored position is the outside position. If tensions are very high within a family, the system may seek to involve an individual outside the family; the police may be called or an extramarital affair begun.

Figure 10.2

Depiction of an Unstable Dyad Transmitting Anxiety to a Third Person, Forming a Triadic Relationship.

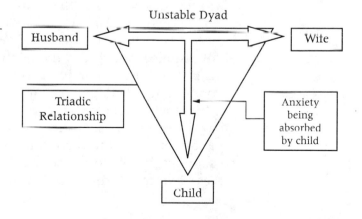

Generally, under moderate degrees of stress, there are two comfortable positions and one uncomfortable position within a triangle.

Differentiation: A Key to Understanding the Self

An essential concept in Bowen's (1976, 1978) theory is differentiation, which has two components: **self/other** and **emotional differentiation.** All individuals are propelled toward growth and separation, counterbalanced with the need for affiliation and togetherness. The need for togetherness is evolutionarily programmed, as it ensures survival of the species. When a family system is well-differentiated, the child can develop his or her identity without becoming entangled in the emotional force field of the other family members in an unhealthy way: The child can learn to think and feel for himself or herself. Conversely, in poorly differentiated families, the emotionality is such that the child is constantly reacting to others; for example, an oppositional child reacts to the emotional insecurity of the parents, who then react with more control, creating more immature behavior.

Self/Other Differentiation: In this cornerstone concept, their level of **fusion** versus **differentiation** defines people. Self/other differentiation refers to the level of closeness and intimacy versus distance between self and other. When the level of differentiation is at a low level, one could describe the relationship as fused or symbiotic. Bowen called this type of anxious attachment **fusion,** "a symbiotic attachment and blurring of boundaries between two people in which the transmission of anxiety is so intense that both people become convinced that they can't survive without the other" (Guerin et al., 1996, pp. 10–11). In this type of relationship, there is a contagious anxiety that traps both members of the dyad. When the level of distance is too great, the relationship could be described as disengaged. There is an optimal level of intimacy/closeness: too close and one is enmeshed, too distant and one is disengaged. In any relationship, there is a process whereby ebb and flow occurs to some degree; at times, one partner may distance or pull away to enjoy aloneness and then return to the relational field, but not to extremes. "These same cycles of closeness and distance appear, although perhaps in less extreme form, in all dyadic relationships—parent and child, brother and sister, husband and wife, and even friend and friend" (Guerin et al., 1996, p. 11). A more differentiated position is a balance between intimacy and differentiation, neither fused or disengaged (see Figure 10.3).

Emotional Differentiation: Emotional differentiation of the self refers to the capacity to distinguish between intellectual and emotional processes. Bowen (1976) writes, "The core of my theory has to do with the degree to which people are able to distinguish between the *feeling* process and the *intellectual* process" (p. 59). Individuals who are the most fused in the spheres of feeling and intellect function the poorest. "Those with the most ability to distinguish between feeling and thinking, or who have the most differentiation of self, have the most flexibility and adaptability in coping with life stresses, and the most freedom from problems of all kinds" (p. 59). When individuals are in the fused position, emotionality predominates their functioning and the intellect is "an appendage of the feeling system" (p. 66). When the level of functioning is higher, the distinction between the emotional and intellectual spheres are clearer. When families are stuck in at a low level of differentiation, they are described as **undifferentiated ego mass.** Bowen describes the difference between the two ends of the spectrum: "A poorly differentiated person is trapped within a feeling world. His effort to gain the comfort of

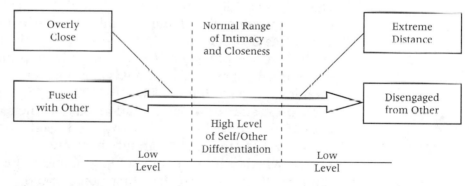

Figure 10.3

Depiction of Level of Differentiation and Continuum of Closeness and Distance.

emotional closeness can increase the fusion, which can increase his alienation from others. There is a lifelong effort to get the emotional life into livable equilibrium. A segment of these emotionally trapped people use random, inconsistent, intellectual-sounding verbalization to explain away their plight. A more differentiated person can participate freely in the emotional sphere without the fear of becoming fused with others. He is also free to shift to calm, logical reasoning for decisions that govern his life. The logical intellectual process is quite different from the inconsistent, intellectualized verbalizations of the emotionally fused person" (p. 67).

Bowen developed a scale to convey the gradations of differentiation from 0 to 100, with profiles of people who fall in the four quadrants. This scale was intended more for theoretical clarification than as a psychometric instrument for clinical or research use. For some people, the level of emotional differentiation can shift; others stay remarkably stable.

Solid Self versus Pseudo-Self: The **solid self** does not participate in fusion experiences and is evident in those at higher levels of differentiation. On the other hand, the **pseudo-self** is the pretend self and can be created by emotional pressure and demand from others. It is the part of us that pretends we are smarter or not as smart as we are or stronger or weaker than we are. Individuals at lower levels of differentiation have a tendency to change and adapt to the expectations of others. An individual in the process of emotional differentiation and self/other differentiation while maintaining emotional contact in relationships with family members is **defining the self.** In a sense, this is giving up the fusion fantasy that if we merge with others we will be protected. The greater our emotional reactivity, the less defined our true or solid self is and the more we are acting out of pseudo-self. According to Bowen (1976), "Most spouses can have the closest and most open relationships in their adult lives during courtship. The fusion of the two pseudo-selfs into a common self occurs at the time they commit themselves to each other permanently, whether it be the time of engagement, the wedding itself, or the time they establish their first home together" (p. 79). It is not uncommon for clinical practitioners to face the faltering of a marriage shortly after any of these points, as the pseudo-self no longer holds in the light of the process of getting acquainted with the true self of the other.

Dysfunctional/Functional Family Systems

In dysfunctional families, the members are caught in a process of emotional reaction that determines behavior. The level of differentiation within the family is low and adaptation to stress is poor. In high-functioning families, more stress can be handled by the family emotional system without symptomatic outbreaks.

Nuclear Family Emotional System: This refers to the way in which a nuclear family functions on an emotional level within one generation. Basic patterns of relationships may replicate the past's being transmitted from one generation to the other. By gathering a careful multigenerational history and reconstruction of the way past generations operated, prediction about future generations may be made.

Family Projection Process: "The process through which parental undifferentiation impairs one or more children operates within the father-mother-child triangle" (Bowen, 1976, p. 81). By this mechanism, undifferentiation is projected to other family members. Some of this can be absorbed in the marriage or as sickness in a spouse, which will reduce the amount projected to the child. Bowen describes the various factors:

> *The children selected for the family projection process are those conceived and born during stress in the mother's life; the first child, the oldest son or oldest daughter, and only child of either sex, one who is emotionally special to the mother, or one the mother believes to be special to the father. Among common special children are only children, and oldest child, a single child of one sex among several of the opposite sex, or a child with some defect. Also important are the special children who were fretful, colicky, rigid, and nonresponsive to the mother from the beginning. A good percentage of mothers have a basic preference for boys or girls, depending upon their orientation in the family of origin. It is impossible for mothers to have equal emotional investment in any two children, no matter how much they try to protest equality for all. (pp. 82–83)*

These children are generally referred to as **triangulated** because they are the focus of the family projection process. In conducting a multigenerational history, one will find almost all families have a child who is more triangulated than others and functions at lower levels of differentiation.

Emotional Cutoff: Some unresolved emotional attachments with parents are handled by cutting the parents off. In these cases, the normal process of healthy separation is foreshortened by emotionally or physically distancing, or staying in physical proximity but being "allergic" to intimacy and closeness (Bowen, 1976, p. 84). Emotional cutoffs are equivalent to the level of emotional differentiation; in other words, an individual who cuts off his or her family in an attempt to start over is carrying the unresolved process to the next generation. Bowen provides the example of a child who continues to live with his parents into adulthood, collapsing into psychosis as a way of isolating himself. There is a continuum with gradations of emotional cutoffs.

Multigenerational Transmission Process: This is a fundamental construct of immense importance in relational systems theory, accounting for the passing of unresolved issues from one generation to another. The family projection process occurs throughout successive generations, often with increasingly fewer levels of emotional differentiation from one generation to the next. In healthy families, the level of differentiation is reasonably consistent throughout generations. Those children who are in triangulated positions generally do less well than siblings who tend to function at the same level of differentiation as their parents.

Sibling Position: Bowen's (1976) research was an adaptation of Toman's (1961) development of 10 basic personality profiles that were based on sibling position. The way these profiles fit with the normal ones can shed light on family and individual functions. For example, an oldest child who functions like a youngest is at a low level of differentiation. Bowen states: "Based on my research and therapy, I believe that no single piece of data is more important than knowing the sibling position of people in the present and past generations" (p. 87).

Emotional Regression: When feelings and conflicts are not appropriately faced and expressed because of lack of differentiation, emotional reactivity and poor communication anxiety builds within the family emotional system. This anxiety can cause regressions that can last for days to years or even lifetimes. The process becomes circular; as the regression deepens and family members are coping poorly, more anxiety is aroused, increasing triangles within the family.

Anxiety

Bowen (1976) believes that all organisms can adapt to anxiety and, in fact, have "built-in mechanisms to deal with short bursts of anxiety" (p. 65). Almost any organism can seem normal if anxiety is at a low level. If anxiety increases, becoming chronic, tension will build in the organism or in the relationship system; this can lead to sickness or dysfunction. "There is also the phenomenon of the infectiousness of anxiety, through which anxiety can spread through the family, or through society" (p. 65).

Acute Anxiety: Acute anxiety results from a real threat, similar to the Freudian construct. This type of anxiety occurs in short intervals and can be absorbed in a person with an adequate level of differentiation. Acute anxiety is fueled by what is happening, as opposed to what might happen.

Chronic Anxiety: Chronic anxiety results from imagined threats and does not dissipate, putting a strain on adaptive capacity. It is long-standing anxiety that may be channeled into physical disorders, emotional dysfunction, or social dysfunction. The person who suffers from chronic anxiety fears what might occur. Chronic anxiety exists in a system of actions and reactions and is generally related to disturbance in the relational matrix. In poorly emotionally differentiated systems, chronic anxiety is the hallmark. Individuals and systems at the lowest level of differentiation have the poorest ability to adapt and are more vulnerable under stress. When these systems are under stress that reaches a certain threshold, symptomatic behavior may result until the equilibrium is reestablished. When ongoing chronic anxiety exists, personality disturbance may result and chronic patterns become consolidated. Relationships tend to be the most common way in which to bind anxiety. Kerr (1988) describes some of the personality configurations and variations possible: "People who deny their need for attachment to others can be just as relationship-dependent as those who constantly seek a relationship.

Loners can bind just as much anxiety by avoiding people as people who constantly seek social contact can bind through that contact. Poorly differentiated people who are loners usually are labeled 'schizoid.' Poorly differentiated people who are consistently involved in tumultuous relationships usually are labeled 'hysterical.' Schizoid people and hysterical people are dealing with the same basic problem: a high degree of emotional need for and reactivity to others. The lower the level of differentiation, the more intense the process" (p. 48).

Flow of Anxiety: Anxiety can flow both in a horizontal and a vertical direction (E. A. Carter, 1978). The **vertical** flow of anxiety refers to the process by which anxiety "derives from patterns of relating and functioning that are transmitted historically down the generations, primarily though the process of emotional triangulating" (McGoldrick & Gerson, 1985, p. 6). For example, in one family, the mother was in an enmeshed relationship with her mother. When one of her female children was born, she identified this one as being "my child" to her husband, which carried with it the expectation that her baby would serve as her caretaker throughout her life. This was the beginning of a symbiotic relationship characterized by the very low levels of differentiation discussed previously.

Horizontal anxiety flows through the nuclear family "as it moves forward through time, coping with the inevitable changes, misfortunes and transitions in the family life cycle" (McGoldrick & Gerson, 1985, p. 6). Vertical and horizontal anxiety can interact to exacerbate family dysfunction. In the above example, the normal developmental transitions that were encountered by the child symbiotically attached to her mother created major crisis points. When she was about to leave for college, the mother threatened to go with her, undermining her daughter's individuation so that she did not go away.

Personality traits and patterns therefore can be anxiety-binding, just as they are in psychodynamic models. Personality traits may be exaggerated in systems that are poorly differentiated. Individuals who become anxious seek to have the burden lifted and may attempt to get others to do things their way. In this process, someone who is bossy then can become the mirror image of someone who is dependent and helpless (Kerr, 1988).

The Birth of Family Therapy

Bowen (1976) describes the beginnings of the family movement at a meeting of the American Orthopsychiatric Society in March 1957 in Chicago: "That was a small and quiet meeting. There were papers on research by Spiegel, Mendell, Lidz, and Bowen. In my paper I referred to the 'family psychotherapy' used in my research since late 1955. I believe that may have been the first time the term was used in a national meeting. However it happened, I would date the family therapy explosion to March 1957. . . . At the national meetings in 1958, the family sessions were dominated by dozens of new therapists eager to report their family therapy of the past year" (p. 55). Family therapy was born in a radical departure from the therapeutic and theoretical orientations of the time.

McGoldrick and Gerson (1985, p. 5) sum up the basic systemic perspective, now termed an *integrative model* (Magnavita, 2000d): "The adaptive efforts of members of the system reverberate throughout many levels of a system—from the biological to the intrapsychic to the interpersonal, i.e., nuclear and extended family, community, culture and beyond (Bowen, 1978; Engel, 1980; Scheflen, 1981)." Although these factors were identified by systemic thinkers, an integrative model of personality that attempts to account for these was not developed. We return to this integrative model in Chapter 12 and explore how these component factors interrelate.

Contemporary Perspectives: Systemically Based Relational Personality Theory

Like many of the other innovative models presented in this text, the development of relational-systemic theory occurred in a dialectic process. The individual-oriented psychodynamic model is at the opposite end of the pendulum swing from the model presented in this chapter. In many regards, the systemic-relational model was "out of the box" in terms of many of the original formulations and the fact that it drew concepts from disciplines other than psychology, utilizing biological, anthropological, and evolutionary theory. The trend of systems theory was developing along separate lines from those of classical personality theory; workers from the two specialties generally did not interact and thus there was not much cross-fertilization. As with the radical behaviorists, many of the family systems workers strove for a "pure form" in their models, rejecting individual models. In almost all of the publications of systemic theory there was an absence of the construct personality, as if systems construct and personality theory were mutually exclusive.

The Thrust to Develop Relational Models of Personality

As we have seen in the developments and models presented so far, by and large, personality theories and constructs emerged primarily out of models of psychotherapy and psychopathology. As the individual model of mental disorders became the mainstream model in psychiatry and the mental health professions, relationally oriented theorists and therapists became dissatisfied and began to explore the possibility of developing a relationally oriented diagnostic system that would be more congruent with systemic theory. The system of classification of mental disorders offered by the various editions of the *DSM*, despite all of its taxonomy difficulties and problems with validity, has advanced the field. The ascendancy of any diagnostic system is of vital importance to the development of theories of personality, as well as to its sister discipline psychopathology. According to Reis (1996), a diagnostic manual "forms an important basis for treatment planning in inpatient and outpatient programs throughout the world. It lies at the core of clinical record keeping, it structures training programs and textbooks, and it is a critical component of reimbursement systems and health care planning" (p. xii). Most contemporary texts on personality theory and personality disorders use the individualistic system as their foundation (Livesley, 1995; Millon & Davis, 1996a; Millon et al., 2000). It also has fueled research by making diagnostic criteria more reliable.

The lack of a system of nosology for systemic-oriented professionals led many in the field to begin to consider the need for developing a relational system. According to Kaslow (1996), "The clear majority of the authors and myriad other family therapy practitioners have been pursuing the quest for a taxonomy of the variety of problems, syndromes, and interactive difficulties that can be subsumed under the broad rubric of dysfunctional family patterns" (p. 3). Kaslow's impetus and those who served on the Collation on Family Diagnosis and Task Force on Diagnosis and Treatment provided a forum for conceptualizing the elements of this system. This sentiment was expressed in the series preface to the *Handbook of Relational Diagnosis and Dysfunctional Family Patterns* by Kaslow: "Our ability to form strong interpersonal bonds with romantic partners, children, parents, siblings, and other relations is one of the key qualities that defines our humanity. These relationships shape who we are and what we become—they can be a source of great gratification or tremendous pain. Yet only in the mid-twentieth century did behavioral and social scientists really begin focusing on couples and family dynamics, and only in the last several decades have the theory and findings that emerged from those studies been used to develop effective therapeutic interventions for troubled couples and families" (p. v).

As we discussed in Chapter 4, relational science is emerging as a new discipline. One of the leading researchers in this exciting field, Ellen Berscheid (1999), writes of the importance of relational science: "We are born into relationships, we live our lives in relationships with others, and when we die, the effects of our relationships survive, in the lives of the living, reverberating throughout the tissue of their relationships" (p. 262).

Understanding Personality through the Relational Triangle Lens

Very few personality theorists have used the relational triangle as a lens through which to view the genesis and coalescence of personality in either normal or abnormal forms. It is almost as if systems thinkers did not read about personality and thus were not able to see how this construct can be useful in theoretical modeling. Bank and Kahn (1982) comment: "Such family-systems theorists avoid speaking about the self or about the feelings inside people . . . there is no individual person in the process of becoming" (p. 6). Guerin, one of the pioneers in the development of the systemic relational model, and his associates expanded on the theoretical formulations of Bowen, developing a typology of various triangular relationships.

Guerin and associates (1996) propose three basic typologies of triangular relationships, with two separate axes. Their first axis defines the area of conflict, whether with a child or marital. The second axis is whether the third person in the triangle is outside the multigenerational family system (an extramarital triangle) or a member of the multigenerational family system (an intrafamilial triangle). This allows for six types of triangles and subtypes (see Table 10.1).

Marital and Adult Triangles: Marital triangles are developed when a couple is not able to resolve their differences: "The implicit or explicit relationship debris, when ignored, makes fertile soil for the triangulation either within the family or externalized and projected outside the family" (Guerin et al., 1996, p. 150). In the long run, triangular configurations don't work and will often lead to the demise

Table 10.1   Triangle Types and Subtypes.

	Marital Triangles	Child or Adolescent Triangles	Adult Individual Triangles
Extra-familial triangles	Extramarital affairs Social network triangles Occupational triangles	School-related triangles Social network/peer triangles	Social network triangles Occupational triangles
Intra-familial triangles	*Family of origin* In-law triangles Primary parental triangles *Nuclear family* Child-centered triangles	*Family of origin* Three-generational triangles *Nuclear family* Symptomatic child triangles Target child triangles Parent and sibling triangles Sibling subsystem triangles Stepfamily triangles	*Family of origin* Primary parental triangles Dysfunctional spouse triangles Sibling subsystem triangles *Nuclear family* Spouse and child triangles

Source: Working with Relationship Triangles by P. J. Guerin Jr., T. F. Fogarty, L. F. Kay, and J. G. Kautto, © 1996. Reprinted by permission of The Guilford Press.

of a relationship. These can be divided into two subcategories: **extramarital** and **intrafamilial.**

Extramarital triangles are typically activated when the family cannot contend with one or more of the intrafamilial category and include extramarital affairs, social network triangles, and occupational triangles:

- **Extramarital affairs triangles** are attempts to deal with anxiety and tension by externalizing the process to a third party. Although temporary, this often serves to reduce the tension and stabilize a marriage. When discovered, an affair can also become a central issue.

- **Social network triangles** involve social groups outside the family that unduly influence an individual. In one couple, the "boys" down at the local bar were the main network for a man in a conflicted marriage. Social clubs and community activities can also serve this function.

- **Occupational triangles** are present when there is an intense emotional attachment that is resented by the spouse and absorbs a significant amount of tension from the marriage. The individual may have abandoned family life for the work family where emotional needs are met instead of in the primary relationship.

Intrafamilial triangles includes in-law triangles, triangles with children, spouse and sibling triangles, and primary parental triangles of each spouse.

- **In-law triangles** exist when an individual has not made a shift from the family of origin to his or her primary relationship. In this triangular configuration, individuals seek to maintain overly reactive emotional links with their family of origin and place secondary importance in their marital relationship. There is a blurring of boundaries with the primary relationship system and an overinvestment in the family of origin at the cost of the nuclear family. A man may go and visit his mother every morning for coffee, ignoring his wife and children in the process; loyalty or idealization of a parent might be maintained so that the spouse is always second-best to Mom or Dad; a parent may be demanding or controlling and expect the triangulated individual to remain faithful.

- **Triangles with children** "are ready made" (Guerin et al., 1996, p. 187). These are very easy triangular relationships to fall into. Recall the example of the child who "looks just like George's mother"; this is a common way triangular relationships are expressed. Children are easy figures to project onto and vulnerable to triangulation because of their underdeveloped emotional systems.

- **Spouse and sibling triangles** exist when an individual is overly invested in a sibling or sibling subsystem (two or more siblings). For example, a man is always bailing his younger sister out of trouble by giving her money and spending excessive time and energy extracting her from bad situations.

- **Primary parental triangles** of each spouse refer to the position each spouse has been in with his or her own parents. Any sensitivity or emotional reactivity that has been cultivated in a primary family of origin triangle is brought to the new relationship. A rebellious daughter may react to her husband's suggestion that she not drive so erratically by speeding up.

Child and Adolescent Triangles

- **School-related triangles** involve parent-teacher conflict that is expressed in a child's symptomatic behavior. For example, an overly involved mother was concerned that the teacher was not providing a suitable educational experience for her son with a learning disability and criticized the teacher in front of the child. The son began to show behavioral problems at school, requiring the intervention of the school psychologist.

- **Social network triangles** involve the adolescent, usually with a group of peers whom the parents find unacceptable. Although to a degree this is a common developmental stage, in some cases it can become extreme. For example, in one family, the mother not so subtly encouraged her son to have his inappropriate friends at home so she could be aware of what they were "up to." She inadvertently strengthened the friends' bond, which resulted in a pattern of substance abuse in the house. The distant and passive father was not involved until the son was arrested.

- **Symptomatic child triangles** involve an overly close and a distant parent in relation to the child. The symptomatic child binds anxiety in the system. Certain temperamental, physical, or emotional vulnerabilities will increase a child's likelihood of becoming a symptom bearer; this may exacerbate physical vulnerabilities such as asthma. The goodness-of-fit paradigm from Chapter 4 is another critical variable; if the fit between the parent and child is not "good enough," the vulnerability for symptomatic outbreak is greater.

- **The target child triangle** involves a child who is special in the eyes of one parent but becomes a target of resentment of the other. This is generally due to anger toward the spouse being displaced on the child. For example, the child may resemble the favored parent, who is idealized and compared to the spouse, who can never measure up.

- **The parent and sibling triangle** involves a symptomatic child and a sibling, most evident in single-parent family constellations. Often, an older child is elevated by "necessity" to an overly responsible position without any real authority. This child has to shift roles, from the parent to the child position, creating stress.

- **The sibling subsystem triangle** is most often evident "in families with anorexia, severe behavior disorders, and psychotic-level process" (Guerin et al., 1996, p. 210). This entails three siblings who are triangulated in an auxiliary triangle. For example, two children may side against an absent father, while a third does not join and is identified as the "troublemaker." The allegiance toward the father may be the primary triangle.

- **The three-generation triangle** typically involves a grandparent, a parent, and a child. In one case, the maternal grandfather undermined the parental authority and function of the parental dyad.

- **Stepfamily triangles** refer to triangular configurations whereby relationships with stepfamilies are distorted. The variants include the wicked stepparent triangle, the perfect stepparent triangle, ghost of the ex-spouse triangle, and the grandparent triangle.

Triangles as Defense Mechanisms: Triangles can be conceptualized as defense mechanisms that are present when there is anxiety and depression (Guerin et al. 1996). "Not surprisingly . . . people shift around in their relationships to defend themselves against experiencing painful feelings—and that's where triangles come in" (p. 117). Guerin and associates provide an example: "A man may handle his loneliness by a close association with his sister, and his wife may handle the resulting distance by developing a keen interest in art. This may be satisfactory to both and, in their view, not worth pursuing further. That triangle may work well until the sister dies, but it may fall apart when the man wants more closeness from his wife and asks her to give up her interest in art. Under stress, a potential triangle becomes not just active but clinically symptomatic" (p. 117).

Triangles can be used to track relationship patterns that occur in one generation but are also useful in examining the multigenerational transmission process. In terms of personality theory, the multigenerational transmission process is a mechanism by which certain personality traits, styles, and disorders may be transferred from one generation to the next.

The Family Genogram

The **family genogram** to assess and record family information and patterns based on Bowen's family systems theory was developed by McGoldrick and Gerson (1985). "A genogram is a format for drawing a family tree that records information about family members and their relationships over at least three generations. Genograms display family information graphically in a way that provides a quick gestalt of complex family patterns and a rich source of hypotheses about how a clinical problem may be connected to the family context and the evolution of both problem and context over time" (p. 1). A genogram usually includes at least three generations of members and critical events that may be influential in the family history. The genogram is a graphic depiction of a family using symbols, such as a circle for female, a square for male, and various lines to symbolize relationships.

Figure 10.4 depicts a three-generation genogram. In the first generation depicted are two marriages, each of which produced two offspring. The Xs through August and Selma indicate their deaths and the dates are recorded underneath. Lines connecting couples indicate marriages, and divorce is indicated by two dashes through the line

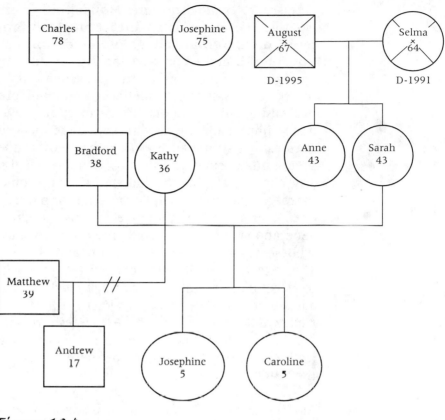

Figure 10.4

Three-Generation Genogram.

connecting the couple. August and Selma's two children are identical twins, depicted by one line that splits. In the second generation there are two marriages: Bradford and Sarah, who have two identical twin girls, Josephine and Caroline; and Kathy and Matthew, who are divorced with one teenage son, Andrew.

There are a number of categories and factors that can be used to understand the unique structure and dynamics of each family (McGoldrick & Gerson, 1985). These are very useful in helping us understand how family dynamics shape the personality of an individual.

Category 1. Family Structure: **Household composition** refers to whether the family is an **intact nuclear family, single-parent household, remarried** or **blended family, three-generation household,** and **extended family,** or **nonfamily.** Various issues emerge from these configurations. When only one parent is raising the children, issues of "loneliness, economic problems, the difficulties raising children alone" (Guerin et al., 1996, p. 42) can have a major impact on the way the system functions and adapts to the stresses and strains of life. In remarried families, other issues may predominate, such as "custody, visitation, jealousy, favoritism, loyalty conflict, stepparent and step-sibling problems" (p. 43). In the three-generation household, a parent or parents live with their parents; issues that predominate in this composition include "cross-generational boundaries, alliances and conflicts" (p. 44), such as who serves the parental function and three-generation triangles. The extended family may occupy a house with nonfamily or extended family members; this might include a housekeeper, nanny, adult member with a psychiatric or medical illness, or a young married couple who do not have the resources to establish separate domicile. It should be remembered that ethnic groups vary dramatically in cultural acceptance of these structures, which influences the family's dynamics and issues.

BIRTH ORDER: This refers to the birth position, number of years between children, and sex of children in the family (Bank & Kahn, 1982). Birth order can have relevance to the psychological development of the individual: "For example, an oldest child is more likely to be over-responsible, conscientious and parental, while the youngest is more likely to be child-like and carefree" (McGoldrick & Gerson, 1985, p. 46). Adler (1928) pioneered conceptions regarding the significance of birth order (Ansbacher & Ansbacher, 1956), and others also have made claims about its importance (Toman, 1976). Adler believed that birth order (ordinal position) and family size were significant factors in personality development. Older children are often pampered and expect others to meet their needs in exaggerated ways. This is complicated when there is an only child who remains enthroned as the center of attention. The second child's upbringing is often more relaxed; he or she is not the center of attention, which can lead to feelings of inferiority. The youngest often is also pampered and coddled excessively but can become competitive in reaction to the older siblings. The empirical evidence concerning birth order is somewhat equivocal, even though a "mountain of data" (Bank & Kahn, 1982, p. 6) supports its importance.

SIBLING BOND: The bonds that siblings develop can also exert a strong influence on personality formation (Bank & Kahn, 1982): "Siblings will use one another as major influences, or touchstones, in search for personal identity" (p. 19).

AGE DIFFERENCES BETWEEN SIBLINGS: Generally speaking, the closer the siblings are in age, the more they will share of the same developmental experiences. When there are great distances, each child may feel more like an only child. Sibling constellations can also be organized in subsystems, for example, the two younger in one subsystem and the two older ones in another. Parental functions may also increase for the older child when there is a great span of years; an older brother may act more like a father than a sibling.

THE FAMILY'S PROGRAM: Preexisting expectations and attitudes can exert a powerful influence on a child's personality development. "For example, Gregory Bateson, named for one of his father's heroes, Gregory Mendel, was perhaps being 'programmed' to aim at great accomplishments as a natural scientist" (McGoldrick & Gerson, 1985, p. 63).

ATTITUDES CONCERNING GENDER ROLES: Another important influence is the way parental attitudes are communicated to the child. Various cultures may have a preference for one sex; in most cases, it is the male. Thus, a child may grow up in a favored position entirely because of his or her sex. In some families, parents communicate their attitudes openly. Some females have been told that their parents are not going to pay for a college education because "girls just get married and have kids," so they don't want to "waste" their money.

Category 2. Life Cycle Transitions—Family Developmental Stages: Each family progresses through a developmental sequence, and at each transition point some restructuring of the family must occur to successfully navigate this. E. A. Carter and McGoldrick (1980) identify six distinct stages in the family life cycle:

1. The launching of the single young adult.
2. The joining of families through marriage.
3. Families with young children.
4. Families with adolescents.
5. Launching children and moving on.
6. Families in later life (p. 17).

"These transitions can be very difficult for some families, whose patterns rigidify at transition points, and who have trouble adapting to new circumstances" (McGoldrick & Gerson, 1985, p. 71). At each stage, various tasks have to be negotiated and responsibilities accepted, shifted, and renegotiated. Additionally, a variety of events can serve to dislocate the family, requiring restabilization to proceed developmentally; examples include divorce and postdivorce blending of families.

Category 3. Multigenerational Repetition of Patterns

PATTERNS OF FAMILY FUNCTIONING: Family patterns tend to repeat themselves over generations, although not always in a linear process. Styles of adaptation or dysfunction may be passed down to successive generations. Numerous symptomatic patterns, such as alcoholism, incest, physical symptoms, violence and suicide, tend to be repeated in families from generation to generation. These patterns may result in **dysfunctional personologic systems (DPSs),** defined as follows (Magnavita, 2000d):

- A dysfunctional family system in which a preponderance of individuals suffers from personality pathology, often observed over generations.
- A lineage of certain types of personality pathology associated with central family themes, dynamics, and triangles (p. 49).

Various types of DPSs have been elaborated, each having various systems themes, patterns of communication, and relational issues (Magnavita, in press-a):

- Addictive dysfunctional personologic system.
- Narcissistic dysfunctional personologic system.
- Covertly narcissistic personologic system.

- Psychotic dysfunctional personologic system.
- Developmentally arrested dysfunctional personologic system.
- Physically/Sexually traumatizing dysfunctional personologic system.
- Depressogenic dysfunctional personologic system.
- Chronically medically ill dysfunctional personologic system.
- Paranoid dysfunctional personologic system.
- Somatic dysfunctional personologic system (p. 60).

FEATURES OF DYSFUNCTIONAL PERSONOLOGIC SYSTEMS: The following features are associated with DPSs:

- Impermeable or weak external boundaries that separate the family system from others.
- Poor boundaries among family members.
- Disturbed levels of communication and overreliance on primitive defenses.
- Reversal of the parent-child relationship.
- Need for family to revolve around narcissistic parent.
- Poor emotional differentiation and regulation.
- Emotional malnourishment.
- Financial instability.
- Multigenerational transmission effects (Magnavita, 2000d, p. 54).

Over generations, there may be evidence of various patterns that are fused or disengaged or where certain patterns are recreated. Certain triangular configurations may also repeat themselves.

Category 4. Life Events and Family Functioning

COINCIDENCES OF LIFE EVENTS: A cluster of events may occur at the same point in development that are change occurrences but have profound effect on the family. The multiple tragedies of the Kennedy family are an example.

CHANGE, TRAUMA, AND TRANSITION: There may be an event or a number of events that affect the family; the loss of parents in a plane crash or multiple family members in war are a few. The system may respond to these in an attempt to accommodate, but they neverthe-less have an influence.

SOCIOECONOMIC AND POLITICAL EVENTS: Social and political events, such as war and social upheaval, can exert a strong influence.

Category 5. Relational Patterns and Triangles: The variety of triangular configurations that have been presented in the previous section pro-vides for an infinite and complex relational matrix. These configura-tions represent various emotionally laden triangles that can shape both individuals and systems.

Category 6. Family Balance and Imbalance

FAMILY STRUCTURE: Various factors indicate that a system is more or less balanced. For example, a spouse who is an only child marrying one who is the youngest of seven children may indicate some poten-tial sources of emotional stress.

ROLES: The roles that are assumed by various family members are also a factor that determines family functioning. In some alcoholic systems, an individual may function as a caretaker, and another as a black sheep.

LEVEL AND STYLE OF FUNCTIONING: Various members of families may function at different levels of capacity that may be informative. When there are extremes in the levels and styles, dysfunction may be evident.

Dysfunctional and Functional Parenting

The impact of parenting on the personality development of a child is a good example of the complexity of relational phenomena and the multiple factors that are involved. Abidin (1995) developed the Par-enting Stress Index to investigate the stressors and characteristics most commonly associated with dysfunctional parenting. He wrote: "In each situation in which the development of dysfunctional pat-terns of parenting occurred and in which children developed behav-ioral and emotional problems, one or more of the factors seemed to be involved: child temperament, parental personality characteris-tics, and family structure and functioning" (p. iii).

The Second Branch of Relational Theory

Rogers's Phenomenology of Experience

Carl Rogers (1902–1987) was a major theorist and clinical innovator in the area of existential-humanistic psychology. Rogers (1951) developed **client-centered therapy.** One of the main tenets of his theory was that humankind has a capacity for self-reflection and unique perceptions and experience, termed **phenomenology.** Rogers believed that people's basic motivation is for **personal growth.** He did not subscribe to the pathology-based models that were dominant at the time. Using language similar to the self psychologist, his conception is that all of us have an **ideal self** that strives for **actualization.**

Rogers is probably most noted for his identification of core conditions necessary for successful therapy, such as unconditional positive regard and genuineness on the part the therapist. Personality development required similar conditions, such as approval from significant figures, unconditional positive regard, and experiences consistent with the self. If an individual's experience does not match his or her self-concept, this incongruence will lead to neurotic or psychotic behavior, depending on the degree to which experience does not reflect the ideal self. The concept of the self and, in particular, the construct self-concept has lead to over 1,000 studies (Hillner, 1984). Rogers, however, is noteworthy for his emphasis on the relational experience that occurs between the therapist and the client.

The Centrality of Relationships in Women's Development

The Stone Center Relational/Cultural Theory: Although a much smaller body of work, the second branch of the relational tree is having substantial impact on the way in which the development of women is conceptualized. Jean Baker Miller (1976) offered a new perspective on the psychology of women in her book *Toward a New Psychology of Women.* "The seeds of the relational theory were presented by Miller, a classically trained psychiatrist," in this work (Silverman, 1999, p. 780). Carol Gilligan (1982) was also interested in women's development; in her book *In a Different Voice*, she examined the difficulties that exist when women are forced into a male-oriented model of psychological development. J. B. Miller, Stiver,

Jordan, and Surrey (1998) discuss the impact of the new model: "The writings of Miller and Gilligan quickly attracted many women in the psychological professions who were becoming more and more dissatisfied with the prevailing theories. Although their work has continued to capture the attention and imagination of growing numbers of women, more than a decade passed before 'mainstream' psychiatry and psychology began to acknowledge, respect, and assimilate these newer approaches" (p. 258).

A number of other theorists building on this work examined the role of gender in women's development. Their combined efforts led to a new understanding of the **centrality of relationships.** This model emphasizes both the relational and **cultural aspects** of women's experience. Judith Jordan (1997), working in conjunction with Miller and Gilligan at the Stone Center at Wellesley College, expanded this work. Jordan, Kaplan, Miller, Stiver, and Surrey (1991) have summarized the core ideas of the Stone Relational Model:

- People grow through and toward relationships throughout the life span.
- Movement toward mutuality rather than movement toward separation characterizes mature development.
- Relational differentiation and elaboration characterize growth.
- Mutual empathy and mutual empowerment are at the core of growth-fostering relationships.
- In growth-fostering relationships, all people contribute and grow or benefit; development is not a one-way street.
- Therapy relationships are characterized by a special kind of mutuality.
- Mutual empathy is the vehicle for change in therapy.
- Real engagement and therapeutic authenticity are necessary for the development of mutual empathy (Jordan, 2000, p. 1007).

Relational Connections/Disconnections: Challenging notions about the importance of autonomy and independence, relational theorists emphasize the importance of relationships that foster growth in others. Women's relationships are centered on connection and mutuality. J. B. Miller et al. (1998) sum up the central features:

- We grow in, through, and toward relationships.
- For women, especially, connection with others is central to psychological well-being.
- Movement toward relational mutuality optimally occurs throughout life, as a result of mutual empathy, responsiveness, and contribution to the growth of each individual and to the relationship (Frager & Fadiman, 1998, p. 260).

Repeated patterns of disconnection lead to states of shame and tension, along with a concomitant desired to connect. According to Jordan (2000):

> *The central paradox in this model suggests that disconnections (defined as breaks in connectedness) occur in relationships all the time (J. B. Miller & Stiver, 1997). Disconnections are ubiquitous; people misunderstand one another, hurt one another, fail one another empathically, and simply let one another down. When someone is hurt in a relationship and can represent her feelings of hurt authentically to the other person, and the other person responds in an empathic, caring way, the disconnection can move back into connection. By this movement, the relationship is actually strengthened and transformed. The connection becomes stronger and more authentic. If, however, the other person does not respond and if the other person has more power, the disconnection will not be reworked. Instead, the less powerful, hurt person will begin to develop strategies of disconnection. He or she will withdraw and present only what is acceptable to the other person in the service of staying in the relationship. But at that moment of withdrawal, the relationship loses much of its authenticity and vitality as the less powerful person keeps increasingly more of herself out of relationship in order to stay in the semblance of relationship. Both people lose out in such interactions.* (p. 1007)

When the pattern of the relationship is characterized by repeated disconnection, the individual may settle into a state of **chronic disconnection.** Gilligan (1982) describes how White adolescent girls often lose their voice and have a drop in self-esteem because of the disconnection they experience; this seems to be a "normative" developmental crisis for adolescent girls. A main feature of disconnection and suffering is isolation. Jordan (2000) writes: "Strategies of disconnection are protective; they allow an individual to keep certain aspects of the experience alive but out of connection. In cases of severe abuse, these strategies of disconnection get carried to other relationships as relational images and expectations and prevent the person from bringing her/himself more fully to the relationships" (p. 1008).

Chronic disconnection is the result of a failure of **mutual empathy.** Mutual empathy is similar to Buber's (1958) conception of the **"I-Thou" relationship.** The I-thou relationship refers to the experience of being touched or impacted in a relationship with another. In the therapeutic process, the I-thou can be contrasted to the neutral, distant, emotionally nonresponsive therapeutic Freudian stance. For most people, mutual empathy is natural: "It is the process of flowing back and forth, of being moved, of feeling safe in sharing one's vulnerability, and of disclosing the impact of the other person on one" (Jordan, 2000, p. 1010).

Cultural context is another important aspect of this theory. Traditional patriarchal cultures endow males with greater power, and so there is a tendency for women to be in relationships that are not mutual. This leads to a disempowering of women that can result in marginalization from the dominant culture. Any factor that marginalizes women is relevant; sexual preference, race, and age are capable of being used by the dominant culture to push women to a marginal position where they experience disconnection (A. Kaplan, 1991).

Rejecting Pathology and Labeling: A distinguishing feature of the Stone Relational Model is that it eschews the use of pejorative labels and is non-pathology-based. Psychological terms and constructs are not reified to the level they often are in other systems. In Frager and Fadiman (1998), J. B. Miller et al. discuss this aspect of the relational model:

> *In this relational approach to the psychology of women, every prior description of women requires reexamination. For example, the diagnosis of dependent personality disorder, and the more general use of the word dependent as pejorative and often pathological, are recast (Stiver, 1991). Women's search for connection, and the relative ease with which they express their vulnerabilities and needs, are often mislabeled as dependent—and, thus, neurotic, regressive and infantile. As the empowering value of relationships for women is recognized, dependency is seen as a positive movement along the path of healthy growth and development. This reframing*

moves us out of a value-laden and blaming mode into an empowering mode. The blaming mode originates in overvaluing independence and self-sufficiency and devaluing relationships which are collaborative and mutually empowering. (p. 262)

Finding Connection in Dysfunctional Families: Families suffering from alcoholism, incest, depression, eating disorders, or catastrophe survival (Holocaust, ethnic cleansing) are caught in the paradox of attempting to find connections among their members. The chronic disconnection in these dysfunctional families can lead to immobilization, which can underlie many symptomatic conditions, "including phobias, addictions, eating disorders, depression, dissociative states, and paranoid ideas, as well as many of the problems labeled as personality disorders (L. S. Brown, 1992). In each of these specific situations, the woman elaborates specific images of herself and others and specific forms of behavior that seem the only ones possible in the framework of the relationship she has constructed" (Miller et al. in Frager & Fadiman, 1998, p. 268). Personality disorder and the construct of defense are in a sense reframed as a **paradox of connection-disconnection,** leaving behind the pathology orientation and instead viewing these as forms of adaptation to the dysfunctional system. This is a point of confluence between the two relational models: Dysfunctional families as well as cultural forces are important in shaping individual personality. It therefore becomes crucial to view the individual as in relationship: "This model is not about *self-development.* We suggest instead that human behavior is about relational development, a constant movement of energy and meaning between people, a deeply contextual experience of personhood. In this perspective the enhancement of relatedness may constitute a greater goal than individual gratification and, ironically, may lead to greater individual fulfillment (Jordan, 1997). Stated more strongly, perhaps the most basic human need is the need to participate in relationship" (J. B. Miller et al. in Frager & Fadiman, 1998, p. 271).

Diagnostic Labels: The use of the *DSM* to diagnose women is fraught with danger, for there is a bias against women in these diagnostic categories. Labeling women as "too emotional" and diagnosing them as hysterical are examples of the bias that exists and the idealization of male psychology—independent, nonfeeling, and rational—as the

Selected Research Findings

- "The effects of familial risk, personality, and expectancies on alcohol use and abuse" (Finn, Sharkansky, Brandt, & Turcotte, 2000). The researchers studied the association among familial risk, personality risk, alcohol expectancies, and alcohol abuse in a cohort of 224 offspring of alcoholics and 209 offspring of nonalcoholics. One pathway to alcohol abuse proceeds from family alcoholism to social deviance and pleasure seeking/excitement.

- "Family processes as resources for African American children exposed to a constellation of sociodemographic risk factors" (Klein, Forehand, & Family Health Project Research Group, 2000). The investigators examined positive functions of African American children who experienced stressors associated with low socioeconomic status. The subjects were 212 mother-child dyads. The results indicated a significant association between mothers who were more supportive and optimal child functioning. Mothers who monitored their children more closely had children with less disruptive behavior and depressive symptoms.

- "Early risk factors for serious antisocial behavior at age 21: A longitudinal community study" (Pakiz, Reinherz, & Giaconia, 1997). The investigators analyzed data collected over 18 years regarding risk factors for serious antisocial behavior in 375 youths living in the community. A constellation of behaviors including acting-out, family dysfunction, aggression, and academic problems were associated with later antisocial behavior in both males and females.

- "Personality and family development: An intergenerational longitudinal comparison" (Schneewind & Ruppert, 1998). In an epoch study investigators followed 570 German families over a sixteen-year period evaluating them on multiple factors. One of the many findings was that there is a powerful intergenerational process whereby child rearing practices go from one generation to another.

- "Are adult children of dysfunctional families with alcoholism different from adult children of dysfunctional families without alcoholism? A look at committed, intimate relationships" (Harrington & Metzler, 1997). The researchers investigated the relationship between dysfunctional families with and without alcoholism. The findings indicate that family dysfunction is significantly related to problem-solving communication in relationships and distress. However, the findings did not support the discriminatory power of dysfunctional alcoholic families.

gold standard of mental health. "Taking issue with this process, Kaplan humorously suggests adding two new characterizations more applicable to male psychopathology, *the independent personality disorder* and the *restricted personality disorder* (1983)" (J. B. Miller et al. in Frager & Fadiman, 1998, p. 261).

Principles of the Relational Models

Philosophical Underpinnings and Assumptions

The major assumption of relational models is that personality and human adaptation need to be understood within the context of the relational matrix, encompassing both dyadic and triadic constellations. The relational models presented in this chapter tend to follow the deductive orientation, in that processes and systems are conceptualized from clinical observation as opposed to amassing data from which laws and relationships will emerge. These theoretical models tend to be more introspective and assume that human behavior cannot be studied from a distant position. Sullivan's notion of the participant-observer characterizes this orientation. Relational theories have been developed by psychotherapists and are often not empirically grounded, although empirical evidence does support them. Rychlak (1968) comments: "Although the personality theories of our well-known psychotherapists often lack the weight of validation, they do not lack meaning for us, they are not without a certain modicum of objectivity and relevance to the population at large, or at least to certain elements within the broader population" (p. 213).

Notions of Normal versus Abnormal

Most of the relational models presented in this chapter steer clear of the conundrum of clearly defining normal versus abnormal personality. In many ways, these models challenge the psychopathology orientation of individualistic personality theory. However, the systemic-relational model uses terms that help us define the continuum of gradations between normal and abnormal, such as functional and dysfunctional. The concept of differentiation is probably the best device for making a determination between levels of functioning. Obviously, those who are at the lower end of the scale, are the most disturbed individuals. This model speaks of dysfunctional systems versus functional systems or of a dimension of functionality. Thus, in my own model of dysfunctional personologic systems, one can assume that at the more severe level there will be evidence of greater personality disturbance in the individual family members over successive generations. The Stone relational model avoids this controversy regarding psychopathology and is constrained and uneasy with pathologic labeling.

Assessment Strategies and Tools

Probably the greatest tool of the relational model emerging from Bowen's, McGoldrick's, and Gerson's pioneering work is the family genogram. This represents a remarkable and unique contribution to the field from the systemic-relational theorists. Various objective instruments and rating scales have been developed to measure communication, parenting style, marital satisfaction, and many other aspects of relationships.

Application of Model

The two relational models share some common features, but there are differences that distinguish them, and they are differentially applied. The main application of the systemic-relational model has been in the development of systems of psychotherapy and models of family functioning. There are two major psychotherapeutic applications: advancing the treatment of dyads and systems, which include couples and families; and understanding family and organizational processes. The cultural-relational model was developed as a psychology of women and will probably have broader application as it becomes more accepted as an alternative to male-dominated notions of personality.

Cultural Influences and Differences

Both of the relational models presented in this chapter are sensitive to cultural differences. Systemic principles seem to have broad application, although this needs to be empirically validated. The cultural-relational model was developed to offer a more culturally sensitive model of development for women and is a unique alternative to the models presented thus far.

Strengths and Limitations of Model

At this point in its evolution, the relational model has great strengths and serious limitations. This model holds great potential for addressing and offering input into important social issues, but there is a dearth of research support for many of the main conceptualizations. A strength of the relational cultural model is its unique attempt to provide a new psychology of women. Relational science has the challenge of developing empirical support to inform federal policymaking, especially on issues concerning family functioning (Berscheid, 1999). The science of this field is "international in character, as well as multidisciplinary" (Berscheid & Reis, 1998, p. 194). Berscheid and Reis summarize: "Relationship science is young, sprawling, dynamic, enthusiastic, and growing at a feverish pace" (p. 253).

Summary

The relational model presented in this chapter has two main branches, relational-systems and Stone Center relational/cultural. Early work studying communication processes in families of schizophrenics emphasized the double-bind communication that they observed in many families. More recent work along this line looks at communication deviance, which is how emotion is expressed (expressed emotion). Current models of psychiatric disorder generally subscribe to the stress-diathesis model, which suggests that stress can exaggerate or trigger a biological vulnerability. A major advance occurred with the development and application of von Bertalanffy's general systems theory. Batteson applied new discoveries about communications theory to the field of psychiatry in an attempt to understand the communication process in schizophrenic families, pioneering an interdisciplinary approach to the topic. Bowen, one of the early founders of family systems theory, conceived of the family as an emotional unit and developed triadic theory, which describes the process that occurs in an unstable dyad when a third party is emotionally pulled in to stabilize the dyad. Bowenian theory offers many useful insights and new constructs for understanding personality development, such as differentiation, conceptions of the self, and the family projection process, to name a few. Ackerman was influential in the early development of a relational diagnostic system. More recently, Kaslow has attempted to further this relational system of diagnosis. Guerin has advanced the range of typologies of triangles, showing how they occur in most human relations, where high levels of anxiety are not being managed and are transferred to a third person. The family genogram developed by McGoldrick and Gerson is a major assessment tool that was inspired by the systems movement. A stage theory of development called the family life cycle shows how families progress through various phases in their development. Magnavita observed a number of dysfunctional personologic systems that tend to spawn personality disorders over generations. Baker and her associates developed a model of women's development that emphasizes the centrality of relationships for women and the cultural aspects, such as discrimination, that affect their development. Women are less concerned than males with autonomy and more concerned with relational connections and disconnections and mutual empathy in relations.

Suggested Reading

Green, H. (1965). *I never promised you a rose garden.* New York: Holt.

Jordan, J. V. (Ed.). (1997). *Women's growth in diversity.* New York: Guilford Press.

Integrative Models of Personality

11

Chapter

Introduction

This, the final theoretical chapter, presents integrative perspectives of personality that attempt to provide unification of the component or module systems that have been presented. As discussed in Chapter 1, this type of theoretical model emphasizes deductive reasoning. Overall, the more comprehensive the theory of personality, the more likely it is to divert from empirical, measurable observations that are used to build the component theories and constructs, especially inductive ones, such as behavioral. Although each of these approaches has its strengths and limitations, both are needed to advance the field of personality.

After a century of substantial work, only a fraction of the literature on personality can be covered in this volume. The prospect of attempting to sort through the extensive material and add to the mosaic is a daunting task indeed. The task of the next century may be to determine the dynamic interactions of these component systems, which is an extraordinarily complex task, similar in some ways to neuroscience's attempt to explain and model consciousness. Even though the various perspectives presented in this text at times seem in contradiction to one another, each model of personality is part of a mosaic that can be seen as a coherent whole. This should allow for a more utilitarian, broader theory with wider application.

The most comprehensive contemporary effort to achieve integration of personality theory based on an **evolutionary** framework has been offered by Millon (1981, 1990, 1996, 1999, 2000). His work is presented in a series of interconnected volumes that have had major impact on the discipline, partly because of their inclusiveness and partly because of their theoretical advancements. Next, attempting to integrate the component systems presented in this volume, the author (Magnavita, 1997, 1999, 2000a, 2000d) emphasizes the **systemic** (cross-sectional analysis: "space") contribution as the primary theoretical scaffold, as compared with Millon's evolutionary (longitudinal analysis: "time") emphasis, in a way that has been useful in conceptualizing normal and disordered personality.

Major Historical Figures

Darwin's Theory of Evolution

Charles Darwin (1859) is one of the intellectual giants of the nineteenth century, whose work continues to have tremendous impact on almost every scientific discipline and is particularly relevant to the theories of Millon and other evolutionarily based psychologists (D. M. Buss, 1984; A. H. Buss & Plomin, 1975, 1984; see Chapter 4). Darwin, a natural scientist, spent many years observing species of plants and animals, recording these while on his famous five-year voyage around the world on the H.M.S. *Beagle*, where he was the official naturalist. Darwin's most influential experience was four weeks he spent in the Galapagos Islands in the Pacific Ocean, very near the equator. Although others had formulated components of his theory of **natural selection,** it was Darwin who assembled all the data and constructed "an unassailable theory" (Leakey & Lewin, 1977, p. 28). He "was an effective synthesizer of existing information; his theory was not entirely new, but he presented it to the world at a time when the intellectual climate was at its most favorable" (p. 28).

Darwin observed that there were a number of different types of finches having a common stock. He hypothesized that species could undergo transformation, yet he did not understand how this occurred. He did not know how selection occurred and led to basic changes in populations. Leakey and Lewin (1977) describe Darwin's scientific leap that led to one of the greatest paradigmatic shifts of all time: "A flash of insight that was to illuminate the whole problem for him came on 3 October 1838, while he was reading 'for amusement' the book on population by Thomas Malthus (1766–1834), asserting that populations tend to increase geometrically unless constrained. Here, it came to him, was the answer: changes that favored an individual would allow it to prosper as compared with others not possessing these new properties; populations of animals with such advantageous mutations thrived, while those with less advantageous traits declined" (pp. 29–30).

Darwin's accomplishment was to demonstrate how, by gradual adaptation to the environment over successive generations, various species diversify and transform themselves through a process he termed **natural selection.** Those best suited in the competitive natural environment survive, and those ill suited decline, a process termed **survival of the fittest.** Accordingly, the origin of man in this theory is linked to other nonhuman primates. This theory of evolution lead to a confrontation with the creationists, an ongoing polemic in contemporary society.

Wilson's Unified Theory of Knowledge

Edward O. Wilson, a biologist who specializes in entomology, spent many years studying the social systems of ants (1971) before tackling the contradictions of human nature. A staunch advocate of evolutionary theory, Wilson (1998) was the main figure in the development of sociobiology (1978), a controversial field due to the emphasis it places on the hereditary foundation of human social behavior. In his book *On Human Nature* (1978), Wilson summarizes his view:

> *The argument to this point: the general traits of human nature appear limited and idiosyncratic when placed against the great backdrop of all other living species. Additional evidence suggests that the more stereotyped forms of human behavior are mammalian and even more specifically primate in character, as predicted on the basis of general evolutionary theory. Chimpanzees are close enough to ourselves in the details of their social life and mental properties to rank as nearly human in certain domains where it was once considered inappropriate to make comparisons at all. These facts are in accord with the hypothesis that human social behavior rests on a genetic foundation—that human behavior is, to be more precise, organized by some genes that are shared with closely related species and others that are unique to the human species. The same facts are unfavorable for the competing hypothesis which has dominated the social sciences for generations, that mankind has escaped its own genes to the extent of being entirely culturally bound. (p. 32)*

Wilson revitalized the question that has been a central one in the social sciences of **nature versus nurture.** The degree to which the nature of genetics accounts for the behavior of humans continues to be controversial. We shall revisit some of these notions and polemics in the final chapter. What is interesting here is the greater degree of interdisciplinary dialogue that is one of the primary achievements of integrative science.

Wilson's Challenge to the Social Sciences: Wilson is interested in the usefulness and power of scientific theorizing. He emphasizes the systemic nature of this endeavor: "The greatest challenge today, not just in cell biology and ecology but in all of science, is the accurate and complete description of complex systems" (1998, p. 85). The power of a theory depends on "its ability to transform a small number of axiomatic ideas into detailed predictions of observable phenomena" (Wilson, 1978, p. 34). Wilson (1998) describes scientific theories as "a product of imagination—*informed* imagination. They reach beyond their grasp to predict the existence of previously unsuspected phenomena. They generate hypotheses, disciplined guesses about unexplored topics whose parameters the theories help define. The best theories generate the most fruitful hypotheses, which translate cleanly into questions that can be answered by observation and experiment" (p. 53).

Wilson (1998) provides a harsh critique of social sciences from his perspective from biological science:

> *Social scientists, like medical scientists, have a vast store of factual information and an arsenal of sophisticated statistical techniques for its analysis. They are intellectually capable. Many of their leading thinkers will tell you, if asked, that all is well, that the disciplines are on track—sort of, more or less. Still, it is obvious to even casual inspection that the efforts of social scientists are snarled by disunity and a failure of vision. And the reasons for the confusion are becoming increasingly clear. Social scientists by and large spurn the idea of the hierarchical ordering of knowledge that unites and drives the natural sciences. Split into independent cadres, they stress precision in words within their specialty but seldom speak the same technical language from one specialty to the next. A great many enjoy the resulting overall atmosphere of chaos, mistaking if for creative ferment. Some favor partisan social activism, directing theory into the service of their personal political philosophies. (p. 182)*

He sees four potential bridges, paraphrased below:

1. Cognitive neuroscience attempting to solve the mystery of consciousness.
2. Human behavioral genetics attempting to tease apart hereditary bases of mental development.

3. Evolutionary biology attempting to explain the hereditary origins of social behavior.

4. Environmental science, the theater in which humans adapt (p. 192).

Wilson delivers a useful report card from a related natural science that is perspicacious. Theodore Millon's theoretical formulations parallel Wilson's evolutionary concepts and the belief in the need for synthesizing. However, before proceeding with Millon's evolutionary theory, another important movement in psychology, touched on in various parts of this text, is reviewed in greater depth because of its direct link to the theory presented in this chapter.

A Trend toward Theoretical Integration

A number of individuals throughout the past century have recognized the need for integrative theoretical models. But it was not until the last quarter of the twentieth century that the movement really began to emerge as a major force in many disciplines. The reason for this delay may be the necessity for sufficient empirical evidence and theoretical model building to accrue in a discipline so young (only 100 years) before a trend toward assimilation and integration could be successful. William James (1890), who was in part responsible for the birth of psychology as an independent scientific discipline, was one of the earliest proponents of integrating seemingly disparate psychological constructs. He was unwilling to accept theoretical consistency over an evolving system that had contradictions about human nature. In other words, he preferred to posit theoretical systems that did not always stay close to the data, in contrast to many of the empiricists of the time. According to Allport (1968), "More than any other psychologist James agonized over problems of systematic eclecticism" (p. 16).

Another prominent figure in personology, Henry Murray (1959), systematically attempted to produce comprehensive scaffolding for his theory of personality that was highly integrative in scope. As ambitious as this was, it likely lacked important aspects of the component systems discovered later that would have afforded him the opportunity to succeed in this daunting task. He had much more data than he could possibly process. Also, computer technology, which might have allowed him to analyze his data more effectively, was not available. It is interesting to note that many of his concepts did not achieve an enduring place in psychology, but his ambitiousness in attempting comprehensive integration continues to inspire, and he had substantial influence on seminal theorists such as Silvan Tomkins (Tomkins & Messick, 1963). Tomkins actually published a work entitled *Computer Simulation of Personality,* but is more widely known for his affect theory (Tomkins, 1962, 1963, 1991).

Allport's Clarion Call for Systematic Eclecticism

Gordon Allport (1968) was among the early proponents of what he called **systematic eclecticism.** The term eclectic has a somewhat negative connotation: "Eclecticism is often a word of ill-repute. An artist or composer, or even a psychologist who is 'eclectic' seems to lack a mind and style of his own" (p. 3). The term has also been used in the field of psychotherapy to describe the use of various techniques often without concern for theoretical anchoring. This is not how Allport conceived of the term, as he describes in his essay, "The Fruits of Eclecticism: Bitter or Sweet?" given as an invited address to the seventeenth International Congress of Psychologists in 1963. Allport describes eclecticism as "a system that seeks the solution of fundamental problems by selecting and uniting what it regards as true in the specialized approaches to psychological sciences" (pp. 5–6). He did not believe that it was possible to "synthesize all plausible theories," yet he believed that it "is still an ideal and a challenge" (p. 6). Allport reminded his readers that eclecticism is not new but was a concept used by philosophers who tried to distill Truth from various philosophical systems (Janet, 1885). He described the lack of synthesis in the field at the time: "The situation at present is that each theorist typically occupies himself with one parameter of human nature, and builds himself a limited model to fit his special data and personal style. Those who concern themselves with either the brain or phenomenology may be said to focus on one important parameter (body-mind); depth psychologists on the conscious-unconscious parameter; trait theorists on the stability-variability parameter; others on self and non-self. Trouble arises when an investigator maintains that his preferred parameter, or his chosen model, overspreads the whole of human personality" (Allport, 1968, p. 10).

Allport (1968) describes **theoretical assimilation** as "the absorption of great ideas into the stream of intellectual history," identifying the works of Darwin, Galton, Pavlov, and Freud as in our "bloodstream" (p. 14). Allport recognized the importance of the discovery of general systems theory, which he believed offered promise, but with a caveat about the potential to lose the construct of personality, which subsequently did prove to be the case. He wrote: "Its chief danger, I feel, is that in the hands of the positivists it loses altogether the concepts of personality and self. Yet properly employed the basic principle of *open system* is, I believe, the most fruitful approach to systematic eclecticism" (p. 17). He discusses the concept of personality as an "open system": "Personality is the most eclectic concept in psychology, and an open system view the most eclectic interpretation of this concept" (p. 22). Allport talked inspiringly about the task ahead: "It was Einstein's ambition to discover the physical unity of the universe. He built on knowledge that was available, and projected his brilliant synthesis into stellar space. The space assigned to us is much less vast. It is within the human skull; its contents weigh about three pounds. But the material contents are not a measure of the scope of consciousness. We are still far behind Einstein. He did not despair. Neither should we" (p. 24).

Allport (1968) realized that system theory was critical, but he did not expand his frame of reference to take into account all that happens outside of the "three pounds" of brain. He was concerned about reductionism and reminded us that a model is an **analogue:** a picture, but not the entity itself. "To say that human behavior is 'like the input and output of a computer' is a substantive model; to say that behavior fits a mathematical theorem is a formal model. Having pointed to a substantive or formal analogy the modelist stops dead in his tracks" (p. 11). He uses an Indian proverb about blind men attempting to describe an elephant as an example of myopic theorizing: "One finds its tail very like a rope; another his hoof like a pillar; to a third the ear is like a saddle. But none is able to characterize the elephant. Similarly, modelists who say man is very like a machine, a pigeon, a mathematical theorem, mistake the part for the whole, and sometimes even mistake the simulata for the thing simulated. Systematic eclecticism works less with models than with theories. And its eventual aim is a comprehensive metatheory of the nature of man" (p. 11).

The integrative movement, as with many others in psychology, has multiple tributaries that feed it. One major contributor to the development of integration was a new spirit of collaboration among psychotherapy innovators who were seeking more effective models to guide psychotherapy. Millon and Davis (1996b) state, "Clearly, those who undertake to propose 'integrative theories' are faced with the formidable task, not only of exposing the inadequacies of single-level theories, but of providing a convincing alternative that is both comprehensive and systematic" (p. 221). In spite of the parochialism that existed during the first half of the twentieth century, integration took hold, first slowly and with trepidation and then in a flood from innovative thinkers such as Allport.

The Influence of the Integrative Psychotherapy Movement

Although the concept of theoretical integration was not new, it began a more formal stage of development in the late 1970s (Arkowitz, 1992). This movement "crystallized into a strong and coherent force" (p. 262). According to Norcross and Newman (1992), "Rivalry among various theoretical orientations has a long and undistinguished history in psychotherapy, dating back to Freud" (p. 3). This dogmatism has also existed in psychotherapy's sister discipline, personality theory. Norcross and Newman believe that this "ideological cold war" may have been a necessary development before a period of "rapprochement" could be reached (p. 3). This interplay is a necessary stage of evolution in the science of personality. In the 1980s, there was a "geometric increase" in this movement, with "more than 200 publications" during this decade devoted to psychotherapy integration (Goldfried & Newman, 1992, p. 60). This burst of publications on theoretical integration in the 1980s marked the end of an era of parochialism and ushered in a new era of interdisciplinary collaboration (Arkowitz & Messer,

1984; Goldfried, 1982; Marmor & Woods, 1980; Norcross & New-man, 1992; Wachtel, 1987).

This interest culminated in a formal movement in the early 1980s to form a network of individuals interested in psychotherapy integration. The Society for the Exploration of Psychotherapy Integration was founded in 1983. The importance of this movement was summarized by Arkowitz (1992): "By expanding our scope beyond theories of psychotherapy and by looking toward areas of theory and research in other areas of psychology (e.g., cognitive sciences, social psychology, health psychology and psychobiology), psychotherapy integration promises to bring psychotherapy back to the field of psychology from which it has become somewhat isolated" (p. 293). This increased activity in psychotherapy integration necessitated a similar development in personality theory, spearheaded almost single-handedly by Millon.

Assimilation and Integration

There are basically two ways a theory can coalesce: theoretical assimilation and theoretical integration. Theoretical models of one persuasion over time may unwittingly absorb features of other systems in an ongoing process of **assimilation;** we discussed Allport's conception of this in the preceding section. Aspects of various theoretical models are absorbed and add to a new synthesis (Messer, 1992). This is not always a conscious process but occurs in all disciplines to one degree or another. Just as evolutionary theory has been assimilated into personality theory, a similar trend occurred when behavior theorists began applying the concept of neurosis to an animal model, called learned helplessness.

The second type of merging of theoretical models is more actively **integrative,** as opposed to "passive" assimilation (passive is not entirely correct, as one needs to read or hear lectures from other disciplines). Here there is an attempt to blend constructs of one model with another to create a "stronger" amalgam that has enhanced utility. This is similar to Allport's concept of systematic eclecticism.

As presented in Chapter 7, the most ambitious attempt to integrate two distinct and somewhat contentious theoretical positions occurred when Dollard and Miller (1950) published *Personality and Psychotherapy: An Analysis in Terms of Learning, Thinking, and Culture.* Arkowitz (1992) writes, "This book went far beyond its usual description as a simple attempt to translate psychoanalytic concepts into behavioral language" (p. 264). It was a major attempt to synthesize and integrate these two models. Not just a translation, then, it represented a new integrative theory of personality.

One of the most influential of the current integrative theorists is Paul Wachtel, who studied at Yale with Miller and Dollard. Wachtel actively sought to develop a model that integrated both psychodynamic and behavioral models, with systemic constructs. Wachtel (1977) published a highly influential book, *Psychoanalysis and Behavior Therapy: Toward an Integration*, in which he built a framework that combined the best features of both models. Wachtel's model, **cyclical psychodynamic theory,** posits that past experiences influence the present environment, often leading to vicious circles. Horney (1945) and Millon (1969) preceded Wachtel with their parallel concepts of "fostering vicious circles" and "self-perpetuating processes," respectively. One of the important components of Wachtel's model, according to Arkowitz (1992), is "the view of causality," which "in this theory is circular and reciprocal, rather than the linear causal views of behavioral and psychoanalytic theories" (p. 269). This is the basis of the second **integrative-systemic model** perspective presented in this chapter. Again, Arkowitz comments on the importance of the way Wachtel conceptualized his model for future efforts:

> It is important to keep Wachtel's original vision in mind. He sought an "evolving framework" for integration rather than a fixed integration of one approach over another. What does the concept of an evolving framework involve? This question may hold the key to one of the most important new directions for psychodynamic-behavioral integration and theoretical integration more broadly. I believe that we may be moving toward what G. E. Schwartz (1991) and others have described as an "open system" model that not only consists of the interaction of its existing components, but also allows for new elements to be introduced and old ones to exist. There is some internal cohesiveness in the system—not all elements can enter readily into it. Some elements either are unable to enter into the system or must change in order to do so. In addition, a change in one element of the system potentially changes the entire system. (p. 273)

Cyclical psychodynamics rejects the notion that there is "fundamental incompatibility among the theoretical viewpoints it attempts to integrate" (Wachtel & McKinney, 1992, p. 335). Wachtel's system "seeks to synthesize key facets of psychodynamic, behavioral, and family systems theories" (p. 335). Wachtel describes the evolution of his model—moving from a theory of psychotherapy to one of personality, much like others presented in this text: "The cyclical psychodynamic approach to theory and to clinical practice developed as an integrative effort to incorporate the observations and concepts of diverse perspectives into a coherent conceptual framework. Over the years, this point of view has evolved so that in certain respects it now resembles a 'theory of personality' in its own right. This is both a sign of progress and a signal of danger. The increasing coherence and comprehensiveness of this point of view are encouraging, as is its fertility in generating new ideas for how to proceed clinically" (p. 364). Wachtel warns that the intent is *not to develop various integrative schools*, but for theorists to maintain the "spirit of the integration movement" so as not to re-create the "parochialism they were designed to transcend" (p. 364). He emphasizes the open-ended nature of this model.

Millon's Evolutionarily Based Integrative Model of Personality

Theodore Millon (1928–) is one of the most influential contemporary personality theorists, coming from a lineage of influential mentors, among others, the famous personologists Gardner Murphy and Henry Murray. More than any other contemporary figure he has been responsible for the resurgence of clinical, academic, and research interest in the field of personality. After the heyday of interest in personality peaked in the mid-twentieth century, with the grand attempts by Murray, Lewin, and Murphy to develop comprehensive systems, personality fell into disrepute. "No longer was personality to be seen as an integrated gestalt, a dynamic system comprising more than the mere sum of its parts. The pendulum swung toward empiricism and positivism; only 'observable' facts were in ascendancy" (Millon, 1984, p. 452). Looking back on that time, it seems as if the study of personality entered the "dark ages,"

during which the rich heritage of early theories was shelved. This period lasted for the next quarter of the twentieth century, until Millon's (1984) invited address and article, "On the Renaissance of Personality Assessment and Personality Theory." In his address and an article that followed, Millon proclaimed: "The long drought is over and a revival of the rich heritage of the Forties and Fifties is under way" (p. 450). Millon's (1983) interests in personality and participation in the task force of the American Psychiatric Association's committee on personality disorders fueled a good part of this renewal. Millon (1984) comments: "With the advent of this official classification, personality disorders not only gained a place of consequence among syndromal categories, but became central to its multiaxial schema" (p. 455).

Millon (1990) is a theorist and empiricist with training and interest in the natural sciences, from which he draws useful concepts and metaphors. His career has been devoted to extending the parameters of psychopathology and clinical diagnosis (1967, 1969, 1996), personality and its disorders (1973, 1981; Millon & Millon, 1974), and assessment and clinical instrumentation (1977) and theory (1990; Millon & Davis, 1996a, 1996b). He reiterates Kurt Lewin's (1936) sentiment that "there is nothing so practical as a good theory." The purpose of theory is to establish the "organizing principles that not only create order but also provide the basis for generating hypotheses and stimulating new knowledge" (p. 14). He does not minimize the complexity of the task, neither does he avoid what he sees as necessary for scientific advancement (Millon, 1987): "To recall thoughts expressed some years ago concerning the character of theory (Millon, 1969), I voiced my chagrin that nature was not made to suit our need for a tidy and well-ordered universe. Quite evidently, the complexity and intricacy of the natural world make it difficult not only to establish clearcut relationships among phenomena, but to find simple ways in which these phenomena can be classified or grouped. In our desire to discover the essential order of nature, we find it necessary to concern ourselves with only a few of the infinite number of elements that could be chosen; in this selection we narrow our choice only to those aspects of nature that we believe best enable us to answer the questions we have posed" (p. 3).

The ease of gathering evidence and establishing a perspective can be problematic. Millon (1990) comments: "It is paradoxical, but true and unfortunate, that personologists learn their subject quite well merely by observing the ordinary events of life. As a consequence of this ease, personologists appear to shy from and hesitate placing trust in the 'obscure and complicating,' yet often fertile and systematizing powers inherent in formal theory, especially theories that are new or that differ from those learned in their student days" (p. 17). "And what better sphere is there within the psychological sciences to undertake such syntheses than with the subject matter of personology. Persons are the only organically integrated system in the psychological domain, evolved through the millennia and inherently created from birth as natural entities, rather than culture-bound and experience-derived gestalts. The intrinsic cohesion of persons is not merely a rhetorical construction, but an authentic substantive unity. Personologic features may often be dissonant, and may be partitioned conceptually for pragmatic or scientific purposes, but they are segments of an inseparable biopsychosocial unity" (p. 12).

Millon (2000) strives for logical and systematically integrated and interrelated domains on which to base theory. He believes that the science of personality would be best served if various domains of knowledge were coordinated. He states:

> *Rather than developing independently and being left to stand as autonomous and largely unconnected functions, a truly mature clinical science, one that is designed to create a synergistic bond among its elements, will embody the following explicit elements:*
>
> 1. Universal scientific principles, *that is, be grounded in the ubiquitous laws of nature, despite their varied forms of expression, providing thereby an undergirding framework for guiding and constructing subject-oriented theories.*
>
> 2. Subject-oriented theories, *that is, explanatory and heuristic conceptual schemas of personality and psychopathology that are consistent with established knowledge in both its own and related sciences, and from which reasonably accurate propositions concerning all clinical conditions can be both deduced and understood, enabling thereby the development of a formal classification system.*
>
> 3. Classification of pathological syndromes and disorders, *that is, a taxonomic nosology that has been derived logically from the theory, and provides a cohesive organization within which its major categories can*

readily be grouped and differentiated, permitting thereby the development of coordinated assessment instruments.

4. Personality and clinical assessment instruments, *that is, tools that are empirically grounded and sufficiently sensitive quantitatively to enable the theory's propositions and hypothesis to be adequately investigated and evaluated, and the categories comprising its nosology to be readily identified (diagnosed) and measured (dimensionalized), specifying the target areas for interventions.*

5. Integrated therapeutic interventions, *that is, planful strategies and modalities of treatment, designed in accord with the theory and oriented to modify problematic clinical characteristics, consonant with professional standards and social responsibilities. (pp. 39–40)*

Theoretical Model

Evolutionary Foundation: Millon's (1990) model is anchored to evolutionary theory. **Personality** is represented as "the more-or-less distinctive style of adaptive functioning that an organism of a particular species exhibits as it relates to its typical range of environments" (p. 21). **Personality disorders** are "particular styles of maladaptive functioning that can be traced to deficiencies, imbalances, or conflicts in a species' capacity to relate to the environments it faces" (p. 21). Millon describes the evolutionary aspects: "During its life history an organism develops an assemblage of traits that contribute to its individual survival and reproductive success, the two essential components of 'fitness' formulated by Darwin. Such assemblages, termed 'complex adaptations' and 'strategies' in the literature of evolutionary ecology, are close biological equivalents to what psychologists have conceptualized as personality styles and structures" (p. 21).

Traits and styles of personality are genetically molded over generations to adapt to the particular environmental demands. In addition, this evolutionary process occurs over the life span of an individual. "What is seen in the individual organism is a shaping of latent potentials into adaptive and manifest styles of perceiving, feeling, thinking and acting; these distinctive ways of adaptation, engendered by the interaction of biologic endowment and social experience, comprise the elements of what is termed personality style" (Millon, 1990, p. 22).

Chaos Theory: Millon (1990) also acknowledges the importance of chaos theory, according to which, all systems have random fluctuations that cannot be explained by linear models. Small shifts may have great impact. "Random fluctuations and irregularities in ostensibly chaotic states may come to form not only complicated rhythms and patterns, but also demonstrate both recurrences and replicated designs . . . here, the same shapes emerge from fluctuations time and again, taking form sequentially on smaller and smaller scales" (p. 31), called fractal patterns (Mandelbrot, 1977).

A Tripartite Model—Three Polarities of Mental Life: In his system, Millon (1990) proposes three polarities of mental life that he uses as the scaffold for conceptualizing the structure and function of personality. Millon acknowledges that Freud (1915/1925), as well as others, advanced these polarities but unfortunately never developed them to explain personality. These are (1) **subject-object** or self-other, (2) **pleasure-pain,** and (3) **active-passive.** Millon (1990) reports that he discovered these principles following a Skinnerian behavioral model, without knowledge of Freud's work. He describes his experience: "Unacquainted with Freud's proposals at the time, and employing a biopsychosocial learning model, the author constructed a framework similar to Freud's 'great polarities that govern all of mental life'" (p. 48). The fact that both Freud and Millon identified these polarities, if not a case of two astute scientists brilliantly distilling the elements of their observations, reflects the best interpretation of assimilative theoretical integration. As we have seen in Chapter 7, Eysenck also developed a tripartite model of personality "matching in most regards the three-part polarity model" developed by Millon (1990, p. 49).

The subcomponents that Millon attaches to each of his polarities include four major theoretical domains, principles of learning, psychoanalytic concepts, components of emotion/motivation, and neurobiological substrates. He arranges the subcomponents in relationship to his evolutionarily predisposed polarities (see Table 11.1). His conceptual model is far-reaching, including components of each of the theoretical models covered in this text, either explicitly stated or suggested.

SUBJECT-OBJECT/SELF-OTHER: The evolutionary basis for the self-other polarity is based on "a balanced though asymmetric parental

Table 11.1   **Correspondence of Evolutionary Polarities and Psychological Constructs**

Psychological Constructs	Evolutionary Polarities		
	Pleasure-Pain	**Passive-Active**	**Self-Other**
Principles of learning	Positive and negative reinforcers of learning	Respondent versus operant modes of behavior	Internal versus external controls of reinforcement
Psychoanalytic concepts	Instinctual aims of the id	Reality apparatuses of the ego	Self-structures versus object relations
Components of emotion/motivation	Pleasant and unpleasant valences of emotion	Low versus high intensities of activation	Competitive versus cooperative dispositions of motivation
Neurobiological substrates	Substrates of mood	Substrates of arousal	Substrates of gender

Source: Toward a New Personology: An Evolutionary Model by T. Millon, © 1990. Reprinted by permission of John Wiley & Sons, Inc.

investment in both the genesis and nurturance of offspring" (Millon, 1990, p. 77). To maximize competitive advantage, males tend to be self-oriented so that their gene pool will have the best chance of survival. Women, on the other hand, tend to lean toward the "other" end of the self-other continuum: "Not only must the female be oriented to and vigilant in identifying the needs of and dangers that may face each of her few offspring, but it is reproductively advantageous for the female to be sensitive to and discriminating in her assessment of potential mates" (p. 78). One can see support from the Stone relational model covered in Chapter 10 in support of this view. Women on the whole may be more motivated than men by connection and relatedness. The following elements are included under the self-other polarity:

- Internal-external, ego-object, self-nonself.
- Self-structures and object relations.
- Cooperation versus competition.
- Neurobiology of gender.

PLEASURE-PAIN: "The pleasure-pain distinction recognizes that sensations, motivations, feelings, emotions, moods, and affects can ultimately be placed on two contrasting dimensions, each possessing separate quantitative extremes (i.e., bipolarities)—events such as attractive, gratifying, rewarding, or positively reinforcing may be experienced as weak or strong, as can those which are aversive, distressful, sad or negatively reinforcing also be experienced as weak or strong" (Millon, 1990, pp. 51–52). The following elements are subsumed under the pleasure-pain polarity:

- Positive and negative reinforcement.
- Instinctual organization.
- Emotion, motivation, mood, and temperament.

ACTIVE-PASSIVE: The active-passive polarity refers to "two primary modes by which living organisms adapt to their ecological environments" (Millon, 1990, p. 64). In the natural sciences, plants are examples of passive adaptation and animals of active adaptation. Plants remain attached to one location and adapt to that particular set of environmental demands. Animals more actively interact with the environment, allowing for shifting to different environments when necessary for survival or enhanced functioning. In terms of personality, those on the passive end of the continuum tend to be phlegmatic and unmotivated. They seem to have little sense of self-efficacy and expect things to come to them rather than to seek them out: "They seem suspended, quiescent, placid, immobile, restrained, listless, waiting for things to happen and reacting to them only after they occur" (Millon, 1990, p. 65). The following domains are identified:

- Conditioning paradigms.
- Ego apparatus.
- Intensities of activation.
- Arousal; neurobiological substrates.

Nosology: Classification of Personality

"Scientific progress requires the logical ordering of a systematic taxonomy" (Millon, 1990, p. 101). Nosology is the classification of entities into their logical categories (Millon, 1987). "Drawing on the threefold polarity framework—pain-pleasure, active-passive, self-other—a series of ten personality 'prototypes' and three severe variants were deduced, of which a few have proved to be 'original' derivations in the sense that they had never been formulated as categories in prior nosologies" (Millon, 1990, p. 107). Millon's system includes the following personality styles/disorders:

- *The Schizoid personality:* Schizoid individuals are those who have deficiencies in their pleasure-pain polarity. They do not have the capacity for either pleasure or pain. They are not much motivated by personal enjoyment, and tend to be apathetic, distant, and listless. They do not seek out human relationships for comfort and pleasure.

- *The Avoidant personality:* Avoidant individuals also have disturbance in the pleasure-pain domain. They are detached, as is the schizoid person. But unlike the schizoid individual, they react strongly to pain, seeking to avoid it at the cost of their mastery and improved coping. They tend to be on guard and vigilant, ready to distance from perceived painful events.

- *The Self-Defeating personality:* Self-defeating individuals have a polarity reversal on the pain-pleasure continuum. Pain may actually be preferred on some level, or at least familiar and more easily tolerated. "Typically acting in an unpresuming and self-effacing way, they often intensify their deficits and place themselves in an inferior light or abject position" (Millon, 1990, p. 118).

- *The Sadistic personality:* Sadistic individuals actually experience pain as pleasurable and thus have a strange reversal of the normal tendencies. They tend to be hostile, contentious, and combative, and indifferent or pleased with their destructiveness. There are various subcategories of this personality. In its extreme form, individuals receive pleasure from brutalizing others.

- *The Dependent personality:* Dependent individuals turn almost excessively toward others. "Behaviorally, these persons display a strong need for external support and attention; should they be deprived of affection and nurturance they will experience marked discomfort, if not sadness and anxiety" (Millon, 1990, p. 120). They tend to look toward others for affection and guidance. They willingly submit to others to maintain others' affection.

- *The Histrionic personality:* Histrionic individuals also have primary imbalance in self-other polarity. Unlike the dependents, who are passive, histrionics are active in attempting to maintain dependence. "They achieve their goal of maximizing protection, nurturance, and reproductive success by engaging busily in a series of manipulative, seductive, gregarious, and attention-getting maneuvers" (Millon, 1990, p. 121). They are often desperate in their search for stimulation and affection.

- *The Narcissistic personality:* Narcissistic individuals have an imbalance in the self-other as well as pleasure-pain polarities. They emphasize reliance on themselves and a sense of superiority. They display "manifest confidence, arrogance, and exploitive egocentricity in social contexts" (Millon, 1990, p. 122). They tend to be egotistic and self-centered, placing a high value on their special status and often appearing pretentious.

- *The Antisocial personality:* Antisocial individuals act to counter pain by exploiting others. They lack empathy for others because of an imbalance in the self-other polarity, with a greater emphasis on themselves than others. "Many are irresponsible and impulsive, actions they see as justified because they judge others to be unreliable and disloyal" (Millon, 1990, p. 122). Insensitive and ruthless behavior lead to victimizing others and then justifying their behavior because of slights or disloyalty.

- *The Passive-Aggressive (negativistic) personality:* Passive-aggressive individuals tend to vacillate between self-other polarities. At times, they are compliant, but quickly can become defiant and stubborn, even at the cost of their own satisfaction. "Feeling intensely, yet unable to restore their ambivalence, they weave an erratic course from voicing their self-depreciation and guilt for failing to meet the expectations of others, to expressing stubborn negativism and resistance over having submitted to the wishes of others rather than their own" (Millon, 1990, p. 123).

- *The Obsessive-Compulsive personality:* Obsessive-compulsive individuals show a proclivity for other-directedness. "They are trapped in an ambivalence; to avoid intimidation and punishment they have learned to deny the validity of their own wishes and emotions and, in their stead, have adopted as 'true' the values and percepts set forth by others" (Millon, 1990, p. 124). They tend to be prudent, perfectionist, self-restrained, and overconforming, but can be oppositional as well.

Severe Personality Disorders: Along with the above personality types, Millon's system accounts for the severe forms of personality disorder. These are characterized by a tendency to decompensate into psychosis, although usually reversible. They also have social deficits, which tend to be more severe than the ones described:

- *The Schizotypal personality:* Schizotypal individuals evidence a level of cognitive dysfunction. They "have difficulty consistently differentiating between self and other strategies, as well as active and passive modes of adaptation" (Millon, 1990, p. 126). They are rather eccentric in behavior and appearance and can appear confused and tangential in their thinking. They tend to prefer isolation and minimal attachments and obligations.

- *The Borderline personality:* Borderline individuals oscillate among all the polarities, which creates instability in most areas of functioning. They have a poorly developed sense of their identity and are characterized by extreme states of emotional dysregulation and often parasuicidal behavior, such as cutting themselves in a mutilating way. They often demonstrate conflicting feelings of rage and love toward their attachment figures.

- *The Paranoid personality:* Paranoid individuals have a deep and pervasive sense of distrust of others. They have a higher than usual sensitivity to interpersonal pain and rejection, and are often described as thin-skinned for their hair-trigger reactions to others. They tend to be irritable and often provoke the very reactions from others that they fear and expect. Their irascibility makes others respond in negative ways, further cementing their paranoid perceptions that others are out to do them harm. Unlike borderline individuals, paranoids are inflexible in their position.

Normal Personality: Millon (1991) states: "The intersection between the study of 'psychopathology' and the study of 'normality' is one of these spheres of significant academic activity and clinical responsibility"

(p. 356). In this schema, normal personality represents a balance among the three personalities. Individual differences may be explained by a person's relative position on the polarities. "A particularly 'healthy' person, for example, would be one who is high on both self and other, indicating a solid sense of self-worth, combined with a genuine sensitivity to the needs of others" (Millon, 1990, p. 107).

Millon (1991) views normality in the same way as abnormality: from an evolutionary perspective. He believes individual **personality styles** are shaped by evolutionary mechanisms that unfold over a lifetime. "In phylogenesis, then, actual gene *frequencies* change during the generation-to-generation adaptive process, whereas in ontogenesis, it is the *salience* or prominence of gene-based traits that changes as adaptive learning takes place. . . . It is the formative process in a single lifetime that parallels gene redistributions among species during their evolutionary history" (pp. 363–364). Two important factors affect the evolutionary process of humans: Humans require a long period of childhood **parental dependence** and nurturing, and there is a complex process of **role modeling.** Humans must be capable of adapting to complex ecological environments where "alternate modes of functioning for dealing both with predictable and novel environmental circumstances" (p. 364) are required. This malleability diminishes as development proceeds, increasing the immutability of the personality style, becoming more resistant to modification:

- *Pleasure-Pain polarity:* An evolutionary model assumes that the aim of life is survival and preservation of life. The pain-pleasure polarity relates to the attraction to life-enhancing activities and repulsion from the life-threatening ones. This polarity subsumes "sensations, motivations, feelings, emotions, moods, and affects" (Millon, 1991, p. 372). An individual may experience each of the polarities as weak or strong. Thus, in one person, negatively tinged affects may be more powerfully associated with what others would experience as pleasurable.

- *Active versus Passive styles:* Those who are **passive** tend to have few strategies that they use instrumentally. "They display a seeming inertness, a phlegmatic lack of ambition or persistence, a tendency toward acquiescence, a restrained attitude in which they initiate little to modify events, waiting for circumstances of their environment to take course before making accommodations" (Millon, 1991, p. 374). Those who are **active** plan strategies and are instrumental in their acts. They "are best characterized by their alertness, vigilance, liveliness, vigor, forcefulness, stimulus-seeking energy and drive" (p. 374). Some tend to be hasty, excitable, and rash; others more deliberate. "Normal" or optimal functioning requires a flexible balance between both active and passive polarities.

■ *Self-Other Orientation:* Self-oriented individuals are more concerned with maintaining a competitive edge over others. They tend to act in an "egotistic, insensitive, inconsiderate, uncaring, and noncommunicative manner" (Millon, 1991, p. 378). Other-oriented individuals tend to be more cooperative and nurturing in their relationships with others. They tend to act in an "affiliative, intimate, empathic, protective, and solicitous" manner (p. 378). Millon believes that there is ample evidence from evolutionary biology to suggest that the self-oriented strategy is a primarily male form of adaptation and the other-oriented strategy a primarily female form.

Instrumentation

Millon believes that a comprehensive theory of personality requires empirically derived instrumentation that is calibrated to measure the constructs elaborated in the previous sections. Six instruments "have been created to operationalize the constructs of the theoretical model" (Millon & Davis, 1996b, p. 317). Millon (Millon & Davis, 1996a) began to develop his instruments in the early 1970s in an attempt to "identify and quantify" personality constructs (p. 158). The most commonly used to assess personality disorders and clinical syndromes, which has gained the stature of the MMPI is the Millon Multiaxial Inventory-III (Millon, Millon, & Davis, 1994).

Intervention and Treatment

Although not the focus of this text, intervention and treatment aspects are essential to understanding Millon's comprehensive effort to have theory, taxonomy, instrumentation, and practical application (i.e., change-oriented intervention) relate logically and be systematically integrated. Those who are interested in the topic of psychotherapy are encouraged to read Millon's (1999) tome, *Personality-Guided Therapy*, wherein he builds the therapeutic scaffold for his theory of intervention in action. Millon terms this therapeutic metamodel **psychosynergy;** it is similar to psychoanalysis developed 100 years earlier in that it attempts a grand unification theory based on his evolutionarily based metapsychology. His fundamental assumption is that effective therapeutic change needs to be guided by understanding personality and interrelated clinical syndromes. Essentially, Millon uses his three polarities as a means of establishing the optimal intervention and draws on available technology and psychotherapeutic methods consistent with his goals. His goal is to balance the polarities and he offers a synopsis of various methodologies to do so. He summarizes the overarching goals of the model: "Depending on the pathological polarity to be modified and the integrative treatment sequence one has in mind, the goals of therapy are (1) to overcome *pleasure deficiencies* in schizoids, avoidants, and depressive styles/disorders; (2) to reestablish *interpersonally imbalanced* polarity disturbances in dependents, histrionics, narcissists, and antisocials; (3) to undo the *intrapsychic conflicts* in sadists, compulsives, masochists, and negativists; and (4) to reconstruct the structural defects in schizotypal, borderline, and paranoid persons" (1999, p. 130).

Systemic Integrative Model of Personality

The model of systemic integrative personality presented in this section is based primarily on the contemporary formulations of Magnavita (1997, 2000d) and Wachtel (1977; Wachtel & Wachtel, 1986). This contemporary integrative model shares many common elements with Millon's, but has a somewhat different emphasis regarding the theoretical foundations. The systemic integrative model shares the following theoretical aspects with Millon's evolutionarily based integrative model: (1) systems theory, (2) chaos theory, (3) integrative blending of components from other models, (4) biosocial basis, and (5) evolutionary theory. The emphasis placed on these foundational theoretical beliefs differs sufficiently to offer a somewhat different perspective. As we have reviewed in the previous chapter on relational models, systems theorists by and large rejected the construct of individual personality. In agreement with Millon, an either/or position does not serve the field well: Too much is lost. "Some systems theorists argue that these larger systems are solely responsible for creating and sustaining person-level pathology, and that individual pathology, in effect, simply does not exist because it is derivable from and can be 'reduced' to these more encompassing systems. The authors . . . philosophically reject such forms of system reductionism" (Millon & Davis, 1996a, p. 212). The model presented in this section is based on the author's attempt to provide a contemporary model that integrates the various theoretical components elucidated in Chapter 4. It is my hope that this will provide a parsimonious scaffold for many of the relevant perspectives on personality presented in this text.

Biopsychosocial Model in a Relational Field

Personality development is an extraordinarily complex process that does not lend itself to simplistic or reductionistic explanations. Therefore, personality style is neither interpersonal, intrapsychic, biological, cognitive, societal, nor developmental in etiology; rather, all these factors contribute to personality (Magnavita, 2000d). Personality is not made up of this collection of static interrelated factors but is a constantly interactive, fluid process that is best explained with a biopsychosocial model in a relational field. Grigsby and Stevens (2000), writing from a neurodynamic perspective, state, "While constitutional factors are unquestionably important, much of a person's character emerges from interactions with parents and other significant people" (p. 315). This model is strengthened by von Bertalanffy's (1948) general systems theory, which stresses the feedback loops and patterns of interrelationships among subsystems (see Figure 11.1).

Chaos Theory

Another model borrowed from the natural sciences that is useful for understanding complex systems is chaos theory, described by Millon in the preceding section. Chaos theory offers a useful perspective consistent with general systems theory on the way complex systems function. Gleick (1987) describes the explanatory power of this theory: "In science as in life, it is well known that a chain of events can

Figure 11.1

The Systemic Interrelationships among the Modular Components of Personality.

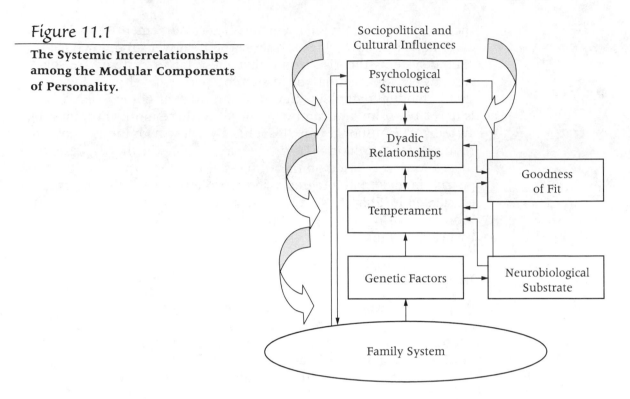

have a point of crisis that could magnify small changes. But chaos meant that such points are everywhere. They were pervasive. In systems like the weather, sensitive dependence on initial conditions was an inescapable consequence of the way small scales intertwined with large" (p. 23).

The study of weather was one of the complex systems that chaos theorists used to develop their model. In the prediction of weather, there was a common joke "known as the **Butterfly Effect**—the notion that a butterfly stirring the air today in Peking can transform storm systems next month in New York" (Gleick, 1987, p. 8). Complex systems are exquisitely sensitive to random fluctuations. In weather, very small fluctuations can give rise to rapid fluctuations with exponential force: "Errors and uncertainties multiply, cascading upward through a chain of turbulent features, from dust devils and squalls up to continent-size eddies that only satellites can see" (p. 20). These random fluctuations, even when small, can have a dramatic impact on the functioning of the entire system. Gleick provides the following illustration: "A man leaves the house in the morning thirty seconds late, a flowerpot misses his head by a few millimeters, and then he is run over by a truck. Or, less dramatically, he misses a bus that runs every hour. Small perturbations in one's daily trajectory can have large consequences" (p. 67). This model rejects the linear nature of natural phenomena. The human being is much too fragile and complex to capture in any static model, so a model that includes the concept of continual motion is useful. For example, a personality disorder is a disorder of a complex system that can be set in motion by the introduction of small events that reverberate throughout the biopsychosoical system. The problem of reducing complex systems to basic elements is described by Mandel (1985) and summarized by Gleick (1987):

> *To Mandel, the discoveries of chaos dictate a shift in clinical approaches to treating psychiatric disorders. By any objective measure, the modern business of "psychopharmacology"—the use of drugs to treat everything from anxiety and insomnia to schizophrenia itself—has to be judged a failure. Few patients, if any, are cured. The most violent manifestations of mental illness can be controlled, but with long-term consequences, no one knows. Mandel offered his colleagues a chilling assessment of the most commonly used drugs. Phenothiazines, prescribed for schizophrenics, make the fundamental disorder worse. Tricyclic antidepressants "increase the rate of mood cycling, leading to long-term increases in the numbers of relapsing psychopathological episodes." Only lithium has any real success, Mandel said, and only for some disorders. (p. 298)*

The problem as Mandel conceptualized it was the reductionistic emphasis on a linear model in what is the most complex organismic system. According to Mandel, the entire paradigm was wrong in the way it describes the linear sequence from gene, to receptor, to syndrome, to drug, to rating scale instead of the nonlinear dynamics of geometrically flowing complex systems. Evolution itself is an example of a chaotic system with a feedback system.

Evolutionarily Based Interrelated Modular Systems

Personality can be thought of as numerous interrelated modular systems that have nonlinear dynamic impact on one another. We have identified the primary modular systems; the challenge is to develop an understanding of the way these systems determine personality. Grigsby and Stevens (2000) argue "that the brain's organization can be understood only within an evolutionary context, in which pattern-recognition and pattern-generating activity is assumed to have been shaped by the pressures of natural selection" (p. 203).

Depicting Nonlinear Processes with Triangular Constructs: According to Grigsby and Stevens (2000), "No matter how predictable a person's behavior, character is not a *thing*, but rather a set of processes that show variability in the probability of their expression from moment to moment" (p. 311). Triangular configurations are helpful in describing a nonlinear model of personality. A triangle is able to depict the potential synergy among the corners. Revisiting the triangular constructs from the previous chapters provides an anchor for many of the modular systems that have been described throughout this book. This is not an attempt to provide a grand unification theory but to begin to depict the components of personality in an arrangement that accounts for the infinite variability in the living system, as opposed to the surface contours that may exist in limited domains. Three triangular configurations depict the regions of personality functions: **intrapsychic-biological, interpersonal-dyadic,** and **relational-triadic.** Within each of these triangular representations are the various modular or component systems (see Table 11.2); we must then attempt to depict how they interrelate. This is an oversimplification for heuristic purposes, but triangular configurations provide a useful model to demonstrate the constant movement of these interacting modules. As in the biopsychosocial model, various theoretical models and constructs may have more explanatory value at one level of abstraction than another. As opposed to the biopsychosocial model, hierarchy is not critical, interrelationships are. For example, the neurobiological substrate has an explanatory scope at the micro level, although the major assumption in this model is that all levels are involved in a series of interconnected feedback loops.

Intrapsychic-Neurobiological Triangle

At the micro level of analysis, we begin with an explanation of the **intrapsychic-biological triangle** (see Figure 11.2). The three corners are (1) affective-cognitive, (2) anxiety, and (3) defense/coping.

Table 11.2   **Component Systems Moving from the Micro to the Macro Level of Analysis**

Micro level of organization: Concerned primarily with inferred psychological structures and dynamic relationships. Includes the extreme microscopic level of neurotransmitter action and genetic predisposition. Theoretical components useful for analysis include psychodynamic constructs, evolutionary theory, cognitive constructs, neurobiological models, temperament, behavioral principles, factor models, and affect theory.

Intermediate level organization: Concerned with the relational field, primarily what occurs in dyadic transaction. Theoretical components useful for analysis include interpersonal models, self-other models, factor theories, object-relations theory, cognitive constructs, evolutionary theory, and learning theory.

Macro level of organization: Concerned with what transpires with triadic relational configurations and multiple overlapping triangles. Theoretical components useful for analysis include systems theory, triadic models, learning theory, and psychodynamic constructs.

Figure 11.2

Intrapsychic-Biological Functions.

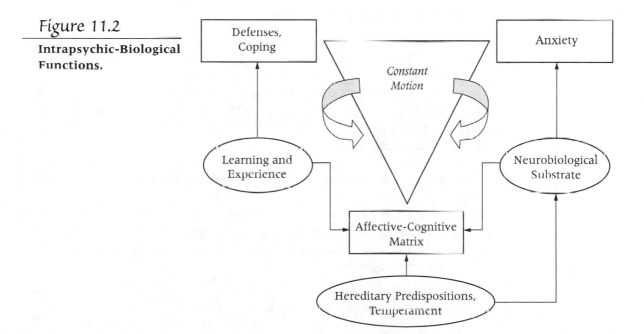

Any increase in one corner will induce a functional increase in the others. For example, if anxiety is increased, both defensive functioning and the affective-cognitive matrix will respond. There is a direct interaction between the psychological structure and the neurobiological structure. The integrity and functioning of the central nervous system, including neurotransmitter action, is taken into account.

- *Affective-cognitive matrix:* The affective-cognitive matrix includes the affect system, cognitive beliefs, and schematic representations and related neurobiological functions such as neurotransmitter action and interactions.

- *Anxiety:* The anxiety corner depicts the level of anxiety within the person-system. This corner also subsumes the neurobiological basis of anxiety.

- *Defense and coping:* The defense/coping corner of the triangle represents the array of defensive operations (elaborated in Chapter 6). These defenses are part of the distinctiveness of an individual's personality but are fluid and not a static system.

Interpersonal-Dyadic Triangle

The **interpersonal-dyadic triangle** begins at the bottom with early experiences and fuels both the current relational matrix corner, which is the array of current relationships, and the expected schematic matrix corner, which is an internalized form of schematic representation (object, cognitive, relational; see Figure 11.3). This depicts the intermediate level of personality phenomena as expressed in interpersonal dynamics.

- *Early relational matrix:* As we have seen throughout this book, the early relational matrix primes the pump of personality organization. These early experiences with attachments—positive, negative, or "good enough"—will begin the process of structuring the personality components of the intrapsychic-dyadic triangle.

- *Current relational matrix:* The current relational matrix includes the dyadic configurations that shape and reinforce personality types and styles. Interpersonal patterns that are evident in all

Figure 11.3

Interpersonal-Dyadic Triangle.

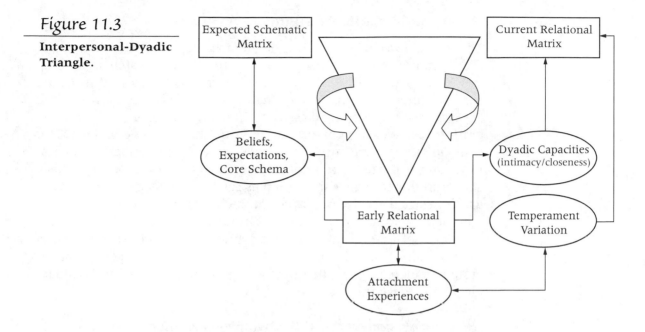

personalities can be observed in this corner, in the way we relate to others. Whether an individual is active-passive- or self-other-oriented can be determined by using two of the Millonian constructs. A particular pattern of behavior then emerges based in part on the matrix that has been incorporated from the early relational experiences.

- *Expected relational matrix·* The expected relational matrix has to do with the core schemata that are stored in the psychobiological system and are projected onto others. This process is what the psychodynamic theorists have termed transference and cognitivists core schema. It relates to the expectancies that an individual will be received in an interpersonal transaction in a particular way regardless of the validity of the other person's response system. Thus, a person with early experience of not being able to trust expects others to act untrustingly (see Chapter 9).

Wachtel's (1977) cyclical psychodynamics construct is useful here to explain the recurrence of relational patterns as well as the reinforcement patterns evident in these reoccurring behavioral sequences.

Relational-Triadic Triangle

The **relational-triadic triangle** depicts the processes that occur among more than two people or to other larger systems (see Figure 11.4). This represents the macroperspective reviewed in Chapter 10. Important in this triangular configuration is that each "person system" is interrelated to others in a complex dynamic operation that seeks to contain anxiety in a homeostatic pattern. This triangle is especially useful in understanding pathological adaptations and patterns of relationships over generations. Because each corner in this triangle can be seen as representing a person, what we are concerned with here is the interactional patterns that occur in complex relational systems. Recall from Chapter 10 that an unstable dyad will often seek a third party to stabilize itself and, in effect, shift anxiety to a third person. At this level, the complexity of the system is increased, as the other triangles are in operation at all levels during these transactions:

- *Person systems at top:* If the two people at the top corners of the triangle are not able to contain anxiety, either because of faulty affect systems, low differentiation, or other factors, anxiety threatens the relationship.

Figure 11.4

Relational-Triadic Triangle.

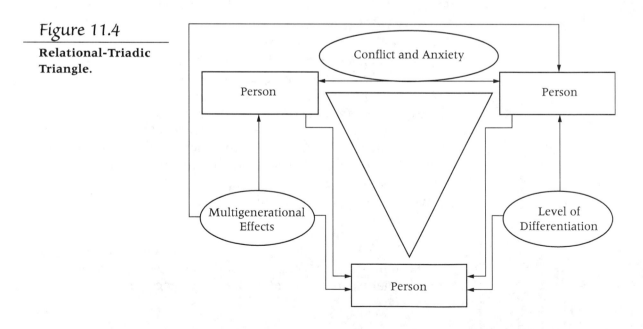

- *Person at the bottom:* If the people at the top do not contain the anxiety, the anxiety will be absorbed and manifested in some type of symptom or behavioral disturbance or, over time, can lead to a personality disorder.

Extreme Variations of Personality

The development course of normal versus aberrant personality is multidetermined, with multiple pathways and opportunities to unfold normally or for the individual and system to develop maladaptive patterns. Any attempt to explain the trajectory is, out of necessity, overly reductionistic. Nevertheless, we can begin to understand the complexity using integrative models.

Why do some individuals develop dysfunctional personality styles and others don't, even from the same family? As you can probably predict at this point in your journey through this text, there are various potential junctures of departure. The basic model is depicted in Figure 11.5. Starting at the bottom, we can trace the trajectory of an individual beginning with genetic vulnerabilities. We also should not forget the lessons from the systems theorists, who believe that even before birth, a family process is in operation defining the self by projections. An individual with a high biological vulnerability, such as affect dysregulation, will have a range of early object bonds that can provide either a secure, an ambivalent, or a faulty attachment. These biological/temperament vulnerabilities can be mitigated by an optimal or "best-fit" dyadic relationship.

Let us say the fit is not good and the parental figure is insufficient in ability or capacity to provide a "good-enough" attachment: this could be the result of a variety of factors, such as mental illness or addiction. This combination of factors shapes the psychological structure of an individual. In this case, the structure of our hypothetical individual is organized at the level of borderline to psychotic. If the family system also has severe dysfunction and in fact is a **dysfunctional personologic system,** the personality adaptation will be either unstable or fragmented. Even in this limited depiction, one can see the possibility of shaping and reinforcing particular personality adaptations. Simply illustrated, an individual toward the left side of the diagram is going to have a greater chance of healthy personality adaptation.

Figure 11.5

Course of Normal and Abnormal Personality.

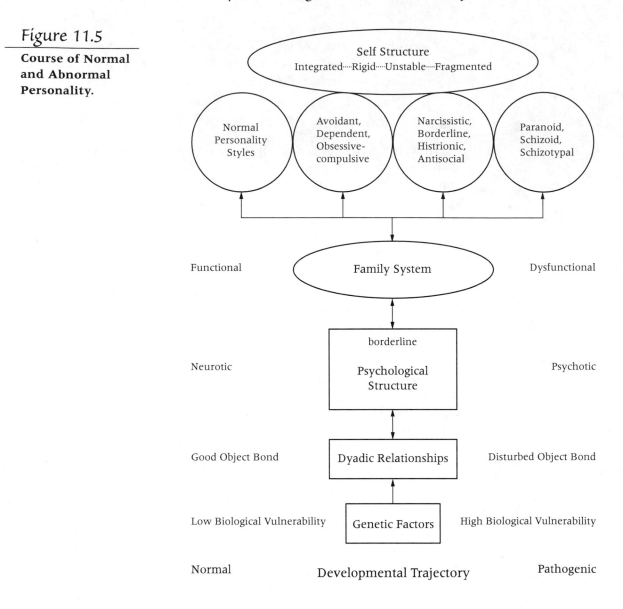

Simple or Complex Models

Multiplicity of Factors: As we have seen, there are a multiplicity of factors that determine who we are and whether our personality will be functional, flexible, and adaptive, or disordered, dysfunctional, inflexible, and maladaptive. In the following chapter, we will deal more directly with the controversy over normal and abnormal, mitigating

Selected Research Findings

- *"Reports of the early home environment in DSM-III-R personality disorders"* (Norden, Klein, Donaldson, Pepper, & Klein, 1995). The researchers assessed a group of 90 outpatients who met criteria for a personality disorder. Using a semistructured interview and self-report inventory, they found that antisocial traits were correlated with poor relationships with both parents and physical abuse. Borderline and self-defeating personality traits were associated with poor parental relationships and sexual abuse.

- *"Factorial elements in Millon's personality theory"* (Choca, Retzlaff, Strack, Mouton, & Van Denburg, 1996). The investigators factor analyzed test items for the 13 scales of the MCMI-II using 1,229 male and female psychiatric patients. The findings suggest that the content of the factors closely match Millon's prototype in five of eight areas. The authors state that their findings provide support for Millon's conceptualizations.

- *"Cluster analysis of narcissistic personality disorders on the MCMI-II"* (DiGuiseppe, Robin, Szeszko, & Primavera, 1975). Researchers administered the MCMI-II along with various other instruments to 742 clients at an outpatient clinic. They conducted a discriminant function analysis and correctly identified 97% of clients in three clusters. They identified the clusters as "true narcissist," "compensating narcissist," and "detached narcissist."

- *"Preschool children's exposure to violence: Relation of behavior problems to parent and child reports"* (Shahinfar, Fox, & Leavitt, 2000). The researchers examined a group of 155 parents and children attending Head Start regarding their exposure to violence. Those who witnessed violence were more likely to have internalizing problems, and those who were victimized externalizing problems.

- *"Family environment characteristics of persons with histrionic and dependent personality disorders"* (Baker, Capron, & Azorlosa, 1996). The investigators examined the families of subjects with dependent and histrionic personality disorders and controls. A group of 30 subjects was selected from an initial pool of 683 undergraduate females. The results suggest that families low on independent functioning and cohesion and high on control are associated with dependent personality. Families high in control and intellectual-cultural orientation were associated with histrionic personality, as well as being high in achievement. The authors state that the findings provide partial support for Millon's theory.

factors, and resiliency, as well as other special issues. At this point in the evolution of personality theory, the primary component systems have likely been identified. The challenge now seems to be to determine how these component systems are organized and influence one another. In addition to the complex nature of the person-systems that we are studying, it seems useful to revisit how chaos theory might be a way to understand how people are infinitely different yet have similar core characteristics.

Paradoxes: There are certain evident paradoxes in the study of personality. One is the contradiction between the integrity and fragility of personality development. As chaos theory suggests, small perturbations may have catastrophic results for personality development. A severe trauma at a particular developmental point can have catastrophic results on personality. Less dramatic events, such as maternal depression, quality of child care, or economic disadvantage, may magnify themselves as the waves of a stimulus reverberate through the personality and family systems.

Principles of the Integrative Models

Philosophical Underpinnings and Assumptions

The philosophical underpinnings of integrative theory include a basic assumption that personality is multidetermined and that it is inconsistent to use reductionistic models to account for the variation evident in personality. Thus, although empiricism is valued, a balance is struck between utility and validation through scientific methods.

Notions of Normal versus Abnormal

As we have seen, there are indexes of what comprises normal and abnormal forms of personality adaptation. Normal adaptation is flexible, adaptive, and balanced; abnormal is inflexible, maladaptive, and imbalanced. The integrative-evolutionary model has very well-articulated formulations of normal and abnormal variations of personality and well-developed, empirically derived instrumentation for measurement. Millon's theory has spawned substantial research and validation of his constructs. His instrumentation has been used to assess coping styles, illness adaptation, medication abuse, and compliance among medically ill patients. The integrative-systemic model has less well-delineated categories of normal and abnormal personality and far less technology in instrumentation. This model looks at normality from a variety of perspectives to gain a comprehensive picture of individuals and their social context and system.

Assessment Strategies and Tools

The integrative model offers an array of assessment tools and strategies to draw on, including projective tests, objective tests, genogram, structured interview, structural interview, videotaped interview, and standardized intelligence testing, from which it creates a profile and draws conclusions. Most of the assessment tools in this text are consistent with an integrative model. Multilevel assessment is a particular strength of this model due to the development of standardized instruments that have substantial reliability and validity in the measurement of personality and personality disorders. This model is consistent with the use of a variety of assessments that can be used to evaluate individual, couple, and family.

Application of Model

One of the major applications of the integrative model is systematic assessment and treatment planning for both personality disturbance and clinical syndromes. The model may also have application for addressing social issues facing our increasingly culturally and ethnically diverse society. Systemic theory is useful in understanding the dynamic movement in larger systems. Processes that encourage dysfunction in various systems can be better understood using this model than an individualistic approach. A major application of the model has been in various forms of integrative psychotherapy that attempt to maximize the technology of change by offering combinations of modalities and types of treatment for mental disorders.

Cultural Influences and Differences

Cultural differences have a place in an integrative model where evolutionary principles are given credence. Various cross-cultural adaptations are related to the particular sociocultural context, which exerts an influence and shapes individuals' personality. Therefore, certain cultural variations in personality are attributed to the necessity of adaptation over generations or a lifetime to the cultural demands. Because a feature of integrative theory is that it is always evolving, it offers the flexibility to adapt to new cultural phenomena as they arise in our ever-changing multinational community.

Strengths and Limitations of Model

The obvious strength of an integrative perspective is its inclusiveness of components from various related areas and disciplines. This can result in broader conceptual power if the integration is logically consistent. The weakness is the potential to become too removed from the empirical basis of scientific psychology and to become too speculative.

Summary

This chapter presents an integrative perspective on personality, which attempts to provide a scaffold for the many components or module systems of personality that have been presented in this text. Wilson, a sociobiologist, harshly criticizes and challenges the social scientist to generate comprehensive theories. There has been a trend toward theoretical integration, beginning with William James. Allport invited the field to become less fractious and called for systematic eclecticism. The psychotherapy integration movement provided a strong impetus for theoretical assimilation and integration. The integrative model is based in various degrees on (1) evolutionary constructs, (2) general systems theory, (3) biopsychosocial model, (4) chaos theory, and (5) integrative trends. Millon is the major figure in the development of a comprehensive integrative-evolutionary model. His model uses the primary scaffold of evolutionary theory to anchor his three polarities: self-other, passive-active, and pleasure-pain. Theoretical consistency is sought, along with a clear nosology (system of classification), empirically derived instrumentation based on the entities measured, and a consistent intervention approach.

The second variation of this model, based on general systems theory, is the integrative-systemic perspective, which also posits three constructs using triangular configurations that suggest the fluidity of the system. These include the intrapsychic-neurobiologic, interpersonal-dyadic, and relational-triadic.

Suggested Reading

Allport, G. W. (1968). *The person in psychology: Selected essays.* Boston: Beacon Press.
Millon, T. (1999). *Personality-guided therapy.* New York: Wiley.

SECTION
Five

SPECIAL TOPICS

Applications, Research, and Future Directions

12

Chapter

Introduction

The last chapter in this text explores a variety of special topics that could not logically be placed in the preceding chapters, whose grounding in the basic component theoretical systems will enhance the reader's understanding of these topics. In doing so, I pose some of the yet unanswered questions and explore controversies in the field of personality, such as stability of traits, sociocultural influences, classification dilemmas, and other important issues. The chapter ends with a brief discussion of some of the exciting new applications of personality theory, for both psychologists and non-psychologists as well as students of other disciplines who are interested in the utility of this subject. Winter and Barenbaum (1999) suggest the following analogy: "Personality may come to be seen as a series of interacting elements, all existing like a series of Windows computer applications. Over time, different personality 'applications' are installed, opened, moved between foreground and background, modified, closed, even deleted. Although the sum total of available 'personality' elements may have limits that are specifiable (though perhaps unique for each person), the current 'on-line' personality may be complex and fluid" (p. 28).

We begin the chapter with a review of some the explicit and implicit general assumptions that have been made in this text for a comprehensive theoretical system:

- Behavior and personality are multidetermined; no one factor can account for the variation in personality.
- Various dynamic systems interact systemically to create an organic process that balances both stability and instability.
- Although each person is unique, there are many clusters of patterns and traits commonly observed.
- There is a certain degree of plasticity to behavior that probably fluctuates at different developmental stages.
- Personality consists of component systems at various levels of analysis, from the biological to the cultural, each having some influence on the totality.
- Personality, although determined, is vulnerable to random fluctuations in the array of component systems.
- Basic drives as well as the drive for attachment fuel personality development.
- Personality has stable components that yet are subject to transformation at various developmental transitions and crisis points in life.

How Stable Is Personality over Time?

One of the interesting issues in the field of personality is whether personality can change or is set. As often quoted from William James, "In most of us, by the age of thirty, the character is set like plaster, and will never soften again" (1902, pp. 125–126). As you have probably surmised from reading this text, personality is often such a diffuse construct, with multiple meanings depending on one's theoretical belief, that one cannot readily answer the question Can personality change? without examining the assumptions and definitions behind it. In fact, this question was explored by leading figures in the field of personality research in *Can Personality Change?* edited by Heatherton and Weinberger (1994). They begin their book with the following:

> *The Jesuit maxim, "Give me a child until he is seven, and I will show you the man," is the thesis of Michael Apted's well-known documentary* 35 Up. *This documentary follows the development of British schoolchildren through*

interviews at ages 7, 14, 21, 28, and 35. A striking aspect of this film is the apparent stability in personality from childhood through adulthood. The child interested in the stars and science becomes a university professor of physics; the boy who finds his childhood troubling and confusing develops an apparent schizotypal personality; the reserved upper-class girl at 7 wears a crested sweater in her pastoral retreat at age 35; a 7-year-old successfully predicts not only his future career, but the schools that he will eventually attend. Are people so stable? Is our personality at age 80 ordained at age 8? (p. xi)

A deeper examination of this controversy requires us to know more about the scientific models that we use when we attempt to answer this question. DiClemente (1994) thoughtfully addresses the question: "The question, Can personality change? is most succinctly answered by, It depends. It depends on how one defines personality and how one defines change. It depends on whether one examines constellations of behaviors, imputed characteristics, or inherited temperament and dispositions. It depends on when and how often one understands stability and the process of change. This equivocal response reflects more the complexity of the question than any attempt to avoid a more definitive response" (p. 175).

Root Metaphors and Personality Theory and Change

Davis and Millon (1994) are also interested in this question but prefer to examine it from a metatheoretical perspective. They explore the philosophy of science in terms of the root scientific metaphors in Heatherton and Weinberger's (1994) volume.

Based on the writing of Pepper (1942), the philosopher of science, Davis and Millon (1994) suggest that four root metaphors are different perspectives with which to address the issue of personality change: (1) formism (analytic-dispersive), (2) organicism, (3) mechanism (analytic-integrative), and (4) contextualism (synthetic-dispersive). Each position has advantages and limitations to understanding the immutable versus the transformative nature of personality.

1. *Formism:* This root metaphor assumes that the natural world has boundaries and categories with which to sort different phenomena. This root metaphor is most strongly affiliated with

trait models of personality. Therefore, personality change in this metaphor is related to changes in traits, as measured by various personality inventories.

2. *Organicism:* This root metaphor views personality theory as an organic whole, best depicted in a unified theory. Basically, this is most consistent with developmental models of personality. Theoretical principles are critical and not "merely a descriptive venture that consists of observing, categorizing, and cross-correlating various phenomena at their face value" (Davis & Millon, 1994, p. 97). The person is emphasized over the context in which one exists. This root metaphor is most closely aligned with psychodynamic and other stage models of personality where stages of change are passed through, each setting the stage for the next transition (**orthogenetic principle;** Werner, 1948).

3. *Mechanism:* This root metaphor is based on the model of a machine, which can range from mechanical to computer. It is basically a reductionist model that attempts to reduce the subject to essential parts and establish laws. This metaphor is most closely aligned with behavioral and cognitive models of personality.

4. *Contextualism:* This root metaphor attempts to establish synthesis, as does the organicism metaphor. In this model, personality cannot be captured with static measures or samples; personality is in dynamic movement and change is itself a category to be understood. There may be no permanent structures. In this model, personality systems are both multidirectional and multidimensional. Personality is therefore always embedded in context and cannot be studied removed from the context. This metaphor is most aligned with the systemic model of personality. The cultural perspective reviewed later in this chapter uses this root metaphor.

Davis and Millon (1994) ponder the prospect of synthesizing these root metaphors. They recognize the limitations of a linear model of personality and suggest a blending of organicism and contextualism. If personality is understood in an open systems model, then personality change is possible. "Numerous terms refer to processes of transformational change, including religious conversion, brainwashing, rehabilitation, and decompensation" (p. 113). In some cases, this change is from a higher to a lower level of functioning or organization, or to a kind of "organization that is simply different" (p. 113).

Stability of Personality

Researchers empirically investigating the stability of personality have primarily been those associated with the Five-Factor Model (see Chapter 9). Various other theorists have speculated, as did James, about the time in life when personality is crystallized. Theorists have ranged from the Freudians, who see personality becoming fairly well established quite early in development, to the Eriksonians, who see personality as progressing naturally through periods of transition and transformation.

Childhood and Early Development: As we have seen, temperament and attachment styles are the precursors to personality development and emerge very early in life (Caspi & Roberts, 1999). The strength of this relationship before age 3 is weak to moderate. However, after age 3, "it is possible to chart connections from the first few years of life" (p. 301) with a fair degree of certainty. In fact, "the second year of life may be the crucial dividing line for predicting later personality differences because of the intercorrelated cognitive-emotional changes that take place during this period" (p. 301).

Adulthood: When is personality set in plaster? There is a lack of sufficient empirical evidence to answer this question (Caspi & Roberts, 1999). Various theorists speculate about the critical period for the crystallization of personality. Psychoanalytic theory posits that at age 5, personality structure is determined; later, psychodynamic theorists pushed the time to late adolescence (Bloom, 1964). Costa and McCrae (1994) agree with James that personality is set around age 30: "Furthermore, life experiences appear to be related to individual differences in personality change well into the fourth decade of life" (Caspi & Roberts, 1999, p. 305). Roberts and Friend-DelVecchio (in press) conducted a meta-analysis that confirmed two essential findings: Personality becomes more stable with time and less stable the longer the interval between observations. The results showed rates of consistency of personality to be .32 in childhood, .55 at 30 years and then level out at .75 between ages 50 and 70. In sum, "The data do not support the conclusion that rank-order consistency peaks at age 50" (Caspi & Roberts, 1999, p. 309).

Using the Five-Factor Model to analyze data from longitudinal and cross-sectional studies, other researchers have found personality to be quite stable over time (Costa & McCrae, 1994). The empirical evidence strongly supports the finding that personality, as measured by the Five-Factor Model, is relatively stable, with a median correlation of .65. Using statistical procedures to eliminate test error, the "stability coefficients usually exceed .90 (Costa & McCrae, 1988, 1992; Costa, McCrae, & Arenberg, 1980), suggesting almost perfect stability in rank order" (Costa & McCrae, 1994, pp. 32–33). Thus, the authors surmise that personality really is set like plaster, then offer a caveat: "But anyone who has lived in an older house knows that plaster is not granite. With time, moisture, and the settling of the house, it begins to crack and crumble" (p. 33). Reviewing many studies, they conclude that the variance in personality as tested by the Five-Factor Model approximates about three-fifths of the variance. They

The Critical Importance of Research

Why, you may ask, is the question *When does personality fully develop?* an important research topic? "The answer to this question is critical for both psychologists and society. It pertains directly to whether we choose to rehabilitate individuals or subject people to long-term, palliative care. For example, if personality becomes fixed at age 20, then psychologists would approach interventions differently if faced with a sociopath at age 15 or a sociopath at 40. Likewise, it may shift the action of a business owner from trying to shape a supervisor's authoritarian management style to simply firing the person" (Caspi & Roberts, 1999, p. 302). Ideas about the malleability of personality are also crucial in trying to determine when public funds should be spent for high-risk populations. Generally speaking, it has been assumed that early childhood interventions are most efficacious, but it may be that the money for social programming is better spent on adolescents. Research has yet to be conducted on this last question, but some of the findings about the stability of personality may be useful in guiding policymakers and social intervention program designers.

also conclude that personality "sets" between age 21 and 30, taking its final form. "We now know that in many fundamental ways, adults remain the same over periods of many years and that their adaptation to life is profoundly shaped by their personality. People surely grow and change, but they do so on the foundation of enduring dispositions" (pp. 35–36). In sum, evidence indicates that personality does not stop developing in childhood, adolescence, or early adulthood. Rather, personality appears to grow increasingly consistent with age and to reach a plateau later in life than originally thought (i.e., age 50).

How Is Continuity Maintained over the Life Span? Assuming that the empirical support is a valid estimate of personality stability of .65 with fluctuations over the life span, what is it that keeps personality stable? Caspi and Roberts (1999) suggest a number of possibilities:

- *The influence of the environment:* The common factor that may explain the stability of personality is the consistency of the environment. Individuals for the most part tend to live in similar environments unless there is a major disruption or catastrophic occurrence, such as war or financial reversal. For example, among families who experienced the Great Depression during the first half of the twentieth century, many have observed the rigidity of certain traits in those most affected.

- *The influence of genetics:* Another way to account for the consistency in personality may be the genetic predisposition of the individual to certain temperament/biological response systems. We have seen that a fair amount of the variability in certain measured personality traits can be accounted for by genetic influence.

- *Transactional processes:* A third way to account for the stability in personality is via the transactional processes that occur in dyadic and triadic relational matrices. There is a degree of stability in the interactional patterns that people develop; these are the relational and cognitive schemata that guide our interactive process.

Livesley, Schroeder, Jackson, and Jang (1994) write: "The temporal stability of personality traits, however, does not mean that personality is immutable. Circumstances do lead to major personality change; modulation in the expression of traits across the life span is typical" (p. 14). How this change occurs is also a crucial area of investigation and theorizing.

How Does the Process of Change Occur?

Caspi and Roberts (1999) write that there is surprisingly little written in the psychological literature on how the process of change occurs. What data do exist come mostly from the empirical research and clinical observations concerning the process of change undergone by individuals in psychotherapy. New lines of research are focused more on the process of change that cuts across theoretical models and also considers how people outside of therapy change. Drawing from theoretical work done in sociology and behavioral models, Caspi and Roberts outline four primary change processes:

1. *Contingency and role acquisition:* This is essentially behavioral theory about how behavior is shaped and maintained. The notion is that personality is shaped and can be modified through parenting contingencies and other role expectations and pressures.

2. *Watching oneself:* To change, one has to have an awareness of sequences of one's behavior and have some insight into their action potential.

3. *Watching others:* Another major change process is in modeling others by observing them. We often develop new behavioral repertories by watching someone else.

4. *Listening to others:* Individuals develop meaning and change behavior through linguistic communication. Language serves the purpose of allowing for symbolic interaction that can modify cognitive-affective patterns that influence behavior. We receive feedback from others that can be used to reinforce our identity and personality or challenge and modify it (pp. 316–318)

Types of Change

Change is a very complex notion. Many investigators believe that there are various types of change, ranging from gradual to radical. Novelists are aware of the various kinds of change that humans undergo. W. Somerset Maugham (1995), in his novel *The Moon and Sixpence,* describes a **gradual** type of change, like a drop of water dripping on a rock, over time wearing it away, and the **rapid transformation** of a rock shattering into fragments. He describes his observations about the types of change in this passage: "Conversion may come under many shapes, and it may be brought about in many ways. With some men it needs a cataclysm, as a stone may be broken to fragments by the fury of a torrent; but with some it comes gradually, as a stone may be worn away by the ceaseless fall of a drop of water" (p. 78).

Conversion Experiences: Conversion experiences are familiar to those in theology and occur when an individual has a profound spiritual awakening that transforms the self. William James (1902) was interested in the phenomenon of transformational change and was not willing to dismiss these reports as pseudoscience not worthy of his attention. He wrote about these in his book *The Varieties of Religious Experience.* Even though many of the cases of religious conversion he wrote about included psychopathological traits in the individual undergoing conversion, he did not think that this discounted the validity of the event. He believed that these transformations were often permanent. James (1902) described such a case: "I was effectively cured of all inclination to that sin I was so strongly addicted to that I thought nothing but shooting me through the head could have cured me of it; and all desire and inclination to it was removed, as entirely as if I had been a suckling child; nor did the temptation return to this day" (p. 217).

Discontinuous Transformational Experiences: W. R. Miller and C'deBaca (1994) offer the example of Ebenezer Scrooge in Dickens's (1843/1984) *Christmas Carol* as an example of the possibility of what they term **quantum change.** The authors comment on the issue: "If radical and sudden shifts in personality do indeed occur, they pose a puzzle of great potential. Nearly all of current scientific psychology is focused on describing, understanding, or influencing gradual incremental change. . . . Quantum transformations, however, suggest at least a different magnitude of change" (p. 257). Subjects in their study told stories which the researchers categorized and presented along with summary statistics (see research section at the end of the chapter). Turning points in people's lives were described in the following ways:

- *Time out from life:* After a period of immobilization because of illness, a major change followed.

- *Moment of choice:* An individual sees clearly that he or she has a definitive choice in how to live.

- *Spiritual conversion:* A powerful religious experience results in intense emotions, and change follows.

- *Trauma:* Major trauma induces an individual to become more compassionate and trusting of others.

- *A voice:* Hearing a voice gives the person an answer or new direction.

- *Catastrophe:* A major catastrophe precedes major change.

- *Switching controls:* After a period of detachment, an individual describes a feeling that someone else took charge of the controls and change ensued.

This type of radical change has now gained the attention of clinicians who believe that efforts should be made to understand and harness these forces (Magnavita, 1997). Mahrer (1997) poses as questions some of the breakthrough problems for advancing the field of psychotherapy:

- How can psychotherapy enable a client to undergo radical, in-depth, qualitative, transformational change toward what the particular client is capable of becoming?

- How can such radical, qualitative changes be accomplished quickly and effectively, even within a single session? How can such radical, qualitative, in-session changes persist and endure into the person's extratherapy world? (p. 84)

Accelerating and deepening the course and impact of psychotherapy and other vehicles of change such as self-help programs and community programs have been a major preoccupation of therapists for over a century. W. R. Miller and C'deBaca (1994) express the excitement of their findings in the following questions: "Science typically proceeds beyond description by hypothesizing principles for organizing and predicting behavior. Who undergoes such transformation, under what conditions? Are there precursors of quantum change? Are there consistent patterns or types? Which changes endure, and why? Within understanding at this level lies the potential for comprehending and developing strategies to induce quantum change. If, as seems to be the case, these are often profoundly positive developmental events, is it possible to facilitate them? Could therapeutic strategies be designed to trigger quantum change? The reorganization of personality is, after all, an historic objective of long-term psychotherapy" (p. 277).

In a review of the literature, Hanna (1996) identified the following variables that are often precursors to change:

- Sense of necessity.
- Willingness to experience anxiety or difficulty.
- Awareness.
- Confrontation of the problem.
- Effort.
- Hope.
- Social support.

Cross-Cultural Conceptions and Mechanisms of Change: The belief that rapid transformational change can occur is something the West is just beginning to acknowledge. Eastern practices and philosophy are increasingly being assimilated into mainstream Western practice and beliefs; notice the rise of Yoga in many communities in North America. Practices such as yoga, meditation, breathing exercises, Tai Chi, Shiatsu massage, as well as many other Eastern practices have been described as deeply transforming (Bankart, 1997).

Transtheoretical Model of Change

Probably one of the most widely cited contemporary models of change, developed by Prochaska, DiClemente, and Norcross (1992) and termed the **transtheoretical model of change** was published in *American Psychologist.* This article announcing the model, "In Search of How People Change: Applications to Addictive Behaviors," is considered groundbreaking, heralding in a paradigmatic shift in the manner in which change is conceptualized. The model is transtheoretical because it presumes to represent an "atheoretical" (not based on any previously existing model but encompassing them all) series of stages that occur in all behavioral change processes;

thus, it is considered a metatheory. While studying addictive processes, Prochaska and his coworkers originally conceived of this model in a linear mode, progressing from one stage to another. They then discovered that most change occurs in a spiral pattern, whereby people move from one stage to another and then back again, cycling through at their own pace. The stages of change in the model:

■ *Precontemplation:* This is the period literally before contemplation. In this stage, there is no recognized intention to change in the future. Individuals in this stage are generally unaware of their problems. Until awareness can be enhanced, it is unlikely that change is going to ensue.

■ *Contemplation:* During this stage of change, individuals are beginning to develop an awareness that a problem exists. They are considering doing something about it but have not yet made a commitment to do so. Individuals in this stage are usually considering the pros and cons of change. Possibly, they have made the statement that they really have to do something about the problem.

■ *Preparation:* During this stage of change, the intention is mobilized, with some, usually small step toward taking more potent action. There may be a reduction in the behavior the individual desires to modify. If it is smoking cessation, the person may cut back from 10 to 5 cigarettes or smoke each one half way and then extinguish it.

■ *Action:* This stage of change is characterized by a modification of the individual's behavior. This usually requires intense focus and awareness, as well as energy. Changing patterns are usually anxiety-provoking as homeostatic patterns are disrupted.

■ *Maintenance:* This stage is the one in which individuals work at maintaining the changes they expended so much energy to enact. An attempt to stabilize the new patterns of behavior and avoid relapse is emphasized.

DiClemente (1994) states: "Personality change is probably best understood as part of the aftereffects of the process of change, rather than more direct and immediate changes" (p. 192). He also believes the process can work at another level. Individuals probably also make deeper changes, and then the behavior or addictive process follows. He describes these two types of change as "top down" and "bottom up" (p. 192). Theoretically, one might describe the intrapsychic emphasis of psychodynamic and cognitive models as emphasizing bottom-up change and behavioral models as top-down change: If you change the behavior the personality will follow.

The Process of Change in Psychotherapy

Psychotherapy and Personality: Personality theory has developed in tandem with the practice of psychotherapy, and understanding change is a topic of interest to both. Greenberg (1994) comments: "One of the most remarkable observations we can make about psychotherapy is that no one really knows how it leads to change. If we scratch beneath the surface of even those who confidently espouse particular theories, we find doubt and a sense of mystery and wonder" (p. 114). Therefore, most of what we know about how individuals change has been reported in the clinical literature for over a century by psychotherapists. There has not really been a systematic, concerted effort outside of psychoanalysis to treat personality disorders until the last quarter of the twentieth century. Milder forms of personality disturbance—**neurotic characters**—were generally considered amenable to psychotherapy, although the common belief was that even these would require a long treatment process (Shapiro, 1989). As we have seen in previous chapters, many pioneering figures, such as Ferenczi, Reich, and Fromm-Reichman, have accepted challenging and refractory cases. Many sought to accelerate treatment and develop effective models. Often, however, we learn the most from the more difficult presentations of personality disorder, called severe personality disorder.

Personality and Psychopathology: "Personality and psychopathology have long been linked conceptually . . . the ancient Greek theory of the four humors represented a very early attempt to relate temperament to personality" (D. Watson & Clark, 1994b, p. 5). Although the dark ages of personality theory in the 1960s to 1980s opened a chasm between the fields of personality and psychopathology, recently there has been a "rapprochement and convergence" between the two (D. Watson & Clark, 1994b, p. 3). "Personologists and psychopathologists currently are studying many common or closely related processes, including cognitive schemas and attributional styles, individual differences in attitudes and affectivity, and life stresses and coping mechanisms" (p. 3). According to Watson and Clark, "Personality traits and psychopathological disorders are, in fact, empirically related" (p. 4). Certain personality traits that occur before (premorbid) the development of psychopathology can act as predisposing factors that increase vulnerability.

A great deal has been learned about personality change during the last 25 years of the twentieth century from efforts to modify severe forms of personality disorder. Otto Kernberg (1984) and Salman Akhtar (1992) have been two of the most prolific and sustained contributors to this effort. More recently, Marsha Linehan (1993) has developed theoretical and technological innovations to understand the process of change in her efforts to increase treatment efficacy. What is apparent from a variety of sources is that these severe forms of personality disorder are extremely difficult to modify without extensive therapeutic intervention that may take years and for some may be a lifelong recovery process.

Personality Modification and Change: Clearly, substantial clinical documentation shows that personality can be negatively altered in a deteriorating process. Helson and Stewart (1994, p. 201) describe O. F. Kernberg's (1980) observations by which narcissistic individuals can deteriorate later in life: "Awareness of the limits of their achievements, he said, produces feelings of envy and rage that lead to defensive devaluation of others and reduce external and internal sources of support. Lacking a normal capacity to integrate the good and the bad, they become introverted in a world that comes to be seen as hostile and devoid of meaning. In a partial test of Kernberg's ideas within a normal sample of women, Wink (1992) showed that extroverted narcissists (who most resembled the familiar conception of this syndrome) were buoyant in their late 20's but had relational failures, did not maintain the careers they started, and failed to grow as their age-mates did from late to early 40's" (p. 210).

An ongoing controversy in the field is whether personality can be modified substantially. There are well-intentioned individuals on both sides of the issue (Magnavita, 1997). Some (McWilliams, 1994) believe that it is virtually impossible to radically alter the personality of an individual, although one can modify some aspects of the various domains of functioning. Others, such as Livesley et al. (1994), believe

"The temporal stability of personality traits . . . does not mean that personality is immutable. Circumstances do lead to major personality change; modulation in the expression of traits across the life span is typical" (p. 14). Reich (1945) suggested: "A compulsive character will never change into a hysteric character." However, he goes on to say, "The whole being of the patient becomes different . . . a change which is often more apparent to people who see the patient only occasionally, at long intervals, than to the analyst" (pp. 117–118).

The Impact of Trauma on Personality: Many studies have shown that trauma can have a powerful impact on personality. "Traumatic events have primary effects not only on the psychological structures of the self but also on the systems of attachment and meaning that link an individual and community" (Herman, 1992, p. 51). The impact of trauma was originally observed in cases of war neurosis or "shell shock" and then in victims of political torture and family abuse. Herman (1992) writes: "Repeated trauma in adult life erodes the structure of the personality already formed, but repeated trauma in childhood forms and deforms the personality" (p. 96). This syndrome has been termed Posttraumatic Stress Disorder (PTSD). The earlier in life abuse occurs and the greater the severity, the more likely that the person will also develop borderline personality. The link between PTSD and borderline syndromes has been confirmed in a number of studies (Herman, 1992). It is evident from a number of perspectives that personality can change for the worse through decompensation and fragmentation, as well as become developmentally derailed.

Psychotherapy's Effectiveness: A century of accumulated clinical and empirical evidence on the effectiveness of psychotherapy can be reduced to two main findings: (1) Psychotherapy is effective and relatively robust in changing a variety of behaviors and disorders, and (2) most psychotherapies produce equivalent results (Greenberg, 1994). Both findings were confirmed in a study completed by *Consumer Reports* ("Mental health," 1994) after receiving responses to questionnaires from 4,100 subscribers. Although there has been some controversy about the validity of the findings because of the absence of a control group, Seligman (1995) concluded: "The *CR* study, then, is to be taken seriously—not only for its results and its credible source, but for its method" (p. 974). The finding of equivalence among the various approaches to psychotherapy has been likened to the Dodo verdict from *Alice in Wonderland* (Carroll, 1962): "Everybody has won and all must get prizes" (Luborsky, Singer, & Luborsky, 1975). Whether the finding of equivalence is a reflection of the similar potency of various approaches or of a lack of sensitivity of measures has yet to be fully determined. There may be **common factors,** such as empathy, problem solving, interest, and awareness, as well as others present in all forms of psychotherapy that account for these findings.

The Nature of Personality Disorders

A theme throughout this text has been the close relationship among the areas of psychopathology, theories of psychotherapy, and theories of personality. Although the focus of this volume is not personality disorders, this topic is so interwoven with the evolution of personality theory that some space should be spent reviewing the essentials. Students and professionals can learn more about disorders of personality in other volumes, many of which have been mentioned throughout the text.

We begin with definitions: *A personality disorder is a repetitive, maladaptive pattern of behavior, thinking, and feeling that is expressed in an interpersonal context.* There needs to be a disruption in functioning either at work or in interpersonal relationships that represents an enduring pattern that is not related to another condition. There are various ways to conceptualize and diagnose a personality disorder, but it is essential to remember that it is not an entity: Personality disorder is a construct used to build a science of nosology (classification) and treatment.

The major ways to classify personality disorders are categorically, dimensionally, structurally, prototypally, and relationally:

1. *Categorical classification:* This classification is the predominant model on which *DSM* is based. In this model, one either has or doesn't have a disorder based on the number of criteria that are met.

2. *Dimensional classification:* This classification system is the predominant one of factor models. Normal and abnormal variants

exist along a spectrum or gradient from normal to a certain statistically derived abnormal point.

3. *Structural classification:* This classification system is used in most psychodynamic models. Personality disorder is diagnosed by an ego functions assessment, determining whether one's structural level is primarily normal, neurotic, borderline, or psychotic. Each of these represents a different level of structural integrity.

4. *Prototypal classification:* This classification, used by the Millonians, combines the categorical and dimensional approaches. Various prototypes can be arranged along a dimensional spectrum.

5. *Relational classification:* Primarily, the systemic and interpersonal theorists focusing on the relational components in dyads and triads use this classification.

Personality Disorders in Children and Adolescents

Related to the various issues covered in this chapter, such as the period of consolidation of personality and stability during the life span, is the question of whether children and adolescents can have personality disorders. The appropriateness of diagnosing children with personality disorder, as well as its prevalence in children, have not been adequately addressed in the empirical literature; in fact, there are few studies on this topic (P. F. Kernberg, Weiner, & Bardenstein, 2000). "For reasons both personal and theoretical, clinicians have been reluctant to make the diagnosis of personality disorder in children and adolescents" (p. 6). There is often a concern with labeling a child with a disorder considered by many inalterable. Others believe that prior to achieving identity consolidation in adolescence, personality is far from fixed. Not diagnosing personality disorders in children when they do exist may cause unnecessary suffering and may be a way of denying the extent of the problem. This is a new area of clinical investigation that is crucial to pursue.

Personality disorders seem apparent in many adolescents seeking mental health treatment. The question is whether this represents an exaggerated phase of normal development or if a personality disorder truly is present. Surprisingly, very few clinicians and researchers have addressed this question in the in-depth manner the problem deserves. It is rather obvious to most people that adolescent personality disorders are a problem. Seeing headlines, as I did the day I wrote this section, about two teenagers fleeing after being arraigned on murder charges in the suspected killings of two professors from a small college town, reinforces this clinical observation. Some clinicians have identified severe personality disorders in adolescents and actively treated them (Masterson, 1972). An excellent portrayal of adolescent personality disorders can be seen in the movie *Girl Interrupted*, which I highly recommend for its accurate depiction of borderline and antisocial adolescent females and their treatment.

Etiology: The Roots of Personality Disorders

Etiology is the study of the cause of a clinical syndrome or illness. What are the factors that cause personality disorders to develop? The psychosocial aspects of personality disorders have been distilled over the past century from a variety of sources and include (Magnavita, 1997):

- Insufficient attachment and responsivity of early caretakers.
- Incidents of sexual and/or physical abuse.
- Patterns of parental neglect.
- Loss of attachments.
- Injuries to self (narcissistic exploitation).
- Unresolved family/interpersonal conflicts (p. 73).

Are Personality Disorders Separate Entities or Variations along a Continuum?

As one might guess, the answer to this question depends on how one views the phenomenon. Personality theorists debate two major perspectives on the nature of personality disorders. One is that personality disorders represent a discrete phenomenon from "normal" personality; in this perspective, a disorder is a different arrangement of component systems than normal would represent. The other view is that personality exists on a continuum, with normal being a position along this continuum. There are advantages and disadvantages to both views and, in fact, both may be necessary. Certain personality types may be evident in all of us. For example, certain individuals tend to be very orderly, logical, and concerned with details—an obsessive style. Others, at a certain point along a theoretical continuum, might have a greater degree of these features and be considered "disordered." Personality disorders such an antisocial and schizotypal may be best conceptualized as separate categories because it is difficult to be a partial antisocial or schizotypal personality. According to Livesley (Livesley et al., 1994), one of the prominent researchers in the field, "The question of whether personality disorder is a variant of normal personality, or whether disorders are discrete categories, remains unresolved" (p. 7).

Can Personality Disorders Be Cured or Modified?

Although it is difficult to answer this question with an unequivocal degree of scientific certainty, there is reason to believe that in some cases, a cure is possible and in others probably not. The research on this topic is scant. There are some psychotherapy outcome studies that support the possibility that personality can be modified even with brief treatment lasting under 40 sessions (Winston et al., 1991, 1994).

There is a modest degree of evidence for both gradual and rapid personality change in extensive clinical case documentation reported in the clinical literature (Magnavita, 1997). For example, F. G. Alexander and French (1946) report a rapid transformation of a young man with a schizoid personality using a brief dynamic therapy model.

Hardiness, Resilience, Stress Response, and Personality

It is puzzling that some individuals who have been raised in less than ideal circumstances survive and even thrive. Clinicians are aware of the variable fate of individuals from the same family. Some seem to do well in spite of abuse, neglect, and trauma; others seem profoundly affected, in that they seem altered or fragmented by negative influences.

The Hardy Personality and Resistance to Illness

Researchers have described an array of protective personality characteristics they term **hardiness** (Kobasa, 1979; Kobasa & Maddi,

1977). It is proposed that hardiness accounts for why some people become physically sick and others under similar circumstances do not. These protective personality characteristics include (1) believing one has **control** over one's circumstances, (2) a sense of **commitment** and purpose in others and activities, and (3) a tendency to view opportunities in life as a **challenge** and opportunity rather than as threats to one's security.

Resilience and Surviving Developmental Disadvantage

Resilience is a term that has been applied to children who seem to develop into well-adjusted individuals despite being raised in very difficult or extreme circumstances. Matsen and Coatsworth (1998) summarize the research:

- *Individual factors*
  - (1) Good intellectual functioning.
  - (2) Appealing, sociable.
  - (3) Easygoing disposition.
  - (4) Self-efficacy, self-confidence, high self-esteem.

- *Family factors*
  - (1) Close relationship to caring parent figure.
  - (2) Authoritative parenting: warmth structure, and high expectations.
  - (3) Socioeconomic advantages.
  - (4) Connections to extended supportive family networks.

- *Extrafamilial context*
  - (1) Bonds with prosocial adults outside the family.
  - (2) Connections to prosocial organizations.
  - (3) Attending effective schools (p. 212).

The strongest of these factors are a strong relationship with caring prosocial adults and intelligence.

Intelligence and Personality: Intelligence is a powerful resiliency factor. Cattell (Cattell, Eber, & Tatsuoka, 1970) believed that intelligence was one of the 16 basic factors in personality. As the other main domain of twentieth-century psychology, intelligence has also been measured and quantified and its nature theoretically pondered (Herrnstein & Murray, 1994). As with the field of personality, there are various theoretical models of intelligence. There is little question that intelligence is an important aspect of personality adaptation, although there is little in the way of empirical support. There is, however, a remarkable body of literature that supports the commonsense observation that overall, individuals with higher levels of intelligence fare better in their social and occupational adjustment and satisfaction than those with lower levels. In a massive review of the literature on intelligence, Herrnstein and Murray (1994) found: "The most basic implication of the analysis is that intelligence and its correlates—maturity, farsightedness, and personal competence—are important in keeping a person employed and in the labor force" (p. 165). They also found that more serious criminal offenders with likely personality disturbance have lower IQ scores than less serious offenders and nonoffenders. Intelligence seems to capture a number of related domains that enhance one's level of adaptation.

Emotional Intelligence: One domain of intelligence has been described as **emotional intelligence** and is also seen as an adaptive capacity. Goleman (1994) makes the case that emotional intelligence is the cornerstone on which character rests. He states that "the bedrock of character is self-discipline; the virtuous life, as philosophers since Aristotle have observed, is based on self-control" (p. 285). Goleman summarizes five domains of emotional intelligence: (1) knowing one's emotions; (2) managing emotions; (3) motivating oneself; (4) recognizing emotions in others; and (5) handling relationships. These factors are similar in scope and function to what is described by the ego psychologists as constituting ego-adaptive capacity. Individuals low on these capacities may have more difficulty adapting to the complex social environment of modern society.

Stress and Type A and B Personalities

Why do some people seem to have a vulnerability not only to emotional disorder but to physical disease process? This question has posed a challenge to personality researchers and clinicians. Originally, the area known as **psychosomatic medicine,** developed in the 1950s as a cross-discipline of psychoanalysis and medicine, studied patterns of behavior observed in certain medical cohorts. These studies shed some light on the interrelationship between personality and disease. This is an area of great interest to health psychologists (see section on future applications in this chapter).

The study of Type A behavior patterns had an inauspicious start. Two cardiologists, Friedman and Rosenman (1974), were studying dietary habits of cardiac patients when a wife of one of the patients offered her observation: "If you really want to know what is giving our husbands heart attacks, I'll tell you. It's stress, the stress they receive in their work, that's what's doing it" (p. 56). Shifting the focus of their investigation to behavioral patterns, they discovered differences in emotional and behavioral attributes of patients prone to cardiac disease; they termed these attributes **Type A**

The "Cancer" Personality?

Theoretical speculations that are not tied to empirical evidence are not only misleading but can be damaging. An example of this type of poor research leading to inaccurate conclusions occurred in the 1950s, when two researchers reviewing the literature on cancer suggested that personality can play a role in its development (Le Shan & Worthington, 1956). "The researchers presented what they considered to be three major threads that ran through all the studies they reviewed: people who had cancer were more likely than those without cancer (1) to be unable successfully to express hostile emotions, (2) to have more unresolved tension concerning a parental figure, and (3) to have more sexual disturbance" (DiMatteo, 1991, p. 38). Unfortunately, this led to erroneous conclusions that the hostility seen in cancer patients was part of what caused the cancer, instead of being a reaction to the illness. Another research team did identify a link between susceptibility to cancer and measures of depression and repression, as measured by the MMPI prior to the diagnosis of cancer (Dattore, Shontz, & Coyne, 1980). At this time, the evidence is too scant to establish that there is indeed a cancer-prone personality. Future research is needed to do so.

---

behavior pattern (TABP). There are three major characteristics of Type A personality: (1) competitive achievement orientation, (2) time urgency, and (3) anger/hostility. As compared with Type A, **Type B personalities** tend to be more easygoing and philosophical about their lives and lower on the three factors. Type A individuals tend to be easily aroused to states of hostility, have a sense of urgency, as if they are always trying to beat the clock, and are impatient. Hundreds of research studies have established a robust relationship between TABP and coronary heart disease.

Sociocultural and Political Influences on Personality Constructs

The influence of societal, cultural, and political forces on how we conceptualize and understand personality cannot be minimized. Lewis-Fernandez and Kleinman (1994) comment: "In a world in which ethnic and cultural pluralism is daily becoming more politically salient, it is striking that North American professional constructs of personality and psychopathology are mostly culture bound, selectively reflecting the experiences of particular cohorts—those who are White, male, Anglo-Germanic, Protestant, and formally educated and who share a middle and upper-middle-class cultural orientation" (p. 67).

As we have discussed, personality cannot be conceived of as a closed system, as the sociocultural and political influences are significant. Cross and Markus (1999) pose some challenging questions about the cultural component of personality and implicit assumptions that are often ignored when considering cultural influences: "These largely implicit assumptions include (1) that social behavior is rooted in and determined by underlying dispositions or traits; (2) that the person's behavior can and should be understood apart from the person's particular social experiences and roles in society; and (3) that positively distinctive or non-normative behavior is particularly diagnostic and 'good' in the sense of valued" (p. 379). Research in personality, according to the authors, "assumes a consensual understanding of what is included in the personological signature of an individual and consensual answers to questions such as 'What or where is the person?' 'What is critical or significant for defining a person?' and 'What is individual behavior and how do we categorize it?'" (p. 379).

The Utility of a Cultural Approach

The cultural approach can be viewed as a "global perspective" generated by "the rise of 'cultural psychology' and the influence of feminist and other critical perspectives from the humanities" (Winter & Barenbaum, 1999, p. 18). Cross and Markus (1999) liken the cultural approach to an MRI, which illuminates brain activity, in that this perspective can also see what might otherwise be obscure (see Table 12.1). They write: "The cultural approach also allows more careful specification of the ways that personality processes and mechanisms are created and maintained by engagement in particular interpersonal and collective processes and milieus" (p. 381). The use of cross-cultural comparisons is a way by which different manifestations of personality can be viewed. Without this tool, "a monocultural personality psychology will fall short of a comprehensive understanding of human behavior" (p. 380).

For example, Western notions of self-esteem are highly contingent on a theory that emphasizes the importance of autonomy. In many other cultures, esteem may be more contingent on social groups. As we saw in Chapter 10 on relational approaches, this is one of the challenges that the Stone relational model has posed: the ascendancy of **connection** for women as opposed to **autonomy.** Cross and Markus (1999) write: "A cultural approach can illuminate what has been hidden, at least within an individualist culture; it makes visible the systems of meanings and practices—the language, the collective representations, the metaphors, the social scripts, the social structures, the policies, the institutions, the artifacts—within which people come to think and feel and act" (p. 380). Cultural values and emphasis on such issues as dependence and autonomy, cooperation versus competition, self versus other, social/family versus individual structures are pertinent to how we understand personality. For example, in many Indian families, hierarchical communication patterns and structures may appear, when viewed through the individualistic Western lens, overly "dependent," "passive," "authoritarian," and "enmeshed."

The way we view and study personality is not "value-free" (Cross & Markus, 1999, p. 383). Eastern and Western approaches differ substantially; thus, Western constructs may not reflect universal personality traits. These constructs may in fact reflect deep structural differences in the human psyche (Doi, 1971). This is

Table 12.1   **Two Approaches to Questions Raised by a Cultural Analysis of Personality**

Question	Independent View of Self	Interdependent View of Self
What is a person?	An autonomous, "free" entity "Possesses" distinctive attributes or processes	An interdependent entity Fundamentally connected to others Part of encompassing social relationships
What are the sources of behavior?	Behavior results from the operation or expression of internal attributes—traits, preferences, attitudes, goals, motives	Behavior results from adjusting to or being responsive to the others with whom one is interdependent; and from restraining or controlling individual desires, tendencies
What is the basis of individual coherence in behavior?	The operation of traits, dispositions, internal attributes	Fulfilling consensual roles; meeting expectations, obligations; conforming to norms
Where is individual agency?	In "choosing" goals; in "making" plans; in "doing what one wants"; in "controlling," mastering, or changing the social world from which one is independent	In "adjusting to" and "attuning with" the standards, expectations, or duties that define one's encompassing relationships and thus the person; in fitting or harmonizing with the social world with which one is interdependent

Source: Handbook of Personality: Theory and Research, 2nd ed. by L. A. Pervin and O. P. John, © 1999. Reprinted by permission of The Guilford Press.

particularly evident in comparing the construct of dependence, which in Japanese culture has very different and socially relevant connotations than in Western conceptions. For the Japanese, dependency is culturally valued, not denigrated, as Westerners are prone to do. As another example, Yang and Bond (1990) examined a mixture of translated and native Chinese "terms for personality attributes and found five to six personality factors among Taiwanese university students, but these factors deviated significantly

Two Different Cultural Perspectives on "Suicidal" Pilots

Toward the end of World War II, American sailors were terrorized and killed by kamikaze pilots. " 'Kamikaze'—literally, 'divine wind,' and originally a poetic name for a typhoon that scattered a Mongol fleet trying to invade Japan in 1281—is one of the few Japanese words firmly in the world's vocabulary" (Sayle, 2001, p. 16). In a small room at a new shrine in Tokyo are housed farewell letters these men wrote to their families prior to their last mission. One 22-year-old ensign wrote, "I attack in four hours. I shall be shining among the clouds, drifting and tumbling forever. This is my last letter. Your loving son" (p. 17). Underneath the display in Japanese is the sentiment: "Foreigners don't understand what this display is about." To the Western mind, this act of self-destruction *is* difficult to understand; to the Japanese, it may be the highest spiritual act of selflessness.

from the components of the Five-Factor Model" (Lewis-Fernandez & Kleinman, 1994, p. 68). The authors caution against assuming a universal personality structure.

Narcissism and the Culture of the "Consumerized Self"

Narcissism is a condition that seems ubiquitous in Western society, "a character pattern that has gained considerable recognition in the last two decades" (Millon & Davis, 1996a, p. 393). How can we explain the rise of narcissism? This form of pathological self-focus, written about by H. Ellis (1898/1933), Freud, Kohut, Winnicott, Kernberg, and others covered in this text, seems to be fueled by cultural forces in Western society. As we saw in Chapter 6, the individual in modern society often seeks to fill the "empty self" with consumer products. This "promise" of completion and self-fulfillment places a great deal of emphasis on materialism and attainment of the perfect body. This can be clearly seen in many facets of Western culture, such as the rise of cosmetic surgery to achieve the transformation of the body-self and rampant consumerism that is fueled by the mass media. Anyone who watches television can bear witness to the obvious messages that are continually bombarding viewers: Buy our product and you will be popular, happy, sexy, successful, and on and on. Within this culture, instant gratification is emphasized at the cost of the more tedious road to self-development. Finding the "real self" is not encouraged. With this, and the reconfiguration of families and institutions, we have a culture that seems in rapid transition (Masterson, 1988).

In a chapter on the cultural influences on personality, Cross and Markus (1999) compare the personal ads in a California newspaper:

> Patel parents invite professional for their U.S.-raised daughter 26 (computer science) and son 24 (civil engineer), family owns construction firm.

> 28, SWM, 6'1", 160 lbs. Handsome, artistic, ambitious, seeks attractive WF, 24–29, for friendship, romance, and permanent relationship (p. 378).

The differences the authors found when comparing these ads between Indian Americans and European Americans were quite striking: "In the Indian American ad, knowing about the person seems to require knowing how the family is located in social space and also about the qualities of the family (e.g., respectable, owns construction firm). In the European American ad, it is the attributes of the individual who will engage in the relationship that are most salient (e.g., ambitious, independent, artistic) and that comprise the majority of the ad. Moreover, the European American ads include references to preferences and ways of spending one's time (loves fine dining and gardening) and seem to draw attention to what is unique and special" (p. 379).

Another manifestation of sociocultural influences on narcissistic disorders may be seen in the development of a relatively new syndrome termed **body dysmorphic disorder.** This disorder is characterized by a deep rejection of certain imagined physical features that seem tied to one's identity. It may be related to mood disorders or obsessive-compulsive behavior (Phillips, McElroy, Keck, Pope, & Hudson, 1993). Whether this is secondary to a severe narcissistic disorder is still unknown and requires further research.

Borderline Syndromes and the Fragmentation of Social Structures

Another arena in which to observe the potential effects of Western culture on personality is the apparent rise of borderline syndromes. Many clinicians, researchers, and theorists believe that cultural and societal forces are fueling the seeming increase in borderline conditions. The increasing fragmentation of the nuclear family and the community, the increased mobility of members of society, the disintegration of well-defined social roles, and the depersonalization of modern technological advances may help explain the phenomenon (Millon, 1992). It is postulated that prior to the industrialization of America, societal expectations were clearer and social roles well defined. This allowed for a cushioning effect for those who might have the biopsychosocial tendencies that create borderline syndromes. Some of the potentially mitigating effects of traditional society have been lost. Millon comments: "I believe, furthermore, that recent cultural changes have led to a loss of key cohering experiences that once protected against problematic parent-child relationships. Traditional societies provided meliorative and reparative relationships (grandparents, aunts, older siblings, neighbors) and institutions (church, school) that offered remedies for parental disaffiliation; such societies provided a backup, so to speak, that insured that those who had been deprived or abused would be given a second chance to gain love and observe models for developmental coherence" (p. 17).

The Cross-Cultural Application of the Five-Factor Model

The Five-Factor Model of personality has been used to map the personality attributes of members of other cultures. According to Cross and Markus (1999), "There is, however, also mounting evidence of its inadequacies as a universal model" (p. 390). Western models such as this may be too focused on personality phenomena not relevant to other cultures. Eastern conceptualizations view personality as more of a process toward self-realization, as opposed to clusters of fixed traits, as Westerner theorists tend to do. "These findings suggest that Western models have ignored potentially important components of personality structure, particularly those that reflect interpersonal relationships and social interaction" (p. 391). The factor model was derived from the lexicon of Western dictionaries and has been criticized by some for this ethnocentric view. "From an interpersonal perspective, current Western theories of personality, such as the Five-Factor Model (McCrae & John, 1992), appear more as highly abstracted expressions of individualistic personalities produced by modern rationalist behavioral environments than as universal human patterns of personality dimensions" (Lewis-Fernandez & Kleinman, 1994, p. 68).

The Rise of Apotemnophilia-Elective Amputation

"In January of this year [2000] British newspapers began running articles about Robert Smith, a surgeon at Falkirk and District Royal Infirmary, in Scotland. Smith had amputated the legs of two patients at their request, and he was planning to carry out a third amputation when the trust that runs the hospital stopped him" (Elliott, 2000, p. 73). If this sounds like a new horror movie, unfortunately it is not. In a cogent and frightening article in the *Atlantic Monthly,* Elliot describes the rise of this new syndrome "apotemnophilia—an attraction to the idea of being an amputee" (p. 73). There are increasing reports of a cluster of "healthy" individuals who are electively seeking out amputations of healthy limbs. There is even an apotemnophilia listserv on the Internet with 1,400 subscribers. In his research, Elliot, who has a medical degree and an interest in how psychiatric disorders spread, writes, "I have been struck by the way wannabes use the language of identity and selfhood in describing their desire to lose a limb" (p. 74). In this context, wannabes are people who want to have an amputation but have not yet achieved their goal. He believes the language of the popular culture shapes this syndrome and others. "We talk of self-discovery, self-realization, self-invention, self-knowledge, self-betrayal, and self-absorption. It should be no great revelation that the vocabulary of the self feels like a natural way to describe our longings, our obsessions, and our psychopathologies" (p. 74). He similarly describes people who have found themselves in Prozac (see Chapter 5).

The Politicization of Personality and Psychopathology

The politics of psychopathology is a fascinating subject that will be only briefly touched on in this text. Throughout, I have reminded the reader that personality, personality disorder, traits, and psychopathology are constructs of a clinical and theoretical science of personality. These are not real entities but constructions that are used in hopes of better understanding human nature and behavior. In an attempt to catalog and understand various aspects of human experience, both "normal" and "abnormal" variants, social scientists have constructed a theory or theories of personality and psychopathology. Language is used to describe these concepts, and as T. Anderson (1996) writes, "Language is not innocent" (p. 119). In so doing, we have created the danger that these constructions then become a way of defining or more dangerously constructing reality. This is the **postmodern social constructionist perspective,** and must be taken seriously (Gergen, 1985). This epistemological perspective contends that the very act of describing is a construction that shapes how we "know" the subject of our study. The very language we employ, the constructs developed, and the theories described can influence cultural patterns. "So, the words we select influence the meanings we come to reach" (T. Anderson, 1996, p. 122). Gergen, Hoffman, and Anderson (1996) describe this process:

> As these terminologies are disseminated to the public—through classrooms, popular magazines, television, and film dramas—they become available to people for understanding of self and others. They are, after all, the "terms of the experts," and if one wishes to do the right thing, they become languages of choice for understanding or labeling people (including the self) in daily life. Terms such as depression, paranoia, attention deficit disorder, sociopathic, and schizophrenic have become essential entries in the vocabulary of the educated person. And when the terms are applied in daily life, they have substantial effects—in narrowing the explanation to the level of the individual, stigmatizing, and obscuring the contribution of other factors (including the demands of economic life, media images, and traditions of individual evaluation) to the actions in question. Further, when these terms are used to construct the self, they suggest that one should seek professional treatment. (p. 103)

T. Anderson (1996) describes this process as a hermeneutic circle: understanding our world through the meaning systems in which we are endowed. We know our world through our senses; if we had microscopic vision, we would know the world in a much different manner than we do with our current visual system. The act of describing or labeling personality and its associated domains forms part of an individual's or a system's future.

Social Contagion Effect: There may in fact be a social contagion that encourages the spread of various psychiatric conditions. Elliott (2000) writes, "The fuzziness around the borders of most mental disorders, along with the absence of certainty about their pathophysiological mechanisms, make them notoriously likely to expand" (p. 83). This suggests that there is an engine to the expansion and reification of psychiatric labels. Certainly, we have witnessed this phenomenon in the last quarter of the twentieth century. The marriage of mental health and surgery has been a dark spot in psychiatry. After immersing himself in the study of elective amputation, Elliott comments on the danger of this slippery slope: "And to be honest, haven't surgeons made the human body fair game? You can pay a surgeon to suck fat from your thighs, lengthen your penis, augment your breasts, redesign you labia, even (if you are a performance artist) implant silicone horns in your forehead or split your tongue like a lizard's. Why not amputate a limb?" (p. 84).

Transient mental disorders have occurred throughout the history of humanity and probably will continue being a testament to the sociopolitical forces. Examples include multiple personality disorders of the late twentieth century and fugue states (loss of memory and identity) in the late nineteenth century in France, seen in young men wandering the country with no sense of identity.

The Controversy in the Development of the **DSM***:* The development and evolution of the diagnostic and statistical manuals have been fraught with controversy that demonstrates the power of the political forces sometimes overshadowing the scientific mission. This process was particularly heated when the *DSM* task force for personality disorders was attempting to establish its categories (Millon, 1983). The main impact of *DSM* was to partition off personality from other clinical syndromes, creating a multiaxial system with personality recorded on Axis II and clinical syndromes on Axis I. The other important feature was to avoid theoretical alliances with any one model of personality in an attempt to create an atheoretical system that could be used by all. One controversy that was received with quite a storm of hostility from nonmedical practitioners was the proposal that mental disorders represent a subset of medical disorders.

Another heated controversy of the time, and one still, is the potential sexual bias in certain personality disorders. Kaplan (1983) suggested that the *DSM* system of classification proposed in the 1980s is biased toward a male conception of psychology. Particularly, the histrionic and dependent personality disorders were said to be but a characterization of traditional female roles pathologized. It was suggested that this represented a social inequality that was reinforced by the diagnostic system. On the other side of the controversy were those who believed that certain personality disorders are more prevalent in women than in men. Offering evidence from the male epidemiological findings, Williams and Spitzer (1983; Kass, Spitzer, & Williams, 1983) suggested that men were overrepresented in the category of antisocial personality and that both sexes were fairly well represented when the overall diagnosis of personality disorder is considered. As presented in Chapter 4, new evolutionary theories postulate that these differences are a natural result of evolutionary forces and are likely different adaptations based on sexual differences and role adaptations.

The Influence of Socioeconomic Forces: The power of socioeconomic forces in the shaping of the science of personality and psychopathology is extraordinary in scope and influence. Disorders such as depression and anxiety have special days or weeks allocated to educating the public about them. Personality disorders do not yet have their own day or week, but it probably won't be long before you will be able to go to a local center and have yourself screened for personality syndromes. Whether this ultimately will do more good or further reify the problem is uncertain.

REIMBURSEMENT FOR MENTAL HEALTH TREATMENT: The political forces that shape the field of personality and psychopathology have strong economic elements that are in operation and cause great tension. Insurance companies that provide reimbursement for mental disorders exert a strong influence on the mental health field. As new ideas and classifications of personality and mental disorders emerge, there is a continual process whereby financial rewards are provided for some and not for others. For example, at the current time, most insurers reimburse disorders that are considered biologically based at a higher rate than those deemed not biologically based. Therefore, disorders such as schizophrenia, severe affective disorders (Bipolar Disorder and Major Depression), and Obsessive-Compulsive Disorder are among those that have **parity** (are reimbursed at an equivalent level) with other physical illnesses. Personality disorders do not have parity. Some insurance providers will not reimburse an individual who qualifies for an adjustment disorder, a relatively common and benign, albeit painful reaction to a stressor in life, but will reimburse for a diagnosis of a personality disorder.

The research findings on the stability and immutability of personality can also be used to justify withholding treatment. "All too often, the fact that personality disorders are on a separate axis is used to justify pessimism about outcome and indeed to withhold treatment" (Livesley et al., 1994). One can see the tension in this economic force. For example, if personality disorders are conceptualized by the psychobiological model presented in Chapter 5, should they then be reimbursed at a higher level than those conceptualized by the relational model presented in Chapter 10? As the reader can see, we are entering a new debate about the ethical delivery of medical service. This relatively new field, called **bioethics,** attempts to find the ethical solutions to the ever increasing and complex problems engendered by medical advances.

COMPETITION FOR RESEARCH FUNDING: This economic pressure is seen not only in the struggle that clinical practitioners wage against insurance companies for reimbursement of mental health service but in the competition for research dollars. Established disorders often receive substantial research support that allows social and medical researchers the opportunity to have sufficient funding for research projects. The politics of what warrants governmental and private funding is influenced by a plethora of often competing forces. Various disorders and syndromes can come in and out of fashion with both the public and review committees who have the power to make or break a research program and affect public acceptance.

Applications of Personality Theory and Future Directions

It is interesting to note that not too long ago, personality theory was in the Dark Ages. No doubt the field is now in the early stage of the Renaissance period. For all intents and purposes, this field is in its infancy and is likely to rapidly expand as we enter a phase in development that is truly multidisciplinary. Fortunately, by and large, the fractionated phase of development is now over as we begin the twenty-first century. What are the potential applications of personality theory and what is the value to society? These are exciting topics to explore as personality theory holds promise in a number of traditional areas of endeavor as well as many newer areas.

Applied Behavioral Health

Personality theory has been applied to the field of behavioral health, concerned with the interface between psychology and physical health, creating a rapidly growing discipline. This area of psychology was originally called **psychosomatic medicine** and focused on the interaction between emotions and somatic process (F. G. Alexander, 1950). Psychosomatic medicine was based on the psychoanalytic model. Conditions such as high blood pressure, asthma, headaches, ulcers, and arthritis were the focus of attention. In the 1960s, the frame widened and a broader field called behavioral medicine emerged, followed in the 1970s by a third discipline that involved "all aspects of illness—prevention, diagnosis, treatment and rehabilitation" (Sarafino, 1994, p. 14). Millon (1982) offered one of the first concise definitions of **clinical health psychology:** "The application of knowledge and methods from substantive fields of psychology to the promotion and maintenance of mental and physical health of the individual and to the prevention, assessment, and treatment of all forms of mental and physical disorder in which psychological influences either contribute to or can be used to relieve an individual's distress or dysfunction" (p. 9).

Behavioral health is interested in identifying the causes and maintenance of such problems as smoking, obesity, chronic illness, and alcoholism. Behavioral health psychologists have also been interested in the relationship between personality and illness. For example, individuals with personalities that tend to be anxious, hostile, and depressed tend to be "disease-prone" (Sarafino, 1994).

The Development of New Models of Psychotherapy

A direct application of personality theory has been in the development of new models of psychotherapy that are effective for the treatment of personality syndromes and related clinical syndromes. It has only been within about the last quarter of the twentieth century that personality was deemed something that could potentially be modified through psychotherapy. Until that time, most clinicians believed that personality could only be modified with years of extensive psychoanalysis. There were exceptions to this throughout the evolution of psychotherapy, but by and large it wasn't until the 1980s that clinical theorists and innovators began to tackle this challenging problem. We are still at the very early stages in the development of effective models of psychotherapy for personality change. This is likely to be an area of significant attention during the first part of the twenty-first century.

Improved Assessment and Treatment of Psychopathological Conditions

Accurately assessing psychopathology saw significant growth in the past century and continues to grow in this century. The close marriage of personality theory, assessment, and psychopathology has been illustrated by the various theoretical models in this text. Earlier in the twentieth century we saw the development of innovative assessment instruments such as the **Rorschach Inkblot Test** and the **Thematic Apperception Test (TAT),** as well as major developments in the standardization and measurement of intelligence. Later, with the development of the **Minnesota Multiphasic Personality Inventory (MMPI)** and especially with computer scoring and interpretation capabilities, major advances in objective/standardized instruments were achieved. Another wave of development took place with the Millon Inventories for measuring personality constructs, as well as many other standardized instruments and clinical interview protocols.

Personality theory is also quite useful in understanding and treating major psychiatric illness. An understanding of the comorbidity of many clinical syndromes and personality disorders and how they should be approached by the clinical mental health professional is enhanced by knowledge of personality theory (Millon, 1999). We know very little at this point about how personality is impacted by the onset and course of major psychiatric conditions, such as Bipolar Disorder, schizophrenia, and pervasive developmental disorders, to name a few. There is a dearth of empirical evidence on the effect severe clinical syndromes such as chronic addictions have on personality; evidence from the clinical literature suggests that personality may deteriorate as a result of these, but little is know about the course and causes. This is an area of clinical research that holds much promise. Certainly, as Millon writes and as clinicians have observed, there is a synergistic relationship between personality and clinical syndromes.

Neuropsychology

Neuropsychology, which studies brain-behavior relationships, a relatively new and rapidly expanding field, is another area that can be enhanced with an understanding of personality theory. We know much about the obvious impact of neuropsychological deficits and insults on personality, but there is much more that needs to be known. There are various neuropsychological conditions that are subtler yet have a major impact on personality. For example, certain types of epilepsy may actually cause a sudden religious conversion, and a mutation of a single gene may emerge in middle adulthood, causing erratic behavior or a "midlife crisis" (Sapolsky, 1998). Severe Obsessive-Compulsive Disorder may also be caused by a neuropsychological disorder. Various neuropsychological conditions result in radical and profound changes in personality, such as in Alzheimer's disease and sometimes epilepsy.

Aging and Extended Life Span: The average life expectancy has dramatically increased during the twentieth century, more than in any other period in the history of humanity. Extended life span has led to a population where it is expected that many will live fuller and more active lives well into their 70s and possibly 80s. Very little research in personality has been conducted with older adults. Social scientists have essentially ignored this population. However, as the population ages, it is critical that we learn as much as possible about interaction among aging, personality, and neuropsychological functioning.

Informed Social Policy and Social Change

Social policy development can be enhanced in many areas, such as welfare reform, child care, juvenile aggression, abusive family relations, drug and alcohol abuse, and teen pregnancy, by the contributions of personality theory (Magnavita, 2000d). Families that do not provide optimal conditions for normal personality development fuel many social problems through the multigenerational transmission process and modeling of parental behavior. For example, personality disorders have an enormous effect on many social conditions and problems. Ruegg and Frances (1995) summarize the societal and personal impact: "[Personality disorders] are associated with crime, substance abuse, disability, increased need for medical care, suicide attempts, self-injurious behavior, assaults, delayed recovery from Axis I and medical illness, institutionalization, underachievement, underemployment, family disruption, child abuse and neglect, homelessness, illegitimacy, poverty, STDs, misdiagnosis and mistreatment of medical and psychiatric disorders, malpractice suits, medical and judicial recidivism, dissatisfaction with and disruption of psychiatric treatment settings, and dependency on public support" (pp. 16–17). The potential exists that advancements in personality theory can have direct application to a number of chronic societal problems.

Enhanced Child Rearing Practices: An integral part of child rearing practices is based on prevailing models of personality theory and development. Recall Watson's behaviorism, which exerted a major influence on child rearing practice of his time. Child rearing practices change dramatically, often from generation to generation. The old adage "Spare the rod and spoil the child," an accepted practice in the early twentieth century, is considered child abuse and an example of "poisonous pedagogy" (A. Miller, 1990). Miller, who has studied the roots of child abuse, has postulated that part of what led to the Holocaust was socially approved (abuse) encouraged by "child experts.'" She believes that the roots of violence was instilled in a generation of Germans, which resulted in an acceptance and immunity to suffering of others. She also believed that the authoritarian parenting style encouraged by "child experts" which encouraged parental dominance and the use of force and humiliation to attain compliance was a deadly combination.

As we have seen, the quality of the parent-child and family relationships have major implications in the development of personality. Effective child rearing practices need to be viewed from the vantage point of developing healthy and functional adults. How do we do so? Ask three experts and often two opposite models are offered, with the third being somewhere in between.

As Western families have become more fragmented as a result of societal trends, many question the influence such issues as divorce and child care have on development. These issues strike an emotional chord in most people. Should couples who are unhappy seek divorce when there are children? Should working or single parents worry about placing their children in day care centers? In a somewhat controversial book, Leach (1994) writes that society turns its back on children after they are born: "The failure of Western societies to do their best for children has only become apparent as cross-cultural and cross-disciplinary research knowledge of childhood has accumulated" (p. 171). The polemics over the effects of day care and quality of day care have not been satisfactorily answered. Leach states: "Postwar changes in families, communities, indeed whole societies, have eroded traditional Western childcare patterns based on an earning male married to a dependent female who nurtured their joint children within the context of extended family support. Settled new patterns have not yet evolved in their place, and because children cannot be left uncared-for while a radical rethink goes on, Western policy-makers have turned to daycare without first asking the crucial questions: how can children's needs best be met within modern socio-economic circumstances?" (p. 69). Personality theory can be an essential tool in helping to examine and guide this process.

Economic Development

The *New York Times* (Uchitelle, 2001) recently announced the arrival of **behavioral economics,** blending psychology with economics. This new discipline was stimulated by two economists in the 1970s, Richard Thaler (Lowenstein, 2001) and George Akerlof, who collaborated with two psychologists, Amos Tversky and Daniel Kahneman (Uchitelle, 2001). Behavioral economics is interested in how human behavior and personality affect economics at both a micro and a macro level. For example, at the macro level, one problem is why some economic boom periods persist while busts may be difficult to reverse. "Their research sheds light on why identity—the traits people assign to themselves and to others—plays a huge and often damaging role in the economy" (p. 1). This new breed of behavioral economists believe that most people who receive a windfall of money will spend it, instead of rationally planning how to best conserve it. In fact, many people are in debt from youth to adult stages of life. They have termed this tendency "hyperbolic discounting," which essentially means that people can rationally plan for money they expect to receive but once received, it is spent ("A bird in the hand is worth two in the bush").

Also under study is why individuals show interest in the environmental movement and volunteerism. At a micro level, along with understanding self-interest, those from this cutting-edge discipline are interested in constructs such as altruism, reciprocity, and loyalty. Other important issues they are studying include how psychological constructs affect how the minimum wage is set and why it is never reduced with downturns in the economy. Some hypothesize that concerns of loyalty and fairness might explain this process.

International Peace Efforts and International Affairs

Another challenge for the twenty-first century is to advance the cause of world peace. It is clear, even to the unsophisticated observer, that many world tragedies have been caused by individuals with major personality disorders, such as Adolf Hitler, Pol Pot, and Saddam Hussein, to name some of the more infamous of the bunch in the twentieth century. A more sophisticated understanding of these individuals can be achieved by the use of personality theory (see Chapter 6), such as was done in World War II by psychologists using psychoanalytic theory on Hitler. Personality theory can also be used to arrive at a deeper appreciation of culturally based differences in personality based on evolution and other theories.

Effective Evaluation of Personnel and Occupational Assignment

It is essential for efficient allocation of resources that appropriate matches be made among personality attributes, skills, and occupational placement. Personality attributes and characteristics play a strong role in occupational choice and preference. A good match will enhance productivity and job satisfaction and a poor one can create dissatisfaction.

Enhancement of Personal Adjustment

The psychology of personal adjustment is based on many factors, including an adaptive personality. An understanding of personality theory can maximize personal knowledge about appropriate choices in occupational and relational decisions and personal growth opportunities. Accumulating evidence about personality development can assist parents in decision making about child care, divorce, and dealing with loss and trauma.

Ecological Psychology

Another relative newcomer is ecological psychology, which deals with the interface between the environment and people. A major challenge for the twenty-first century is safeguarding the environment. The increasing pollution of the planet has dire consequences if the pattern continues. The dynamics of why humans tend to disregard and destroy the environment can be examined through the lens of personality theory. Solving this problem will require a multinational interdisciplinary team that understands the complex dynamics of individual and group dynamics as well as international conflict and resolution strategies.

Organizational Behavior

Personality has a central place in organizational development and management. Certain personality types influence organizations either in a positive fashion, as in a charismatic leader, or in a negative, as in a dictatorial or authoritarian one. Personality theory can be applied to enhance organizational health and development.

Forensic Science

Forensic science is a blend of criminology, law, psychology, pathology, and other specialties that are interested in solving and preventing crimes using scientific methods. Profiling is just one of the tools of the forensic scientist; it is a technique used by law enforcement agencies to provide profiles of individuals for solving crimes and predicting who will be an offender. **Racial profiling** has recently come to the public's attention. It relies on one characteristic of an individual—his or her race—and so is a form of discrimination.

Personality profiling is used to establish the possible characteristics of perpetrators of crime. Most of us know from the media that the FBI and other agencies use profiling as a way to catch serial killers and mass murderers. Profiling is also used by the CIA to assess the personality characteristics and motivation of terrorists and other dangerous figures who may be mentally ill or personality disordered. The Secret Service also uses profiling to protect the president. As personality theory becomes more advanced, it is likely to become a major tool for law enforcement, not only on a national level but, as greater sophistication develops, on a local level.

Future Directions: Multiple Perspectives and Interdisciplinary Emphasis

The future of personality theory depends on attracting individuals from diverse disciplines who can see in multiple perspectives. Winter and Barenbaum (1999) sum up the diversity that has been a part of the field: "A final 'lesson' from the history of personality involves the background and training of many of its great figures over the past century. Consider that Freud started as a neurologist; Murray, as a surgeon with a doctorate in biochemistry; and Cattell, with an extensive background in statistics. Rogers enrolled in theological seminary before he turned to psychology, Eysenck originally planned to study physics, and Kelly was first an aeronautical engineer and then taught public speaking. Even Gordon Allport blended his studies of psychology with social ethics" (p. 20).

Personology is a truly integrative interdisciplinary science that will continue to expand and assist in understanding and, hopefully, solving many of the problems facing humans in contemporary society. "As our society increasingly recognizes the diversity of the persons we claim to interpret and analyze, personality psychology needs to insure that its theorists and researchers in the 21st century are drawn from a diverse (academic and extraacademic) background and that they are given diverse experiences as a part of their professional training" (Winter & Barenbaum, 1999, p. 20).

Summary

The final chapter presents a variety of issues and controversies in the field of personology. Personality seems to set at about age 30 and remains relatively stable over time, perhaps becoming stronger as development proceeds. In most theories, one's personality goes through various stages of transformation over the life span. The Five-Factor Model shows that a median correlation of .65, between personality characteristics at various points in development, is seen in many studies. The environment, genetics, and transactional processes may maintain continuity of personality over one's life span. Various models of personality emphasize different aspects of continuity, and various types of change have been postulated to understand how personality is transformed. A major model, the transtheoretical model of change, views change as a spiral process rather than a linear one.

Change has been studied in clinical work with individuals with personality disorders; in fact, some of the models in this text were developed for that purpose. Researchers and clinicians have been interested in the impact of trauma on personality development and functioning. One controversy is whether children should be diagnosed with personality disorders; many clinicians believe such diagnosis is supported by phenomena seen in clinical practice.

Certain individuals who are hardy and resilient are less prone to develop psychopathology. Researchers have investigated Type A and B behavior patterns and their relation to cardiac illness; Type As are more likely to suffer from heart attacks. Sociocultural and political forces exert a strong influence in determining what is pathological and what is normal. Racism and cultural marginalization can be misinterpreted as pathology. Some believe narcissism is related to our consumer-driven culture and borderline syndromes to societal fragmentation and family instability and dysfunction. Various applications of personality theory continue to develop as the field enters the second century of contemporary scientific personality theory.

Suggested Reading

Miller, J. B. (1976). *Toward a new psychology of women*. Boston: Beacon Press.

Millon, T., & Davis, R. (2000). *Personality disorders in modern life*. New York: Wiley.

Pollack, W. S., & Levant, R. F. (Ed.). (1998). *New psychotherapy for men*. New York: Wiley.

Sue, D. W., & Sue, D. (1999). *Counseling the culturally different: Theory and practice* (3rd ed.). New York: Wiley.

References

Abidin, R. R. (1995). *Parenting stress index: Professional manual* (3rd ed.). Odessa, FL: Psychological Assessment Resources.

Ackerman, N. W. (1937). The family as a social and emotional unit. *Bulletin of the Kansas Mental Hygiene Society.*

Ackerman, N. W. (1958). *The psychodynamics of family life: Diagnosis and treatment of family relationships.* New York: Basic Books.

Ackerman, N. W. (1967). The emergence of family diagnosis and treatment: A personal view. *Psychotherapy: Theory, Research, and Practice, 4*(3), 125–129.

Adler, A. (1924). *The practice and theory of individual psychology.* New York: Harcourt Brace.

Adler, A. (1928). Characteristics of first, second and third children. *Children, 3*(5), 14–52.

Adorno, T. W., Frenkel-Brunswik, E., Levinson, D. J., & Sanford, R. N. (1950). *The authoritarian personality.* New York: Harper.

Ainsworth, M. D. S. (1967). *Infancy in Uganda: Infant care and the growth of attachment.* Baltimore: Johns Hopkins University Press.

Akhtar, S. (1992). *Broken structures: Severe personality disorders and their treatment.* Northvale, NJ: Aronson.

Alexander, F. G. (1950). *Psychosomatic medicine: Its principles and applications.* New York: Norton.

Alexander, F. G., & French, T. M. (1946). *Psychoanalytic therapy: Principles and applications.* New York: Ronald Press.

Alexander, F. G., & Selesnick, S. T. (1966). *The history of psychiatry: An evaluation of psychiatric thought and practice from prehistoric times to the present.* New York: Harper & Row.

Alexander, J., & Barton, C. (1995). Family therapy research. In R. H. Mikesell, D. D. Luster-

man, & S. McDaniel (Eds.), *Integrating family therapy: Handbook of family psychology and systems theory* (pp. 199–215). Washington, DC: American Psychological Association.

Allport, G. W. (1963, August). *The fruits of eclecticism: Bitter or sweet?* Washington, DC: Seventeenth International Congress of Psychologists.

Allport, G. W. (1968). *The person in psychology: Selected essays.* Boston: Beacon Press.

Allport, G. W., & Odbert, H. S. (1936). Trait-names: A psych-lexical study. *Psychological Monographs, 47*, 1–171.

American Psychiatric Association. (1994). *Diagnostic and statistical manual of mental disorders* (4th ed.). Washington, DC: Author.

Amick, D. J., & Walberg, H. J. (1975). *Introductory multivariate analysis: For educational, psychological and social research.* Berkeley, CA: McCutchan.

Anderson, J. R. (1990). *Cognitive psychology and its implications* (3rd ed.). New York: Freeman.

Anderson, T. (1996). Language is not innocent. In F. W. Kaslow (Ed.), *Handbook of relational diagnosis and dysfunctional family patterns* (pp. 119–125). New York: Wiley.

Ansbacher, H. L., & Ansbacher, R. R. (Eds.). (1956). *The individual psychology of Alfred Adler.* New York: Basic Books.

Arkowitz, H. (1992). Integrative theories of therapy. In D. K. Freedheim (Ed.), *History of psychotherapy* (pp. 261–303). Washington, DC: American Psychological Association.

Arkowitz, H., & Messer, S. B. (Eds.). (1984). *Psychoanalytic therapy and behavior therapy: Is integration possible?* New York: Plenum Press.

Arnkoff, D. B., & Glass, C. R. (1992). Cognitive therapy and psychotherapy integration. In

D. K. Freedheim (Ed.), *History of psychotherapy: A century of change* (pp. 657–694). Washington, DC: American Psychological Association.

Baker, J. D., Capron, E. W., & Azorlosa, J. (1996). Family environment characteristics of persons with histrionic and dependent personality disorders. *Journal of Personality Disorders, 10*(1), 82–87.

Balint, M. (1968). *The basic fault: Therapeutic aspects of regression.* London: Tavistock.

Bandura, A. (1997). *Self-efficacy.* New York: Freeman.

Bank, S. P., & Kahn, M. D. (1982). *The sibling bond: The first major account of the powerful emotional connections among brothers and sisters throughout life.* New York: Basic Books.

Bankart, C. P. (1997). *Talking cures: A history of Western and Eastern psychotherapies.* New York: Brooks/Cole.

Barlow, D. H. (1988). *Anxiety and its disorders: The nature and treatment of anxiety and panic.* New York: Guilford Press.

Bartlett, F. (1932). *Remembering.* Cambridge, MA: Cambridge University Press.

Bateson, G. (1944). Cultural determinants of personality. In J. McV. Hunt (Ed.), *Personality and the behavior disorders* (Vol. 2, pp. 714–735). New York: Ronald Press.

Bateson, G., Jackson, D., Haley, J., & Weakland, J. (1956). Toward a theory of schizophrenia. *Behavioral Science, 1,* 251–264.

Beck, A. T. (1976). *Cognitive therapy and emotional disorders.* New York: International Universities Press.

Beck, A. T., & Emery, G. (with Greenberg, R. L.). (1985). *Anxiety disorders and phobias: A cognitive perspective.* New York: Basic Books.

Beck, A. T., & Freeman, A. (1990). *Cognitive therapy of personality disorders.* New York: Guilford Press.

Beck, A. T., Rush, A. J., Shaw, B. F., & Emery, G. (1979). *Cognitive therapy of depression.* New York: Guilford Press.

Benjamin, L. S. (1974). Structural analysis of social behavior. *Psychological Review, 81,* 392–425.

Benjamin, L. S. (1979). Structural analysis of differentiation failure. *Psychiatry: Journal for the Study of Interpersonal Processes, 42,* 1–23.

Benjamin, L. S. (1986). Adding social and intrapsychic descriptors to Axis I of *DSM-III.* In T. Millon & G. L. Klerman (Eds.), *Contemporary directions in psychopathology: Toward the DSM-IV* (pp. 599–638). New York: Guilford Press.

Benjamin, L. S. (1993). *Interpersonal diagnosis and treatment of personality disorders.* New York: Guilford Press.

Benjamin, L. S. (1994). Good defense makes good neighbors. In H. R. Conte & R. Plutchik (Eds.), *Ego defenses: Theory and measurement* (pp. 38–78). New York: Wiley.

Benjamin, L. S. (1996). An interpersonal theory of personality disorders. In J. C. Clarkin & M. F. Lenzenweger (Eds.), *Major theories of personality disorders* (pp. 141–220). New York: Guilford Press.

Berns, S. B., Jacobson, N. S., & Gottman, J. M. (1999). Demand-withdraw interaction in couples with a violent husband. *Journal of Consulting and Clinical Psychology, 67*(5), 666–674.

Berscheid, E. (1983). Emotion. In H. H. Kelly, E. Berscheid, A. Christensen, J. H. Harvey, T. L. Huston, G. Levinger, E. McClintock, L. A. Peplau, & D. R. Peterson (Eds.), *Close relationships* (pp. 110–168). New York: Freeman.

Berscheid, E. (1994). Interpersonal relationships. *Annual Review of Psychology, 45,* 79–129.

Berscheid, E. (1999). The greening of relationship science. *American Psychologist, 54*(4), 260–266.

Berscheid, E., & Ammazzalorso, H. (2001). Emotional experience in close relationships. In G. J. O. Fletcher & M. S. Clark (Eds.), *Blackwell handbook of social psychology:*

Interpersonal processes (pp. 308–330). Malden, MA: Blackwell.

Berscheid, E., & Lopes, J. (1997). A temporal model of relationship satisfaction and stability. In R. J. Sternberg & M. Hojat (Eds.), *Satisfaction in close relationships* (pp. 129–159). New York: Guilford Press.

Berscheid, E., & Reis, H. T. (1998). Attractions and close relationships. In D. T. Gilbert, S. T. Fiske, & G. Lindzey (Eds.), *The handbook of social psychology* (4th ed, pp. 193–281). New York: McGraw-Hill.

Bischof, L. J. (1970). *Interpreting personality theories* (2nd ed.). New York: Harper & Row.

Bleuler, E. (1911). *Dementia praecox or the group of schizophrenias* (J. Zinkin, Trans.). New York: International Universities Press.

Bloland, S. E. (1999, November). Fame: The power and cost of a fantasy. *Atlantic Monthly*, 54–62.

Bloom, B. S. (1964). *Stability and change in human characteristics.* New York: Wiley.

Bornstein, R. F., & O'Neill, R. M. (2000). Construct validity of the Rorschach Oral Dependency (ROD) Scale: Relationship of ROD scores to WAIS–R scores in a psychiatric impatient sample. *Journal of Clinical Psychology, 53*(2), 99–105.

Bowen, M. (1976). Theory in the practice of psychotherapy. In P. J. Guerin (Ed.), *Family therapy: Theory and practice* (pp. 42–90). New York: Gardner Press.

Bowen, M. (1978). *Family therapy in clinical practice.* New York: Aronson.

Bowlby, J. (1969). *Attachment and loss. Volume I: Attachment.* New York: Basic Books.

Bowlby, J. (1973). *Attachment and loss. Volume II: Separation: Anxiety and anger.* New York: Basic Books.

Bowlby, J. (1980). *Attachment and loss. Volume III: Loss: Sadness and depression.* New York: Basic Books.

Bremner, J. D., Narayan, M., Staib, L. H., Southwick, S. M., McGlashan, T., & Charnery, D. S. (1999). Neural correlates of memories of childhood sexual abuse in women with and without posttraumatic stress disorder. *American Journal of Psychiatry, 156*(11), 1787–1795.

Brody, S., & Siegel, M. G. (1992). *The evolution of character: Birth to 18 years a longitudinal study.* Madison, CT: International Universities Press.

Brown, G., Goowin, F., Ballenger, J., Goyer, P., & Mason, L. (1979). Aggression in humans correlates with cerebrospinal fluid metabolites. *Psychiatric Research, 1*, 131–139.

Brown, G. W., Birley, J. L. T., & Wing, J. K. (1972). Influence of family life on the course of schizophrenic disorders: A replication. *British Journal of Psychiatry, 121*, 241–258.

Brown, L. S. (1992). A feminist critique of the personality disorders. In L. S. Brown & M. Ballou (Eds.), *Personality and psychopathology: Feminist reappraisals* (pp. 206–228). New York: Guilford Press.

Buber, M. (1958). *I and thou.* New York: Charles Scribner's Sons.

Buckley, P. (Ed.). (1986). *Essential papers on object relations.* New York: New York University Press.

Burns, K. A., Chethik, L., Burns, W. J., & Clark, R. (1997). The early relationship of drug abusing mothers and their infants: An assessment at eight to twelve months of age. *Journal of Clinical Psychology, 53*(3), 263–277.

Buss, A. H., & Plomin, R. (1975). *A temperament theory of personality development.* New York: Wiley.

Buss, A. H., & Plomin, R. (1984). *Temperament: Early developing personality traits.* Hillsdale, NJ: Erlbaum.

Buss, D. M. (1984). Evolutionary biology and personality psychology: Toward a conception of human nature and individual differences. *American Psychologist, 39*, 1135–1147.

Buss, D. M. (1999). Human nature and individual differences: The evolution of human personality. In L. A. Pervin & O. P. John (Eds.), *Handbook of personality: Theory and research* (pp. 31–56). New York: Guilford Press.

Buss, D. M. (2000a). *The dangerous passion: Why jealousy is as necessary as love and sex.* New York: Free Press.

Buss, D. M. (2000b, June). Prescription for passion. *Psychology Today,* 54–61.

Caine, D. B. (1999). *Within reason: Rationality and human behavior.* New York: Pantheon Books.

Campbell, D. T., & Stanley, J. C. (1963). *Experimental and quasi-experimental designs for research.* Chicago: Rand McNally College Publishing.

Carroll, L. (1962). *Alice's adventures in wonderland.* Harmondsworth, Middlesex: Penguin Books. (Original work published 1865)

Carter, E. A. (1978). Transgenerational scripts and nuclear family stress: Theory and clinical implications. In R. R. Sager (Ed.), *Georgetown family symposium: 1975–1976* (Vol. 3). Washington, DC: Georgetown University.

Carter, E. A., & McGoldrick, M. (Eds.). (1980). *The family life cycle: A framework for family therapy.* New York: Gardner Press.

Carter, R. (1998). *Mapping the mind.* Berkeley, CA: University of California Press.

Caspi, A., & Roberts, B. W. (1999). Personality continuity and change across the life course. In L. A. Pervin & O. P. John (Eds.), *Handbook of personality: Research and practice* (pp. 300–326). New York: Guilford Press.

Cattell, R. B. (1945). The description of personality: III. Principles and findings in factor analysis. *American Journal of Psychology, 58,* 69–90.

Cattell, R. B., Eber, H. W., & Tatsuoka, M. M. (1970). *The handbook for the Sixteen Personality Factor Questionnaire.* Champaign, IL: Institute for Personality and Ability Testing.

Charcot, J. M. (1982). Physiologie pathologique: Sur le divers etats nerveux determines par phypotization chez les hysteriques [Pathological physiology: On the different nervous states hypnotically induced in hysterics]. *CR Academy of Science Paris, 94,* 403–405.

Chase, A. (2000, June). Harvard and the making of the unabomber. *Atlantic Monthly,* 41–65.

Chess, S., & Thomas, A. (1986). *Temperament in clinical practice.* New York: Guilford Press.

Choca, J., Retzlaff, P., Strack, S., Mouton, A., & Van Denburg, E. (1996). Factorial elements in Millon's personality theory. *Journal of Personality Disorders, 10*(4), 377–383.

Chomsky, N. (1965). *Aspects of the theory of syntax.* Cambridge, MA: MIT Press.

Chrzanowski, G. (1977). *Interpersonal approach to psychoanalysis: Contemporary views of Harry Stack Sullivan.* New York: Gardner Press.

Clarkin, J. F., & Lenzenweger, M. F. (Eds.). (1996). *Major theories of personality disorder.* New York: The Guilford Press.

Clarkin, J. F., Yeomans, F. E., & Kernberg, O. F. (1999). *Psychotherapy for borderline personality.* New York: Wiley.

Cloninger, C. R. (1986a). A systematic method for clinical description and classification of personality variants: A proposal. *Archives of General Psychiatry, 44,* 573–88.

Cloninger, C. R. (1986b). A unified biosocial theory of personality and its role in the development of anxiety states. *Psychiatric Developments, 3,* 167–226.

Cloninger, C. R., Adolfsson, R., & Svrakic, D. M. (1996). Mapping genes for human personality. *Nature Genetics, 12,* 3–4.

Cloninger, C. R., Svrakic, D. M., & Przybeck, T. R. (1993). A psychobiological model of temperament and character. *Archives of General Psychiatry, 50,* 975–990.

Clore, G. C. (1994). *Why emotions are felt.* In P. Ekman & R. J. Davidson (Eds.), *The nature of emotions: Fundamental questions* (pp. 103–111). New York: Oxford University Press.

Coley, R. L., & Chase-Lansdale, P. L. (1998). Adolescent pregnancy and parenthood:

Recent evidence and future directions. *American Psychologist, 53*(2), 152–166.

Cook, T. D., & Campbell, D. T. (1979). *Quasi-experimentation: Design and analysis for field settings.* Chicago: Rand McNally College Publishing.

Coolidge, F. L., Thede, L. L., & Jang, K. L. (2001). Heritability of personality disorders in childhood: A preliminary investigation. *Journal of Personality Disorders, 15*(1), 33–40.

Costa, P. T., & McCrae, R. R. (1985). *The NEO Personality Inventory manual.* Odessa, FL: Psychological Assessment Resources.

Costa, P. T., Jr, & McCrae, R. R. (1988). Personality in adulthood: A six-year longitudinal study of self-reports and spouse ratings on the NEO Personality Inventory. *Journal of Personality and Social Psychology, 54,* 853–863.

Costa, P. T., Jr, & McCrae, R. R. (1992). Trait psychology comes of age. In T. B. Sondergger (Ed.), *Nebraska symposium on motivation: Psychology and aging* (pp. 169–204). Lincoln: University of Nebraska Press.

Costa, P. T., Jr, & McCrae, R. R. (1994). Set like plaster? Evidence for the stability of personality. In T. F. Heatherton & J. L. Weinberger (Eds.), *Can personality change?* (pp. 21–40). Washington, DC: American Psychological Association.

Costa, P. T., Jr, McCrae, R. R., & Arenberg, D. (1980). Enduring dispositions in adult males. *Journal of Personality and Social Psychology, 38,* 793–800.

Cramer, P. (1982). *Manual for scoring defenses.* Unpublished manuscript, Williams College, Williamstown, MA.

Cramer, P. (1987). The development of defense mechanisms. *Journal of Personality, 55*(4), 599–614.

Cramer, P. (1991). Anger and the use of defense mechanisms in college students. *Journal of Personality, 59*(1), 39–55.

Cramer, P. (1995). Identity, narcissism, and defense mechanisms in late adolescence. *Journal of Research in Personality, 29,* 341–361.

Cramer, P. (1997). Identity, personality, and defense mechanisms: An observer-based study. *Journal of Research in Personality, 31,* 58–77.

Cramer, P. (1998a). Defensiveness and defense mechanisms. *Journal of Personality, 66*(6), 879–894.

Cramer, P. (1998b). Freshman to senior year: A follow-up study of identity, narcissism, and defense mechanisms. *Journal of Research in Personality, 32,* 156–172.

Cramer, P., Blatt, S. J., & Ford, R. Q. (1988). Defense mechanisms in the anaclitic and introjective personality configuration. *Journal of Consulting and Clinical Psychology, 56*(4), 610–616.

Cramer, P., & Gaul, R. (1988). The effects of success and failure on children's use of defense mechanisms. *Journal of Personality, 56*(4), 729–742.

Cross, S. E., & Markus, H. R. (1999). The cultural constitution of personality. In L. A. Pervin & O. P. John (Eds.), *Handbook of personality: Theory and research* (2nd ed, pp. 378–396). New York: Guilford Press.

Cushman, P. (1992). Psychotherapy to 1992: A historically situated interpretation. In D. K. Freedheim (Ed.), *History of psychotherapy: A century of change* (pp. 21–64). Washington, DC: American Psychological Association.

Daley, S. E., Burge, D., & Hammen, C. (2000). Borderline personality disorder symptoms as predictors of 4-year romantic relationship dysfunction in young women: Addressing issues of specificity. *Journal of Abnormal Psychology, 109*(3), 451–460.

Damasio, A. (1999). *The feeling of what happens: Body and emotion in the making of consciousness.* New York: Harcourt Brace & Company.

Darwin, C. R. (1859). *On the origin of the species by means of natural selection.* London: Murray.

Darwin, C. R. (1871). *The descent of man and selection in relation to sex.* London: Murray.

Darwin, C. R. (1998). *The expression of the emotions in man and animal* (3rd ed.). New York: Oxford University Press. (Original work published 1872)

Dattore, P. J., Shontz, F. C., & Coyne, L. (1980). Premorbid personality differentiation of cancer and noncancer proneness. *Journal of Consulting and Clinical Psychology, 48*(3), 388–394.

Davanloo, H. (1978). *Basic principles and technique in short-term dynamic psychotherapy.* New York: Spectrum.

Davanloo, H. (Ed.). (1980). *Short-term dynamic psychotherapy.* New York: Aronson.

Davidson, R. J. (1994). On emotion, mood, and related affective constructs. In P. Ekman & R. J. Davidson (Eds.), *The nature of emotions: Fundamental questions* (pp. 51–55). New York: Oxford University Press.

Davis, R. D., & Millon, T. (1994). Personality change: Metatheories and alternatives. In T. F. Heatherton & J. L. Weinberger (Eds.), *Can personality change?* (pp. 85–119). Washington, DC: American Psychological Association.

de Jongh, A., Muris, P., ter Horst, G., & Duyx, M. P. M. A. (1995). Acquisition and maintenance of dental anxiety: The role of conditioning experiences and cognitive factors. *Behaviour Research and Therapy, 33*(2), 205–210.

Dennett, D. C. (1991). *Consciousness explained.* Boston: Little, Brown.

Depue, R. A. (1996). A neurobiological framework for the structure of personality and emotion: Implications for personality disorders. In J. F. Clarkin & M. F. Lenzenweger (Eds.), *Major theories of personality disorders* (pp. 347–390). New York: Guilford Press.

Deutsch, H. (1965). *Neurosis and character types: Clinical psychoanalytic studies.* New York: International Universities Press.

Diamond, J. (2001, February, 17). Think tank: Freud, influential yet unloved. *New York Times,* p. B11.

Diaz-Marsa, M., Carrasco, J. L., & Saiz, J. (2000). A study of temperament and personality in anorexia and bulimia nervosa. *Journal of Personality Disorders, 14*(4), 352–359.

DiClemente, C. C. (1994). If behaviors change, can personality be far behind? In T. F. Heatherton & J. L. Weinberger (Eds.), *Can personality change?* (pp. 175–198). Washington, DC: American Psychological Association.

DiGiuseppe, R., Robin, M., Szeszko, P. R., & Primavera, L. H. (1995). *Journal of Personality Disorders, 9*(4), 304–317.

Dillard, J. P. (1991). The current status of research on sequential-request compliance techniques. *Personality and Social Psychology Bulletin, 17,* 283–288.

DiMatteo, M. R. (1991). *The psychology of health, illness, and medical care.* Pacific Grove, CA: Brooks/Cole.

Doi, T. (1971). *The anatomy of dependence.* New York: Kodansha International.

Dollard, J., & Miller, N. E. (1950). *Personality and psychotherapy: An analysis in terms of learning, thinking, and culture.* New York: McGraw-Hill.

Donald, M. (1991). *Origins of the modern mind: Three stages in the evolution of culture and cognition.* Cambridge, MA: Harvard University Press.

Dykman, B. M., & Johll, M. (1998). Dysfunctional attitudes and vulnerability to depressive symptoms: A 14-week longitudinal study. *Cognitive Therapy and Research, 22*(4), 337–352.

Eagle, M. N., & Wolitzky, D. L. (1992). Psychoanalytic theories of psychotherapy. In D. K. Freedheim (Ed.), *History of psychotherapy: A century of change* (pp. 109–158). Washington, DC: American Psychological Association.

Eagly, A. H., Makhijani, M. G., & Klonsky, B. G. (1992). Gender and the evaluation of leaders: A meta-analysis. *Psychology Bulletin, 111,* 3–22.

Eifert, G. H., & Evans, I. M. (Eds.). (1990). *Unifying behavior therapy: Contributions of paradigmatic behaviorism.* New York: Springer.

Ekman, P. (1998). Preface to the third edition. In C. Darwin (Ed.), *The expression of the emotions in man and animals: Definitive edition* (3rd ed, pp. xiii–xvii). New York: Oxford University Press.

Ekman, P., & Davidson, R. J. (Eds.). (1994). *The nature of emotions: Fundamental questions.* New York: Oxford University Press.

Ellenberger, H. (1970). *The discovery of the unconscious.* New York: Basic Books.

Elliott, C. (2000, December). A new way to be mad. *Atlantic Monthly,* 73–84.

Ellis, A. (1974). Rational-emotive theory: Albert-Ellis. In A. Burton (Ed.), *Operational theories of personality* (pp. 308–344). New York: Brunner/Mazel.

Ellis, A., & Harper, R. A. (1961). *A new guide to rational living.* NJ: Prentice-Hall.

Ellis, H. (1933). Auto-erotism: A psychological study. *Alienist and Neurologist, 19,* 260–299. (Original work published 1898)

Emery, R. E., & Laumann-Billings, L. (1998). An overview of the nature, causes, and consequences of abusive family relationships: Toward differentiating maltreatment and violence. *American Psychologist, 53*(2), 121–135.

Engel, G. L. (1980). The clinical application of the biopsychosocial model. *American Journal of Psychiatry, 137*(5), 535–544.

Erikson, E. (1970, December 21). The quest for identity [Special report]. *Newsweek,* 84–89.

Erikson, E. H. (1950). *Childhood and society.* New York: Norton.

Erikson, E. H. (1958). *Young man Luther.* New York: Norton.

Erikson, E. H. (1959). *Identity and the life-cycle: Selected papers* (Psychological Issues Monograph No. 1). New York: New York University Press.

Erikson, E. H. (1968). *Identity youth and crisis.* New York: Norton.

Erikson, E. H. (1970). *Gandhi's truth: On the origins of militant nonviolence.* New York: Norton.

Eysenck, H. J. (1947). *Dimensions of personality.* London: Routledge.

Eysenck, H. J. (1952a). The effects of psychotherapy: An evaluation. *Journal of Consulting Psychology, 16,* 319–324.

Eysenck, H. J. (1952b). *The scientific study of personality.* New York: Macmillan.

Eysenck, H. J. (1953). *The structure of human personality.* New York: Wiley.

Eysenck, H. J. (Ed.). (1960). *Behavior therapy and the neurosis.* London: Pergamon Press.

Eysenck, H. J. (Ed.). (1981). *A model for personality.* Berlin, Germany: Springer-Verlag.

Eysenck, H. J. (1982). *Personality, genetics, and behavior: Selected papers.* New York: Praeger.

Eysenck, H. J., & Eysenck, M. W. (1985). *Personality and individual differences: A natural science approach.* New York: Plenum Press.

Ezriel, H. (1952). Notes on psychoanalytic group therapy: Interpretation and research. *Psychiatry, 32*(15), 119–126.

Fenichel, H., & Rapaport, D. (Eds.). (1954). *The collected papers of Otto Fenichel* (2nd ed.). New York: Norton.

Ferenczi, S. (1933). The confusion of tongues between adults and children: The language of tenderness and passion. In M. Balint (Ed.), *Final contributions to the problems and methods of psycho-analysis* (Vol. 3, pp. 156–167). New York: Brunner/Mazel.

Ferenczi, S., & Rank, O. (1925). *The development of psychoanalysis.* New York: Nervous and Mental Disease Publishing Co.

Finn, P. R., Sharkansky, E. J., Brandt, K. M., & Turcotte, N. (2000). The effects of familial risk, personality, and expectancies on alcohol use and abuse. *Journal of Abnormal Psychology, 109*(1), 122–133.

Fishman, D. B., & Franks, C. M. (1992). Evolution and differentiation within behavior therapy: A theoretical and epistemological review. In

D. K. Freedheim (Ed.), *History of psychotherapy: A century of change* (pp. 159–196). Washington, DC: American Psychological Association.

Fosha, D. (2000). *The transforming power of affect.* New York: Basic Books.

Frager, R., & Fadiman, J. (1998). *Personality and personal growth.* New York: Longman.

Frances, A., & Widiger, T. A. (1986). Methodological issues in personality disorders diagnosis. In T. Millon & G. L. Klerman (Eds.), *Contemporary directions in psychopathology: Toward the DSM-IV* (pp. 381–400). New York: Guilford Press.

Franklin, A. J. (1998). Treating anger in African American men. In W. S. Pollack & R. F. Levant (Eds.), *New psychotherapy for men* (pp. 239–258). New York: Wiley.

Freedman, M. B., Leary, T. F., Ossorio, A. G., & Coffey, H. S. (1951). The interpersonal dimension of personality. *Journal of Personality, 20,* 143–161.

Freud, S. (1925). The instincts and their vicissitudes. In *Collected Papers* (Vol. 4). London: Hogarth. (Original work published 1915)

Freud, S. (1966). *The complete introductory lectures on psychoanalysis* (James Strachey, Ed. and Trans.). New York: Norton.

Friedman, L. A., & Rosenman, R. H. (1974). *Type A behavior and your heart.* New York: Alfred A. Knopf.

Frijda, N. H. (1994). Emotions are functional, most of the time. In P. Ekman & R. J. Davidson (Eds.), *The nature of emotions: Fundamental questions* (pp. 112–122). New York: Oxford University Press.

Fromm, E. (1959). *Sigmund Freud's mission.* New York: Harper & Row.

Fromm-Reichmann, F. (1950). *Principles of intensive psychotherapy.* Chicago: University of Chicago Press.

Frost, A. K., Reinherz, H. Z., Pakiz-Camras, B., & Gianconia, R. M. (1999). Risk factors for depressive symptoms in late adolescence: A longitudinal community study. *American Journal of Orthopsychiatry, 69*(3), 370–381.

Gagnon, M., & Ladouceur, R. (1992). Behavioral treatment of child stutterers: Replication and extension. *Behavior Therapy, 23*(1), 113–129.

Galton, F. (1892). *Hereditary genius: An inquiry into its laws and consequences.* London: Macmillan.

Gardner, H. (1985). *The new mind's science: A history of the cognitive revolution.* New York: Basic Books.

Gay, P. (1988). *Freud: A life for our time.* New York: Norton.

Gergen, K. J. (1985). The social constructionist movement in modern psychology. *American Psychologist, 40,* 266–275.

Gergen, K. J. (1991). *The saturated self: Dilemmas of identity in contemporary life.* New York: Basic Books.

Gergen, K. J., Hoffman, L., & Anderson, H. (1996). Is diagnosis a disaster? A constructionistic trialogue. In F. W. Kaslow (Ed.), *Handbook of relational diagnosis and dysfunctional family patterns* (pp. 102–118). New York: Wiley.

Geschwind, N. (1979). Specializations of the human brain. *Scientific American, 241*(3), 180–199.

Gilbert, P., & Steven, A. (1994). Assertiveness, submissive behaviour and social comparison. *British Journal of Clinical Psychology, 33*(3), 295–306.

Gilligan, C. (1982). *In a different voice.* Cambridge, MA: Harvard University Press.

Gleick, J. (1987). *Chaos: Making a new science.* New York: Viking/Penguin.

Goldenson, R. M. (1970). *The encyclopedia of human behavior: Psychology, psychiatry, and mental health* (Vol. 2). New York: Doubleday.

Goldfried, M. R. (1982). *Converging themes in psychotherapy: Trends in psychodynamic, humanistic, and behavioral practice.* New York: Springer.

Goldfried, M. R., & Merbaum, M. (Eds.). (1973). *Behavior change through self-control.* New York: Holt, Rinehart and Winston.

Goldfried, M. R., & Newman, C. F. (1992). A history of psychotherapy integration. In J. C. Norcross & M. R. Goldfried (Eds.), *Handbook of integrative psychotherapy* (pp. 47–93). New York: Basic Books.

Goleman, D. (1994). *Emotional intelligence.* New York: Bantam Books.

Goode, E. (1999, November 2). 100 years ago, a book ignited the study of the mind. *New York Times,* p. F4.

Goode, E. (2000, January 15). What provokes a rapist to rape? Scientists debate the notion of an evolutionary drive. *New York Times,* B9, B17.

Goode, E. (2001, February 20). What's in an inkblot? Some say, not much. *New York Times,* pp. F1, F4.

Gray, N. S., Pickering, A. D., & Gray, J. A. (1994). Psychoticism and dopamine D2 binding in the basal ganglia using single photon emission tomography. *Personality and Individual Differences, 17,* 413–434.

Green, H. (1964). *I never promised you a rose garden.* New York: Holt.

Greenberg, L. S. (1994). The investigation of change: Its measurement and explanation. In R. L. Russell (Ed.), *Reassessing psychotherapy research* (pp. 114–143). New York: Guilford Press.

Greenspan, S. I. (1997a). *Developmentally based psychotherapy.* Madison, CT: International Universities Press.

Greenspan, S. I. (1997b). *The growth of the mind: And the endangered growth of intelligence.* Reading, MA: Perseus Books.

Grier, W., & Cobbs, P. (1968). *Black rage.* New York: Basic Books.

Griffin, D. (1992). *Animal minds.* Chicago: University of Chicago Press.

Grigsby, J., & Stevens, D. (2000). *Neurodynamics of personality.* New York: Guilford Press.

Gross, J. J. (1999). Emotion and emotion regulation. In L. A. Pervin & O. P. John (Eds.), *Handbook of personality: Theory and research* (2nd ed, pp. 525–552). New York: Guilford Press.

Guerin, P. J. (1976). Family therapy: The first twenty-five years. In P. J. Guerin (Ed.), *Family therapy: Theory and practice* (pp. 2–22). New York: Gardner Press.

Guerin, P. J., & Chabot, D. R. (1992). Development of family systems theory. In D. K. Freedheim (Ed.), *History of psychotherapy: A century of change* (pp. 225–260). Washington, DC: American Psychological Association.

Guerin, P. J., Fogarty, T. F., Fay, L. F., & Kautto, J. G. (1996). *Working with relational triangles: The one-two-three of psychotherapy.* New York: Guilford Press.

Guntrip, H. (1971). *Psychoanalytic theory, therapy and the self: A basic guide to the human personality in Freud, Erikson, Klein, Sullivan, Fairbairn, Hartmann, Jacobson and Winnicott.* New York: Basic Books.

Guttman, L. (1966). Order analysis of correlation matrixes. In R. B. Cattell (Ed.), *Handbook of multivariate experimental psychology.* Chicago: Rand McNally.

Haley, J. (1959). The family of the schizophrenic: A model system. *Journal of Nervous and Mental Disease, 129,* 359–374.

Hammond, M. V., Landry, S. H., Swank, P. R., & Smith, K. E. (2000). Relation of mothers' affective development history and parenting behavior: Effects on infant medical risk. *American Journal of Orthopsychiatry, 70*(1), 95–103.

Hanna, F. J. (1996). Precursors of change: Pivotal points of involvement and resistance in psychotherapy. *Journal of Psychotherapy Integration, 6*(3), 227–264.

Hare, R. D. (1991). *Manual for the Hare Psychopathy Checklist–Revised.* Toronto, Canada: Multi-Health Systems.

Harlow, H. F. (1961). The development of affectional patterns in infant monkeys. In B. M. Foss (Ed.), *Determinants of infant behaviour* (Vol. 1). New York: Wiley.

Harlow, H. F., & Zimmerman, R. R. (1959). Affectional responses in the infant monkey. *Science, 130,* 421–432.

Harrington, C. M., & Metzler, A. E. (1997). Are adult children of dysfunctional families with alcoholism different from adult children of dysfunctional families without alcoholism? A look at committed, intimate relations. *Journal of Counseling Psychology, 44*(1), 102–107.

Hartmann, H. (1958). *Ego psychology and the problem of adaptation.* New York: International Universities Press.

Hartmann, H. (1964). *Essays on ego psychology: Selected problems in psychoanalytic theory.* New York: International Universities Press.

Hazel, J. (Ed.). (1994). *Personal relations therapy: The collected papers of H. J. S. Guntrip.* Northvale, NJ: Aronson.

Heatherton, T. F., & Weinberger, J. L. (Eds.). (1994). *Can personality change?* Washington, DC: American Psychological Association.

Hebb, D. O. (1949). *The organization of behavior: A neuropsychological theory.* New York: Wiley.

Helson, R., & Stewart, A. (1994). Personality change in adulthood. In T. F. Heatherton & J. L. Weinberger (Eds.), *Can personality change?* (pp. 201–225). Washington, DC: American Psychological Association.

Herman, J. L. (1992). *Trauma and recovery.* New York: Basic Books.

Herrnstein, R. J., & Murray, C. (1994). *The bell curve: Intelligence and class structure in American life.* New York: Free Press.

Hetherington, E. M. (Ed.). (1998). Applications of developmental science [Special issue]. *American Psychologist, 53*(2), 89–272.

Hetherington, E. M., Bridges, M., & Insabella, G. M. (1998). What matters? What does not? Five perspectives on the association between marital transitions and children's adjustment. *American Psychologist, 53*(2), 167–184.

Hibbard, S., Farmer, L., Wells, C., Difillipo, E., Barry, W., Korman, R., & Sloan, P. (1994). Validation of Cramer's Defense Mechanisms manual for the TAT. *Journal of Personality Assessment, 63,* 197–210.

Hibbard, S., & Porcerelli, J. (1998). Further validation for the Cramer Defense Mechanism manual. *Journal of Personality Assessment, 70,* 460–483.

Higgins, M. B. (Ed.). (2000). *American odyssey: Letters and journals, 1940–1947 by Wilhelm Reich.* New York: Farrar, Straus and Giroux.

Hilgard, E. R., & Bower, G. H. (1975). *Theories of learning* (4th ed.). Englewood Cliffs, NJ: Prentice-Hall.

Hilliard, R. B., Henry, W. P., & Strupp, H. H. (2000). An interpersonal model of psychotherapy: Linking patient and therapist developmental history, therapeutic process, and types of outcome. *Journal of Consulting and Clinical Psychology, 68*(1), 125–133.

Hillner, K. P. (1984). *History and systems of modern psychology: A conceptual approach.* New York: Gardner Press.

Hjelle, L. A., & Ziegler, D. J. (1976). *Personality theories: Basic assumptions, research, and applications.* New York: McGraw-Hill.

Holi, M. M., Sammallahti, P. R., & Aalberg, V. A. (1999). Defense styles explain psychiatric symptoms: An empirical study. *Journal of Nervous and Mental Disease, 187*(11), 654–660.

Horner, A. J. (Ed.). (1994). *Treating the neurotic patient in brief psychotherapy.* Northvale, NJ: Aronson.

Horner, A. J. (1995). *Psychoanalytic object relations therapy.* Northvale, NJ: Aronson.

Horney, K. (1937). *The neurotic personality of our time.* New York: Norton.

Horney, K. (1945). *Our inner conflicts.* New York: oNorton.

Horney, K. (1950). *Neurosis and human growth.* New York: Norton.

Horney, K. (1967). *Feminine psychology.* New York: Norton.

Horowitz, M., Marmar, C., Krupnick, J., Wilner, N., Kaltreider, N., & Wallerstein, R. (1984).

Personality style and brief psychotherapy. New York: Basic Books.

Howard, K. I., Kopta, S. M., Krause, M. S., & Orlinsky, D. E. (1986). The dose-effect relationship in psychotherapy. *American Psychologist, 41*(2), 159–164.

Hubel, D. H. (1979). The brain. *Scientific American, 241*(3), 45–53.

Hubel, D. H., & Wiesel, T. N. (1979). Brain mechanisms of vision. *Scientific American, 241*(3), 150–162.

Hull, C. L. (1943). *Principles of behavior: An introduction to behavior theory.* New York: Appleton-Century-Crofts.

Hull, C. L. (1952). *A behavior system: An introduction to behavior theory concerning the individual organism.* New Haven, CT: Yale University Press.

Hundert, E. M. (1990). *Philosophy, psychiatry and neuroscience: Three approaches to the mind.* New York: Oxford University Press.

Hunt, M. (1993). *The story of psychology.* New York: Doubleday.

Isaac, S., & Michael, W. B. (1979). *Handbook in research and evaluation: For educational and behavioral sciences.* San Diego, CA: Edits Publishers.

Iversen, L. L. (1979). The chemistry of the brain. *Scientific American, 241*(3), 134–149.

Izard, C. (1994). Intersystem connections. In P. Ekman & R. J. Davidson (Eds.), *The nature of emotions: Fundamental questions* (pp. 356–361). New York: Oxford University Press.

James, W. (1890). *The principles of psychology.* New York: Henry Holt and Company.

James, W. (1902). *The varieties of religious experience.* New York: Dolphin Books.

Janet, P. (1885). *Victor Cousin et son oeuvre.* Paris: Clamann Levy Editor.

Jasny, B. R., & Kennedy, D. (2000). The human genome. *Science, 291*(5507), 1153.

Jones, A. C. (1985). Psychological functioning in Black Americans: A conceptual guide for use in psychotherapy. *Psychotherapy, 22,* 363–369.

Jordan, J. V. (Ed.). (1997). *Women's growth in diversity.* New York: Guilford Press.

Jordan, J. V. (2000). The role of mutual empathy in relational/cultural therapy. *Journal of Clinical Psychology/In Session: Psychotherapy in Practice, 56*(8), 1005–1016.

Jordan, J. V., Kaplan, A., Miller, J. B., Stiver, I., & Surrey, J. (1991). *Women's growth in connection.* New York: Guilford Press.

Jung, C. G. (1923). *Psychological types.* New York: Harcourt Brace.

Kandel, E. R. (1979). Small systems of neurons. *Scientific American, 241*(3), 67–76.

Kaplan, A. (1991). *Some misconceptions and reconceptions of a relational approach* (Work in progress, No. 49). Wellesley, MA: Stone Center Working Paper Series.

Kaplan, M. (1983). A woman's view of *DSM-III. American Psychologist, 38*(7), 786–792.

Kaslow, F. W. (Ed.). (1996). *Handbook of relational diagnosis and dysfunctional family patterns.* New York: Wiley.

Kass, F., Spitzer, R. L., & Williams, J. B. W. (1983). An empirical study of the issue of sex bias in the diagnostic criteria of *DSM-III* Axis II personality disorder. *American Psychologist, 38*(7), 799–801.

Kelly, G. (1955). *The psychology of personal constructs.* New York: Norton.

Kendler, K. S., Myers, J. M., & Neale, M. C. (2000). A multidimensional twin study of mental health in women. *American Journal of Psychiatry, 157*(4), 506–513.

Kernberg, O. F. (1976). *Object relations theory and clinical psychoanalysis.* New York: Aronson.

Kernberg, O. F. (1980). Pathological narcissism in middle age. In O. F. Kernberg (Ed.), *Internal world and external reality* (pp. 135–153). Northvale, NJ: Aronson.

Kernberg, O. F. (1984). *Severe personality disorders: Psychotherapeutic strategies.* New Haven, CT: Yale University Press.

Kernberg, O. F. (1994). Aggression, trauma, and hatred in the treatment of borderline patients. In J. Share (Ed.), *Borderline personality disorder: The psychiatric clinics of*

North America (pp. 701–714). Philadelphia: Saunders.

Kernberg, O. F. (1996). A psychoanalytic theory of personality disorders. In J. F. Clarkin & M. F. Lenzenweger (Eds.), *Major theories of personality disorders* (pp. 106–140). New York: Guilford Press.

Kernberg, O. F., Selzer, M. A., Koenigsberg, H. W., Carr, A. C., & Appelbaum, A. H. (1989). *Psychodynamic psychotherapy of borderline patients.* New York: Basic Books.

Kernberg, P. F., Weiner, A. S., & Bardenstein, K. K. (2000). *Personality disorders in children and adolescents.* New York: Basic Books.

Kerr, M. E. (1988, September). Chronic anxiety and defining self. *Atlantic Monthly,* 35–57.

Kiesler, D. J. (1983). The 1982 Interpersonal Circle: A taxonomy for complementarity in human transactions. *Psychological Review, 90,* 185–214.

Kiesler, D. J. (1986). The 1982 Interpersonal Circle: An analysis of *DSM-III* personality disorders. In T. Millon & G. L. Klerman (Eds.), *Contemporary directions in psychopathology: Towards DSM-IV* (pp. 571–597). New York: Guilford Press.

Kimble, G. A. (1985). Conditioning and learning. In S. Koch & D. E. Leary (Eds), *A century of psychological science* (pp. 284–321). New York: McGraw-Hill.

Klein, D. F. (1967). The importance of psychiatric diagnosis in prediction of critical drug effects. *Archives of General Psychiatry, 16,* 118–126.

Klein, D. F. (1970). Psychotropic drugs and the regulation of behavior at activation in psychiatric illness. In W. L. Smith (Ed.), *Drugs and cerebral function.* Springfield, IL: Thomas.

Klein, K., Forehand, R., & Family Health Project Research Group. (2000). Family processes as resources for African American children exposed to a constellation of sociodemographic risk factors. *Journal of Child Clinical Psychology, 29*(1), 53–65.

Klein, M. (1975). *The writings of Melanie Klein* (Vols. 1–4). London: Hogarth.

Klein, M. H., Kupfer, D. J., & Shea, M. T. (1993). *Personality and depression.* New York: Guilford Press.

Klerman, G. L., & Weissman, M. M. (1986). The interpersonal approach to understanding depression. In T. Millon & G. L. Klerman (Eds.), *Contemporary directions in psychopathology: Toward the DSM-IV* (pp. 429–456). New York: Guilford Press.

Klerman, G. L., Weissman, M. M., Rounsaville, B. J., & Chevron, E. S. (1984). *Interpersonal psychotherapy of depression.* New York: Basic Books.

Kobasa, S. C. (1979). Stressful life events, personality, and health: An inquiry into hardiness. *Journal of Personality and Social Psychology, 37,* 1–11.

Kobasa, S. C., & Maddi, S. R. (1977). Existential personality theory. In R. Corsini (Ed.), *Current personality theories.* Itasca, IL: Peacock.

Kohut, H. (1971). *The analysis of the self.* New York: International Universities Press.

Kohut, H. (1984). *How does analysis cure?* Chicago: University of Chicago Press.

Kohut, H. (1986). Forms and transformations of narcissism. In A. P. Morrison (Ed.), *Essential papers on narcissism* (pp. 61–87). New York: New York University Press.

Kohut, H., & Wolf, E. S. (1986). The disorders of the self and their treatment: An outline. In A. P. Morrison (Ed.), *Essential papers of narcissism* (pp. 175–196). New York: New York University Press. (Original work published 1978)

Kraepelin, E. (1904). *Lectures on clinical psychiatry.* New York: Wood.

Kramer, P. D. (1993). *Listening to Prozac: A psychiatrist explores antidepressant drugs and the remaking of the self.* New York: Viking/Penguin Books.

Krech, D., Crutchfield, R. S., & Ballachey, E. L. (1962). *Individual in society.* New York: McGraw-Hill.

Kretschmer, E. (1925). *Physique and character.* New York: Harcourt Brace.

Kuhn, T. (1970). *The structure of scientific revolutions.* Chicago: University of Chicago Press.

Kuyken, W., & Brewin, C. R. (1999). The relation of early abuse to cognition and coping in depression. *Cognitive Therapy and Research, 23*(6), 665–677.

LaForge, R., Leary, T. F., Naboisek, H., Coffey, H. S., & Freedman, M. B. (1954). The interpersonal dimension of personality: II. An objective study of repression. *Journal of Personality, 23,* 129–153.

Langer, W. C. (1972). *The mind of Adolf Hitler: The secret wartime report.* New York: Basic Books.

Lathrop, R. G. (1969). *Introduction to psychological research: Logic, design, analysis.* New York: Harper & Row.

Lazarus, R. S. (1991). *Emotion and adaptation.* New York: Oxford University Press.

Leach, P. (1994). *Children first: What our society must do—and is not doing—for our children today.* New York: Alfred A. Knopf.

Leakey, R. E., & Lewin, R. (1977). *Origins.* New York: Dutton.

Lear, J. (1998). *Open minded: Working out the logic of the soul.* Cambridge, MA: Harvard University Press.

Leary, T. (1957). *Interpersonal diagnosis of personality: A functional theory and methodology for personality evaluation.* New York: Ronald Press.

Leeper, R. W., & Madison, P. (1959). *Toward understanding human personality.* New York: Appleton-Century-Crofts.

Le Shan, L. L., & Worthington, R. E. (1956). Personality as a factor in the pathogenesis of cancer: A review of the literature. *British Journal of Medical Psychology, 29,* 49–56.

Levin, J. D. (1998). *The Clinton syndrome: The president and the self-destructive nature of sexual addiction.* Rocklin, CA: Prima.

Levitan, R. D., Parikh, S. V., Lesage, A. D., Hegadoren, K. M., Adams, M., Kennedy, S. H., & Goering, P. N. (1998). Major depression in individuals with a history of childhood physical or sexual abuse: Relationship to neruovegetative features, mania, and gender. *American Journal of Psychiatry, 155*(12), 1746–1752.

Lewin, K. (1936). *Principles of topological psychology.* New York: McGraw-Hill.

Lewis-Fernandez, R., & Kleinman, A. (1994). Culture, personality, and psychopathology. *Journal of Abnormal Psychology, 103*(1), 67–71.

Linehan, M. M. (1993). *Cognitive-behavioral treatment of borderline personality disorder.* New York: Guilford Press.

Lipset, D. (1980). *Gregory Bateson: The legacy of a scientist.* Englewood Cliffs, NJ: Prentice-Hall.

Livesley, W. J. (Ed.). (1995). *The DSM-IV personality disorders.* New York: Guilford Press.

Livesley, W. J., Schroeder, M. L., Jackson, D. N., & Jang, K. L. (1994). Categorical distinctions in the study of personality disorder: Implications for classification. *Journal of Abnormal Psychology, 103*(1), 6–17.

Loeber, R., & Stouthamer-Loeber, M. (1998). Development of juvenile aggression and violence: Some common misconceptions and controversies. *American Psychologist, 53*(2), 242–259.

Loehlin, J. C. (1992). *Genes and environment in personality development.* Newbury Park, CA: Sage.

Loftus, E. (2000, December). The most dangerous book you may already be reading. *Psychology Today,* 32–35, 84.

Loftus, E., & Ketcham, K. (1994). *The myth of repressed memory: False memories a collection of sexual abuse.* New York: St. Martin's Press.

Lorenz, K. Z. (1957). Der Kumpanin der Umvelt de Vogels. J. Orn. Berl, 83. In C. H. Schiller (Ed.), *Instinctive behavior.* New York: International Universities Press. (Original work published 1935)

Lowenstein, R. (2001, February 11). Exuberance is rational or at least human. *New York Times Magazine,* 68–77.

Luborsky, L., & Crits-Christoph, P. (1997). *Understanding transference: The core conflictual relationship theme method* (2nd ed.). Washington, DC: American Psychological Association.

Luborsky, L., Singer, B., & Luborsky, L. (1975). Comparative studies of psychotherapies: Is it true that "Everyone has won and all must get prizes"? *Archives of General Psychiatry, 32,* 995–1008.

Lundin, R. W. (1969). *Personality: A behavioral analysis.* New York: Macmillan.

Magnavita, J. J. (1993a). The evolution of short-term dynamic psychotherapy. *Professional Psychology: Research and Practice,* 24(3), 360–365.

Magnavita, J. J. (1993b). On the validity of psychoanalytic constructs in the 20th century. *Professional Psychology: Research and Practice,* 25(3), 189–199.

Magnavita, J. J. (1997). *Restructuring personality disorders: A short-term dynamic approach.* New York: Guilford Press.

Magnavita, J. J. (1999). Challenges in the treatment of personality disorders: When the disorder demands comprehensive integration. *Journal of Clinical Psychology/In Session: Psychotherapy in Practice,* 4(4), 5–17.

Magnavita, J. J. (2000a). Integrative relational therapy of complex clinical syndromes: Ending the multigenerational transmission process. *Journal of Clinical Psychology/In Session: Psychotherapy in Practice,* 56(8), 1051–1064.

Magnavita, J. J. (2000b). Introduction: The growth of relational therapy. *Journal of Clinical Psychology/In Session: Psychotherapy in Practice,* 56(8), 999–1004.

Magnavita, J. J. (2000c). Psicoterapia psicodinamica para los trastornos de personalidad: Teoria, metodos y fases de tratamiento acelerado [Psychodynamic psychotherapy for personality disorders: Theory, methods and phases of accelerated treatment]. *Argentina Journal of Clinical Psychology, 9,* 211–225.

Magnavita, J. J. (2000d). *Relational therapy for personality disorders.* New York: Wiley.

Magnavita, J. J. (in press-a). A century of the "scientific" study of personality: How far have we come? [*Contemporary Psychology,* Book Review.] T. Millon, R. Davis, C. Millon, L. Escovar, & S. Meagher (Eds.), *Personality disorders in modern life.* New York: Wiley.

Magnavita, J. J. (Ed.). (in press-b). *Comprehensive handbook of psychotherapy: Vol. I. Psychodynamic/object relations.* New York: Wiley.

Mahler, M. S., Pine, F., & Bergman, A. (1975). *The psychological birth of the human infant: Symbiosis and individuation.* New York: Basic Books.

Mahoney, M. J. (1974). *Cognitive and behavior modification.* Cambridge, MA: Ballinger.

Mahoney, M. J. (1977). Reflections on the cognitive-learning trend in psychotherapy. *American Psychologist, 32,* 5–13.

Mahrer, A. R. (1997). What are the "breakthrough problems" in the field of Psychotherapy? *Psychotherapy,* 34(1), 81–85.

Malan, D. H. (1963). *A study of brief psychotherapy.* New York: Plenum Press.

Malan, D. H. (1976). *The frontier of brief psychotherapy: An example of the convergence of research and clinical practice.* New York: Plenum Medical Book Company.

Malan, D. H. (1979). *Individual psychotherapy and the science of psychodynamics.* London: Butterworth.

Mandel, A. J. (1985). From molecular biological simplification to more realistic central nervous system dynamics: An opinion. In J. O. Cavenar (Ed.), *Psychiatry: Psychobiological foundations of clinical psychiatry.* New York: Lippincott.

Mandlebrot, B. (1977). *The fractal geometry of nature*. New York: Freeman.

Marmor, J., & Woods, S. E. (Eds.). (1980). The interface between behavior therapy and psychodynamic methods. *British Journal of Medical Psychology, 39*, 11–23.

Masson, J. M. (1984). *The assault on truth: Freud's suppression of the seduction theory*. New York: Farrar, Straus and Giroux.

Masson, J. M. (1990). *Final analysis: The making and unmaking of a psychoanalyst*. New York: Addison-Wesley.

Masten, A. S., & Coatsworth, J. D. (1998). The development of competence in favorable and unfavorable environments. *American Psychologist, 53*(2), 205–220.

Masters, W. H., & Johnson, V. E. (1966). *Human sexual response*. Boston: Little, Brown.

Masterson, J. F. (1972). *Treatment of the borderline adolescent: A developmental approach*. New York: Wiley.

Masterson, J. F. (1988). *The search for the real self: Unmasking personality disorders of our age*. New York: Free Press.

Matsen, A. S., & Coatsworth, J. D. (1998). The development of competence in favorable and unfavorable environments. *American Psychologist, 53*(2), 205–220.

Maugham, W. S. (1995). *The moon and sixpence*. New York: Barnes & Noble Books.

McCrae, R. R., & John, O. P. (1992). An introduction to the Five-Factor Model and its applications. *Journal of Personality, 60*, 174–215.

McCullough Vaillant, L. (1997). *Changing character: Short-term anxiety-regulating psychotherapy for restructuring defenses, affects, and attachments*. New York: Basic Books.

McGoldrick, M., & Gerson, R. (1985). *Genograms in family assessment*. New York: Norton.

McLoyd, V. C. (1998). Socioeconomic disadvantage and child development. *American Psychologist, 53*(2), 185–204.

McWilliams, N. (1994). *Psychoanalytic diagnosis: Understanding personality structure in the clinical process*. New York: Guilford Press.

Mead, M. (1964). *Anthropology: A human science*. New York: Van Nostrand.

Meichenbaum, D. H. (1977). *Cognitive-behavior modification*. New York: Plenum Press.

Meissner, W. W. (1981). Meissner's glossary of defenses. In H. I. Kaplan & B. J. Sadock (Eds.), *Modern synopsis of comprehensive textbook of psychiatry* (3rd ed., pp. 137–138). Baltimore: Williams & Wilkins.

Menninger, K. (1958). *Theory of psychoanalytic technique*. New York: Basic Books.

Mental health: Does therapy help? (1995, November). *Consumer Reports*, 734–739.

Messer, S. B. (1992). A critical examination of belief structures in integrative and eclectic psychotherapy. In J. C. Norcross & M. R. Goldfried (Eds.), *Handbook of integrative psychotherapy* (pp. 130–165). New York: Basic Books.

Meyer, D. F. (1997). Codependency as a mediator between stressful events and eating disorders. *Journal of Clinical Psychology, 53*(2), 107–116.

Miklowitz, D. J. (1995). The evolution of family-based psychopathology. In R. H. Mikesell, D. D. Lusterman, & S. McDaniel (Eds.), *Integrating family therapy: Handbook of family psychology and systems theory* (pp. 183–197). Washington, DC: American Psychological Association.

Miller, A. (1990). *For your own good*. New York: Moonday Press

Miller, G. A. (1956). The magical number seven plus or minus two: Some limits on our capacity for information processing. *Psychological Review, 63*, 81–97.

Miller, J. B. (1976). *Toward a new psychology of women*. Boston: Beacon Press.

Miller, J. B., & Stiver, I. P. (1997). *The healing connection*. Boston: Beacon Press.

Miller, J. B., Stiver, I. P., Joran, J. V., & Surrey, J. L. (1998). The psychology of women: A relational approach. In R. Frager & J. Fadiman (Eds.), *Personality and personal growth* (pp. 258–277). New York: Longman.

Miller, W. R., & C'deBaca, J. (1994). Quantum change: Toward a psychology of transformation. In T. F. Heatherton & J. L. Weinberger (Eds.), *Can personality change?* (pp. 253–280). Washington, DC: American Psychological Association.

Millon, T. (Ed.). (1967). *Theories of psychopathology.* Philadelphia: Saunders.

Millon, T. (1969). *Modern psychopathology: A biosocial approach to maladaptive learning and functioning.* Philadelphia: Saunders.

Millon, T. (Ed.). (1973). *Theories of psychopathology and personality* (2nd ed.). Philadelphia: Saunders.

Millon, T. (1977). *Millon Clinical Multiaxial Inventory manual.* Minneapolis, MN: National Computer Systems.

Millon, T. (1981). *Disorders of personality: DSM-III: Axis II.* New York: Wiley.

Millon, T. (1982). On the nature of clinical health psychology. In T. Millon, C. J. Green, & R. B. Meagher (Eds.), *Handbook of clinical health psychology* (pp. 1–27). New York: Plenum Press.

Millon, T. (1983). The *DSM-III:* An insider's perspective. *American Psychologist, 38*(7), 804–816.

Millon, T. (1984). On the renaissance of personality assessment and personality theory. *Journal of Personality Assessment, 48*(5), 450–466.

Millon, T. (1987). On the nature of taxonomy in psychopathology. In C. Last & M. Hersen (Eds.), *Issues in diagnostic research* (pp. 3–85). New York: Plenum Press.

Millon, T. (1990). *Toward a new personology: An evolutionary model.* New York: Wiley.

Millon, T. (1991). Normality: What we learn from evolutionary theory? In D. Offer & M. Sabshin (Eds.), *The diversity of normal behavior* (pp. 356–404). New York: Basic Books.

Millon, T. (1992). The borderline construct: Introductory notes on its history, theory, and empirical grounding. In J. F. Clarkin, E. Marziali, & H. Munroe-Blum (Eds.), *Borderline personality disorder: Clinical and empirical perspectives* (pp. 3–23). New York: Guilford Press.

Millon, T. (1996). *Personality and psychopathology: Building a clinical science.* New York: Wiley.

Millon, T. (1999). *Personality-guided psychotherapy.* New York: Wiley.

Millon, T. (2000). Toward a new model of integrative psychotherapy. *Journal of Psychotherapy Integration, 10,* 37–53.

Millon, T., & Davis, R. D. (1996a). *Disorders of personality: DSM-IV and beyond.* New York: Wiley.

Millon, T., & Davis, R. D. (1996b). An evolutionary theory of personality disorders. In J. F. Clarkin & M. F. Lenzenweger (Eds.), *Major theories of personality disorder* (pp. 221–346). New York: Guilford Press.

Millon, T., Davis, R., Millon, C., Escovar, L., & Meagher, S. (2000). *Personality disorders in modern life.* New York: Wiley.

Millon, T., & Klerman, G. L. (Eds.). (1986). *Contemporary directions in psychopathology: Toward DSM-IV.* New York: Guilford Press.

Millon, T., Millon, C., & Davis, R. D. (1994). *Millon Clinical Multiaxial Inventory-III.* Minneapolis, MN: National Computer Systems.

Millon, T., & Millon, R. (1974). *Abnormal behavior and personality.* Philadelphia: Saunders.

Mitchell, S. (1988). *Relational concepts in psychoanalysis.* Cambridge, MA: Harvard University.

Mowrer, O. H. (1947). On the dual nature of learning: A reinterpretation of "conditioning" and "problem solving." *Harvard Educational Review, 17,* 102–148.

Mowrer, O. H. (1950). *Learning theory and the personality dynamics.* New York: Arnold Press.

Muris, P., Steerneman, P., Merckelbach, H., & Meesters, C. (1996). The role of parental fearfulness and modeling in children's fear. *Behaviour Research and Therapy, 34*(3), 265–268.

Murray, H. A. (1938). *Explorations in personality.* New York: Oxford University Press.

Murray, H. A. (1943). *Thematic Apperception Test.* Cambridge, MA: Harvard University Press.

Murray, H. A. (1959). Preparations for the scaffold of a comprehensive system. In S. Koch (Ed.), *Psychology: A study of science* (Vol. 3, pp. 7–54). New York: McGraw-Hill.

Murray, H. A., & Morgan, C. D. (1935). A method for investigating fantasies. *Archives of Neurology and Psychiatry, 34,* 289–306.

Nathanson, D. L. (Ed.). (1996). *Knowing feeling: Affect, script, and psychotherapy.* New York: Norton.

National Institute of Mental Health. (1995). *The neuroscience of mental health II: A report on neuroscience research: Status for mental health and mental illness.* Rockville, MD: U. S. Department of Health and Human Services.

Nauta, W. J. H., & Feirtag, M. (1979). The organization of the brain. *Scientific American, 241*(3), 88–111.

Neisser, U. (1967). *Cognitive psychology.* New York: Appleton.

Newell, A., Shaw, C. J., & Simon, H. (1963). Empirical explorations with the logic theory machine: A case study in heuristics. In E. A. Feigenbaum & J. Feldman (Eds.), *Computers and thought.* New York: McGraw Hill.

Newell, A., & Simon, H. (1972). *Human problem solving.* Englewood Cliffs, NJ: Prentice Hall.

Nichols, M. (1984). *Family therapy: Concepts and methods.* New York: Gardner Press.

Norcross, J. C., & Goldfried, M. R. (Eds.). (1992). *Handbook of psychotherapy integration.* New York: Basic Books.

Norcross, J. C., & Newman, C. F. (1992). Psychotherapy integration: Setting the context. In J. C. Norcross & M. R. Goldfried (Eds.), *Handbook of psychotherapy integration* (pp. 3–45). New York: Basic Books.

Norden, K. A., Klein, D. N., Donaldson, S. K., Pepper, C. M., & Klein, L. M. (1995). Reports of the early home environment in *DSM-III-R* personality disorders. *Journal of Personality Disorders, 9*(3), 213–223.

Ogilvie, D. M., & Ashmore, R. (1991), Self: With other representation as a unit of analysis in self-concept research. In R. C. Curtis (Ed.), *Relational self* (pp. 282–314). New York: Guilford Press.

Ornstein, P. H. (Ed.). (1978a). *The search for the self: Selected writings of Heinz Kohut: 1950–1978. Volume 1.* New York: International Universities Press.

Ornstein, P. H. (Ed.). (1978b). *The search for the self: Selected writings of Heinz Kohut: 1950–1978. Volume 2.* New York: International Universities Press.

Pakiz, B., Reinherz, H. Z., & Giaconia, R. M. (1997). Early risk factors for serious antisocial behavior at age 21: A longitudinal community study. *American Journal of Orthopsychiatry, 67*(1), 92–101.

Panksepp, J. (1994). Basic emotions ramify widely in the brain, yielding many concepts that cannot be distinguished unambiguously—yet. In P. Ekman & R. J. Davidson (Eds.), *The nature of emotions: Fundamental questions* (pp. 186–88). New York: Oxford University Press.

Pavlov, I. P. (1927). *Conditioned reflexes: An investigation of the physiological activity of the cerebral cortex* (G. V. Anrep, Trans.). New York: Oxford University Press.

Pepper, S. C. (1942). *World hypotheses: A study in evidence.* Berkeley: University of California Press.

Perry, J. C. (1992). Perry's defense rating scale. In G. E. Vaillant (Ed.), *Ego mechanisms of defense: A guide for clinicians and researchers* (pp. 253–259). Washington, DC: American Psychiatric Press.

Pervin, L. A. & John, B. P. (Eds.). (1999). *Handbook of personality: Theory and research* (2nd ed.). New York: Guilford Press.

Phillips, K. A., McElroy, S. L., Keck, P. E., Pope, H. G., & Hudson, J. L. (1993). Body dysmorphic disorder: 30 cases of imagined ugliness. *American Journal of Psychiatry, 150,* 320–309.

Piaget, J. (1926). *The language and thought of the child.* New York: Harcourt Brace.

Pickering, A. D., & Gray, J. A. (1999). The neuroscience of personality. In L. A. Pervin & O. P. John (Eds.), *Handbook of personality: Theory and research* (2nd ed, pp. 277–299). New York: Guilford Press.

Pine, F. (1990). *Drive, ego, object, and self: A synthesis for clinical work.* New York: Basic Books.

Pinker, S. (1997). *How the mind works.* New York: Norton.

Pinto, C., Dhavale, H. S., Nair, S., & Patil, B. (2000). Borderline personality disorder exists in India. *Journal of Nervous and Mental Disease, 188*(6), 386–388.

Planalp, S. (1987). Interplay between relational knowledge and events. In R. Burnett, P. McGhee, & D. D. Clarke (Eds.), *Accounting for relationships: Explanation, representation and knowledge* (pp. 175–191). New York: Methuen.

Plomin, R., & Caspi, A. (1999). Behavioral genetics and personality. In L. A. Pervin & O. P. John (Eds.), *Handbook of personality: Theory and research* (2nd ed, pp. 251–276). New York: Guilford Press.

Pretzer, J. L., & Beck, A. T. (1996). A cognitive theory of personality disorders. In J. F. Clarkin & M. E. Lenzenweger (Eds.), *Major theories of personality disorders* (pp. 36–105). New York: Guilford Press.

Prochaska, J. O., DiClemente, C. C., & Norcross, J. C. (1992). In search of how people change: Application to addictive behaviors. *American Psychologist, 47*(9), 1102–1114.

Rachman, A. W. (1997). *Sándor Ferenczi: The psychotherapist of tenderness and passion.* Northvale, NJ: Aronson.

Ramey, C. T., & Ramey, S. L. (1998). Early intervention and early experience. *American Psychologist, 53*(2), 109–120.

Rayner, E. (1991). *The independent mind in British psychoanalysis.* Northvale, NJ: Aronson.

Redfield Jamison, K. (1995). *An unquiet mind: A memoir of moods and madness.* New York: Alfred A. Knopf.

Redfield Jamison, K. (1999). *Night falls fast: Understanding suicide.* New York: Alfred A. Knopf.

Reich, W. (1945). *Character analysis* (3rd ed.). New York: Noonday Press.

Reis, D. (1996). Foreword. In F. W. Kaslow (Ed.), *Handbook of relational diagnosis and dysfunctional family patterns* (pp. ix–xv). New York: Wiley.

Reiser, M. F. (1990). *Memory in mind and brain: What dream imagery reveals.* New York: Basic Books.

Ridley, M. (2000). *Genome: The autobiography of a species.* New York: HarperCollins.

Rilling, M. (2000). John Watson's paradoxical struggle to explain Freud. *American Psychologist, 55*(3), 301–312.

Roberts, B. W., & Friend-DelVecchio, W. (in press). Consistency of personality traits form childhood to old age: A quantitative review of longitudinal studies. *Psychological Bulletin.*

Robins, R. W., Norem, J. K., & Cheek, J. M. (1999). Naturalizing the self. In L. A. Pervin & O. P. Oliver (Eds.), *Handbook of personality: Theory and research* (2nd ed, pp. 443–477). New York: Guilford Press.

Rogers, C. (1951). *Client-centered therapy.* Boston: Houghton Mifflin.

Rorschach, H. (1951). *Psychodiagnostics, a diagnostic test based on perception.* New York: Grune & Stratton. (Original work published 1942)

Rotter, J. B. (1954). *Social learning and clinical psychology.* Englewood Cliffs, NJ: Prentice-Hall.

Ruegg, R., & Frances, A. (1995). New research in personality disorders. *Journal of Personality Disorders, 9*(1), 1–48.

Ruiz, D. M. (1997). *The four agreements: Wisdom book.* CA: Amber-Allen.

Rychlak, J. F. (1968). *A philosophy of science for personality theory.* Boston: Houghton Mifflin.

Rychlak, J. F. (1973). *Introduction to personality and psychotherapy: A theory-construction approach.* Boston: Houghton Mifflin.

Rychlak, J. F. (2000). A psychotherapist's lessons from the philosophy of science. *American Psychologist, 55*(10), 1126–1132.

Salter, A. (1949). *Conditioned reflex therapy: The direct approach to the reconstruction of personality.* New York: Creative Age Press.

Sapolsky, R. M. (1998). *Biology and human behavior: The neurological origins of individuality* (Audiocassette tapes). Springfield, VA: The Great Courses on Tape, The Teaching Company Limited Partnership.

Sarafino, E. P. (1994). *Health psychology: Biopsychosocial interactions* (2nd ed.). New York: Wiley.

Sayers, J. (1991). *Mothers of psychoanalysis: Helen Deutsch, Karen Horney, Anna Freud & Melanie Klein.* New York: Norton.

Sayle, M. (2001, March). Tokyo: The kamikazes rise again. Notes & Dispatches. *Atlantic Monthly,* 16–17.

Scarr, S. (1998). American child care today. *American Psychologist, 53*(2), 95–108.

Schaefer, E. S. (1965). Configurational analysis of children's reports of parent behavior. *Journal of Consulting Psychology, 29,* 552–557.

Scheflen, A. (1981). *Levels of schizophrenia.* New York: Brunner/Mazel.

Scheier, M. F., & Carver, C. S. (1992). Effects of optimism on psychological and physical well-being: Theoretical overview and empirical update. *Cognitive Therapy and Research, 16*(2), 201–228.

Scherer, K. R. (1994). Emotion serves to decouple stimulus and response. In P. Ekman & R. J. Davidson (Eds.), *The nature of emotions: Fundamental questions* (pp. 127–130). New York: Oxford University Press.

Schneewind, K. A., & Ruppert, S. (1998). *Personality and family development: An intergenerational longitudinal comparison.* Hillsdale, NJ: Erlbaum.

Schwartz, G. E. (1991). The data are always friendly: A systems approach to psychotherapy integration. *Journal of Psychotherapy Integration, 1,* 55–69.

Schwartz, J. (1999). *Cassandra's daughter: A history of psychoanalysis.* New York: Viking/Penguin.

Seligman, M. E. (1995). The effectiveness of psychotherapy: The Consumer Reports study. *American Psychologist, 50*(12), 965–974.

Seligman, M. E. P. (1975) *Helplessness: On depression, development, and death.* San Francisco: Freeman.

Seligman, M. E. P. (1990). *Learned optimism.* New York: Alfred A. Knopf.

Seligman, M. E. P. (1996). *The optimistic child.* New York: HarperCollins.

Serketich, W. J., & Dumas, J. E. (1996). The effectiveness of behavioral parent training to modify antisocial behavior in children: A meta-analysis. *Behavior Therapy, 27*(2), 171–186.

Shahinfar, A., Fox, N. A., & Leavitt, L. A. (2000). Preschool children's exposure to violence: Relation of behavior problems to parent child reports. *American Journal of Orthopsychiatry, 70*(1), 114–125.

Shannon, C., & Weiner, W. (1949). *The mathematical theory of communication.* Urbana: University of Illinois Press.

Shapiro, D. (1989). *Psychotherapy of neurotic character.* New York: Basic Books.

Sheldon, W. H., & Stevens, S. S. (1942). *The varieties of temperament: A psychology of constitutional differences.* New York: Harper & Brothers.

Sheldon, W. H., Stevens, S. S., & Tucker, W. B. (1940). *The varieties of human physique: An introduction to constitutional psychology.* New York: Harper & Brothers.

Shneidman, E. S. (Ed.). (1981). *Endeavors in psychology: Selections from the personology of Henry A. Murray.* New York: Harper & Row.

Siegel, D. J. (1999). *The developing mind: Toward a neurobiology of interpersonal experience.* New York: Guilford Press.

Siever, L. J., & Davis, K. L. (1991). A psychobiological perspective on the personality disorders. *American Journal of Psychiatry, 148,* 1647–1658.

Siever, L. J., Klar, H., & Coccaro, E. (1985). Biological response styles: Clinic implications. In L. J. Siever & H. Klar (Eds.), *Psychobiological substrates personality* (pp. 38–66). Washington, DC: American Psychiatric Press.

Sifneos, P. E. (1988). Alexithymia and its relationship to hemispheric specialization, affect, and creativity. *Psychiatric Clinics of North America, 11,* 287–292.

Sifneos, P. E. (1990). Short-term anxiety-provoking psychotherapy (STAPP): Termination outcome and videotaping. In J. K. Zeig & S. G. Gilligan (Eds.), *Brief therapy: Myths, methods, and metaphors* (pp. 318–326). New York: Brunner/Mazel.

Silverman, T. (1999). The Internet and relational theory. *American Psychologist, 59*(4), 780–781.

Simon, H. (1969). *The sciences of the artificial.* Cambridge, MA: MIT Press.

Simon, H. (1991). *Models of my life.* New York: Basic Books.

Skinner, B. F. (1948). *Walden two.* New York: Macmillan.

Skinner, B. F. (1953). *Science and human behavior.* New York: Free Press.

Skinner, B. F. (1972). *Beyond freedom and dignity.* New York: Bantam Books.

Skinner, B. F. (1979). *The shaping of a behaviorist.* New York: Alfred A. Knopf.

Skynner, A. C. R. (1976). *Systems of family and marital psychotherapy.* New York: Brunner/Mazel.

Smith, M. L., Glass, G. V., & Miller, T. I. (1980). *The benefits of psychotherapy.* Baltimore: Johns Hopkins University Press.

Spearman, C. (1904). "General intelligence," objectively defined and measured. *American Journal of Psychology, 16,* 201–293.

Sperry, L. (1999). *Cognitive therapy of DSM-IV personality disorders: Highly effective interventions for the most common personality disorders.* Philadelphia: Brunner/Mazel.

Spitzer, R. L., Williams, J. B. W., & Gibbon, M. (1987). *Structured clinical interview for the DSM-III-R personality disorders* (SCID-III). New York: New York State Psychiatric Institute, Biometrics Research.

Staats, A. W. (1975). *Social behaviorism.* Homewood, IL: Dorsey Press.

Staats, A. W. (1981). Social behaviorism, unified theory, unified theory construction, and the zeitgeist of separatism. *American Psychologist, 36,* 240–256.

Stampfl, T. G. (1966). Implosive therapy: The theory, the subhuman analogue, the strategy, and the technique. In S. G. Armitage (Ed.), *Behavior modification techniques in the treatment of emotional disorders* (pp. 12–21). Battle Creek, MI: Veterans Administration.

Stein, J. (Ed.). (1975). *The Random House college dictionary* (Rev. ed.). New York: Random House.

Steinberg, M. (2000a). *Stranger in the mirror. Dissociation: The secret epidemic of our time.* New York: Cliff Street Books.

Steinberg, M. (2000b, December). Dr. Marlene Steinberg responds: "It's the 'gold standard'." *Psychology Today, 34,* 84.

Stevens, C. F. (1979). The neuron. *Scientific American, 241*(3), 55–65.

Stiver, I. (1991). The meanings of "dependency" in female-male relationships. In J. V. Jordan, A. G. Kaplan, J. B. Miller, I. P. Stiver, & J. L. Surrey (Eds.), *Women's growth in connection* (pp. 143–161). New York: Guilford Press.

Stolorow, R., & Atwood, G. E. (1992). *Contexts of being.* Hillsdale, NJ: Analytic Press.

Strupp, H. H., & Howard, K. I. (1992). A brief history of psychotherapy research. In D. K. Freedheim (Ed.), *History of psychotherapy: A century of change* (pp. 309–334). Washington, DC: American Psychological Association.

Sue, D. W., & Sue, D. (1999). *Counseling the culturally different: Theory and practice* (3rd ed.). New York: Wiley.

Sullivan, H. S. (1953). *The interpersonal theory of psychiatry.* New York: Norton.

Sullivan, M. J., Tripp, D. A., & Santor, D. (2000). Gender differences in pain and pain behavior: The role of catastrophizing. *Cognitive Therapy and Research, 24*(1), 121–134.

Suomi, S. J. (1991). Primate separation models of affective disorders. In J. Madden (Ed.), *Neurobiology of learning, emotion, and affect* (pp. 195–214). New York: Raven Press.

Talbot, M. (1998, May 24). Attachment theory: The ultimate experiment. *New York Times Magazine,* Sec. 6, pp. 24–30, 38, 46, 50, 54.

Thomas, A., & Chess, S. (1977). *Temperament and development.* New York: Brunner/Mazel.

Thomas, A., Chess, S., & Birch, H. G. (1968). *Temperament and behavior disorders in children.* New York: New York University Press.

Thompson, C. (1952). *Psychoanalysis: Evolution and development.* London: Allen & Unwin.

Thurstone, L. L. (1938). *Primary mental abilities.* Chicago: University of Chicago Press.

Tierney, P. (2000). *Darkness in El Dorado: How scientists and journalists devastated the Amazon.* New York: Norton.

Toman, W. (1961). *Family constellation.* New York: Springer.

Toman, W. (1976). *Family constellation: Its effects on personality and social behavior* (3rd ed.). New York: Springer.

Tomkins, S. S. (1962). *Affect imagery consciousness: Volume I: The positive affects.* New York: Springer.

Tomkins, S. S. (1963). *Affect imagery consciousness: Volume II: The negative affects.* New York: Springer.

Tomkins, S. S. (1991). *Affect imagery consciousness: Volume III: The negative affects: Anger and fear.* New York: Springer.

Tomkins, S. S., & Messick, S. (Eds.). (1963). *Computer simulation of personality: Frontier of psychological theory.* New York: Wiley.

Tompson, R. A., & Nelson, C. A. (2001). Developmental science and the media: Early brain development. *American Psychologist, 56*(1), 5–15.

Trijsburg, R. W., Van T' Spijker, A., Van, H. L., & Hesselink, A. J. (2000). Measuring overall defensive functioning with the Defense Style Questionnaire: A comparison of different scoring methods. *Journal of Nervous and Mental Disease, 188*(7), 432–439.

Tsien, J. Z. (2000, April). Building a brainier mouse. *Scientific American,* 62–68.

Uchitelle, L. (2001, February 11). Some economists call behavior a key. *New York Times,* Sec 3, pp 1, 11.

Vaillant, G. E. (1977). *Adaptation to life.* Boston: Little, Brown.

Vaillant, G. E. (Ed.). (1992). *Ego mechanisms of defense: A guide for clinicians and researches.* Washington, DC: American Psychiatric Press.

von Bertalanffy, L. (1942). Theoretical models in biology and psychology. In D. Krech & G. S. Klein (Eds.), *Theoretical models and personality theory.* Durham, NC: Duke University Press.

von Bertalanffy, L. (1948). *General systems theory.* New York: Braziller.

von Bertalanffy, L. (1952). Theoretical models in biology and psychology. In D. Krech & G. S. Klein (Eds.), *Theoretical models and personality theory.* Durham, NC: Duke University Press.

von Bertalanffy, L. (1954). *Problems of life.* New York: Wiley.

von Bertalanffy, L. (1968). *General systems theory.* New York: Braziller.

Von Neumann, J., & Morgenstern, O. (1944). *Theory of games and economic behavior.* Princeton, NJ: Princeton University Press.

Wachtel, P. L. (1977). *Psychoanalysis and behavior therapy: Toward an integration.* New York: Basic Books.

Wachtel, P. L. (1987). *Action and insight.* New York: Guilford Press.

Wachtel, P. L., & McKinney, M. K. (1992). Cyclical psychodynamics and integrative psychodynamic theory. In J. C. Norcross & M. R. Goldfried (Eds.), *Handbook of integrative psychotherapy* (pp. 335–370). New York: Basic Books.

Wachtel, P. L., & Wachtel, E. F. (1986). *Family dynamics in individual psychotherapy: A guide to clinical strategies.* New York: Guilford Press.

Wada, J. A. (Ed.). (1976). *Kindling.* New York: Raven Press.

Watson, D., & Clark, L. A. (1994a). Emotions, moods, traits, and temperaments, conceptual distinctions and empirical findings. In P. Ekman & R. J. Davidson (Eds.), *The nature of emotions: Fundamental questions* (pp. 89–93). New York: Oxford University Press.

Watson, D., & Clark, L. A. (1994b). Introduction to the special issue on personality and psychopathology. *Journal of Abnormal Psychology, 103*(1), 3–5.

Watson, J. B. (1913). Psychology as the behaviorist views it. *Psychological Review, 20,* 158–177.

Watson, J. B. (1924). *Behaviorism.* Chicago: University of Chicago Press.

Watson, J. B. (1930). *Behaviorism* (2nd ed.). Chicago: University of Chicago Press.

Watson, J. B., & Rayner, R. (1920). Conditioned emotional reactions. *Journal of Experimental Psychology, 3*(1), 1–14.

Watson, J. D., & Crick, F. H. C. (1953). Molecular structure of nucleic acid: A structure for deoxyridose nucleic acid. *Nature, 17,* 737–738.

Watson, R. I. (1963). *The great psychologists.* Philadelphia: Lippincott.

Watson, R. I. (1971). *The great psychologists* (3rd ed.). Philadelphia: Lippincott. (Original work published 1963)

Weiss, B. (2001, March/April). The other side of science [Review of the book *Darkness in El Dorado: How scientists and journalists devastated the Amazon*]. *Psychology Today,* 78.

Weissman, M. M., Markowitz, J. C., & Klerman, G. L. (2000). *Comprehensive guide to interpersonal psychotherapy.* New York: Basic Books.

Werner, H. (1948). *Comparative psychology of mental development.* New York: International Universities Press.

Westen, D. (2000). The efficacy of dialectical behavior therapy for borderline personality disorder. *Clinical Psychology Science and Practice, 7*(1), 92–94.

Westen, D., & Gabbard, G. O. (1999). Psychoanalytic approaches to personality. In L. A. Pervin & O. P. John (Eds.), *Handbook of personality: Theory and research* (2nd ed, pp. 57–101). New York: Guilford Press.

White, J. L., & Parham, T. A. (1990). *The psychology of Blacks.* Englewood Cliffs, NJ: Prentice Hall.

Wiener, N. (1948). *Cybernetics or control and communication in the animal and the machine.* New York: Wiley.

Wiesel, T. N. (1982). The postnatal development of the visual cortext and the influence of the environment [Nobel lecture reprint]. *Bioscience Reports, 2,* 351–377.

Wiggins, J. S. (1979). A psychological taxonomy of trait-descriptive terms: The interpersonal domain. *Journal of Personality and Social Psychology, 37,* 395–412.

Wiggins, J. S. (1982). Circumplex models of interpersonal behavior in clinical psychology. In P. Kendell & J. N. Butcher (Eds.), *Handbook of research methods in clinical psychology.* New York: Wiley.

Wiggins, J. S. (Ed.). (1996). *The five-factor model of personality: Theoretical perspectives.* New York: Guilford Press.

Wiggins, J. S., & Trobst, K. K. (1999). The fields of interpersonal behavior. In L. A. Pervin & O. P. John (Eds.), *Handbook of personality:*

Theory and research (pp. 653–670). New York: Guilford Press.

Williams, J. B. W., & Spitzer, R. L. (1983). The issue of sex bias in *DSM-III:* A critique of "a woman's view of *DSM-III*" by Marcie Kalpan. *American Psychologist, 38*(7), 793–798.

Wilson, E. O. (1971). *The insect societies.* Cambridge, MA: Harvard University Press.

Wilson, E. O. (1975). *Sociobiology: The new synthesis.* Cambridge, MA: Harvard University Press.

Wilson, E. O. (1978). *On human nature.* Cambridge, MA: Harvard University Press.

Wilson, E. O. (1998). *Consilience: The unity of knowledge.* New York: Alfred A. Knopf.

Wink, P. (1992). Three types of narcissism in women from college to midlife. *Journal of Personality, 60,* 597–605.

Winnicott, C., Shepherd, R., & Davis, M. (Eds.). (1989a). *Psychoanalytic explorations: D. W. Winnicott.* Cambridge, MA: Harvard University Press.

Winnicott, C., Shepherd, R., & Davis, M. (Eds.). (1989b). The squiggle game. *Winnicott: Psychoanalytic explorations* (pp. 299–317). Cambridge, MA: Harvard University Press.

Winnicott, D. W. (1988). *Human nature.* New York: Schocken Books.

Winston, A., Laikin, M., Pollack, J., Samstag, L., McCullough, L., & Muran, C. (1994). Short-term dynamic psychotherapy of personality disorders. *American Journal of Psychiatry, 151*(2), 190–194.

Winston, A., Pollack, J., McCullough, L., Flegenheimer, W., Kestenbaum, R., & Trujillo, M. (1991). Brief therapy of personality disorders. *Journal of Nervous and Mental Disease, 179*(4), 188–193.

Winter, D. G., & Barenbaum, N. B. (1999). History of modern personality theory and research. In L. A. Pervin & O. P. John (Eds.), *Handbook of personality: Theory and research* (2nd ed, pp. 3–27). New York: Guilford Press.

Wolpe, J. (1958). *Psychotherapy by reciprocal inhibition.* Stanford, CA: Stanford University Press.

Wolpe, J. (1960). Reciprocal inhibition as the main basis of psychotherapeutic effects. In H. J. Eysenck (Ed.), *Behavior therapy and the neurosis* (pp. 88–113). New York: Pergamon Press.

Wolpe, J. (1969). *The practice of behavior therapy.* New York: Pergamon Press.

Wundt, W. (1874). *Principles of physiological psychology* (5th ed, Vol. 1, E. B. Titchener, Trans.). New York: Macmillan.

Wundt, W. M. (1904). *Grundzuge der physiologischen psyhologie [Principles of physiological psychology]* (5th ed., Vol. 1, E. B. Titchener, Trans.). New York: Macmillan.

Wynne, C. (1999, December). Do animals think? *Psychology Today, 32*(6), 50–53.

Wynne, L. C., & Singer, M. T. (1963). Thought disorder and family relations of schizophrenics: I. A research strategy. *Archives of General Psychiatry, 9,* 191–198.

Yang, K. S., & Bond, M. H. (1990). Exploring implicit personality theories with indigenous or imported constructs: The Chinese case. *Journal of Personality and Social Psychology, 58,* 1087–1089.

Young, J. E. (1994). *Cognitive therapy for personality disorders: A schema-focused approach* (Rev. ed.). Sarasota, FL: Professional Resource Exchange.

Young-Bruehl, E. (1988). *Anna Freud: A biography.* New York: Summit Books.

Ziv, B., Russ, M. J., Moline, M., Hurt, S., & Zendell, S. (1995). Menstrual cycle influences on mood and behavior in women with borderline personality disorder. *Journal of Personality Disorders, 9*(1), 68–75.

Author Index

Subject Index